Smoking Policy: Law, Politics, and Culture

Smoking Policy: Law, Politics, and Culture

Edited by
ROBERT L. RABIN
STEPHEN D. SUGARMAN

New York   Oxford
OXFORD UNIVERSITY PRESS
1993

Oxford University Press

Oxford   New York   Toronto
Delhi   Bombay   Calcutta   Madras   Karachi
Kuala Lumpur   Singapore   Hong Kong   Tokyo
Nairobi   Dar es Salaam   Cape Town
Melbourne   Auckland   Madrid

and associated companies in
Berlin   Ibadan

Published by Oxford University Press, Inc.
200 Madison Avenue, New York, NY 10016

Library of Congress Cataloging-in-Publication Data

Smoking policy : law, politics, and culture / edited by Robert L.
Rabin and Stephen D. Sugarman.
p.   cm.
Includes bibliographical references and index.
ISBN 0-19-507231-6
1. Smoking—Law and legislation—United States.   I. Rabin, Robert L.
II. Sugarman, Stephen D.
KF3812.3.A75S66   1993   344.73'0424—dc20   [347.304424]   92-33045

2 4 6 8 9 7 5 3 1

Printed in the United States of America
on acid-free paper

Acknowledgments

We would like to express our appreciation to the University of California's Tobacco-Related Disease Research Program for funding the research and writing of this book. The Earl Warren Legal Institute of the University of California at Berkeley sponsored and administered the project. The authors are especially grateful to the following professional colleagues for making presentations to the project members at an ongoing seminar we held in Berkeley, during the 1990–91 academic year, as we began work on our individual projects: Kenneth Warner, Neil Collishaw, Richard Daynard, Abe Krash, Michael Pertschuk, Thomas C. Schelling, and Robert Tollison. We benefited greatly from the information and advice they provided. In addition, Mark Pertschuk, Phillip Lee, Milton Silverman, David Perlman, and Althea Mueller provided assistance to individual authors.

The contributors to this volume also received valuable research assistance from Ellen Auriti, Thomas Burke, Charis Cussins, Dennis Galvan, Dan Gentry, Jaclyn Hausman, Donald Kelly, Kelly Klaus, Iona Mara-Drita, William Nelson, Michael Quinn, Karen Stark, and Deborah Stone. We owe a special note of gratitude to Kelly Klaus for his work in compiling the References list and handling the final stages of production. An earlier version of Chapter 6 appeared in the April 1992 Stanford Law Review.

Stanford, California   R.L.R.
Berkeley, California   S.D.S.
December 1992

Contents

Contributors

Robert L. Rabin is the A. Calder Mackay Professor of Law, Stanford University.

Stephen D. Sugarman is the Agnes Roddy Robb Professor of Law, University of California, Berkeley.

Joseph R. Gusfield is Professor Emeritus of Sociology, University of California, San Diego.

Robert A. Kagan is Professor of Political Science and Law, University of California, Berkeley.

Helen Halpin Schauffler is Assistant Professor of Health and Medical Care Policy and Politics, Department of Social and Administrative Health Sciences, School of Public Health, University of California, Berkeley.

Michael Schudson is Professor of Communication and Sociology, University of California, San Diego.

Gary T. Schwartz is Professor of Law, University of California, Los Angeles.

Jerome H. Skolnick is the Claire Clements Professor of Law, University of California, Berkeley.

David Vogel is Professor of Business and Public Policy, Haas School of Business, University of California, Berkeley.

Franklin E. Zimring is the William G. Simon Professor of Law and Director of the Earl Warren Legal Institute, University of California, Berkeley.

Smoking Policy: Law, Politics, and Culture

1

Overview

Robert L. Rabin and Stephen D. Sugarman

Dimensions of the "Smoking Problem"

Risks to Self

In 1989, the U.S. Surgeon General released a report summarizing the progress achieved in the campaign to eliminate cigarette smoking that had begun twenty-five years earlier with the landmark publication of the 1964 Surgeon General's Report, *Smoking and Health* (U.S. DHHS 1989; U.S. DHEW 1964a). Although smoking had declined substantially during the ensuing years, the 1989 report was filled with arresting statistical evidence of the toll in mortality and disease associated with continuing tobacco use. In 1985, approximately 390,000 deaths in the United States could be attributed to cigarette smoking. Smoking was identified as the source of 87 percent of lung cancer deaths, 82 percent of chronic obstructive pulmonary disease fatalities, 40 percent of chronic heart disease deaths in individuals under 65 years of age, and a substantial number of other chronic diseases and deaths. More recent figures indicate cigarette smoking is responsible for an estimated 434,000 annual deaths in this country (U.S. DHHS 1992, p. 106).

By any measure, 434,000 annual deaths is a staggering number of fatalities. It exceeds the total U.S. battlefield casualties in World War II; it constitutes a mortality rate far greater than the sum of deaths that result from drinking, driving, working, and recreational activities. All told, more than one in six deaths from all causes can be traced to tobacco use. Plainly, smoking is the leading source—by a wide margin—of avoidable mortality (U.S. DHHS 1989, pp. 153–61).

Risks to Others

In addition to the risks to smokers, recent scientific findings show that nonsmokers also suffer adverse health effects from sustained exposure to environmental tobacco smoke (ETS). An important document summarizing these findings is another relatively recent Surgeon General's Report, *The Health Consequences of Involuntary Smoking* (U.S. DHHS, Surgeon General 1986). The report brought to public attention the notable findings that "side-stream" smoke is at least as rich in carcinogens as inhaled tobacco smoke, and that reliable studies indicate that "passive

3

smokers" have a significantly higher rate of lung cancer than those relatively unexposed to tobacco smoke, as well as suffering aggravation of various respiratory conditions (U.S. DHHS, Surgeon General 1986, Ch. 2; National Research Council 1986).

Even more recent inquiries, including a 1992 report prepared by the U.S. Environmental Protection Agency and a paper published by the American Heart Association, confirm the link between ETS and lung cancer, as well as a wide variety of respiratory conditions, and report on a linkage with heart disease (U.S. EPA 1992; "Environmental Tobacco Smoke" 1992). These studies attribute to ETS exposure approximately 3,000 annual lung cancer deaths, between 150,000 and 300,000 lower respiratory ailments in young children, and an estimated 37,000 annual cardiovascular disease-related deaths.

Risk Awareness

Public awareness of the dangers of smoking appears to be quite high, even though the initial federal warning requirement imposed in 1965 was rather bland. All that the much heralded Federal Cigarette Labeling and Advertising Act required was: "Caution: Cigarette Smoking May Be Hazardous to Your Health." Nonetheless, in the following years the media provided a steady flow of increasingly alarming reports on the risks of smoking, and, in 1984, Congress enacted a new set of rotating health warnings that are far more explicit about the hazards of smoking than the initial proviso.

At present, public opinion polls confirm that smoking hazards have become common knowledge; for example, by 1986, 92 percent of the public, including 85 percent of current smokers, believed that smoking causes lung cancer (U.S. DHHS 1989, Ch. 4). As for the perception of danger to others, a 1989 Gallup survey commissioned by the American Lung Association found that 86 percent of nonsmokers think that ETS is harmful ("Environmental Tobacco Smoke" 1992).

Smoking Patterns

Given the widespread acknowledgment of the dangers of smoking, it is not surprising that tens of millions of Americans have quit. In 1990, only about 25 percent of adult Americans smoked, according to the Centers for Disease Control, the lowest percentage recorded since the agency began tracking smoking data in 1955. Indeed, since 1987 the percentage of smokers has been dropping at 1.1 percent a year, more than double the rate of decrease in the preceding twenty years ("Smoking Declines at a Faster Pace" 1992).

Nevertheless, many of those who smoked in 1964 and who are still alive continue to smoke. Moreover, millions of Americans have taken up the habit since then, typically beginning in adolescence. As a result, tens of millions of Americans smoke today.

Regulatory Background

In the forty years before the publication of *Smoking and Health*, not only was there no serious thought given to banning cigarette smoking, but there was virtually no regulation at all of tobacco sale or use. To the contrary, for decades our government *promoted* smoking—from subsidies to tobacco growers through free distribution of cigarettes to soldiers during wartime. A tobacco prohibition movement had realized some success in several states before World War I. But by the 1920s, political initiatives aimed at regulating smoking were moribund, and earlier prohibitory laws were repealed. To be sure, laws remained on the books formally restricting the access of the young to tobacco products, but these appear to have been largely ineffectual.

Popular culture between World War I and Vietnam portrayed smoking positively. In movies of the 1940s and 1950s, the cigarette is as ubiquitous as the handgun. Indeed, from Humphrey Bogart to John Garfield to Robert Mitchum, smoking was an accepted symbol of being cool and in control of the situation. In fact, role models in all walks of life—the arts, sports, the professions—were promoting the smoking habit.

The regulatory politics of the era reflects that popular acceptance. Quite simply, the starting point for restrictive regulatory action is the perception of a social problem. As long as smoker's cough, tobacco after-taste, and smoke-filled rooms and sporting arenas were regarded at most as minor annoyances and only vaguely perceived as posing health concerns—annoyances and concerns that were far outweighed by the perceived pleasures and positive connotations of smoking—tobacco use was a highly unlikely candidate for regulatory sanctions.

The hard evidence that smoking is seriously harmful is relatively recent in origin. Although studies of the health consequences of smoking date back to the 1930s, the magnitude of the risks associated with tobacco use—in particular, the risk of lung cancer—as well as the extent of the causal connection were widely recognized in this country only with the publication of the 1964 Surgeon General's Report. That report stated, in unequivocal terms, that "cigarette smoking is a health hazard of sufficient importance in the United States to warrant appropriate remedial action."

The tobacco industry has long disputed the causal link between cigarette smoking and disease in the course of defending lawsuits for money damages brought by smokers and their survivors. Yet, as early as the 1964 report, a substantial body of data linked smoking and lung cancer. And by 1989, the Surgeon General was able to summarize twenty-five years of further studies and conclude that causal connections had been established between smoking and a range of cancer risks—lung, laryngeal, oral, and esophageal—as well as pulmonary diseases, heart disorders, and infant growth retardation. While it remains possible that some yet undiscovered personality or genetic constituent triggers both the propensity to smoke and the various diseases with which smoking has been linked, most of the scientific community rejects this possibility and considers the association between smoking and health risks well established.

With the widespread publicity of the findings in the 1964 report, tobacco use was added, virtually overnight, to the political agenda. Since the mid-1960s social attitudes about smoking have changed dramatically, and political activity addressing the conduct of smokers and the tobacco industry has increased correspondingly. Within a year of the report, Congress enacted the Federal Cigarette Labeling and Advertising Act of 1965, requiring the initial health warnings on cigarette packages. This legislation was followed by the Public Health Cigarette Smoking Act of 1969, banning the advertising of cigarettes on television and radio. The ensuing years have witnessed an incessant stream of further initiatives, principally in state and local legislative arenas (as well as efforts in the courts), aimed at controlling the use of tobacco.

What is the theory behind this regulation, both existing and proposed? What are the justifications for restricting tobacco sale and use? As we discuss in the next section, there is no single answer to these questions, because there are many different senses in which the health risks of smoking can be viewed as "a problem" warranting governmental intervention. Furthermore, as we point out, each perspective in turn implies different governmental responses. The implications of this diversity of outlook and associated solutions, as well as the desirability of further regulation, are addressed in the final section of this chapter.

An Array of Perspectives on "The Problem"

The perspectives discussed in this section begin with those that treat smoking as a risk to self, and the interventions implied range from noncoercive measures to strongly paternalistic government action. The presentation starts with informed choice—the perspective linked to the least coercive of intervention strategies—and moves along a rough continuum to smoking as immoral behavior, the perspective associated with the most assertive level of government involvement. After discussing these various viewpoints on risk to self, we turn to a perspective that focuses on the harm to others from smoking.

Informed Choice

At first blush, the wonder may be that a product as lethal as cigarettes has been allowed to remain in the marketplace at all. Yet, as a general matter, our society does not lightly impose bans on dangerous and deleterious products; witness the continuing controversy over cheap and easily concealed handguns, and consider the exception that might well be taken to underscore the rule—the disastrous experience with alcohol under Prohibition.

Instead, the traditional social goal with respect to consumer goods in America is that product use should reflect informed choice. Although our society largely relies upon the competitive economy to ensure that choice, this does not mean there is no place for public policy interventions. On the contrary, certain "market failures" are customarily thought to justify government regulation. When a product is dangerous, competitors cannot necessarily be counted upon either to provide a safer version or to inform the public through advertising.

This concern is sometimes explained as "safety doesn't sell"—a slogan that rests on the assumption that any claim to have a "safer" variant of a product only serves to emphasize the inherent danger of the product, and to scare off buyers altogether. And if the sales people resist promoting safety, then the production people have less of an incentive to concentrate on safety, facing instead greater pressure either to cut costs or to emphasize style or performance. Alternatively, when an industry does market safety any genuine risk may be unduly downplayed.

In either case, where risks are small, a further concern is that consumers will have difficulty rationally deciding whether or not to run them—some people perhaps foolishly discounting the danger, others unnecessarily exaggerating it. These considerations help explain why we assign safety-promoting roles to federal agencies such as the Food and Drug Administration, the Consumer Product Safety Commission, the Federal Aviation Administration, the National Highway Traffic Safety Administration, and the Federal Trade Commission.

In the context of "the smoking problem" an informed choice perspective starts with the commitment that individuals should decide for themselves whether or not to smoke. It assumes that, even though smoking is very dangerous, it is not inherently an irrational choice; rather, as long as individuals understand the hazards involved, they should be free to engage in risky activity that provides them with personal satisfaction. But as a corollary to this perspective, government's role is then to ensure truly informed individual decision making. Such an outlook, of course, is consistent with the various warning requirements enacted to date.

Yet, perhaps merely telling people that smoking causes cancer, heart disease, and the like is not sufficient. The informed choice perspective arguably requires, among other things, that those who take up or resume smoking, as well as those who continue to smoke or consider quitting, understand the magnitude and potential time dimension of the risks of smoking, the methods of quitting and their availability, the relative riskiness of competing brands and methods of smoking, alternative sources of similar pleasures, and so on. Moreover, because true informed choice requires that people not be seduced into self-delusion about the dangers of smoking, there may be, from this perspective, a legitimate governmental interest in the way tobacco products are promoted that is not restricted to policing outright misrepresentation and deception.

In sum, relying on an informed consumer choice orientation, a case can be built for government intervention beyond the existing required warnings and the current ban on electronic media advertising.

Advocates who see the problem as one of insufficiently informed choice are likely to concentrate on policies such as publicly funded (possibly tobacco-tax funded) community- and physician-based education programs, additional required disclosures about product risk printed on tobacco product packages and promotional materials, further controls on the style and content of cigarette advertisements and promotions, and public health-oriented and information-based mass media campaigns about smoking, including such related matters as information about cessation programs and alternative products.

For many, however, the solution to the smoking problem goes beyond ensuring informed choice.

Prevention and Child Protection

A second perspective on the smoking problem concentrates on the young. We have a long tradition in America of governmental intervention to protect children and youth, drawing on the idea that their immaturity prevents minors from making the sort of informed choice adults can make. Immaturity can preclude adolescents from sensibly considering large consequences before they act—especially long-term consequences. Hence we force young people to stay in school; we restrict their right to marry and to work in certain jobs; we allow them to dishonor their contracts; we don't allow them to vote or purchase alcohol; we subject them to curfews; and so on.

The child protection perspective on smoking emphasizes the fact that an overwhelming proportion of smokers begin when they are minors and that teenage smokers probably discount the future risk to themselves—especially because they probably think they can always quit. Yet it turns out that large numbers do not (and perhaps cannot) stop smoking, even though most adult smokers say they want to quit and have tried, unsuccessfully, to do so.

The child protection view also dovetails with the goal of long-term elimination of tobacco use through prevention. The idea is that if we can keep teenagers from starting to smoke, then the smoking problem as a cause of disease and death will largely solve itself over time. This view assumes that, in the great majority of cases, if people do not begin smoking in adolescence, relatively few will ever start to smoke at all. Whatever the accuracy of that assumption, from this perspective current adult smokers are not the real concern; rather, public policy efforts should be aimed at the next generation.

Advocates of governmental policies targeting children are likely to promote a variety of initiatives: school and community education, restrictions or bans on advertisements and promotions thought to be attractive to youths (including tobacco company sponsorship of sporting and pop culture events, free distribution of cigarette samples, and billboard ads), public sponsorship of mass media antismoking advertising aimed at youths, bans or tight controls on sales of cigarettes through vending machines, stringent penalties and enforcement of laws forbidding the sale of tobacco products to minors, and steep taxes on tobacco products (on the assumption that young, would-be smokers are especially sensitive to price). The general idea here is to make smoking "uncool," and to combine that strategy with making teenage access much more difficult.

Some people who want government to serve the best interests of children view the key role as one of empowering parents, on the theory that parents, in general, can be most counted on to want the best for their children. But this vision has been largely absent from the tobacco debate, perhaps because it is not clear which policies would be appropriate to help parents influence their children's use of tobacco, or perhaps because young people are typically most rebellious against their parents at the age when they begin to smoke. Of course, parents who themselves smoke are thought to be part of the problem and not a likely source of the solution.

Even if people were inappropriately seduced into smoking as teens, if they all quit on becoming adults most people would probably consider the smoking problem relatively trivial. But, although many teen smokers do later quit, many others do not. This brings us to a third perspective on the smoking problem.

Smokers as Addicted Victims

Our society often extends special compassion towards those who are considered "victims." Victims of violent crimes, accidents, fraud, and natural disasters are some obvious examples. Although "innocent" and "victim" are often conjoined, this is not always the case. Indeed, one way to try to elicit sympathy for people engaged in what is widely viewed as socially deviant or personally irresponsible conduct is to label them victims—drug abusers, unwed teenage mothers, and prostitutes come to mind. Victims are typically seen to be entitled to help from society, especially when they have been victimized by impersonal forces, either natural or social. They are also thought to have rights against identifiable victimizers.

In the context of smoking, the standard liberal position in American politics (as explained earlier) is that once adults have been assured informed choice, the role of government ends. After all, the adventurous among us get great satisfaction out of risky activities ranging from sky-diving to skiing, and most would agree that government has no business interfering with these informed choices. Why should smoking be regarded differently?

Those who see smokers as victims respond to this claim of individual autonomy by arguing that smoking is unlike these other voluntary activities because smokers are addicted to tobacco use, and, as a result, do not have the opportunity to exercise personal choice to quit. In short, current smokers have been duped. They were lured into smoking, and large numbers are now stuck with a habit they cannot seem to break. Whereas the informed choice viewpoint implicitly assumes that some people will truly prefer to smoke (notwithstanding its dangers), this perspective assumes that smoking is really in the self-interest of virtually no one. Smoking is effectively considered an irrational choice, one that nearly all smokers now regret (Goodin 1989, pp. 27–28).

The addiction claim draws heavily on studies summarized in the 1988 Surgeon General's Report, *The Health Consequences of Smoking: Nicotine Addiction*, and rests on two premises; namely, that a substance is "addictive" if: (1) once regular use has commenced, physiological effects, establishing a dependency, are evident in its users, and (2) when termination of use is attempted, physiological impediments arise which a user has a very difficult time overcoming (U.S. DHHS, Surgeon General 1988; Goodin 1989, pp. 25–28). Although the data in support of these two propositions appear to be very strong, the conclusions to be drawn from the empirical findings are less clear-cut than might appear on first impression.

The 1988 Surgeon General's Report provides voluminous evidence of the physical consequences associated with the use of nicotine, the prime addictive substance in tobacco. Through studies of animals and humans, cigarette smoke has been traced directly to the bloodstream and thence into the brain and nervous system where alterations in function have been clearly identified. Related studies have revealed two classic characteristics of addictive behavior: (1) the development of "tolerance," the graduated need for larger amounts of the substance (nicotine) to reach a steady state of physical equipoise, and (2) the occurrence of "reenforce-ment," the ability selectively to discriminate among substances (in blind tests) to satisfy the craving for the substance.

Similarly, the empirical findings are impressive that a withdrawal syndrome occurs when nicotine use is terminated. Studies have documented changes in mood, behavior, and physical functioning, such as increases in restlessness, anxiety, irri-tability, somatic and physical complaints, and food intake, as well as lapsed concen-tration and weight gain. Other studies have documented involuntary physical reac-tions, including changes in heart rate, cortical arousal, psychomotor reactions, and sensitivity to visual stimuli. On the whole, these behavioral changes appear to be particularly pronounced in the first week or so of smoking deprivation, and seem to be rapidly reversed once smoking is resumed.

However, there are at least two problems with this analysis. First, what about the 50 percent quit-rate among smokers (U.S. DHHS, Surgeon General 1989, pp. 285–92)? Doesn't such a substantial population of ex-smokers largely undermine the argument that the physiological effects of withdrawal make it very difficult to quit? Indeed, this reaction seems to have motivated the juries which have been distinctly unsympathetic to victims' claims in the cigarette-cancer tort litigation. Put differently, even if it is hard to quit, just how difficult is it? Unfortunately, the Surgeon General's report doesn't really answer this question.

Second, it is possible to raise an objection to the 1988 report that cuts still deeper. Don't other personal obsessions that we would not dream of controlling in ways proposed for smoking also qualify as "addictions" under the report's defini-tion? Consider the runner whose daily routine is incomplete without a five-mile early morning workout. It is not fanciful to think that such a person, upon being suddenly sidelined for an indefinite period, might suffer considerable anxiety, stress, irritability, difficulty in concentrating, and most of the other effects associ-ated with nicotine withdrawal. Has not our runner experienced a "physiological" reaction? And what difference does it make whether we label it "physiological" or "psychosomatic"? Don't the sorts of behavioral manifestations associated with quit-ting smoking frequently accompany the sudden, permanent (or so perceived) cessa-tion of many passionate "habits" that provide sustenance to an individual's basic psychic needs?

Yet our political culture has resisted telling individuals that to take up such habits is bad for them because later they will find it very hard to stop. We don't try to curtail skiing, for example, just because many children get the ski "bug" and some, as adults, go on to become ski "bums"—remaining "addicted" for longer than their bodies can take it and leaving the slopes only when injured. Or consider the avid mountaineer. Would high-altitude climbing be legislatively prohibited if new epi-demiological data and lab studies indicated, to the chagrin of all concerned, that there is a significant relationship between such climbing and fatalities from coro-nary heart disease—and yet "hooked" climbers continued their sport in the face of these findings? It seems highly unlikely.

To be persuasive, then, the perspective that sees smokers as victims must be able to distinguish the case of tobacco use from other habits, routines, and even "addic-tions" that are, by consensus, regarded as best left unregulated. Such a case might be built upon three related factors. First, consider the *magnitude of abuse*. Virtually *all* cigarette smokers are at risk of the most serious physical consequences; there is no documented safe level of smoking, and, in any event, almost all smokers quickly develop a tolerance that places them in the category of substantial users. Contrast, for example, the drinking habit. While excessive drinking is a serious social problem—generating a heavy toll on family life and worker productivity—and can be traced directly to a substantial number of deaths and physical disabilities, it remains the case that most individuals who regularly drink keep it under control, and that, in moderation, alcohol use has no harmful consequences.

A second factor that distinguishes tobacco use from most other hedonistic activities is the *magnitude of the risk* associated with smoking. It may be unwise to eat sweets or potato chips obsessively; it may be courting danger to sky-dive or ski at every opportunity. But the probability of very serious personal harm occurring from any of these activities does not come close to the risk of dire consequences associated with smoking. A recent study published by researchers at the National Cancer Institute estimated that more than 90 percent of the 92,000 expected lung cancer deaths among U.S. males and more than 78 percent of an estimated 51,000 deaths among women in 1991 would be attributable to smoking. Indeed, even without considering secondary smoke or coronary heart disease fatalities, smoking was estimated to account for 30.6 percent of the more than 500,000 total cancer deaths (Shopland et al. 1991). While these figures do not tell us the prospects of any particular individual contracting a smoking-related fatal disease, they indicate the singular dimensions of the aggregate risk associated with tobacco use.

A third distinguishing characteristic of tobacco use is the *magnitude of difficulty in breaking the habit*. Although the 1988 Surgeon General's report is disappointingly thin on this point, nonetheless, in the final analysis, smoking does seem distinctive on this dimension too. The crucial point is that smokers typically use cigarettes to deal with an exceedingly wide range of everyday social activities. Whether coping with bad news, enjoying a good meal, beginning a difficult work assignment, or simply facing the break of another day, the habituated smoker draws a measure of continuing sustenance, ego-strength, even companionship from a cigarette. By contrast, most forms of compulsive personal satisfaction, whether it be skiing, sky-diving, or some other activity, play a far more compartmentalized role in satisfying the emotional needs of "hooked" individuals—and consequently can be more easily targeted for replacement by substitute activities.

Like smoking, drinking seems to play a pervasive role as a multiple-function support system for a substantial number of dependent persons. Nonetheless, as we have indicated, most alcohol users simply do not fall prey to a multiple-function dependency syndrome.

It is precisely these multiple-function, nonsubstitutable characteristics of tobacco use that, we believe, best explain why large numbers of smokers continue to maintain the habit. In the crunch, the smoker concludes that the utility of smoking simply exceeds the perceived risks. Does that, in turn, mean that we would violate smokers' own risk/utility preferences by getting them to quit? Not necessarily, when one considers the latent character of the health risks.

Unlike the sky-diver, skier, or even the alcoholic, the typical smoker has no feedback mechanism in the course of her daily routine to trigger a sense of imminent jeopardy to physical condition. Indeed, given the long-term nature of the harm from smoking, and the potential for avoiding serious physical consequences by quitting "soon," tobacco use takes on an especially sinister character: cumulative physical debilitation goes largely unnoticed, and, whenever extrinsic risk information is assimilated, a rationale is at hand for discounting one's concern—the risk can be addressed at a later point in time.

While these distinctive characteristics of smoking obviously do not suggest that quitting is impossible, they do make a strong case for giving greater credence to the confirmed smoker's expressions of regret than one might extend in other contexts.

What policies follow from the perspective that sees smokers as victims? For those adhering to this perspective, the tobacco companies are the primary wrong-doers; but, of late, others are also seen to victimize smokers by shunning them in various ways. Initiatives might include (a) allowing tort damage claims by smokers against the tobacco companies (or, in the alternative, creating a smoking victims' compensation fund, analogous to the federal Black Lung program for victims of mining-related diseases) and (b) adopting smokers' rights laws that protect smokers from discrimination in employment, and perhaps assure them a reasonable place to smoke during the workday.

Yet perhaps not all smoking "victims" need remain so. After all, victims of other "addictions" do sometimes solve their problems. Often they turn to support net-works for help in this process. Alcoholics Anonymous and similar groups that have been set up for people with other "addictions" (such as cocaine and gambling) fall in this category. Indeed, Americans these days apparently join private self-help pro-grams in droves whenever they are trying to break habits that, while providing some pleasure, are thought to be undesirable on balance. Weight loss programs for dieters are a prime example. The basic idea of these schemes is to impose constraints on one's own conduct in order to help achieve what one "really" wants.

In the tobacco context, the public policy problem would seem to be that, even if smokers mostly want to quit, the mere availability of schemes to help them do so does not appear to suffice. Hence, the "smokers as victims" perspective is also likely to favor the provision of free smoking-cessation programs—if not funded by the tobacco companies, then through employers or ordinary health insurance.

In any event, a perspective that depends upon some notion of addiction seeks to avoid the claim that its supporters are inappropriately paternalistic toward others. But not everyone finds paternalism objectionable—particularly, if it is addressed to behavior regarded as immoral.

Smoking as Immoral Behavior

Still another outlook, then, is that smoking reveals a self-destructive weakness of character; smoking, in short, is socially unacceptable, deviant conduct. It is one more form of "substance abuse" to be eliminated because of its degenerate quality. This, of course, is how many people feel about cocaine and heroin—quite apart from the question of whether their use leads to crime.

Our collective stance toward immoral conduct in America is highly variable—

putting aside such conduct that is condemned for its harm to others. While some want to restrict attacks on such behavior to rhetoric, religion, and individual conscience, others, notwithstanding the American experience with alcohol under Prohibition, are keen to use the muscle of the state against a wide range of conduct viewed as offensive to social norms.

This view seeks forcefully to pressure smokers to stop smoking, and would do so even if they were bothering no one else, and even if they continued to smoke in the face of the softer measures described above that might discourage teens from starting and help "victims" to quit.

Strongly coercive policies adopted from this perspective might include conditioning most jobs and other "essentials" on not being a smoker, adding onerous taxes to the sale of tobacco products, imposing radical limits on where tobacco products can be sold, and possibly even criminalizing of tobacco use (perhaps along with a "methadone" sort of strategy, under which smokers might be provided a nicotine arm patch while being weaned from cigarettes).

Protecting Non-Smokers

A final outlook sees smokers as villains. This perspective regards the central problem as one of smokers injuring innocent nonsmokers, rather than themselves. Smokers are considered much like other scoundrels in our society who violate the liberal maxim to avoid encroaching on the rights of others.

Grounding smoking regulation in the harm that it causes to others avoids the victimless-crime thicket confronting the previously discussed perspective. Once the rationale for regulatory action is located in the domain of general public health and welfare legislation, it takes on the coloration of a traditional exercise of the state's police power. Those who engage in activities imposing health and safety risks on the public have routinely been subjected to governmental control through regulatory standards backed up by criminal or other sanctions.

Lodging the strongest grievances here are those third parties who object to being involuntarily subjected to second-hand tobacco smoke. Their complaints have become conspicuously louder in the wake of the recent findings, discussed at the outset of this chapter, that "passive smoking" is not only an eye, nose, and throat irritant to many and a hazard to the allergic few, but also a source of cancer, heart disease and serious respiratory illnesses, just as it is to smokers themselves.

In addition, smokers are assailed for imposing financial harms on nonsmokers; for example, by disproportionately claiming benefits from public and group health insurance plans, thereby increasing their cost to nonsmokers, and by necessitating more frequent cleaning of clothes and other items that absorb smoke.

In the past, when smoking was widely accepted in the culture, the burden of avoiding harm fell on nonsmokers, who had the duty to get out of the way. But from a perspective that views smokers as injuring innocent third parties, the tables are turned: smokers must be made to stop their wrongdoing or at least to internalize into the cost of smoking those externalities they impose on others.

From a policy standpoint, however, the data on ETS, as alarming as they may sound, need to be kept in perspective. The studies summarized in the 1986 report, indicating a statistically significant increase in lung cancer, as well as those showing less conclusive evidence of linkage to other serious diseases, draw exclusively on cohorts involving household exposure of nonsmoking to smoking spouses. More recent studies suggest similar adverse consequences for the children of parents who smoke. Without question, the elevated risk for nonsmoking spouses and children of long-term smokers is a finding of major import.

But what follows from such results? Is a spouse who continues to live with someone who insists on smoking in the home entitled to governmental help? Are parents who smoke around their children guilty of child abuse? Certainly our traditional answers to both of these questions would be "no."

Furthermore, it does not inexorably follow from the intrafamily studies that government should limit tobacco exposure in public spaces such as restaurants, common carriers, and sports arenas. To the contrary, occasional exposure to sidestream smoke by patrons of such facilities more likely has a *de minimis* effect on health, even among those who are heavily exposed in other settings.

On the other hand, under some circumstances, sustained worksite exposure may impose even greater health risks on employees than those experienced by nonsmoking spouses in the home. Many worksites are more enclosed and have poorer ventilation than the typical household setting. In many instances, the average number of hours per week of ETS exposure will be greater at work if smoking is allowed. And in many situations, the number of smokers per cubic foot of enclosed space will exceed that of the typical household. Brief reflection, however, makes it clear why reliable data on ETS health risks in the workplace are virtually impossible to collect. Nonsmokers rarely work in a fixed milieu over a long period of time, insulated from personnel changes among fellow workers and status changes in their own lives.

Despite the lack of data, it may well be that the various public spaces where there is least concern for health risks to *patrons* pose the strongest case for attentiveness to workplace health risks. In airplanes, restaurants, and enclosed sports arenas, for example, the turnover of minimally exposed patrons is irrelevant from the health perspective of the long-term service personnel whose average level of tobacco smoke exposure remains high.

The upshot is that, while public policies in furtherance of this perspective on the smoking problem are likely to focus on "zoning" controls on where people can smoke, it remains unclear just where those controls are justified. Should nonsmokers be assured the right to smoke-free use of public spaces, workplaces, public transit, and so on? The key question here is similar to many current issues of environmental risk assessment. Is government intervention warranted, based upon an extrapolation from reasonably clear cases to contexts where greater scientific uncertainty exists?

In the real world, of course, regulation is never undertaken in a political vacuum. And whatever the subtleties of the data, public opinion seems to have crystallized on the issue: 77 percent of nonsmokers (who now account for roughly three-quarters of the voting public) believe that smokers should abstain in the presence of nonsmokers ("Environmental Tobacco Smoke" 1992). This strong expression of sentiment against passive exposure to smoking undoubtedly reflects more than just a reaction to the health data, however discerning that perception may be. Almost certainly, it also reflects a growing lack of tolerance for the "annoyance costs" of exposure to secondary smoke, as well—costs that were largely ignored a generation ago.

Moving beyond zoning to the financial side, some who see smokers as wrong-doers call for measures such as differentials in premium contributions to group health insurance by smokers and nonsmokers (to go along with existing differentials in individual health and life insurance policies) and special taxes or charges imposed on smokers to pay for the extra public medical costs they incur. This perception of unfair economic advantage (to smokers) reflects empirical assumptions that are not beyond dispute. It has been pointed out, for example, that smokers claim less from the Social Security and pension systems because they die earlier, and yet they pay premium contributions that fail to take this consideration into account. More generally, some economists have argued that the old-age cross-subsidization just mentioned, when combined with the special taxes exacted on cigarette consumption, offset the aggregate added health and other costs that smokers impose on non-smokers (Manning et al. 1991).

In this section, our primary intention has been to examine the norms underlying the wide array of impulses to regulate. Next, we consider some implications of these perspectives in the arena of public policy.

The Policy Arena

Perspectives on the "Smoking Problem" Reflected in Current Policy

Law and policy making concerning smoking is a product of special interest politics. Smokers' rights groups, which might be regarded as analogous to the National Rifle Association or the Sierra Club, in fact are little developed, and have to date played no significant role in fighting antismoking laws. This perhaps is explained by the fact that, unlike those who love to hike or shoot, smokers don't really have the same unambiguously affirmative commitment to their behavior.

Instead, the lead has been taken by the tobacco industry—most importantly the manufacturers, but also the growers, retailers, and others who benefit from financially healthy tobacco companies. It should be noted, as well, that on advertising control and smokers' rights issues, the American Civil Liberties Union (ACLU) has thrown in with the tobacco industry, because the issues here are representative of that organization's broader Bill of Rights concerns.

On the tobacco control side, the dominant players are elite public health interests like the American Lung Association and the American Cancer Society, and more recently (as discussed by Helen Schauffler in chapter 9), related insurer and employer interests. (At the local level, grass-roots citizens groups do seem to be exercising growing power, as well.) Whether or not it is true that the increasing clout on the public health side can balance the power of the tobacco companies more effectively than in the past, as some believe, that hardly ensures current public policies that reflect current public opinion.

These caveats notwithstanding, and with due regard to the fact that tobacco control policies are by no means uniform at the state and local levels, we find it revealing to consider the ways in which current policy reflects the array of perspectives just described.

One take on current policy is that there is not only substantial support for the informed choice model, but also a reasonably strong belief that informed choice exists. Consider, initially, the fact that lawsuits against the tobacco companies, as explained by Robert Rabin in chapter 6 and Gary Schwartz in chapter 7, have failed largely on the ground that juries conclude that smokers were aware of the risks they were taking and made the choice to smoke anyway. Consider also, that in the United States (as discussed by Robert Kagan and David Vogel in chapter 2), apart from the radio and TV ban, there is now little regulation of ads for tobacco products and only modest required disclosures of the risks of smoking on the product and in promotional materials.

At the same time, current policy does not much reflect the view of smokers as victims. Not only have their lawsuits failed, as just mentioned, but, as Helen Schauffler explains in chapter 9, smoking cessation is little supported either through coverage in health insurance plans or through direct public subsidy. By contrast, under the spur of state-mandated benefit laws, nearly all insured health plans cover treatment for alcoholism and drug abuse.

We take note of the fact, discussed by Stephen Sugarman in chapter 8, that many states have recently adopted smokers' rights laws. While these laws might be considered a countertrend, they seem more aimed at heading off the possibility of a strong movement to discriminate against how workers behave during leisure time than to enable smokers to fight back against widespread existing victimization.

On the other hand, protection of nonsmokers is a growing theme. One strategy of the strong and spreading attack on passive smoking is to designate where people can and cannot smoke—a strategy, as Robert Kagan and Jerome Skolnick explain in chapter 4, that seems to have been largely effective in the United States where enacted. A very different form of nonsmoker protection has been a focal point of recent attention: eliminating economic cross-subsidization by "making smokers pay," through, for example, differential group health insurance premiums. But this movement, as Helen Schauffler discusses in chapter 9, is still largely in the talking stage.

Despite the many laws on the books concerning the illegality of cigarette sales to minors, our society does not yet seem very serious about the child protection perspective. In most places, those laws are not effectively enforced; in only a limited number of areas are cigarette vending machines inaccessible to youths; in comparison with Canada and Europe, taxes on cigarettes remain low (as Robert Kagan and David Vogel show in chapter 2); and outside California it is not easy to find mass media campaigns against smoking aimed at teenagers. Indeed, to the contrary, as discussed by Michael Schudson in chapter 10, young people are very well aware of Joe Camel, the Marlboro Man, and other tobacco company-initiated advertising symbols.

Nor do we seem to be moving toward condemning smoking as immoral through coercive public actions. Again, smokers do not face daunting excise taxes, and efforts to condition jobs on nonsmoking status are being stymied. Yet, at the same time, smoking is becoming an increasingly stigmatized form of conduct in the private culture—a theme explored by both Joseph Gusfield in chapter 3 and Franklin Zimring in chapter 5.

Value and Policy Conflict

Previously we set out several social outlooks on the smoking problem and suggested various specific policy initiatives that might be taken to correspond with the different perspectives. In this section, we want to suggest some of the ways in which the "fit" between values and policy may be far from perfect. By doing so, we hope to provide a clearer understanding of what is at stake in opting for one set of policy initiatives over another.

To begin with, similar policies may sometimes be invoked in support of dissimilar perspectives on the nature of the smoking problem. For example, a call for oppressive cigarette taxes may win the support of both those who connect smoking with the immaturity of children and those who connect it with the immorality of adults. These compatibilities may facilitate that special sort of political logrolling that sometimes infuriates students of the legislative process, in which the votes necessary to pass a certain law are obtained even though it is impossible to state a coherent legislative purpose that had the support of the majority.

On the other hand, some tobacco-control policies are quite incompatible with diverse perspectives on the smoking problem. High taxes may fit some outlooks as just noted, but not "informed choice" or "smokers as victims." Legal liability of tobacco companies to smokers may serve "smokers as victims" but not "informed choice"—assuming there was sufficiently informed choice in the first place. Smokers' rights laws may support "informed choice" and "smokers as victims" but hardly "smoking as immoral behavior."

Precision is important, because policies that may appear at first blush to be compatible with different outlooks turn out on more careful scrutiny to be irreconcilable. Consider, for example, the question of cigarette taxes. Modest taxes may be justified to provide "protection for nonsmokers" by making smokers pay their way, but not the heavy taxes sought by the "child protection" and "immorality" perspectives. Regulation of advertising provides another illustration. The sort of controls justified by the "child protection" perspective are quite different from those supported from the "informed choice" or the "smoking as immoral behavior" perspectives.

Because there are divergent views of the smoking problem, those who want public intervention may not agree readily on what that intervention should be. This is not to suggest, however, that a person cannot coherently believe that there is more than one aspect to the smoking problem. For example, in principle one could blend the viewpoints of "child protection" and "informed choice"; or hold both the outlooks "child protection" and "smokers as victims"; or endorse "smoking as immoral behavior," "protection of nonsmokers," and "child protection" perspectives. Nevertheless, as already suggested, any package of policies put together in support of multiple viewpoints is likely to create some internal tensions and inconsistencies.

This potential for tension is generally shown by the fact that the different outlooks intersect the dimension of coercion at quite different points. Coercion is the antithesis of "informed choice," and it is not comfortably congruent with "smokers as victims"; on the other hand, the "smoking as immoral behavior" viewpoint seems consistent with strong coercive measures, while "child protection" endorses sharp coercion only of youths, and "protection of nonsmokers" favors coercion essentially only regarding location.

Sometimes policies advocated from differing viewpoints are neither mutually reenforcing nor incompatible. They are simply aimed at different targets. Consider, for example, tough enforcement of laws forbidding sales to minors and subsidization of smoking cessation programs. In more awkward fashion, this pattern may also pave the way to political logrolling. Yet the more general problem remains that differing outlooks do not make for a clear tobacco-control policy agenda.

Why are there competing outlooks on the smoking problem? At the most basic level, it is probably a matter of contrasting values. The respective ideas that smoking is immoral, a regrettable habit to be broken, or a perfectly permissible private adult behavior reflect very different starting points.

There may also be sharp disputes about "the facts." As discussed earlier, is smoking really a matter of choice, or is it largely an addiction? If the latter, smokers may seem less immoral, less like villains, and more like victims; so too, compensation rather than cessation may be the most feasible amelioration. By contrast, if smoking is better understood to be voluntary, then it becomes easier to support penalties for harming others and for bearing the consequences of harm to oneself; at the same time, it makes cessation appear more promising. And how powerful is tobacco advertising and promotion? Do relatively few people enter or remain in the market in response to it, or is marketing responsible for seducing countless youths and for keeping even more adults on the hook?

Finally, what does the existing patchwork pattern of governmental activity and social norms suggest about the need for continuing activity on the political front? Has the array of sensible political initiatives been utilized to full effect, or does much remain to be done in the public policy sphere? On this score there is disagreement as well, and it is to these questions that we turn in our final section.

Assessing the Need for Stronger Tobacco Control Measures

Since the Surgeon General's 1964 report, a sea change has taken place in attitudes toward smoking in America. As we noted at the outset, the proportion of adults who smoke is radically lower and continues to drop. Among elites, a smoker is increasingly the unusual exception. As Joseph Gusfield discusses in chapter 3, health and fitness are "in" and smoking is decidedly "out." Not only is smoking at odds with the images of today's leaders, heroes, and idols, but also it rarely seems part of the persona of today's attractive rebels. Smokers are increasingly marginalized and considered reckless, although perhaps viewed with sympathy, by America's cultural trend-setters. In such company, smokers are often on the defensive—apologetic, sheepish, and self-deprecating. In short, if the pattern of the past two decades continues much longer, smokers will be proportionately few indeed.

In view of this trend, perhaps all the agitation by antismoking advocates is alarmist, seeking inappropriately strong government initiatives when such action may not be all that critical. Patience may accomplish the objectives of virtually all the perspectives on the smoking problem that we have discussed.

To be sure, this sharp downward trend in the proportion of Americans who smoke has come about in an environment of governmental policy interventions to reduce smoking. Thus, one critical question is whether those policies aimed at cutting the smoking rate have themselves made an important difference. Or, by contrast, has smoking behavior been transformed largely in response to a combination of the Surgeon General's reports and changing cultural norms, which, through subtle processes, make unfashionable certain behaviors that were formerly chic? Unfortunately, it is not easy to answer these questions. In chapter 5, Franklin Zimring cautions us that, *a priori*, it is as plausible that the widespread rejection of smoking by elites is what brings about antismoking legislation as it is that antismoking laws bring down the smoking rate.

Indeed, a host of critical policy questions remain unanswered. Do higher taxes on tobacco have any long-lasting impact on consumption levels? Or do people, if necessary, simply adjust by determinedly smoking more of each cigarette? Do advertising controls really curtail or prevent smoking? Michael Schudson in chapter 10 argues that advertising is almost surely far less persuasive than most people believe. Aren't teenagers primarily influenced by peers anyway, and don't they smoke at very high levels in many places where there is virtually no advertising, such as Eastern Europe? And regardless of what message the tobacco companies are trying to send, or conceal, aren't most people already aware of the information on the risks of smoking?

Robert Kagan and Jerome Skolnick, in chapter 4, observe that American laws restricting where people can smoke seem to have received a boost from catching the tide of cultural change at just the right moment. But then again, in the present climate in the United States, there may be no need to translate social pressures into further governmental edicts. After all, local ordinances or not, a growing number of employers are adopting smoking control policies, many of which radically restrict or prohibit smoking on the job; and a steadily increasing number of food and entertainment establishments are at a minimum assuring that nonsmokers can enjoy themselves in a smoke-free (or largely smoke-free) environment independent of local ordinances. For example, a 1991 survey found that 85 percent of responding companies had smoking policies, up from 36 percent in 1986. Moreover, 34 percent of the respondents prohibited smoking in all company buildings, as compared with only 2 percent in 1986 (BNA 1991).

Moreover, most of the smoking control measures that promise to be effective may already have been enacted. Similarly, most adult smokers who are most likely to be influenced to quit by public policy interventions may already have done so. If these two points are accurate, then new interventions will face a steep uphill battle, and the returns may be marginal compared with those of the recent past.

From still another perspective, some people who favor a smoke-free America would nevertheless want to restrict government's role to that appropriate to the informed choice approach, on the ground that, in the long run, the only really effective strategy is to convince people to decide for themselves that smoking is too dangerous. From this vantage point, any heavier government pressure on people to stop smoking promises to be counterproductive.

There is also the question of civic relations. Although many nonsmokers feel validated by having legal rights to assert against smokers, this may not be the best way to resolve conflicts over social behavior in our society. It is not only that recognizing new legal rights contributes to our sense that America is drowning in law and litigation, but also that pursuing the "rights" approach may undercut modes of dispute resolution that help to ensure that both parties comfortably feel part of the same community in the long run.

Finally, smoking control policies carry costs. There are, of course, the direct financial costs that go along with educational programs, antismoking media campaigns, subsidized smoking cessation schemes, and the like—although these might well be funded out of cigarette taxes. And there are administrative costs, both public and private, that are almost always incurred in any regulatory program. But beyond these economic burdens, there are other important, albeit less tangible, costs associated with at least some of the policies discussed above. For example, as Stephen Sugarman discusses in chapter 8, when employers or insurers discriminate against those who smoke outside of work, various privacy losses are incurred by smokers (and sometimes nonsmokers as well), the social value of individualized fair treatment is threatened, and the principle of collective responsibility may be violated in areas of American life where it has long held sway. As a further example, discussed by Michael Schudson in chapter 10, certain proposed controls on cigarette promotion jeopardize traditional free-speech values. This is not to say that such controls would be unconstitutional; yet the values underlying the First Amendment may nonetheless be bruised. And as a final example, explored in somewhat different ways by Helen Schauffler in chapter 9, Franklin Zimring in chapter 5, and Stephen Sugarman in chapter 8, several tobacco control policies would have the *de facto* effect of bearing down hardest on ethnic minorities and the poor.

However, we are not necessarily opposing tougher antismoking public policies. After all, powerful responses are still available to those who are unpersuaded by this litany of caution. First, many of the tobacco control policies we have discussed in fact have only spotty adoption. While there are a burgeoning number of laws addressed to workplace and public space smoking controls, many states and communities are still without them. In like fashion, some states have raised tobacco taxes recently, but many others have not. Some states and localities have invested substantially in school-based antismoking education, or in antismoking ads on TV, or have banned cigarette vending machines from places readily accessible to children, but many have not. Therefore, for many tobacco-control advocates one part of getting the job done right is to make at least some of these extant policies far more comprehensive.

Second, despite the downward trend in smoking, tobacco control advocates are apt to have two major concerns. The initial fear is that if new smoking control programs are not adopted, the downward trend may be arrested. In the long run, perhaps one-quarter of all American adults might continue to smoke. In short, easing up on regulation in the hope that social disapproval will take care of things can be regarded as just too risky. This fear is fueled by the fact that new smokers are increasingly from the ranks of poorer and less-educated young people. This leads to the further worry that, without continued pressure from smoking-control activists, the American middle class may lose interest in attacking the problem—particularly since cigarette smoking does not seem to promote criminal behavior in the way that illicit drug use does, and does not seem to promote the sort of threat of injury to innocent victims associated with alcohol abuse.

The other great concern is that even if the downward trend in smoking behavior continues on its current path, millions of people will die before the rate gets anywhere near zero. These deaths might be avoided if the downward rate can be accelerated by some combination of the policy initiatives discussed above.

What, then, is the appropriate public policy stance on smoking and tobacco? The chapters that follow are not centrally designed to provide a blueprint answer, even though some of the authors do include their own judgments along with their analysis. Rather, these studies describe and analyze several important policy choices. We present those appraisals to help decision makers fashion policy that is sensitive to the many competing perspectives in this critical area of social concern.

2

The Politics of Smoking Regulation: Canada, France, the United States

Robert A. Kagan and David Vogel

Which is more remarkable?

- Twenty-five years after their hazards have been widely publicized, cigarettes—highly addictive, extremely dangerous, and unnecessary products—continue to be sold and consumed in huge volumes.
- Within the last decade or two, despite the objections of economically powerful tobacco industries and of millions of smokers (a sizable proportion of the electorate), virtually every democratic industrialized nation has enacted laws that curtail cigarette advertising, impose new taxes on cigarettes, and prevent smoking in public places where citizens have long been accustomed to light up at will.

The answer depends on one's vision of politics. If you expect democratic governments to take all effective measures to prevent disease and suffering, the continued availability of cigarettes would appear to represent a shocking and perverse example of interest-group politics, in which the economic and political power of the tobacco industry has subverted governmental pursuit of "the public interest." If, on the other hand, you expect interest-group pressures to drive political action or you are skeptical about the capacity of government to change everyday habits, then it does seem remarkable that governments have made such extensive efforts to restrict the marketing and use of tobacco products.

Neither perspective is entirely right or wrong. The politics of tobacco regulation is most appropriately understood in terms of the ongoing *interaction* between interest-group politics and the politics of ideas about "the public interest." This chapter, therefore, focuses on how the relative potency of interests and ideas has been affected by institutional arrangements, governmental structure, and political culture. Specifically, we examine how political institutions in the United States, in comparison with those in two other countries—Canada and France—have shaped the struggle for laws regulating the sale and use of tobacco products.[1]

The Politics of Smoking: An Overview

In all economically developed countries, cigarette smoking is by far the most important preventable cause of cancer, heart disease, and premature death. Around the world, millions of people will die this year from smoking cigarettes—more than will die from being hit by automobiles or from the effects of pollution. Thus, public health officials and others have called for tough legal restrictions on cigarette marketing and use, as well as for educational campaigns that encourage smokers to quit and persuade youngsters not to begin.

Underlying this campaign for legal change are two simple ideas: (1) it is wrong to market products of limited social utility that cause widespread addiction and disease; and (2) governments have an obligation to take measures against preventable causes of widespread disease and suffering. These ideas have given rise to scores of laws regulating hazardous foods, drugs, and other products, along with pollution control and other public health regulations.

Against these simple moral claims for regulation, however, are arrayed some very powerful material interests as well as some competing ideals. In the United States, Canada, and France, the tobacco industry is large, profitable, and politically potent. Each country has a substantial tobacco-growing agricultural sector.[2] Cigarette manufacturing in the United States and Canada is dominated by a handful of huge private companies, which increasingly have diversified into packaged foods and other products and hence are very important employers and advertisers. In France, the cigarette market until recently was dominated by a state-owned monopoly. In each country, governments receive substantial revenues from cigarette taxes.

In the United States and Canada, tobacco company advertising expenditures represent a very important source of income for magazines, newspapers, advertising agencies, and the billboard industry. By their generous sponsorship of sporting events, arts organizations, civil rights organizations, and charities, tobacco companies have won both visibility and political allies. Tobacco companies also have been major sponsors of speaking engagements and political contributions for politicians, and have been able to buy the services of outstanding lobbyists and lawyers.

Millions of smokers, too—until recently, a majority of adult males in each of the three countries—presumably also oppose large tax increases and laws that would prohibit them from smoking in offices, railway terminals, airplanes, and restaurants. For decades, cigarette smoking has been a deeply ingrained custom, carried on in many settings, woven into the routines of social life. And cigarettes are addictive; many smokers find it all but impossible to quit. One might expect them, therefore, to be an easily mobilized, intense, antiregulatory political constituency. All in all, if politics and law reflect powerful interests, then one would expect the tobacco industry, along with its allies in the advertising media and the vast army of smokers, to be effective in blocking enactment of regulations and taxes that significantly restrict or discourage smoking.

The smokers' interests, moreover, are "ideal" as well as material, and they can appeal to strongly held values. Why, they might argue, should a democratic government go beyond informing and warning consumers that tobacco products are dangerous? Why shouldn't people for whom cigarettes provide pleasure or alleviate stress be able to choose for themselves whether to take the associated risks? Believing in the primacy of individual choice, many nations allow their citizens to choose a wide variety of risky activities. They can speed downhill on skis. They are permitted to indulge in rich desserts or heavy beer drinking while never exercising. They can engage in promiscuous sex without using condoms or other precautions against AIDS or other sexually transmitted diseases. In the United States, they can keep a loaded handgun in a bedside nightstand.

At the practical level, moreover, the legal landscape is littered with failed governmental attempts to prohibit unhealthful and addictive but widespread private indulgences, ranging from the American effort to ban alcoholic beverages during the 1920s to current futile efforts in many countries to extirpate the sale and use of heroin, cocaine, and other narcotics.

In sum, both powerful material interests and significant competing ideas— freedom of individual choice, hostility to state paternalism—are arrayed against demands for legal restrictions on cigarette marketing and use. From this perspective, it *is* rather remarkable that by 1992, virtually every democratic industrialized nation had enacted or was threatening to enact tobacco control measures that have gone well beyond requiring warning labels on cigarette packages and advertisements. These regulations include prohibitions against cigarette smoking in commercial airlines, stores, restaurants, offices and other public places, bans on cigarette advertising, and the imposition of costly excise taxes that in some countries exceed the price of the cigarettes themselves. In all these instances, the interests of the tobacco industry and its allies have been overridden.

The upsurge of tobacco regulation must be seen, therefore, as the product not only of everyday interest-group politics but also of a broader cultural movement. Everywhere, richer societies have been swept by the politics of environmental purification, with rising demands to remove chemical pollutants from the air, the water, and the workplace and to ban or regulate potentially dangerous compounds in food supplies and beverages (Douglas and Wildavsky 1982). Similarly, increasing numbers of people have become concerned about the health hazards associated with smoking. In previously heavy-smoking countries like the United States and Canada, by 1980 at least half the adult population did *not* smoke. Their number includes countless family members and friends of smokers who suffered and died from lung cancer and emphysema. Many nonsmokers are annoyed by tobacco smoke, some find it nearly intolerable, and those exposed to it continuously, it is now realized, are endangered. Many smokers—a majority in some countries—report that they would like to quit and have attempted to do so, often repeatedly. Like Ulysses, they might want someone else to tie them to the mast, preventing them from compulsively doing what they themselves believe is against their long-term interest. In addition, many addicted smokers may support regulations that would help prevent their children from taking up the habit.

But while many individual nonsmokers (and smokers) might prefer tougher controls on tobacco, they are not organized. Effective antitobacco legislation, therefore, has emerged only through aggressive, imagininative, and determined leadership—what James Q. Wilson (1980) calls "entrepreneurial politics." That leadership can come from a variety of sources—governmental public health officials, academic public health researchers, charitable organizations concerned with cancer and disease prevention, specialized antitobacco lobbying organizations and nonsmokers' rights organizations, and politicians who feel that anticigarette crusading would be electorally advantageous or personally gratifying.

Against the financial resources of the tobacco industry, the antitobacco policy entrepreneurs must deploy the power of ideas. Their challenge has been to redefine the social acceptability of smoking and tobacco marketing to mobilize political support for legal restrictions on both. In some polities, such as France, the antismoking activists have employed an "inside" strategy: well-placed elites in the public health establishment quietly attempted to persuade the minister of health and other key cabinet members that tougher regulations and higher excise taxes would be wise public policy. In the United States, with its far more fragmented political system, antismoking advocates more often (although not exclusively) pursued an "outside" strategy, seeking to persuade governments to act by first influencing public opinion. Their tools have been grass-roots organizing and lobbying, efforts to "demonize" tobacco companies as callous drug pushers, and a guerrilla war of local bans designed to delegitimate smoking as a social practice. In Canada, advocates successfully combined "inside" and "outside" strategies.

The Two Phases of Tobacco Regulation

In most countries that have regulated tobacco products, controls seem to have come in two waves. Phase I regulations primarily sought to enable citizens to make more informed choices. They required cigarette companies to print health warnings on cigarette packages, and in some cases, in magazine and billboard ads. Additionally, Phase I regulations in many countries banned TV and radio ads for tobacco products, on the theory that the seductive power of Marlboro cowboys galloping across television screens would overwhelm the health warnings on the packages.

In many richer countries, after the enactment of Phase I measures, cigarette smoking rates gradually fell, although it is unclear to what extent the decline was stimulated by the legally required warning labels and by TV ad bans—as opposed to the diffusion of public health research findings and intensifying cultural concerns about health, hidden chemical risks, and longevity. In any case, by 1990 American economist Thomas Schelling (1991, p. 1) could write:

> Half the men who ever smoked in this country have quit, and nearly half the women. In my generation three-quarters of young men smoked; the fraction is now less than one-third and going down. Fifty million [American] people have quit smoking, and a hundred million who would have become smokers since 1945 did not.

A 1985 Gallup poll reported that 94 percent of Americans surveyed believed that smoking was hazardous to health, most recognizing that it could lead to respiratory cancer and heart disease. The original legislative goals seemed to have been met. Almost everyone was informed about tobacco's hazards.

Or were they? Antismoking activists pointed out that if fifty million Americans had quit, fifty million still smoked. Even more disturbing, in almost every country, young people continued to take up smoking in large numbers, especially young women and especially youngsters from the lower classes. Banned from television, private tobacco corporations rechanneled millions of advertising dollars into magazines, billboards, and sponsored sporting events. Some studies indicated that consumers did not read the small warning labels in carefully composed cigarette ads and did not fully understand the probability, variety and severity of smoking-related health hazards (Warner et al. 1986).[3]

Through the 1980s, therefore, antismoking activists sought to generate a second wave of controls. If Phase I regulations reflected the liberal state's responsibility to make information available in the marketplace of ideas, Phase II regulations were partly based on a more paternalistic ethos: governments should also ensure that citizens actually learn what they should and actually act in ways that are in their self-interest.[4] Thus antismoking activists called for (and in some countries, obtained) laws requiring larger, starker, more specific warning labels on cigarette packages.[5] They urged total bans on mass media advertising and on tobacco company sponsorship of athletic events. They demanded much higher cigarette taxes, high enough to discourage use.

Simultaneously, there emerged a new breed of antismoking entrepreneurs with a rather different Phase II control strategy. In many countries, grass-roots antismoking organizations sprang up, lobbying for laws and regulations that would prohibit smoking in public places and offices. Thus they sought to regulate the behavior not of cigarette companies but of individual smokers. By compulsory ostracism and inconveniencing of smokers, moreover, they hoped to encourage more smokers to quit and to brand smoking as a socially unacceptable behavior.

This "nonsmokers' rights" movement received new legitimation from a series of research findings, culminating in the U.S. Surgeon General's report for the year 1986, revealing that nonsmokers (such as spouses and children) who had systematically been exposed to cigarette smoke had a significantly elevated risk of contracting lung cancer. The activists could now argue that smoking violated the classical liberal maxim: one person's liberty ends where her actions harm others. Before, your coworker's smoking might have only annoyed you. Now, you could assert, it endangered you. Soon, proposals to ban smoking from workplaces, universities, airplanes, and waiting rooms catapulted onto the legislative agenda in many localities and nations.

Figure 2.1 provides a simplified map of the variety of Phase I and Phase II tobacco control laws. The horizontal dimension tracks the anticipated legal *beneficiaries*, dividing them into (a) smokers and potential nonsmokers (to be helped, somewhat paternalistically, "for their own good"); and (b) nonsmokers (to be protected from smokers). The vertical dimension is based on the *stringency* or *degree of intrusiveness and control* the laws seek to achieve, while simultaneously suggesting the temporal development of tobacco control measures. Thus, in the "paternalistic" column, Phase I regulation begins with governmental funding and circulation of research findings about the hazards of smoking. Moving toward greater stringency, governments require tobacco companies to provide warning labels and then to remove their advertisements from broadcast media.

In Phase II, "paternalistic" regulation increases in stringency, banning all adver-

Beneficiaries of Smoking Control Laws

	Smokers and Potential Smokers	Non-Smokers
Less Stringent and Intrusive	**Phase I Paternalism:** Government research and information Mandatory warnings by tobacco companies TV, radio ad bans	
More Stringent and Intrusive	**Phase II Paternalism:** Ban on print, billboard ads and promotional activities by tobacco companies Increased excise taxes on cigarettes Vending machine restrictions	**Non-Smokers' Rights:** Spot-zoning and use restrictions directed at: *businesses *individuals

Figure 2.1. A Typology of Smoking Regulations

tising. Moving from the regulation of tobacco companies to the "regulation" of individual smokers (and potential smokers), governments enact almost prohibitory excise taxes. The lower right-hand quadrant encompasses "rights-protecting" regulation, which for the most part developed only during Phase II, in the 1980s. In this category, governments, seeking to protect nonsmokers (not smokers, at least ostensibly), began by requiring businesses and employers to provide nonsmoking areas. The most stringent regulations have gone further, banning smoking in public and private spaces where nonsmokers congregate.

A Comparative Perspective: Tobacco Regulation in Canada and France

Viewed in comparative terms, the United States was quick to enact Phase I controls, requiring warnings on cigarette packages and banning cigarette advertising on television and radio. But by the late 1980s and early 1990s, many nations had instituted more stringent Phase II paternalistic measures. Eighteen countries had banned *all* tobacco advertising and sponsorship, while the United States imposed no significant restrictions on tobacco advertising after 1970. Whereas the average price of a pack of cigarettes in the United States was about $1.70 in 1991 (of which about 28 percent reflected state and federal taxes), in most other industrial nations cigarettes sold for $3 to $5 a pack, with taxes accounting for 60 to 70 percent of the retail price. On the other hand, the United States has been an aggressive protector of nonsmokers' rights, imposing more restrictions on where smokers can light up than almost any other country.

The sources of these differences are illuminated by comparing the politics of tobacco regulation in America with parallel struggles in Canada, which in recent years has been aggressive in both paternalistic controls and nonsmokers' rights protection, and in France, which, reversing American priorities, has been strong in enacting Phase II paternalistic measures but weak in protecting nonsmokers.

Canada

In 1991, Canada led the world, or was close to the lead, in restricting cigarette marketing, in deterring use through taxation, and in directly regulating cigarette use.

Marketing. The 1988 national Tobacco Products Control Act banned all ciga- rette advertising and promotions in newspapers and magazines.[6] The act also pro- hibited ads on billboards and transit posters (after January 1, 1991), and at points of sale (after 1992). It restricted brand-name tobacco promotions of arts and sports events[7] and prohibited use of tobacco brand names on nontobacco products (such as t-shirts, mugs, hats). The act also required large and forceful health warnings (including the statement that smoking is addictive) on cigarette packs and bill- boards.

Taxation. In the spring of 1989, Canada's minister of finance sharply increased federal cigarette taxes by about 80 percent, and in 1991 by 60 percent more. Adding tobacco and general sales taxes imposed by Canadian provinces, Canadian taxes on cigarettes were pushed up to about 76.5 percent of the total price paid by consumers—slightly higher than most Western European countries[8] and much high- er than the United States. In the spring of 1991, the retail price of a Canadian pack of cigarettes was almost Can$6.00, compared with about $1.70 (U.S.) in America.

Use. The 1988 national Non-Smokers' Rights Act banned smoking (except for designated, vented smoking rooms) in all federal government workplaces, jails and prisons, and federally regulated private workplaces (banks, broadcasting studios, transport companies). It banned smoking on all domestic airline flights (as of July 1990), Air Canada's international flights, intercity buses, most passenger train seats, and transport terminals.

Canada had not always been so ambitious. Bolstered by the tendency of Cana- dian smokers to dislike American cigarettes,[9] Canada has a substantial tobacco growing region in southern Ontario, with over 2,500 tobacco farms and dedicated representatives in Parliament (Underwood et al. 1987). Canada's tobacco compa- nies (Imperial Tobacco, Rothman's, Benson and Hedges, and RJR-Macdonald) regularly appoint prominent politicians or their family members to their corporate boards of directors and until recently poured thousands of dollars into sponsorship of popular private sports and performing arts organizations (Kyle 1990, p. 10). In the late 1960s, at the urging of governmental public health officials, a parliamentary committee recommended legislation restricting and eventually prohibiting tobacco advertising and promotion, but these initiatives were blunted by tobacco industry pressure. The bill was withdrawn when the industry adopted a voluntary advertising code, which included withdrawal of radio and television advertising and an agree- ment to print mild health warnings on the side of each pack (Lachance and Col- lishaw 1989, p. 32; Mintz 1990).[10]

No significant regulatory measures were enacted by the national government until more than fifteen years later. In 1986, when Air Canada announced an experimental ban on smoking, tobacco firms asked their employees to boycott those flights. In 1987, when the national government again introduced a bill that sought to ban cigarette advertising, the Canadian Tobacco Manufacturers' Council (CTMC) placed full-page paid advertisements in major daily newspapers, discounting the need for the law. As late as May 1986, Health Minister Jake Epp told Parliament that he did not think advertising should be banned, since little evidence existed that it would significantly reduce cigarette smoking (Corelli 1987, p. 24). Tobacco firms also organized and financed a massive letter-writing campaign by small shopkeepers, targeted at locally elected members of Parliament (MPs), to create the appearance of grass-roots opposition to the government bill (Lachance and Collishaw 1989, p. 44; Mintz 1990).

To overcome this opposition, it took both "inside" pressure from Health Ministry officials and political action by "outsiders"—confrontational grass-roots antismoking advocacy organizations, particularly the Non-Smokers' Rights Association (NSRA). Led by its publicity-smart executive director C. Garfield Mahood and by lawyer David Sweanor, NSRA sought to revive the effort to ban cigarette advertising. Prominent among NSRA's tactics were populist appeals to public opinion, intended "to attach," as Mahood put it, "an air of criminality to tobacco industry executives and their dishonest, callous marketing practices" (Mintz 1990, p. 31). Thus in 1986, when tobacco firms were attempting to persuade the government that strengthening the industry self-regulatory advertising code was preferable to legal restrictions on marketing, NSRA published a series of dramatic full-page ads in mass circulation newspapers and magazines. One asserted that more than 300,000 Canadians had died from tobacco-related disease since the code had been adopted, while "the government sits in legislative silence." Another demanded to know why, since tobacco is addictive, it is exempted from the food and drugs law, and why, if it is hazardous, it is exempted from the hazardous products law (Mintz 1990, pp. 35–36).[11]

NSRA also urged large nonpolitical health organizations, such as the Canadian Cancer Society (CCS), to join it in lobbying for advertising restrictions. As a governmental health official put it, when

> the CCS embraced . . . advocacy ardently, the media and the politicians took notice. It was one thing for the tobacco industry to go up against a group perceived by some as militant anti-smokers, but quite another for it to oppose a reputable, historically conservative, broad-based and volunteer driven charitable organisation. (Lachance and Collishaw 1989, p. 35)

In 1987, the CCS asked its volunteers to sign and send 35,000 black-bordered cards to their MPs, in memory of each Canadian estimated to have died annually from tobacco-related diseases. Similarly, the Canadian Medical Association (CMA) organized members to lobby MPs in their home constituencies, and in September 1987, the CMA president publicly asked all CMA members to vote against any MP who opposed the tobacco legislation (Lachance and Collishaw 1989, p. 36).

The antitobacco coalition simultaneously worked the channels of mass communication and inside political gamesmanship. The NSRA and other coalition leaders gave detailed briefings to newspaper publishers and editors. In 1988, five leading Ontario daily newspapers voluntarily decided to reject tobacco ads; they were followed by the Montreal *Gazette*, Eastern Canada's largest paper (Mintz 1990, p. 34). Major newspapers were persuaded to support the Tobacco Products Control Bill in their editorials (Kyle 1990, p. 11). When the bill appeared stalled in the House of Commons, the antitobacco coalition mounted a coordinated telephone campaign to lobby the Government Party Leader in the House (Lachance and Collishaw 1989). They worked with an opposition party back-bencher, Lynn McDonald, who in 1986 had introduced a nonsmokers' rights bill that prohibited smoking in some workplaces and transportation services; this helped induce the Conservative government to introduce its own Tobacco Products Control Bill and Nonsmokers' Rights legislation (Kyle 1990, pp. 9, 11; Mintz 1990, p. 34). By the time the Tobacco Products Control Bill was being discussed in Parliament (1987–88), 62 percent of Canadians polled by Gallup supported the planned ban on advertising and only 30 percent opposed it (Kyle 1990, p. 9). By the time it was voted on, the government's Tobacco Products Control Bill had been endorsed by all three major political parties in Canada.

Of course, the Canadian tobacco industry, like its counterparts in other countries, did not give up. In 1991, its lawyers persuaded a Quebec Superior Court judge to declare the federal ban on tobacco advertising an unconstitutional restriction of the right to free speech, a "form of paternalism . . . unacceptable in a free and democratic society" (Goad 1991). But the tobacco companies' legal victory, even if sustained on appeal, will have come too late. The highly publicized legislative struggle over the Tobacco Products Act and the Non-Smokers' Rights Act legitimated further public and private anticigarette measures, and further delegitimated cigarette smoking in Canada.

Most important, the Canadian finance minister suddenly became willing to promote major increases in cigarette excise taxes, explicitly acknowledging that it was desirable to do so even if they would result in a decline in revenues. Provincial finance ministers followed suit. British Columbia raised its tobacco tax by 34 cents a pack, pushing total taxes there to $2.79 a pack—compared with 66 cents across the border in the State of Washington.[12] Similarly, the enactment of the federal government's Non-Smokers' Rights Act stimulated similar legislation by local and provincial governments. By 1991, 150 Canadian municipalities (compared with only 39 in a 1986 survey) had enacted ordinances of varying stringency restricting smoking in stores and workplaces (Collishaw 1991; Calgary Health Services 1986).

Tobacco Politics in France: Regulation Without Agitation

Tobacco regulation in France has been considerably more centralized than in Canada (or the United States). It has been less affected by popular pressure and mobilization, and more by elite bargaining among bureaucrats and health officials. Perhaps as a result, France has not gone as far as Canada or the United States in regulating *smokers*' behavior via local workplace and public place restrictions on use. But it has gone further than America in enacting Phase II "paternalistic" controls— prohibitions on advertising and promotion, and high cigarette taxes.

The dominant player in the French tobacco market is the state-owned SEITA (*Societe d'Exploitation Industrielle des Tabacs et Allumettes*), which was established during the Napoleonic era and enjoyed monopoly powers until the 1970s. Production of leaf tobacco, too, is relatively centralized: a small number of increasingly large farms are organized into twelve regional marketing boards, which in turn come together in a powerful trade association able to set policy for the entire leaf tobacco production sector (Bell 1985). Thirty-nine thousand government-licensed *debits de tabac* (tobacconist shops) enjoy a *de facto* monopoly on retail distribution. Finally, the price of tobacco products is regulated by law, which fosters an ongoing close relationship between SEITA and the regulatory authority—the Ministry of Finance. Since the early 1980s, however, SEITA has steadily lost half its market to imports, largely from Philip Morris, RJR, and Rothman's. Young consumers, especially women (La Vecchia et al. 1991, pp. 99, 103) turned in increasing numbers to "blonde" cigarettes—made of light-colored Virginia or burley tobacco ("Tobacco Products in France" 1988; "Cigarettes in France" 1985).[13] Still, taxes on SEITA revenues are politically valuable, generating almost $5.5 billion for the government in 1990, some 2.3 percent of the national budget (Gooding 1992, p. 50).

In 1976, eleven years after the U.S. government required warning labels, six years after Congress had banned TV ads, and six years after Canada's proposed law triggered similar "voluntary" restrictions by its tobacco industry, Simone Veil, an activist minister of health, initiated France's Phase I legislation. It banned tobacco advertising from television, radio, billboards, and movies, mandated a very mild—indeed, almost deceptive—warning on all cigarette packages (*"Abus Dangereuse"*—"Overuse is Hazardous"), called for antismoking educational campaigns in French schools, and barred smoking from some government and transportation facilities.

Veil's original regulatory proposals had been harsher. They were watered down in negotiations within the French cabinet, under pressure from SEITA. Officials in the Finance and Budget Ministries worried that the tobacco control measures would reduce the revenues that SEITA generated for the French treasury. In the years following the enactment of the Veil law, most of its provisions—with the exception of the TV, radio, and billboard ban—were only partially enforced (Hirsch). Educational campaigns were ill-financed, and bans on movie ads and on smoking in transport and government facilities were largely ignored.

If the French government was not inclined to regulate SEITA aggressively, it was more than willing to tax cigarettes for revenue purposes, especially after foreign cigarette companies began to make inroads into the French market. By 1986, French taxes amounted to 75 percent of the retail price of a pack of cigarettes, higher than in any European country save Denmark (Hagan and Carey 1988, p. 348; Dalla-Vorgia 1990) and far exceeding American levels. Nevertheless, per capita consumption of tobacco products did not decline in France between 1975 and 1985, as it did in the United States and Canada during this same time period (Laugeson and Meads 1991). Consumption among French elites remained high, and French smoking rates, in comparative terms, greatly exceeded those for Canada and the United States.[14]

In contrast to Canada (and the United States), therefore, the French antitobacco movement did not include grass-roots organizations that channeled popular antismoking sentiment into pressure for regulatory action. Rather, the chief external pressure group in France was the "Smoking or Health Medical Association," a loose organization of doctors and academicians who treated smoking as a public health concern, rather than as an individual rights or an anti–tobacco-company issue. This group set out to sensitize health care professionals to the dangers of smoking, assuming from the start that "some members will be in a position to contact influential persons" in the government to advance their agenda (Freour 1986, p. 388–7).

In 1986, one member of the group, medical professor Albert Hirsch, was asked by the minister of health to write the first official report on tobacco use in France, to mark the tenth anniversary of the Veil law (Hirsch, p. 1). The Hirsch report's call for stronger restrictions went unheeded until 1988, when a press conference and a series of articles in *Le Monde* by members of the Smoking or Health Medical Association, endorsed by two French Nobel Prize laureates, called for more aggressive governmental action. Members of the group began to meet repeatedly with "present, past, and future political leaders, deputies and senators, and high administrative personnel" (Hirsch, p. 2). They first focused on the enormous national health toll taken by smoking-induced diseases, and second, stressing a more directly paternalistic theme, they "denounced the manipulations represented by conditioning the young and the impoverished through the advertising of dangerous products" (Hirsch, p. 2).

By 1989, the group had convinced the health minister, Claude Evin, to back proposals further restricting tobacco advertising and use, and to seek still higher cigarette prices. The doctors' group and Evin enlisted support of sympathetic media organizations to pressure reluctant cabinet ministers—the finance minister feared the inflationary and revenue effects of increased prices and reduced sales, the communications minister had reservations about the legality of extending the ad ban, and the sports and culture ministers were concerned about the economic impact of proposed sponsorship bans (Hirsch, pp. 2–4; Riding 1990; Michalowska and Rosenbaum 1990).

To the extent that the mass of the French citizenry was involved in the process, it was used primarily as an "opinion resource"—elites in the media, government, and the medical community frequently referred to polls showing public support for new ad and use restrictions, but showed no interest in mobilizing popular pressure to support these reforms (Ibrahim 1990; Cohen-Solal 1982, pp. 20–23; Hirsch, pp. 3–4). Like the French struggle against alcohol abuse, the antitobacco movement, led by the professional medical establishment, had a decidedly elitist quality. Just as the French temperance movement had seen better-educated middle-class wine drinkers seeking to change the "unhealthy" habits of working class consumers of hard liquor, so did the tobacco control movement tend to reflect the interests of better-educated, wealthier social groups. Just as workers associations had resisted temperance in the 1930s and 40s, so the Communist Party weighed in against tobacco controls (Brennan 1990; Giles 1990; "France to Ban Tobacco and Alcohol Advertising" 1990).

Cabinet consensus on the new regulations revolved around a technical, economic decision: to remove tobacco product prices from the consumer price index (Tempest 1990; "Parliament Gives Boost to Antismoking Campaign" 1990). This meant cigarette prices could be increased without negative effects on cost-of-living indicators, which in turn would have affected wages and benefit levels. Several weeks after the European Parliament passed nonbinding restrictions on tobacco advertising and use, the French government in late March 1990 announced plans to extend the tobacco ad ban to all print media (by 1993) and to movies (presumably a recommitment to the Veil provision), to ban sponsorships under the name of tobacco products, to extend the ban on smoking in government and transportation facilities, to strengthen the mandatory warnings on cigarette packages,[15] and to raise the price of tobacco products 15 percent (Ibrahim 1990; "French Ad Ban" 1990b). In the French political system, once the executive has made its decision, the route to legal approval is swift. In June, the cabinet decision was made official. The lower parliamentary house, the National Assembly, approved the measure some weeks later. Senate ratification was the only remaining obstacle to final passage.

Tobacco interests seemed not to respond until the late spring of 1990, when the crucial internal political struggle was almost over. Philip Morris threatened to move the Grand Prix race, sponsored by its Marlboro brand, out of France. Sports associations, particularly from the auto and motorcycle racing industries, protested loudly about the loss of tobacco firm subsidies. The Association of Advertising Agencies argued that an ad ban would violate principles of free speech, but mostly stressed the adverse economic effect on the film and newspaper industries. Although there was reportedly "much parliamentary protest," the new regulations passed the upper house in mid-December 1990 (Riding 1990; "France to Ban Tobacco and Alcohol Advertising" 1990).

Underscoring the elite-bargaining origin of the new laws, initial public reaction was rather hostile.[16] French media reported a sense of frustration and resignation over yet another act of government paternalism ("France to Ban Tobacco and Alcohol Advertising" 1990). A popular political cartoonist drew a series in *Le Figaro* depicting French smokers as outcasts, forced to wear demeaning armbands; antitobacco people were portrayed as American-style puritans. Yet there have been no signs of public protest (beyond grumbling and satire) from either the smoking public or the tobacco industry.[17]

On the other hand, while France (like Canada, and unlike the United States) has aggressively restricted ads and taxed tobacco companies, it has failed to match or even approach American and Canadian restrictions on smokers' behavior. In France's centralized political system, nonsmokers' rights groups have had only limited success. One journalist observed in mid-1990:

> To date, the only *non fumeur* sections in restaurants are found in imported American fast-food establishments. The population remains basically untouched by such American issues as secondary smoke inhalation and no smoking in elevators. (Tempest 1990)

Nevertheless, the national government did enact a law, taking effect November 1, 1992, that restricts smoking in shops, restaurants, workshops, and offices ("Stubbed Out" 1992). But unlike the United States and Canada, where smoking bans reflect intense grass-roots lobbying and have met with high levels of compliance (Kagan and Skolnick, this volume), the new French law's effects on behavior remain far from certain.

In terms of our typology of control measures, France has emphasized "paternalistic" interventions. It has sought to help smokers and young potential smokers resist the direct risks of addiction—by banning advertising, greatly increasing cigarette prices, and mounting antismoking ad campaigns (Gooding 1992). The French government has been far less aggressive than Canada (or the United States) in protecting nonsmokers from the real but less intense risks of "secondary smoke." These priorities perhaps reflect the domination of French policy making by medical and public health elites, rather than by grass-roots nonsmokers' rights activists (as in the United States and to some extent in Canada). Perhaps, too, those priorities reflect French political culture and tradition, which endorse strong governmental controls over business entities, policy making by elite-educated bureaucrats who are relatively insulated from political pressure groups, and, at the same time, fierce popular resistance to moralistic social control of individual beliefs and lifestyle choices. "As a rule," a reporter observes, "the French detest being told what to do" (Tempest 1990). And French elites, it bears reemphasizing, have been far slower than their Canadian and American counterparts to quit smoking.

Tobacco Control Politics in the United States

Phase I Regulation in the Federal Government

In the late 1800s and the early part of this century, a number of American states enacted tobacco use restrictions, most of which faded away with the decline of the temperance movement, by or before the 1930s (U.S. DHHS, Surgeon General 1989, pp. 555, 608–09). In the 1950s, the federal Food and Drug Administration (FDA) occasionally reprimanded tobacco manufacturers who attributed health value or medicinal properties to their products, but the FDA dodged accumulating scientific evidence concerning the health hazards of tobacco. Although in the mid-1960s the Federal Trade Commission (FTC) had suggested placing restrictions on tobacco advertising, industry interests were sufficiently well represented in key congressional committees to block such initiatives.[18] Both tobacco company political muscle and regulatory timidity undergirded pre-1965 inaction on tobacco.

In contrast to Congress, the FTC, and the FDA, the federal Public Health Service was quite willing to advocate interventionist governmental policies. Its specialized knowledge and focus on improving primary health care seemingly authorized it to make recommendations about private behavior (Raffel and Raffel 1989, pp. 263–314). The Surgeon General's 1964 report, summarizing existing research on the health hazards of smoking, galvanized (or shamed) federal regulators and legislators into action. In 1965, Congress mandated warning labels on cigarette packages. In 1967, the Federal Communications Commission (FCC) required licensees who broadcast cigarette commercials to provide free media time for antismoking public service announcements. In 1970, Congress enacted a total ban on broadcast advertising for tobacco products.

In seeking to regulate cigarettes, however, public health officials faced a very effective counterlobbying effort by the tobacco industry. Tobacco lobbyists, drawing upon the support of legislators from tobacco growing states—many of whom occupied key congressional positions—managed to water down the warning label required by the 1965 bill until it was a vague, conditional statement that failed to state fully the causal link between cigarettes and health hazards as emphasized in the 1964 Surgeon General's report.[19] Moreover, the industry's supporters in Congress succeeded in adding a provision to the 1965 act that preempted state governments from promulgating more stringent warning label or advertising regulations, and forbade additional federal regulatory restrictions on tobacco advertising for three years (Pertschuk 1986, pp. 32–38; U.S. DHHS, Surgeon General 1989, pp. 474–85).

By the end of the three-year hiatus, the FTC and the FCC, led by liberal, consumer-protection–oriented presidential appointees, were preparing a series of new ad restrictions. Meanwhile, the antitobacco public-service announcements (PSAs) required by the FCC in 1968 were apparently having a significant effect. Between 1966 and 1970, the number of smokers who expressed concern about the health effects of cigarettes increased from 47 percent to 69 percent. Per capita cigarette sales declined 6.9 percent during the three years of PSAs, in contrast to a 2 percent increase during the three previous years (U.S. DHHS, Surgeon General 1989, pp. 497–98; McAufliffe 1990; Mitchell and Mulherin 1988, pp. 855–62). Tobacco companies decided that no press would be preferable to bad press, thus paving the way for Congress's 1970 prohibition of TV and radio ads for cigarettes (Pertschuk 1986, pp. 38–39). In the next three years (1971–73), as tobacco companies diverted advertising dollars from broadcasting into print media and billboards, per capita cigarette sales in the United States grew by 4.1 percent.

When compared with the federal government's concurrent regulatory stance vis-à†vis civil rights, the environment, pesticides, and other potentially dangerous consumer products, the restrictions imposed on the tobacco industry through 1972 were fairly mild. The ambitious goals and standards set by other regulations—for example, the Clean Water Act Amendments of 1972 required "zero discharge" of pollutants into the nation's waterways by 1985—make the cigarette labeling requirements and restrictions on broadcast advertising seem modest indeed. Congress did not establish the goal of "zero smoking," or even mandate a percentage reduction in smoking, as it did in the case of motor vehicle emissions. Although the federal government had taxed tobacco products since the Civil War, Phase I antismoking efforts did not raise excise taxes to discourage smoking (U.S. DHHS, Surgeon General 1989, pp. 527–29, 610–12; "Tax and Price Support Issues" 1986). Likewise, federal regulators and legislators did not seriously consider restrictions on where cigarettes could be smoked (Pertschuk 1986, pp. 32–44).

Phase II Regulation at the Federal Level

Phase I regulation, however mild, coincided with a far-reaching decline in smoking behavior. By 1988, only 28 percent of the adult American population smoked, compared with 37 percent in 1970 and 42 percent in 1967. Among the educated population, at least, smoking was now viewed as a public nuisance, a sign of weakness, or even a vice. On the other hand, tens of millions of Americans still smoked. Teenagers, particularly young women and particularly from the lower classes, continued to take up smoking at a high rate.[20] Consequently, throughout the

1980s tobacco companies still enjoyed a huge and profitable market, bolstered by continued growth in export sales. Using their profits as leverage, they acquired large packaged-food companies. By 1991, Philip Morris (maker of Marlboros) was the fourth-largest corporation in the world, measured by stock market value. In 1986, the Tobacco Institute, the industry's chief lobbying arm, had an annual budget of more than $20 million and a staff of more than 100 (Langley 1986). In 1988 the institute gave more honoraria to members of Congress than any other interest group; in addition, the institute and individual tobacco companies have contributed large sums to candidates for federal office during each election cycle (Matlack 1990, pp. 452–55).

Philip Morris cleverly allied itself with liberal causes. It became the major corporate sponsor of the Coalition on Human Needs, a leading lobbying group on issues of hunger and poverty. It was among the leading corporate patrons of the arts. In 1990, it launched a two-year $60 million national tour to commemorate the Bill of Rights (Freeman 1988a; Rothstein 1990). Equally important, cigarette companies spent $2.58 billion per year on advertising and promotion, which in turn represents a vital source of revenue for publishers of magazines and newspapers and for the billboard industry (Warner et al. 1986, pp. 368–69).

The industry still faced important political challenges in Washington. During the 1980s, pressure from the new breed of antismoking activists, as in Canada, persuaded the large national "health voluntaries"—the American Cancer Society, Heart Association and Lung Association—to create a joint lobbying body in Washington, the Coalition for Smoking or Health. Led by skilled lobbyists, the Coalition claimed some victories in the 1980s:

- A 1984 congressional law prescribed four separate warnings, more specific and emphatic than earlier ones, that tobacco companies must inscribe, in rotation, on cigarette packs and ads.[21]
- A 1985 act extended advertising limits and warning labels to smokeless tobacco products.
- A 1983 law increased federal excise taxes from 8 to 16 cents per pack, and a 1990 budget deficit compromise added another 8 cents a pack (U.S. DHHS, Surgeon General 1989, pp. 527–31).
- In 1986, the General Services Administration, responsible for office space for 890,000 federal employees, prohibited smoking except in designated areas configured to protect nonsmokers from involuntary exposure. The Department of Defense restricted smoking in common work areas and embarked on an antismoking campaign for the armed forces. The Veterans Administration also established smoke-free environments in its medical centers and outpatient clinics (see Leichter 1991, p. 137; U.S DHHS, Surgeon General 1989, pp. 574–75).
- In 1987, a coalition of national health organizations, activist antitobacco lobbyists, and airline flight attendants pushed through legislation banning smoking on all flights of two hours or less. Two years later Congress, in another major legislative defeat for the industry, voted to ban smoking on all domestic flights.

• In 1990, the Interstate Commerce Commission banned smoking on all regularly scheduled interstate buses.

However, these defeats for the tobacco industry must be placed in perspective. Congressional sponsors were unable to enact legislation banning (or even regulating) print media advertising. Unlike the Canadian and French governments, the U.S. federal government did not impose consumption-discouraging tobacco taxes or even increase cigarette taxes enough to keep up with inflation. Nor, despite activists' hopes, did the federal government subsidize antismoking TV ad campaigns, designate cigarette smoke a workplace hazard under the Occupational Safety and Health Act, list cigarettes as a dangerous food or drug, stop subsidizing tobacco farmers, or discourage the export of American cigarettes. Beginning in 1989, President Bush's secretary for Health and Human Services, Louis Sullivan, repeatedly pronounced cigarettes a major health threat. But while his moral exhortations were important, they were not accompanied by any significant policy changes at the federal level. According to the Tobacco Institute's own "scorecard," Congress failed to adopt any of the 160 anticigarette bills introduced in 1985–86; the smoking ban on airline flights under two hours represented its only legislative defeat in the 100th Congress.

The tobacco industry's political effectiveness was in part due to its cultivation of political allies. To defeat proposed legislation restricting cigarette print media advertising, the tobacco industry established the Freedom to Advertise Coalition, which included the American Association of Advertising Agencies, the Outdoor Advertising Association of America, and the Association of National Advertisers. The industry's position was also supported by magazine and newspaper publishers and by the influential American Civil Liberties Union, which announced its strong opposition to cigarette advertising restrictions on First Amendment grounds (Warner et al. 1986; Barlas 1990; Agnew 1987; Victor 1987). Consequently, although a number of bills restricting cigarette advertising were introduced by congressional liberals,[22] they never reached the floor of either house (Matlack 1990; Garrison 1987; Cosco 1988; Vestal 1989; Pertschuk 1990).

The federal government's failure to increase federal cigarettes taxes in real dollars also reflected the tobacco industry's successful recruitment of allies— including the Committee Against Regressive Taxation (which included alcoholic beverage companies) and Citizens for Tax Justice (CTJ), a labor-backed Washington lobby that advocates higher income taxes on businesses and the wealthy and opposes excise taxes on goods consumed by workers and the poor. (The Tobacco Institute furnishes 15 percent of CTJ's budget.)

The industry's political effectiveness was also enhanced by its generous financial support for minority and women's groups, including the Congressional Black Caucus Foundation, the Congressional Hispanic Caucus, the National Women's Political Caucus, the NAACP, the United Negro College Fund, and the National Urban League, in addition to various local, community-based organizations (Novak 1989; Levin 1988). In addition, tobacco companies are among the major advertisers in minority-owned newspapers and magazines. Some civil-rights leaders endorsed the industry's argument that restrictions on smoking discriminate against minorities, since blacks smoke at higher rates than whites (35.6 percent versus 29.4 percent). A number of women's magazines, financially dependent on cigarette advertising, have hesitated to publish articles on the hazards of smoking (Warner et al. 1991). Most important, black, Hispanic, and women's groups have not been prominent in supporting any national legislative initiatives to restrict or discourage cigarette smoking.

Phase II Local Regulation: Non-Smokers' Rights Rampant

While tobacco-industry lobbying and political resistance to tax increases have tempered the movement toward stronger *federal* tobacco control laws, American antismoking activists have been more successful in prodding local governments to enact restrictions on smoking. In the late 1970s and the 1980s, scores of homegrown pressure groups emerged throughout the country, often nicknamed "GASPs"— "Groups Against Smoking Pollution." As their name indicated, GASPs identified more with the environmental movement than with the more paternalistic, treatment-oriented "health voluntaries." Dr. Stanton Glantz, a leading researcher-activist, wrote:

> Activists should state that they are not "antismoker" but rather environmentalists concerned with clean indoor air for everyone. The issue should be framed in the rhetoric of the environment, toxic chemicals and public health rather than the rhetoric of saving smokers from themselves. (Glantz 1987, p. 750)

Like many environmental groups, GASPs adopted a populist, uncompromising tone, quick to label tobacco companies as murderers and quick to demand enforceable legal rights to clean, smoke-free air, thus driving smokers from offices, restaurants, and public places. The GASPs grew from the local level up, relying on "networking" organizations like California's Americans for Nonsmokers' Rights (ANR). Surviving on limited budgets, ANR and the GASPs have lobbied most successfully in city councils and county boards of governance, rather than in state legislatures, where tobacco industry money and lobbying skills have remained relatively effective.

The local activists have campaigned not only for restrictions on smoking (nonsmokers' rights) but also for Phase II "paternalistic" measures—for example, ordinances banning vending machine sales (to limit access to cigarettes by minors), the elimination of advertising on billboards, and the imposition of higher local excise taxes. As of June 1991, twenty Minnesota cities had outlawed cigarette vending machines, and, to prevent illegal sales to minors, the state legislature had restricted vending machines to bars and employee lunchrooms, unless outfittted with an automatic lock that a store clerk must operate (Banner 1991). A New York City ordinance now permits cigarette vending machines only in taverns and bars, and they must be at least 25 feet from the entrance. Bypassing the state legislature, ANR and other antismoking groups in 1988 successfully sponsored a voter initiative that added a huge (by American standards) 25 cents a pack to California's cigarette tax, and mandated use of a portion of those revenues for an antismoking media advertising.[23] In 1991, the California Legislature banned free distribution of tobacco products as a promotional technique.

The local activists' most striking successes, however, have been in enacting local ordinances and organizational policies that restrict smoking. These "spot-zoning" measures, pushing smokers into special sections of restaurants and office buildings, and, in the more stringent cases, banishing them to inconvenient outdoor locations, received a further stimulus from the 1986 Surgeon General's report. Summarizing existing research, the report asserted that nonsmokers who experience prolonged exposure to others' tobacco smoke have significantly elevated risks of incurring cancer, heart, and lung ailments, along with eye and respiratory irritation (U.S DHHS, Surgeon General 1986; Altman 1990; Peterson and Massengill 1986). In 1990, the Environmental Protection Agency (EPA) reported that exposure to environmental tobacco smoke resulted in 3,800 deaths annually (Kerr 1990; Rosewicz and Karr 1990). These findings enabled nonsmokers' rights activists to intensify their arguments for governmental restrictions on smoking without having to resort to the kind of paternalistic arguments that remain suspect in American political culture. Although the activists' underlying goals may be paternalistic—to induce inconvenienced smokers to quit, to delegitimate smoking and thereby discourage smokers and potential smokers—their arguments could now take a classically libertarian form: "Your freedom to choose to smoke ends where my airspace, and my right to breathe unhazardous air, begins," or "You smokers have no right to impose involuntary risks on me."

By mid-1988, 380 local communities had passed laws restricting smoking in public places, four times as many as in 1986 (Brandt 1990, p. 168; U.S. DHHS, Surgeon General 1989, pp. 556–74; Rosewicz and Karr 1990). By 1991, it was estimated that about 450 had done so. Thirty-eight state legislatures had restricted smoking in workplaces. Many of these laws simply mandated segregation of smokers, requiring employers to formulate their own policies. More aggressive laws stipulated that in resolving questions about the size and location of nonsmoking areas, nonsmokers' preferences should prevail. And increasingly, both ordinances and organizational policies have demanded totally smoke-free workplaces. This has been especially common in California, home to at least 200 local laws. The city of Walnut Creek passed an ordinance banning smoking completely in all stores, shopping malls, restaurants, and other public places. The Oakland Coliseum, an outdoor major league baseball stadium, banned smoking in all seats and common areas.[24] The University of California banned smoking in all indoor places, including professors' offices. In the spring of 1991, a top tobacco industry lobbyist was quoted as saying, "Nothing anywhere in the world compares with what is going on right now in California. Nothing" (Flinn 1991)[25]

The tobacco industry, of course, has attempted to combat the guerrilla war of grass-roots nonsmoker's rights groups. Spending lavishly on contributions to key legislative leaders, tobacco companies have bottled up proposed antismoking laws in the California State Assembly (Flinn 1991). In some other states, such as Illinois, Florida, Pennsylvania, and Oklahoma, the tobacco industry prevailed on the legislature to enact mild "nonsmokers' rights" laws that explicitly preempt municipalities from enacting more stringent measures. Tobacco interests have also won "smokers' rights" laws in about half the states, forbidding, among other things, discrimination against smokers in hiring decisions (Sugarman, this volume). Philip Morris has attempted to develop a grass-roots smokers' rights organizations, circulating a glossy newsletter to all members that advises them how to lobby against restrictive local ordinances (Freeman 1988b; Westerman 1990; Kerr 1990; "Smoking Is Not a Civil Right" 1990a).

However, even with Philip Morris's generous support and encouragement, American smokers have not been mobilized into an aggressive political force, analogous to the National Rifle Association's effective advocacy against gun control laws. Although fifty-six million Americans smoke, only ten thousand belong to smokers' rights organizations (Freeman 1988b). Nor is there much evidence that smokers have rebelled in large numbers when told they can no longer smoke in a particular venue. On balance, the tobacco companies' resistance to the nonsmokers' rights movement seems to be a rear-guard action. As the proportion of nonsmokers grows and the example of successful spot-zoning laws spreads, one can expect the continuing spread of such local ordinances and voluntary restrictions by employers. Strong at the center of government, tobacco companies seem unable to combat the efforts of thousands of decentralized activists in local communities.

Finally, the decentralized nature of the American antismoking movement has manifested itself in that characteristically American phenomenon, the product liability lawsuit. Activist private lawyers, maintaining extensive communication networks among themselves, have brought numerous suits against tobacco companies. Alleging that their clients had contracted diseases such as emphysema or cancer at least in part due to deceptive advertising, or due to deliberate sale of a product known to cause cancer, the suits have asked for multimillion dollars in compensatory or and punitive damages. Thus far, no plaintiff has collected a single damage award. Juries have been disinclined to grant compensation to victims who seemed in large measure responsible for their own unhappy fate (Rabin, this volume; Schwartz, this volume). But the lawsuits represent a huge threat to the American tobacco firms. Even one or two awards by sympathetic juries could unleash a torrent of expensive-to-defend lawsuits and an even more dangerous flood of adverse publicity (Daynard 1988).

Indeed, the lawsuit threat may help explain why tobacco companies so stubbornly have refused to admit any conclusive causal link between smoking and cancer or heart disease, even though that stubborn refusal is politically costly—it outrages antismoking activists and many lawmakers, and depletes the tobacco companies' credibility with the public at large. But such an admission, the tobacco companies' lawyers probably tell them, could stimulate a new assault by scores of plaintiffs' lawyers.[26]

Conclusion

During the last quarter century, the United States, Canada, and France have all intensified governmental regulation of smoking. But tobacco controls in the three nations have differed in timing and focus, reflecting variations in national political structure and political traditions.

The United States was the first to act forcefully. But in recent years, its fragmented governmental system and its individualistic political culture have impeded antitobacco activists' efforts to obtain stronger "paternalistic" laws—high cigarette taxes, prohibitions on advertising and promotional activities. But this very individualism and governmental decentralization have abetted enactment of intrusive nonsmokers' rights laws, especially at the local level of government.

In France and Canada, well-developed traditions of public authority, combined with political structures in which business interests have less capacity to block governmental action, have enabled central governments to substantially increase taxes on cigarettes and enact sweeping restrictions on cigarette advertising. Canada has gone beyond France, however, in enacting restrictions on where smokers may smoke, partly because of Canada's more communitarian political culture and partly because it resembles the United States in its greater political openness to grass-roots nonsmokers' rights activists.

If American political structure and culture enabled tobacco companies to fend off tougher restrictions in the 1980s and early 1990s, why was the United States able to take the lead in Phase I regulations concerning cigarette marketing? Perhaps it was because the 1960s and early 1970s were a special historical period. Distrust of established institutions, fanned by the Vietnam War, ignited one of America's periodic outbursts of populist idealism (Huntington 1983). Interest-group activism in civil rights, consumer protection, and environmentalism overwhelmed normal incremental policy-making processes. Unable to activate the multiple veto points in Washington's fragmented power system, business interests saw their autonomy eroded in many spheres of activity (Vogel 1989; Kagan 1991, p. 392).

As a result, during the 1960s and 1970s, the U.S. federal government was on the cutting edge of virtually every dimension of health, safety, and environmental regulation, including the regulation of smoking. In no other capitalist nation did such a large and effective network of public interest organizations develop or was there such widespread public support for protecting the public's health and safety by imposing legal restrictions on business. The 1965 and 1970 congressional statutes requiring warning labels on cigarette packs and banning broadcast advertising can be seen as part of this more general political dynamic.

Why, then, is the United States now trailing behind Canada and France in paternalistic smoking regulation, while acting *more* aggressively in protecting nonsmokers from smokers?

The answer does not seem to flow in a straightforward manner from interest-group theories of politics. The American tobacco industry was not significantly stronger in the 1980s, when it did reasonably well in Washington, than it was in the 1965–70 period, when Phase I measures were enacted. And its economic and political strengths have not enabled it to prevail in scores of state and local governmental battles. The American automotive industry is economically more important than the tobacco industry, yet this has not prevented Congress from enacting increasingly strict and costly motor vehicle emissions and fuel economy requirements. Tobacco and cigarette production is not significantly less important to the

Canadian and French economies, yet those governments have enacted stricter advertising and promotion regulations, as well as far heavier taxes, than has the American government.

On the other side of the interest-group equation, American antismoking forces were far better organized and enjoyed far more popular support in the 1980s than in the 1960s (when a larger proportion of the population smoked cigarettes). Whatever cultural forces led Americans to become so intolerant of the risks associated with industrial activity and consumption goods during the 1960s and 1970s have not diminished; if anything, Americans' obsession with threats to their physical health has increased during the last decade. One might well have expected that a people so concerned with their diet and exercise would have successfully pressured their national government into the vanguard of the antismoking effort, instead of lagging behind Canada and (in some respects) France. In many other areas American federal health and safety regulations remain the world's strictest. Why not for smoking?

Part of the explanation, we think, stems from structural features of the American political system, particularly its fragmentation of political authority. In the American federal government, power is divided between the legislative and executive branches. Within each branch, power is further decentralized: party discipline is weak in the legislature and power is vested in numerous committee and subcommittee chairs. In the executive branch, many administrative agencies are relatively independent.

In many other nations, the senior official responsible for public health has been at the forefront of new national initiatives to restrict smoking. In France and Canada, for example, once their respective health ministers were persuaded of the need to introduce legislation banning cigarette advertising, all that was then required was the agreement of a handful of other key cabinet members—particularly the finance minister or the prime minister. This is not to say that the approval of legislation was then a foregone conclusion. But it meant that a major hurdle had been surmounted: political party discipline could then be trusted to help the government overcome whatever additional obstacles tobacco interests might put in the path of legislation.

In the United States, in contrast, while Health and Human Services Secretary Sullivan was vocal in opposing smoking during the late 1980s and early 1990s, the executive branch could not easily be brought to speak with one voice on the issue. Even if the executive branch were to unite in support of an advertising ban, it would have to pass a number of committees and subcommittees in both houses of Congress—many of which contain legislators who are more responsive to business constituents and campaign contributors than to the priorities of their political party leaders.

Due to the fragmentation of power in the U.S. Congress, executive, and political party system, American tobacco industry lobbyists find it easier than their Canadian or French counterparts to locate a sympathetic committee chair or executive official who will serve as a blocking point in the enormously complicated process of passing a restrictive law. (The same applies, of course, in most state legislatures.) Conversely, in the United States, antitobacco activists seeking restrictive laws have to win the support of a far larger number of politicians than their Canadian or French counterparts. Moreover, in America, even the private sector activist organizations, at least at the national level, have been more fragmented than their Canadian counterparts, weakening their capacity to lobby effectively against tobacco interests.

A legislative proposal to significantly increase taxes on cigarettes for the purpose of discouraging consumption would confront a similar set of hurdles. Most critically, its fate would be decisively affected by the key House and Senate committees responsible for writing tax legislation as well as the preferences of the Office of Management and Budget and the Department of the Treasury—none of whose primary concerns have anything to do with public health. It would also face an additional obstacle, one which has less to do with American institutions than with contemporary American politics: in the United States, unlike in France and Canada, the political party that controlled the executive branch of government during the 1980s and early 1990s was opposed in principle both to tax increases and to the use of taxes to influence social behavior. At the same time, the fact that increased cigarette taxes would hit poor and black Americans particularly hard probably has reduced the enthusiasm for such a measure on the part of liberal Democrats who would otherwise be likely to support regulations to improve the public's health. Organized labor, another element in the Democratic electoral coalition, also has been unsupportive of stringent tobacco regulation and regressive cigarette taxes.[27]

The fragmentation of power in America also helps explain why the United States, while falling behind Canada and France in enacting national controls on tobacco advertising and in imposing consumption-deterring taxes, nevertheless has remained at the cutting edge with respect to nonsmokers' rights regulations. If tobacco interests have been reasonably effective in finding key veto points in Congress, it has been far harder for them to do so in hundreds of city councils. Thus a distinctive characteristic of antismoking politics in America is its decentralized, ad hoc, grass-roots character, in which highly motivated "guerrilla" bands of antismoking activists roam the local political scene pushing for discrete tactical victories—a local ordinance against vending machines here, a corporate ban on workplace smoking there. Conversely, in France, where governmental power is centralized, pressures for change have come from a small, medically trained public-health elite and there have been relatively few local no-smoking rules.[28]

But political structure does not tell the whole story. If fragmentation of power in Washington has made it harder for antitobacco forces to marshal effective political support for more stringent federal legislation, why have environmentalists, advocates for the handicapped, and civil-rights groups managed to win enactment of stringent regulatory laws in the late 1980s and early 1990s? Political culture is a second and even more important explanatory factor.

American liberalism condemns the abuse of power, violation of individual rights, and unequal treatment. When assaults on those values can be dramatically illustrated—as when advocates can point to oil spills, acid-choked lakes, dramatic racial inequality, and discrimination against disabled workers—interest-group advocates and ambitious politicians can often secure the enactment of legislation that condemns industrial pollution or unfair and harmful behavior. But American liberalism provides less support for laws and regulations that smack of paternalism (Vogel 1991). Thus tobacco activists have been unable to obtain laws designed to protect smokers from themselves—prohibitive taxes and sweeping bans on cigarette advertising. Exposure to air pollution is involuntary. Corporate industry can be "blamed" for it. But in an individualistic culture, when smokers voluntarily buy cigarettes and inhale the smoke, blaming the tobacco companies seems discordant to many.

The same logic holds with respect to local politics. Governmental decentralization has enabled American antitobacco groups to outflank tobacco industry lobbyists, gaining local victories of a kind that the industry effectively blocked in Washington. But local activists have not persuaded state and local governments to levy Canadian-level cigarette taxes, or to prohibit billboard cigarette ads. Here, too, *political culture* appears to be the operative explanatory factor. For, with the exception of restrictions on vending machines, most American local antismoking measures are not paternalistic, at least in form and ideology. Their ostensible purpose is not to protect the health of smokers; it is to improve the welfare of nonsmokers. Conversely, advertising bans are opposed as unduly restrictive of freedom of speech and individual freedom of choice. High taxes, designed to induce smokers to stop, are denounced as unduly paternalistic as well as regressive and oppressive.

In both Canada and France, on the other hand, national political traditions support much stronger state taxation in order to serve collective ends. Seymour Martin Lipset argues that whereas the American political creed is characterized by antistatism, individualism, populism, and egalitarianism, "Canada has been and is a more . . . elitist, law-abiding, statist, collectivity-oriented . . . society," more inclined to accept governmental authority and control, to feel that liberty must be circumscribed by obligations to the community (Lipset 1991, pp. 8, 28, 44; see also Grimond 1991, pp. 3–4). Canadians, according to opinion polls, are considerably more willing than Americans to approve laws banning cars from downtown areas, forbidding loud portable-radio playing, prohibiting handgun ownership, and banning door-to-door salemen (Lipset 1991, pp. 98–99). In Canada, governmental welfare state guarantees tend to be much more generous than in the United States, and acceptance of high taxes to pay for them also is greater (Ostry 1985, p. 263; Grimond 1991, p. 14).

France, even more than Canada, has a statist political culture, in which government is expected to take a leading role in shaping society. Compared with Canada, and of course with the United States, French governmental involvement in and control of business is more extensive and less controversial. France also has a tradition of interventionist public health, social welfare, and family policy, justified in part by an overt nationalistic concern for preserving and protecting French civilization. This political tradition could be invoked to support high tobacco taxes and restrictions on advertising cigarettes. On the other hand, French culture includes a strain of resistance to "moralistic" social controls on individual lifestyle choices. Many French people still appear to view controls on *where* people may smoke as an unjustified intrusion on individual choice, rather than as a health-based restriction on behavior that unjustifiably endangers others. Hence France has not been as quick as Canada or the United States to enact nonsmokers' rights laws, and its people have been much less willing to comply with them.

American liberalism, more mistrustful of governmental authority than the Canadians or the French, has played into the hands of tobacco companies' resistance to high taxes and controls on advertising. But American liberalism also supports enactment of legal rights that empower individuals to protect themselves from (or obtain compensation for) intrusions or injuries unjustifiably imposed by businesses and fellow citizens. Hence in the United States, where people are highly sensitive to evidence regarding certain kinds of health risks, the political system, especially at the local level, has been very responsive to demands for enactment of nonsmokers' rights laws. Only in America has the legal system provided incentives for private lawsuits, which, although still unsuccessful, have demanded huge compensation awards against tobacco companies for deceiving unsuspecting customers.

Ironically, the idea of individual liberty also has provided U.S. tobacco-industry lobbyists with their few legislative successes in recent years. While they have been strikingly unsuccessful in blocking passage of nonsmokers' rights acts, they have won enactment of a number of state laws forbidding employer discrimination against workers and job applicants who smoke while off the job.

On balance, therefore, Americans have made a much more serious effort to protect the health of nonsmokers than smokers, even though the latter are clearly much more at risk. Yet this priority is consistent with the general thrust of American health and safety regulation. Americans treat "secondary smoke" like they treat toxic air pollutants or minute quantities of cancer-causing chemicals in the workplace. In each case the principle is the same: do not expose individuals to involuntary hazards or dangers—however remote. Yet there are important political benefits, and ultimately important public health benefits, to be gained from the efforts to protect American nonsmokers. As the locally based nonsmokers' rights movement gathers momentum, socially marginalizing the act of cigarette smoking itself, the growing preponderance of nonsmoking voters exerts pressure in Washington and in state capitals to enact still more aggressive antismoking measures, including *paternalistic* ones such as higher cigarette taxes.[29]

The last point, too, suggests that it is important not to exaggerate the significance of national differences in the regulation of smoking. In all three countries, the general thrust and direction in public policy is toward progressively more restrictive controls on tobacco products. Year by year, the evidence concerning the deadly health effects of tobacco is more widely disseminated and better understood. In a world in which large numbers of people, particularly among elites in richer nations, have good prospects for long and economically abundant lives, fatalism declines. Politically active citizens increasingly demand governmental efforts to eliminate preventable harms, and governments are hard-pressed not to respond. Ten years from now, it would be surprising if the United States had not imposed stronger paternalistic controls on tobacco and France did not have more effective nonsmoker's rights laws.

Notes

1. This study is in the tradition of a well-established literature within both political science and sociology on comparative public policy. The authors are particularly grateful to Neil Collishaw for providing materials concerning the Canadian experience.

2. Tobacco farming, and a way of life that has grown up around it, dominates sections of southern Ontario and large sections of Virginia, North Carolina, Tennessee, and Kentucky. In France, tobacco farms, organized into regional marketing boards, dominate the market for traditional *brune* French cigarettes.

3. Tobacco companies, for their part, point out that studies do not demonstrate a clear causal link between advertising and smoking rates.

4. Antismoking activists might argue that in seeking to ensure that consumers make fully informed (but still free) choices, they are only pursuing the liberal ideal of free choice. We simply wish to indicate that restricting advertising and requiring warning labels concerning relatively well-known hazards is more "paternalistic" than simply enabling research on smoking and health to circulate through the media and school curricula.

5. A 1976 Swedish law requires 16 different warning statements that must appear in rotation on cigarette packages. One of the six rotating labels required in Great Britain must say, "More than 30,000 People Die Each Year in the UK from Lung Cancer." Ireland requires a label that says "SMOKING KILLS!" (U.S. DHHS, Surgeon General 1989, p. 486).

6. There was one big exception to the ad ban: ads in foreign magazines circulating in Canada were not prohibited.

7. Here too there was loophole: while tobacco companies could not display brand names at sporting events, the act allowed them to display corporate names. Canadian tobacco companies responded by setting up new corporations named after popular brands, and displayed these new "corporate names" where they would be shown by TV cameras broadcasting sports events.

8. According to a study done in 1986, the proportion of tax in relation to the retail price of common packets of cigarettes in various European countries was as follows: Spain, 52 percent; Greece, 60 percent; Portugal, 68.5 percent; Belgium, 70 percent; Netherlands, 71.3 percent; Italy, 71.5 percent; Germany, 73.5 percent; Ireland, 74 percent; United Kingdom, 74.8 percent; France, 75 percent; Denmark, 87 percent (O'Hagan and Carey 1988, citing European Commission 1986).

9. During the 1980s, Canadian cigarette imports from the United States averaged less than 1 percent of total Canadian cigarette consumption (Collishaw 1991).

10. The Canadian cigarette companies' side-of-package message stated, "Warning: Health and Welfare Canada advises that danger to health increases with amount smoked—avoid inhaling." By the time Canadian cigarette companies withdrew from television advertising, the public broadcast network, the CBC, had already decided to refuse tobacco commercials, as had several private radio and TV stations (Lachance and Collishaw 1989).

11. Similarly, in 1988, when the Canadian Parliament was considering the Tobacco Products Control Act and was besieged by tobacco industry lobbying tactics, the NSRA placed full-page ads in leading newspapers linking Canada's Prime Minister Brian Mulroney with former close aide William Neville, newly appointed president of the Canadian Tobacco Manufacturers' Council, under the headline "HOW MANY THOUSANDS OF CANADIANS WILL DIE FROM TOBACCO INDUSTRY PRODUCTS MAY LARGELY BE IN THE HANDS OF THESE TWO MEN" (Kyle 1990, p. 11). And in late 1987, when members of Parliament had been bombarded by 200,000 constituent letter prewritten by cigarette companies, NSRA published an ad in 22 newspapers headlined, "WILL TOBACCO INDUSTRY DECEPTION OUTMUSCLE PARLIAMENT?" (Mintz 1990, p. 34).

12. In New Brunswick, federal and provincial taxes in May 1991 were $3.73 a pack, compared with 61 cents in Maine. Ontario's taxes total $3.06, nearby Michigan's 51 cents. One reported result of the high Canadian taxes has been accelerated declines in cigarette purchases, especially among teenagers. Another has been a good deal of cross-border shop-

ping, as well as smuggling of untaxed cigarettes (Reynolds 1991; "Canadian Fired Up Over Cigarette Tax" 1991).

13. Smokers of *brune* cigarettes tend not to inhale as much as smokers of the lighter variety; like pipe and cigar smokers, *brune* smokers tend to hold smoke in their mouth, placing themselves at greater risk of mouth and upper-respiratory cancers (La Vecchia et al. 1991, pp. 95–99).

14. According to one recent article (Gooding 1992, p. 52), in France today, "38 percent of people in France smoke, as compared to 29 percent in the United States, and smoke lies heavy almost everywhere in the land. . . . Sixty percent of all eighteen-year-olds are smokers."

15. The currently required front-of-pack message, much larger than the old "ABUS DANGEREUX," is "NUIT GRAVEMENT A LA SANTE" ("Seriously endangers health"), and the backs of cigarette packs must warn that smoking is harmful to others and dangerous to unborn children, and causes cardiovascular disease and cancer (Gooding 1992, p. 54).

16. This contrasts, of course, with the positive public reaction to Canada's strict Phase II laws, which had been preceded by active public debate, as both proponents and opponents sought to mobilize popular support.

17. According to a 1992 report (Gooding 1992, p. 54), "Tobacco dealers in Becsancon, angry at a vigorous new municipal campaign to reduce smoking, put up posters everywhere that said DON'T SMOKE! DON'T DRINK! DON'T MAKE LOVE! DON'T DRIVE YOUR CAR! YOU COULD DIE FROM IT!"

18. As Michael Pertschuk points out, the influence of Earle Clements, tobacco lobbyist and former senator from Kentucky, proved instrumental in sidetracking initiatives throughout the 1960s and into the 1970s. A large number of Democratic senators, particularly those elected in 1958 when Clements was chair of the Senate Democratic Campaign Committee, owed the former Senator a great political debt, repayment of which he frequently called for in terms of strategic intervention at crucial points in committee hearings and floor votes on behalf of tobacco interests (see Pertschuk 1986, pp. 34–40).

19. In 1965 the FTC proposed a regulation calling for a mandatory label on all cigarette packages and advertisements, stating, "CAUTION: Cigarette smoking is dangerous to health. It may cause cancer and other diseases." The law Congress enacted in 1965 required warnings only on packages (not ads), saying, "Caution: Cigarette Smoking May Be Hazardous to Your Health."

20. In 1982, 60 percent of noncommissioned military personnel smoked, compared with fewer than 25 percent of junior officers (Schelling 1991, n. 9, citing Department of Defense, 1982 Worldwide Survey of Alcohol and Nonmedical Drug Use Among Military Personnel, p. 162). In 1985, a nationwide survey indicated that while 40 percent of men with less than a high-school education smoked, only 23 percent of college grads smoked. For women, the comparable percentages were 31 percent and 17 percent (Schelling 1991, p. 5, citing U.S. DHHS, Surgeon General 1988, p. 571). A 1988 survey indicated that 34 percent of high school dropouts smoked, compared with 16 percent of college graduates ("U.S. Smoking Declines to 28%" 1991).

21. The prescribed warnings must state, in turn: (1) "Smoking Causes Lung Cancer, Heart Disease, Emphysema, and May Complicate Pregnancy"; (2) "Quitting Smoking Now Greatly Reduced Serious Risks to Your Health"; (3) "Smoking by Pregnant Women May Result n Fetal Injury, Premature Birth, and Low Birth Weight"; and (4) "Cigarette Smoke Contains Carbon Monoxide." The format of the warnings, however, was basically unchanged. They were not changed in shape, as the FTC had recommended, and were not required to take up a larger proportion of the ads or package surface (see U.S. DHHS, Surgeon General 1989, pp. 476–80, 612; Beltramini 1988, pp. 26–32; Popper and Murray 1989).

22. Representative Henry Waxman's bill called for strong restrictions on the content and imagery in cigarette ads, larger warning labels, and bans on vending machine sales, free distribution of cigarettes, and certain sponsorships by tobacco companies. As of 1990, more than forty members of Congress had joined a congressional antismoking task force.

23. In 1987, thirty-one states considered cigarette tax hikes, typically promoted on health grounds, and eleven states adopted them (Leichter, 1991, p. 130). Still, in 1987, although taxes exceeded 25 cents per pack in twelve states (led by Minnesota's 38 cents per pack), the average state tax was only 18 cents, or about 14 percent of the retail price per pack—about the same as the federal tax, and hence far lower than Canadian and French taxes.

24. The coliseum management provided some small indoor rooms, equipped with television sets tuned to the game, to which patrons who could not do without a cigarette could repair.

25. Throughout the 1980s, cigarette consumption per capita in California remained about one-third lower than the national average, even as the latter declined by 25 percent.

26. Decentralized anti-tobacco activists have also used lawsuits for paternalistic ends. Thus a suit by activist lawyers compelled a Massachusetts convenience store chain to agree to demand positive age-identification from young would-be tobacco buyers.

27. In contrast, both Canada and France already impose heavy, regressive taxes on consumer goods, so the ideological and economic significance of taxing one particular product even more heavily is marginal. In addition, both Canada and France (unlike the United States) have government-financed national health-care programs. Hence it can more easily be argued that heavy taxation of cigarettes simply forces smokers to pay their fair share of the extra costs their tobacco-induced illnesses impose on nonsmoking taxpayers.

28. Canada, like the United States, has a federal system. A significant amount of governmental power resides in provincial and municipal legislatures and executives. There, too, local nonsmokers' rights ordinances have become common. But since power in the Canadian national government itself is less fragmented than in the United States, Canadian activist organizations, themselves far better coordinated—and hence better funded—than their fragmented American counterparts, have been better able to counterbalance tobacco-company politicking in the nation's capital. In this sense, the decentralized character of the American antismoking movement reflects its political weakness at the national level; by and large, the major victories it has been able to win are local ones.

29. See "Criticized Panel Backs the Condemnation" 1990; Briggs 1988.

3

The Social Symbolism of Smoking and Health

Joseph R. Gusfield

The mirror images of tobacco as harmful and immoral and smoking as harmless and innocently pleasurable have spiralled through Western history since tobacco was first brought to Europe (Gottsegen 1940; Best 1979; Troyer and Markle 1983). Though our economic, political and legal institutions have often been dominated by one or another assessment, both positive and negative images of tobacco have been a part of American life. The two concerns of health and morality have appeared in the perception of tobacco and its uses. The pleasures of smoking have been countered at times by claims of its bad effects on health, at times by its perception as an evil habit associated with vicious living. Dual images and dual criteria have been embodied in institutional practices and the recurring interests of various segments of the American population. Neither the rejecting nor the appreciative view of smoking has entirely disappeared from American life.

Health and morality are by no means always, or even often, separate and unconnected domains. In the history of American medicine matters of health and matters of morality have often been interconnected. To be ill has sometimes seemed to be a result of evil living and sometimes its cause (Rosenberg 1962; Starr 1982; Tesh 1988, Chs. 1, 2). In recent years, many aspects of illness have been construed as resulting from lifestyle choices—as the direct consequences of chosen behavior (Zola 1972; Crawford 1977; Crawford 1979). How we eat, drive automobiles, accept stress, drink alcohol, exercise, conduct sexual relations, lead sedentary lives, use drugs, and smoke tobacco are widely understood today as important to the health of the individual.

A healthy lifestyle and a moral one might seem unrelated to each other. It is logically possible to see each as separate: as different and distinct frames within which to interpret, assess, and adjudge human actions. However, what is logical is not necessarily sociological. Prescriptions for healthful living, of which nonsmoking is now a part, are also prescriptions for being a particular kind of person leading a particular kind of life (Tesh 1988; Glassner 1989).

The frames of morality and health are not as divergent as they appear at first sight. The story of the antismoking movement in the past three decades is a story of its leadership by the elite of medical science supported by the official imprimatur of the national government as health agency. The credibility of the scientific research elite is the salient point in any comparison of the current antismoking movement with that of the early twentieth century in the United States. The antismoking campaigns of the early twentieth century were set in the frame of moral concerns. The present campaigns have been framed in the context of health, an appeal to rational thought devoid of moral judgments. Yet that has not eliminated the moral quality of the issue nor eradicated the significance of emerging social distinctions. The cigarette has been defined in a way different from the earlier twentieth-century movement—yet not as different as it first appears. In the context of the health consciousness of the past three decades, smoking has taken on a symbolic meaning in which moral and social issues are significant. What began as an appeal to considerations of the smoker's health has accrued meanings that make the smoker an object of moral as well as health concerns. With the rising interest in the environmental smoke produced by smokers, the moral condemnation of smoking has been accentuated.

The Moral Condemnation of Smoking

The Movement Against the "Tyrant in White"

The early campaign against smoking originated in the last twenty years of the nineteenth century. By 1890, twenty-six states had passed legislation prohibiting the sale of cigarettes to minors. By the end of 1909, seventeen states had prohibited the sale of cigarettes altogether. By 1917, the movement was clearly in retreat, yet twelve states still maintained prohibitory laws (Gottsegen 1940, p. 184; Troyer and Markle 1983, pp. 34–35).

This early movement was chiefly directed against the cigarette itself, rather than against smoking in general. This first antismoking crusade was triggered by a great increase in the consumption of cigarettes, an object that one writer in 1909 referred to as "the tyrant in white" ("A Counterblast Against Tobacco" 1909). Hand-rolled cigarettes had been in use for several centuries, especially in Europe. However, it was not until the 1880s that a mass market was possible in the United States (Sobel 1978, Chs. 1, 2; Schudson 1984, Ch. 5). Three developments made mass consumption feasible. One was the invention of the Bonsack cigarette-rolling machine in 1884 (Wagner 1971; Sobel 1978, Ch. 2).[1] The second was the invention of the portable and safe matchbook, in use by the 1890s (Sobel 1978, pp. 66–71; Whelan 1984, pp. 39–40). The third development was less technological than organizational. James Buchanan Duke organized the cigarette industry when, in the 1880s, he combined several firms to form the American Tobacco Company (Sobel 1978, Ch. 2).

The production and consumption of cigarettes rose dramatically from the mid-1880s, when the estimated per capita consumption of cigarettes was approximately 8.1. By 1900 it was approximately 34.7. By 1920 it had increased to approximately 470.5 (Gottsegen, cited in Troyer and Markle 1983, p. 34). Until then, cigars, pipes, and chewing tobacco had been the dominant forms of tobacco consumption in the United States, and adult men had been almost the entire market for tobacco products.

The cigarette introduced a new commodity and made possible a new set of meanings to smoking. It was distinctly smaller, easier to light, and milder than its competitors. As such, it became more accessible to two groups for whom smoking had been under a restrictive taboo: women and young people, especially boys. In this period concerns for the harmful effects of cigarettes on health played a minor role. The moral and social consequences of smoking cigarettes loomed large in the themes that appeared in editorials, in news and magazine stories quoting partisans of the antismoking organizations, and in professional medical and scientific journals.[2] Cigarettes were becoming a symbol of moral looseness coupled with a minimized respect for the authority of the male adult—the cigar and pipe smoker.

The following themes appeared in the newspapers and magazines of the period. However, it would be misleading to impute a high level of consensus to this public discussion. Not only were different themes sounded by different people but there was much disagreement, both within the ranks of nonsmokers and between smokers and nonsmokers.

The Threat to Male Dominance. During the nineteenth century in America, smoking was a major symbol and sign of the adult male in American life. The segregation of the genders and all that it implied was dramatically portrayed in the exclusivity of smoking as a masculine form of pleasure. New technology however, made it much easier for women to pursue the pleasures of smoking. Cigarettes could be easily hidden in purses, and the newly invented safety match added to convenience and safety. The fact that women were beginning to smoke reinforced the notion that cigarettes posed a social threat. Complaints of women's smoking appeared in the newspapers, opposing so-called "continental habits" and supporting "good manners" ("A Good Beginning" 1908). A New York assemblyman, introducing his annual bill to prohibit the sale of cigarettes, expressed a sentiment appearing often in the public discourse of the period:

> Do you know that any number of our High School girls, as well as boys, smoke cigarettes, and do you know that many foolish women are beginning to believe that it is real smart to learn to smoke cigarettes? . . . Women in society have taken to smoking cigarettes and persons who are on the ragged edge of society think they have as much right. All roads to ruin are open when [boys and girls] begin to smoke. ("Says Schoolgirls Smoke" 1905).

Although it was not until several years after World War I that public smoking became acceptable for women (Schudson 1984, Ch. 5), cigarettes had already begun to be a symbol of equality between men and women. Whatever the intent of the smoker, the use of cigarettes assumed a political meaning.

As the cigar and pipe were symbolic of male power, the cigarette suffered among male consumers in the 1900s from identification with effeminacy. That impediment to a more rapid development of the cigarette market among men was not to be overcome until after World War I.

The Moral Threat to Youth. With the beginnings of mass marketing of the cigarette, smoking was available to the adolescent. Characteristically, cigarettes were sold in packs of ten and it was sometimes possible to buy one at a time. In marketing them, especially for young men, Duke's advertisers often provided free cards with pictures of alluring young women (Sobel 1978, Ch. 2).

Opponents associated cigarettes with depravity. The cigarette was described as an accompaniment to crime, lust, insobriety, and a general looseness of social obligations. Sometimes this was attributed to the peers with whom the young smoker associated. Sometimes it was seen in the image of the "cigarette fiend" directly affected by the inhalation of smoke. This notion is analogous to more recent discussion of the effects of illegal drugs on the behavior of the addict (Inciardi 1986, Chs. 3, 4). Occasionally the cigarette was portrayed in association with prostitutes, and the woman user seen as a victim of loose morality brought about by the evil weed. Studies were cited establishing an association between cigarette smoking and crime ("Some Cigaret Figures" 1914; Boyers 1916; Hubbell 1904). This theme is consistent with the constant fear of the "dangerous classes" and youth, which was common in the nineteenth century and has continued to today (Gusfield 1991; Kett 1977; Monkkonen 1975).

Illustrative of this view was the following from Charles Buckley Hubbell, President of the Board of Education of New York City:

> Boys of ten, twelve and fourteen years of age, naturally bright, were observed to be losing the power of concentration and application of mind. . . . Further investigation disclosed the fact that very many of these boys stole money from their parents, or sold all sorts of articles that they could lay their hands on, in order that they could gratify an appetite that fed on its own indulgence. (Hubbell 1904, p. 377)

Loss of Efficiency. The cigarette, some believed, caused a loss of productivity in the work force and led to a decline in mental abilities. Studies indicated most students who smoked did poorly in their school grades (Carter 1906, pp. 488ff.). Nonsmoking was seen as a prerequisite to an efficient school performance. The smoker was less likely to succeed; the nonsmoker had a headstart in the game of life. (This belief seems to have reappeared [Robb 1991].)

The themes of immorality, crime, and inefficiency sometimes appear together in the public discussions of cigarettes. Not everyone believed the assertions claiming that cigarettes were responsible for these problems; nevertheless, such associations were sufficiently prominent in the public discussion as "fact" that the cigarette's social meanings were apparent. It represented a challenge to authority, ranging from a mild aura of naughtiness and "continental" sophistication to outright rebelliousness.

Polluting Effects of Smoking. The traditional segregation of the genders when only men smoked had been defended as a concern for the sensibilities of women, for whom smoke was assumed to be distasteful. The same argument, in reverse, was used by the Non-Smoker's Protective League to support laws that banned smoking in public buildings and transportation facilities. Such laws were passed in a number of localities, although their enforcement is less certain. Smoke was, for some, an impure substance and contact with it polluting. The cigarette smoker was portrayed as a physical threat to the nonsmoker.

Medical Harm. Physiologists and professors of medicine had begun to study the effects of smoking at the beginning of the twentieth century. They investigated the effects of smoking on blood pressure and on certain ailments of the eye (tobacco ambylopia) (Dunn 1906; Bruce et al. 1909; "The Pharmacology of Tobacco Smoke" 1909). Such studies were generally experimental and clinical, and the results were mixed. No large-scale epidemiological study appeared during this period.

Several medical professors were scornful of intuitive judgments about health and morality found in the antismoking movements. Most, however, agreed that the prime focus was and should be on the cigarette, if only because the smoker inhaled much more often than with other means of consuming smoke.

But at no time in the early movement were health concerns at the center of the public discussion of cigarette smoking. There was no consensus, among either medical researchers or the lay public, that the physiochemical consequences of cigarette smoking were very harmful to the health of the smoker or the nonsmoker.

By the time the United States entered into World War I, all of the major themes of today's antismoking movement were in place in some or most of the population. The popularity of the cigarette in post–World War I America owes little to a changed perception of its healthful or unhealthful properties that new research might have produced. The use of cigarettes increased considerably among women, and American men shifted their habit from cigars, pipes, and chewing tobacco to cigarettes. The total amount of tobacco in use in the United States remained stable between 1918 and 1940, while the sale of cigarettes increased greatly (Schudson 1984, p. 182).

The Social Acceptance of the Cigarette

The antismoking movement collapsed in the wake of World War I. Many elements are associated with the rise of the cigarette habit and its acceptance by both genders of the American buying public. An adequate social history has not yet appeared, although several elements of the story can be suggested. The carrying convenience of cigarettes, in contrast to pipes and cigars, supported their wide distribution to American soldiers. The association of the soldier with cigarette smoking did much to change the view among men that cigarettes were effeminate and also gave the cigarette an aura of patriotism (Troyer and Markle 1983, pp. 40–47). The taboo against women smokers, which was weakened by the development of the cigarette, was further weakened as the cigarette came to be identified as a symbol of demand for equality of the sexes (Schudson 1984, Ch. 5). By the early 1920s, all state legislation barring the sale of cigarettes to adults had been repealed.

The mildness of cigarettes, as compared with other forms of tobacco, aided its acceptance among women, as among men. During the 1920s, especially among urban, somewhat cosmopolitan and sophisticated women, smoking became the symbol of the modern. As Schudson expresses it, the cigarette was "connected to the young, the cosmopolitan and the naughty" (Schudson 1984, p. 196). It was during the 1920s that smoking in public, although not yet on the streets, became acceptable conduct for women, especially in American cities.

Public Health: The Current Movement Against Smoking

In understanding the shift in smoking behavior in American life, it becomes clear that health concerns played a small role, if any, before the 1950s.

And until 1964, while some intuitive feeling that smoking was harmful existed among a number of Americans, there was no widely accepted authority that settled the factual question of the healthfulness of smoking. Unlike the moral orientations of the earlier campaigns, the present movement has been directed as an aspect of public health. The earlier movement was largely led by voluntary associations. The present movement has been sparked and directed primarily by public health agencies of government, especially the federal government. It has found its authority in the research of medical science.

For much of its history in Western societies there has been some sense that smoking might be harmful, some hope that it is not, and very little fact to support either claim. How great is the real risk of disease from smoking? The average citizen must look to others—epidemiologists, medical clinicians—to make such determinations. But what others? Who "owns" the cigarette question?

By the late 1940s in the United States, cigarette smoking had become common in all classes and genders. Its possible negative effects on health were not a public issue and cigarette smoking in general was not perceived as a public problem. By the mid-1960s this was no longer the case. A public consensus had developed that smoking cigarettes is harmful to health; that it significantly heightens the risks of developing lung cancer, heart trouble, and other diseases. That consensus is largely the work of scientific research, governmental and news reporting, and the emergence and activism of voluntary medical organizations. It represents the hegemony of medical science over the culture of health.

Divisions often exist not only about the wisdom of public policies but also about the very facts that constitute the conditions that are named as "problems." As it operates in social actions, "reality" is not something given in the nature of things, plain for all to see and agree upon. Events and conditions have to be attended to and interpreted. The current American birth rate and the gross national product are aggregated facts that cannot be directly perceived by individuals. We depend on institutions and persons that accumulate data and transmit them to an interested audience. It is in this sense that I consider the belief in the harmful effects of cigarettes as an example of "the social construction of reality" (Berger and Luckmann 1967; Spector and Kitsuse 1977).

In the early antismoking movement the body of research on the negative effects of smoking was too scattered, too conflicting, and too unavailable to the public to serve as an authoritative guide to behavior—a guide that was difficult for the individual to ignore or to impeach. While surveys at the time indicated a public acceptance and appreciation of "science" as an institution and scientists as disinterested investigators, scientific research had little of the institutional structure that has since emerged over the past fifty years (LaFollette 1990). Nor was the role of government in medical research as central as it became after World War II (Brandt 1990). But by the time the Surgeon General issued the report of 1964, social conditions had become favorable to the transmission and credibility of medical science and the position of the federal government as a source of authoritative advice and activity in the promotion of health.

The Emergence of a Scientific Elite

World War II was an enormous stimulus to the development of science in the United States. The construction of the Lawrence Livermore Laboratory at University of California and the successful Manhattan Project to create the atomic bomb demonstrated what might be accomplished by governmental subsidization of scientists in large-scale projects (Davis 1968; Nelkin 1987). Although there had been earlier instances of such subsidization, as a general policy of the federal government it is largely a recent creation.

By 1964, a structure of science had emerged that made possible the development of a range of medical studies and their dissemination to an attentive public. Large-scale epidemiological research was itself a relatively new development in medical science, addressing the smoking problem in a novel language. The institutions responsible for developing and disseminating knowledge about tobacco use were those charged with the functions of maintaining and improving the health of the nation. Among these, the Public Health Service and the Surgeon General's Office of the federal government were preeminent.

Research findings were now more easily transmitted to the general public. By 1964, science reporting had become a part of journalism and the science reporter was a specialist on many newspapers and newsmagazines. William Laurence of the *New York Times* and Milton Silverman of the *San Francisco Chronicle,* pioneers in the field, had begun their careers as science reporters in the late 1930s. This meant that some reporters now read certain scientific journals regularly and were attentive to work they saw as significant for their readers.[4] In the medical field this meant that the reports published in the *Journal of the American Medical Association*, the *New England Journal of Medicine*, *Lancet*, and several other journals for published studies were now accessible to the public. The *Reader's Digest* played a significant role as well in reporting the medical research on smoking, especially in the 1950s. The public was better educated than in the past and was now exposed to television as well as print media (Nelkin 1987; Pfohl 1984).

Since the early antismoking movement, a nonprofessional medical establishment has developed in the form of organizations that support research and seek to persuade the public of healthful forms of living. Among these are the American Cancer Society (ACS), the American Heart Asssociation, and the American Lung Association. The ACS has been the major source of funds for some of the most widely cited epidemiological studies of smoking both before and after 1964.

Lastly, the federal government became a major player in the game of health promotion. The Department of Health, Education, and Welfare was not established in the United States until the 1950s. Before then, medicine had not been considered a major concern of the federal government, even though government sanitary engineers had played a paramount role in public health activities that greatly improved the country's resistance to major infectious diseases. That the Surgeon General's Report was received with a high degree of credibility suggests the trust that government and science had gained by 1964.

Of course medical science in the past had often played a large role in affecting personal behavior and public action. The discovery of germ-produced disease, the spread of immunizing vaccinations, and the work of sanitary engineers are all highly significant developments in the relations between medical science, government, and the individual. What is new, however, is the great increase in health-consciousness in a public fed a daily diet of newspaper, magazine, and television stories of the latest scientific research, the newest discovery, the most recent advice on how to prevent illness and improve health. Such material is a major part of the more general concern for healthy living charactetrized as the "health fitness movement."

Medical Science and the Health Effects of Smoking

The modern study of the health effects of smoking might be dated from 1900, from 1925, or from 1938 (Wagner 1971, pp. 69ff). Such studies, however, made little impression on the public. Yet a sense of harm connected with tobacco smoking in all forms was present in the nineteenth century and earlier (Wagner 1971; Best 1979). That intuition was strengthened by the first antismoking movement and continued as an element of American culture after the movement ceased to be an active force in public policy. During the 1930s and 1940s there was a growing consciousness that smoking was unhealthy. Several studies found a strong statistical association between heavy cigarette smoking and the incidence of lung cancer, which was on the rise in the United States (Brandt 1990). These studies rang alarms, but too softly to be heard. It was finally in the 1950s that a number of prospective epidemiological studies on the risks of smoking were undertaken, especially in the United States, Canada, and England. By the late 1950s these studies had developed in importance so that major news magazines reported their findings in featured studies, sometimes with critics as well ("Cigarettes" 1958; Cort 1959; "Do They—or Don't They?" 1959; "Smoking and Cancer" 1955, 1958, 1959; "Latest on Smoking and Cancer" 1955; "What is Known and Unknown" 1957; "What Britons Are Told" 1957). The demand for a governmental review of this material was growing. In December 1959, Surgeon General Burney issued a statement condemning smoking as unhealthy ("Dr. Burney's Alarm" 1959).

The studies of the 1950s formed the major bases for the conclusions of the Surgeon General's report of 1964. Issued in January of that year and accompanied by a televised press conference, the report marked the definitive beginning of a medical and public consensus that tobacco is harmful to health.

1964: The Emergence of Consensus

The alacrity with which the Surgeon General's Report of 1964, and subsequent reports, were accepted as reality is indicative of the legitimacy of the scientific and the governmental medical agencies in American life. Once issued, the report's conclusions were treated by the mass media as certain and authoritative.

In 1959, *Newsweek*, in its medicine section, described the question of the harmful effects of cigarette smoking as still awaiting "a final, undebatable medical answer" ("Do They—Or Don't They?" 1959, p. 80). In 1962, the magazine began a story of the announcement that the Surgeon General would review the question with the phrase, "No one can say with certainty that cigarettes cause cancer" ("Smoking and Health" 1962a, p. 74). In a later issue, *Newsweek* described the steps in developing that report as "an attempt to settle one of medicine's most controversial questions" ("Smoking and Health" 1962b). When the report did appear, in January 1964, *Newsweek* gave it two and one-half pages and implicitly criticized the long wait before the government agreed with other countries and American health agencies. However, *Newsweek* now described the belief in the health hazard of smoking as having "the full weight" of U.S. authority. It referred to the report itself as "the official judgment" ("Cigarette Smoking is a Health Hazard" 1964, p. 48).

The Surgeon General's conclusions were reported elsewhere by the press in similarly definitive terms. The *New York Times* began an editorial with the statement, "Now it is official" ("The Smoking Report" 1964). In the same edition, on the front page, the *Times* stated that the Report "found no doubt about the role of cigarette smoking in causing cancer of the lungs" (Sullivan 1964). *Time* Magazine stressed the way in which the "impartial committee of top experts" unanimously supported what was already known about the harmful effects of smoking ("The Government Report" 1964).

That the report was quickly accepted by public segments is seen by the decline in cigarette sales and numbers of Americans who said, in surveys, that they had stopped smoking. 1964 was a watershed year. Per capita consumption of tobacco in the United States decreased continuously from a high of 4,345 cigarettes in 1963 to 3,971 in 1969 (U.S. Department of Agriculture 1990, pp. 100, 106). Surveys of the American population also show a continuous decline in percentage of smokers since 1965 (U.S. DHHS, Office of Smoking and Health 1986, pp. 19–20; U.S. DHHS, Surgeon General 1988, pp. 565–66).

Medical Knowledge and the Public

To refer to the hegemony of science is to call attention to the way in which the institution of science, medical science in this instance, creates a believable reality, based on scientific research. Scientists may have to convince each other of the "facts" but they do not have to go far to be the source of the construction of the "real" character of smoking and health. The very attention of the news media is itself an important element in the definition of truth about smoking. The construction of that reality is an important part of the role that medical science plays.

What is the status of the knowledge of the medical consequences of smoking? David Bloor makes a distinction between "high-status knowledge" and "low-status knowledge" (Bloor 1992). For much of the public that has been aware of the Surgeon General's reports, the condemnation of smoking rests on the certainty of verified knowledge. Such knowledge is the property of those uninvolved in the complexities of the investigations; it is low-status knowledge. For those involved in the production of the knowledge the result of research is more complex; it is high-status knowledge. Probability, revision, and qualification are more the rule in epidemiological studies that depend on talking to human beings or utilizing records produced by human beings. The 1964 Surgeon General's report is no different in that respect. Its claims rest heavily on epidemiological studies, although clinical and experimental research were taken into account (U.S. DHEW 1964a).

The epidemiological studies on which the writers of the report based much of their conclusions were seven prospective studies, in which data on smoking habits were drawn from a population and the same population followed over a period of 10–15 years ("longitudinal" studies). Despite consistent findings, the studies presented problems in interpretation. Some of these problems are recognized and dealt with in the report. The authors themselves suggest four major deficiencies in the study populations on which the research was based (U.S. DHEW 1964a, pp. 94–96). First, the samples were entirely male and were not representative of the total populations of American, British, or Canadian men studied. The samples of respondents were better educated than the total populations from which they were drawn. Second, reporting of deaths was incomplete, especially where they depended on volunteers' reports. Third, even though smokers had higher death rates than nonsmokers, the death rates of both groups, corrected for age, were below the national average, especially so for nonsmokers. As the authors of the report point out, this suggests that the nonsmokers were an especially healthy group. Lastly, the study populations did not include people in hospitals, who probably would have increased the numbers of those who died during the sampled periods. In addition, the almost exclusive use of volunteers in gathering data in two of the largest studies (70 percent of the total populations studied) led to ignorance of the number and character of nonrespondents or how a large part of the population was sampled. A number of other criticisms and qualifications have been made in the medical and other journals where the validity of public health conclusions about smoking have been debated (Burch 1983, 1984; Eysenck 1986; Sterling 1975; Lilienfield 1983; Weiss 1975).

What I wish to convey by this discussion is the distinction between conclusions derived from wise, informed judgments and those very rare conclusions in human studies that can be presented with certainty.[4] The authors of the report were aware of many of the defects of the studies. They write, at one point, that "any answer to the question to what general population of men can the results be applied must involve an element of unverifiable judgment" (U.S. DHEW 1964a, p. 94).

An essential part of the report's conclusions is developed around a specific perspective toward the concept of causation. Given that most smokers do not develop lung cancer and that some nonsmokers do develop lung cancer, the concept of a single linear cause, necessary or sufficient, is rejected. Indeed, the authors of the report developed a complex view of cause which was itself an innovation in epidemiology (Burch 1983; Brandt 1990). It utilized criteria based on consistency, strength, specificity, temporality, and coherence of the statistical associations between smoking and death rates. No single criterion or study is sufficient, but a number of different criteria, taken together, establish a test (U.S. DHEW 1964a, pp. 181–89).

> As already stated, statistical methods cannot establish proof of a causal relationship in an association. The causal significance of an association is a matter of judgment which goes beyond any statement of statistical probability. (U.S. DHEW 1964a, p. 182)

The authors of the report, aware of the immense difficulties in achieving certainty, defend their conclusions and recommendations by stressing the interrelated elements of the consistency, strength, specificity, temporality, and coherence of the associations found in the various studies (U.S. DHEW 1964a, pp. 183–86). Thus, despite their differences, all of the studies found similar relative risks for lung cancer. All report a dose-effect phenomenon: heavy smokers were more likely to die earlier and of lung cancer than were lighter smokers; lighter smokers more than ex-smokers; and ex-smokers more than nonsmokers.

Medical researchers operating in the arena of public problems face this dilemma: if they wait until they possess "certain" proof, they may never have answers for a public eager to know the best advice. An editorial in the *American Journal of Public Health* makes the case. While the precise importance of smoking can be debated, wrote the editor, "[T]here can be no question that wide-spread cessation of smoking would result in more good than harm. To dilute the importance of smoking is to foolishly divert us from an important goal" (Ibrahim 1976, p. 133).

The summary of the report, published nine months later, cautiously stated:

> On the basis of prolonged study and evaluation of many lines of converging evidence, the Committee makes the following judgment: CIGARETTE SMOKING IS A HEALTH HAZARD OF SUFFICIENT IMPORTANCE IN THE UNITED STATES TO WARRANT APPROPRIATE REMEDIAL ACTION. (U.S. DHEW 1964b, p. 6)

In discussing the possible causative role of smoking in coronary disease, the report's authors finds such a role, though not proven, strongly enough suspected to warrant countermeasures. They conclude:

> IT IS ALSO MORE PRUDENT TO ASSUME THAT THE ESTABLISHED ASSOCIATION BETWEEN CIGARETTE SMOKING AND CORONARY DISEASE HAS CAUSATIVE MEANING THAN TO SUSPEND JUDGMENT UNTIL NO UNCERTAINTY REMAINS. (U.S. DHEW 1964b, p. 10)

In public discourse, however, the distinction between the guarded character of "judgment" and the certainty of "cause" gets lost. In the arena of public knowledge, qualifications and conceptual difficulties gave way to consensus and certainty. The *San Diego Union* began its front-page story on the 1964 report with the sentence, "Heavy cigarette smoking is the principal cause of cancer of the lungs" ("Cigarettes Called Peril to Health" 1964, p. 1). American Cancer Society materials currently use several different terms. Sometimes they refer to smoking being "responsible" for harm; sometimes to "cause" and sometimes to "may cause." (American Cancer Society 1982, 1987a, 1987b). A statement mandated to be placed on the walls of

California hotels and restaurants that permit smoking reads: "WARNING: This Facility Permits Smoking and Tobacco Smoke is Known to the State of California to Cause Cancer." In these forms, public discourse is informed by a more ordered and certain perception of harm than given by the necessarily fragile and limited character of wise judgment.

The Culture of Healthful Living

The Surgeon General's report and the media's reporting were couched in the language of health. While such language does not disappear, in the three decades since the report a distinct moral tone has been added; the individual's responsibility to follow the advice of medical science becomes a significant element in health or illness. To some extent, we have returned to the moral rhetoric of the earlier movement.

The Meanings of Illness

The Surgeon General's reports on smoking, published annually since 1964, do not occur in a vacuum. They are congruent with and add to a more general shift in the perception of health and medicine which is still occurring in American life. In the remainder of this chapter, I want to consider divergent conceptions of health and medicine and the place of smoking in them.

The smoking issue may be described in more general terms to highlight the idea of health as an aspect of morality. Illness may be, and has been, seen as a sign of deficient moral character; epidemics can become symbols of communal malfeasance. This Sodom and Gomorrah story is especially clear in illnesses such as venereal disease and AIDS. Here the transmission of disease depends on human behavior. This viewpoint is to be contrasted with that perspective in which medical science focuses on the nonpurposive, nonhuman forms of disease instigation. Illness is seen as a result of factors external to individual character or behavior (Tesh 1988). The individual's health is less a result of harmful living than of chance, genetics, and environment. Attention is thus directed toward treatment of disease rather than toward educating people to change their behavior.

While the search for a cure for cancer is still dominated by the latter view, in the cases of smoking, lung cancer, and coronary disease, lifestyles and personal habits have assumed a great importance as ways of preventing illness. To see cancer or heart trouble as consequent on a lifestyle is to shift, to some degree, the nature of the disease and responsibility for its occurrence onto the person. In this fashion, medicine comes to emphasize prevention of diseases by proper living, rather than treatment by chemical or physical means.

Who then is the healthful person? What is the lifestyle enjoined by the transformation of health from the domain of the medical institution to the domain of the individual? Since the 1970s, the public has been exposed to the idea that the healthful person incorporates the pursuit of good health into his or her daily life, at work and at leisure. He or she eats nutritiously, avoiding excess fats, watching caloric intake, and aiming at weight reduction. Exercise is a part of leisure; jogging, fitness activity, cycling are all aspects of daily routine. Drinking alcohol is risky behavior and should be limited or eliminated. Smoking is a foolish risk and should not be a part of life. "Safe sex" should be the rule. Health is not the absence of illness but something pursued in the very way we behave (Stone 1986; Zola 1972; Gusfield 1992). This emphasis on the adoption of healthful styles of living can be considered a social movement—the health-fitness movement (Goldstein 1991). It has been advocated and supported by work of the health "establishment," including government and voluntary medical associations such the American Health Association (U.S. DHEW 1979).

The individual becomes the focus of responsibility for his or her own health. A further example is found in the rise of the nutritional approach to health, which was met with skepticism and resistance by medical science in the 1950s and early 1960s but has become a major element in American orientations toward good health (Belasco 1989; Gusfield forthcoming; Schwartz 1986; Goldstein 1991). What we eat and how much we eat have come to be viewed as major elements in preventing or developing illness.

The role of government in this endeavor at preventive medicine is furthered by the increased role of federal and state governments in financing medical care and the greatly enhanced costs of physician and hospital services. Preventive medicine has virtues for public finance when compared to the one-on-one costs of treating and hospitalizing ill patients.

The Smoker as Responsible Victim

The advice of the health organizations, including government, has been a major part of the health-fitness movement. That advice includes the underlying "moral message" of the movement. In its focus on preventive behavior, the rhetoric of the advice distinguishes between responsible and irresponsible people. Smokers are foolish, ignorant, or lacking in the kind of character necessary for healthfulness. The reward of a healthful lifestyle is long life; the punishment of unhealthy living is early death. The avoidance of risk is a virtue; the acceptance of risk is vice.

The Surgeon General's reports on smoking, from 1964 until the early 1980s, and the news coverage that transmitted them, are largely addressed to a public that is to be persuaded to stop smoking or never to begin to smoke. Their rhetoric makes an appeal to a disciplined self-control. People are asked to act in a rational fashion by developing habits that minimize risk and giving up habits that maximize risk. It is assumed that sensible people will desire a longer and more healthful life. Only fools or addicts will begin smoking or make no efforts to stop. The person who persists in smoking is a victim of his or her own ignorance, stupidity, or lack of self-control. In any case the smoker falls short of the character enjoined by authoritative medical science.

The Healthful Public

In describing the public response to the Surgeon General's reports, I have not differentiated parts of the population from one another. The image of the healthful citizen as a model to be followed is, however, more prevalent in some segments of the population than others. Not everyone is a follower of medical news in the popular culture of contemporary America.[5] Not everyone places the trust in science described above. Not everyone makes health the cornerstone of life depicted in the model of the healthful citizen.

Our knowledge of the segments of population that are attuned to medical science and incorporate health recommendations into their lives is still meager. Nevertheless, all studies report that the college-educated public is the prime recipient and appreciator of health news and advice (U.S. DHHS, Surgeon General 1989, Ch. 5; U.S. DHHS, Office of Smoking and Health 1986; Schoenborn and Boyd 1989; Pierce et al. 1989; Fiore et al. 1989). Lesser, but significant, differences exist between income levels (Goldstein 1991; Williams 1990; Fuchs 1979).

In the years since 1964, the Surgeon General's reports have consistently presented three important findings in respect to smoking:

1. The cessation of smoking and the absence of initiation into smoking is more often found among better educated than less educated persons. This is especially true of the gap between college-educated and non-college-educated persons. It is also truer of men than of women. (This latter finding is reversed in other forms of health behavior in the health-fitness movement, such as alcohol use and dieting, where women are more responsive to health advice.)

2. That difference has been continuous and has increased over the years since 1964. White-collar workers are less likely to smoke than are blue-collar workers and employed workers more likely to smoke than unemployed workers. High-school students expecting to attend four-year colleges are less likely to smoke than are students not expecting to continue education past high school. These indices of smoking and cessation from smoking show the close association between compliance with health advice and markers of social class and status. While studies indicate a high level of knowledge of the harmful effects of smoking at all social levels, the response to health information is structured along lines of social stratification.

3. While both men and women have decreased their usage of cigarettes, the decrease has been considerably greater among men than women. At present the prevalence of smoking among women is only slightly less than among men. Moreover, as new smokers, women are beginning to smoke in larger percentages than are men.

The Social Symbolism of Commodities

Styles of daily living are part of a person's "cultural capital" (Bourdieu and Passeron, 1977); they are signs of membership in networks of people of similar styles. In Veblen's terms, they are signs that the claimant to a status and to a group membership is a person of worth and not someone of a different and less valuable culture (Veblen 1934).

Refraining from smoking becomes necessary to the style of health-oriented, rational, risk-aversive people. Following the prescriptions of medical science demonstrates that they are people of virtue. It shows that they take a measured, self-controlled attitude toward their lives and behavior. They are people who have heard the calls of medical research and have the will to avoid the indulgences toward which a consumer-oriented market beckons their participation. To cease smoking demonstrates the capacity for self-control which has so often been a mark of American self-help movements.

Creating Moral Boundaries:
Smokers as Victims and Villains

In the health-fitness movement smoking has been described as a habit hurting the smoker. Since the early 1980s, however, this situation has changed. With the research and publicity about passive smoking, the smoker has become troubling to others, to nonsmokers, as well.

The appearance of research on passive smoking, its dissemination to the antismoking public, and the recent wave of legislative and administrative polices based on conceptions of passive smoking have widened the distinctions between the smoker and nonsmoker. By the 1990s, the smoker was not only a foolish victim of his or her habit but also an obnoxious and uncivil source of danger, pollution, and illness to others. The early movement against the cigarette and the current movement against smoking take on growing similarities.

Smoking and the Creation of Moral Boundaries

In a recent case challenging the use of gender as a screening device in health insurance rates, the Supreme Court gave voice to the now more common usage of the unhealthy life style as a point of differentiation between Americans:

> [W]hen insurance risks are grouped, the better risks always subsidize the poorer risks. Healthy persons subsidize medical benefits for the less healthy . . . persons who eat, drink, or smoke to excess may subsidize pension benefits for persons whose habits are more temperate. . . . To insure the flabby and the fit as though they were equivalent risks may be more common than treating men and women alike.[6]

What is noteworthy in this opinion is the consciousness of healthful and unhealthful lifestyles as bases for boundaries of significance in American society. "Excess" and "temperate" are used in this context as terms of opprobrium and approval as are "flabby" and "fit."

Before the emergence of the antismoking movement, the issue of smoking did not warrant enough significance to make it a part of descriptions of people. While parents may have cautioned their teenaged children against it, smoking occupied the same status as drinking: an adult pleasure which children might be expected to experiment with before adulthood. It might be a chastised act among teenagers, but by itself it was an ambiguous dereliction. This has changed, and smoking has become a matter of note, of distinction. Even in personals ads today modes of eating, drinking and smoking are elements of self-description ("Classified Ads—Personal" 1991). Smoking or nonsmoking has become an issue; a behavior toward which a stand must be taken. As a source of social distinctions it has been given a moral status. "Substance abuse" has added smoking to form a new trinity: alcohol, cigarettes, and drugs.

For Americans in the middle years (25–60), lower-class and less educated people have higher death and illness rates than their opposites (House et al. 1990). There is some evidence that differences in lifestyles, perhaps more than access to medical care, explain such class differences in health (Williams 1990). It is beyond the scope of this chapter to disentangle the ways in which differences in class affect styles of health behavior. A credible argument can be made for the view that income, education and occupation create a social millieu that deeply influences access to information, dispositions to self-control, and exposure to smoke and to smoking pressures (Navarro 1976; Tesh 1988).

I do not want to overstate the differences between lifestyles and social groups. For one thing, according to the National Institute of Health surveys for 1987, in all educational levels today most people are nonsmokers. In 1985 smokers made up approximately 18 percent of those with 16 or more years of education but they made up only approximately 34 percent of those with less than twelve years of education (Pierce et al. 1989). Nor are class and education levels fully congruent. In American society, as compared with other nations such as France, the cultures of classes and other groups are only loosely homogeneous (Lamont forthcoming).

A better way to think about the boundaries developing in American society is to think about health habits and fitness as emergent criteria by which people judge each other, with smoking behavior serving as an important indicator (Troyer and Markle 1983). In this respect consciousness of smoking as a boundary marker is more likely to be shared in the professional, college-educated, expert-oriented upper middle class than in social classes with opposite attributes.

Passive Smoking: The Smoker as Pariah

During the early 1980s, the public became aware of research on what is known as "involuntary smoking" or "passive smoking." This research, carried out in several countries, has investigated the effect of ambient cigarette smoke on the health of nonsmokers (U.S. DHHS, Surgeon General 1986, Ch. 2; Repace 1985, Ch. 1). The dominant research has consisted of epidemiological studies of the children of smokers and the nonsmoking spouses of smokers.

While the effects on nonsmokers of different periods and different circumstances of exposure to smoke is still undergoing debate, discussion, and further investigation, passive smoking has already had a profound impact on the antismoking movement and on the moral meanings of smoking and smokers. Scientific support for belief in the danger of smoking for nonsmokers has been the intellectual basis for legislation and policy to prohibit smoking in many public areas and to segregate smokers from nonsmokers in many public and work areas.[7]

Before the 1980s, smokers had been viewed in public discourse as people who should be troubling to themselves. Now they were becoming people troubling to others as well. In this fashion smokers have become similar in the public eye to users of alcohol and illicit drugs (Gusfield 1991).

The emergence of research into passive smoking has turned the distaste of smoke into a positive source of exclusion. The smoker is on the defensive as the act of smoking is increasingly banished from many social circles and the smoker so frequently admonished not to smoke. The mandatory exclusion of smoking from public places including outdoor seating areas in stadia furthers the public definition of the smoker as pariah.

As we have seen in the materials on the early antismoking movement, a belief in the polluting effects of smoking and a distaste for proximity to smoke has been a part of American culture for a long time. In public discourse and policy it remained in the background until recent years. Now it is forcefully and often legally revived. Cigarettes have come to assume the status of "dangerous object." The *New York Times*, in an editorial sounding the theme of the shift in the status of the smoker, wrote:

> What a difference a few years and a few Surgeon-General's Reports can make. Only yesterday the nonsmoker was perceived as odd man (or woman) out. Today it's the smoker who stands out. Only 30 per cent of adults smoke now, and they may be feeling a bit hounded. ("Clearing the Air for Nonsmokers" 1984, p. A38)

Public policy cannot wait until scientific criticism has been answered. It draws on the already present sense of the polluting character of smoke to which the 25 years of the contemporary antismoking movement has been added. The resulting pressure for legal measures to segregate smokers has produced a continuing set of local and state measures banning or limiting smoking in public areas.

In recent years, a variety of policies have been put in place that implicitly and symbolically create the definition of the smoker as pariah: someone to be excluded from casual sociability unless he or she abides by the rules of nonsmoking (Schauffler, this volume; Sugarman, this volume). Individual life insurance and hospitalization health insurance now require higher premiums for the smoker than the nonsmoker (Stone 1986). The physical segregation of the smoker on airplanes is now supplanted by the elimination of smoking from all domestic flights in the United States. Smoking is bracketed increasingly with other vices such as drinking and drug abuse. When New York City recently outlawed smoking in public places, the law exempted bars from its provisions, again associating smoking with marginally acceptable areas of behavior. Norms of civility in many social circles now restrict the smoker from smoking in the presence of others (Kagan and Skolnick, this volume). Smoking is an indulgence if granted at all by hosts and often requires the smoker to exclude himself or herself temporarily from sociability.

The moral boundaries between smokers and nonsmokers are now widened by actual physical boundaries. Whenever the smoker steps outside to smoke he or she acts out the symbolism of the pariah being cast from the community. As smoking takes on the attributes of social deviance, of unsocial action, it is even more able to play the role of a social divider. It symbolizes the inability to be aware of or to respect medical science—a sign of a less-educated person.

Public Health and the Individual

The antismoking campaigns and the health-fitness movement have raised again the issues of paternalism and civil liberties. Such issues have always dogged public health efforts to create an environment that would minimize risks to the individual entailed by unhealthy behavior (Beauchamp 1988). Whether public policy should intervene in the free market of business supply and consumer choice has been a question in the movement against the cigarette as it has in other similar public health activities. The developing norms of smoking act to segregate the smoking act rather than prohibit it entirely (Kagan and Skolnick, this volume). To smoke or not to smoke, to cease or not to cease, are still consumer choices.

The effort to eradicate the cigarette in American life is another stage in the public control and self-control of individual life through science and reason. It is in this sense that the health movement and the component promotion of nonsmoking are a facet of modernization. The extension of discipline and forethought to the body as a continuation of the self presupposes and reinforces an image of the noble person. As eating, drinking, smoking, physical movement, and leisure are objects of expert, professional advice and law, the individual who shuns the hegemony of the health elite risks both early death and social censure.

By contrast, the resistance by some to the advice of medical science and public health reflects a distrust of law, social norms, and other constraints on individual action. This resistance is a facet of the glorification of the uniqueness and expressiveness of the "authentic" person in American culture. It symbolizes an individualism that has long been seen as accentuated in the United States as compared with other democratic and modernized societies (Beauchamp 1988, Ch. 5; Lukes 1973; Riesman et al. 1950; Bellah et al. 1985).

In the context of that cultural tension between the individual and the public the cigarette becomes a symbol of rebellion and individuality. A recent movie, *The Fabulous Baker Boys*, illustrates the point. This is the story of two brothers who work as a dual piano team playing popular music in night clubs and cocktail lounges. The film is set in the present. The bourgeois brother lives in the suburbs with his family. The other lives in sleazier quarters in the city. The cigarette smoking of the less-conformist brother is an issue between the two of them. A female singer, who hints of a past as a prostitute, joins the duo. Her smoking and that of the more "outcast" brother establishes a contrast to the conventional brother. In the end, the Bohemian brother gives up his job playing the kind of popular music he hates to devote himself to the jazz world of his black friends. The "hero" has opted for the authenticity of impulse and risk. Smoking is a sign of his identity; a symbol of his opposition to convention and comfort. The cigarette has been given a "heroic" meaning.

From a standpoint of rational concern with health such attitudes may appear frivolous, foolish, romantic, and hedonistic. What medical science advises is a disciplined orientation toward the body based on avoidance of risk. The rational person seeks to maximize life at an acceptable level of bodily comfort. The costs of indulgence in harmful behavior clearly outweigh whatever may be the transient benefits of bodily neglect. A rational orientation toward life and leisure consists in constant consciousness of how each action contributes to health and longevity. Instant gratification, impulsive behavior, and habit-forming activities are a threat to wellness.

The contrast in perspectives is also illustrated in the necessarily public, aggregated character of the research material on smoking. In almost all of the material on the risks of smoking, the differences in death rates between smokers and non-smokers are stated in relative rather than absolute terms. Thus we know that the chances of a smoker dying of lung cancer during the 10–15 period studied for the 1964 report was approximately ten times that of a nonsmoker. This way of reporting the data tells us nothing about the absolute chance of dying of lung cancer. For example, in the data of the 1964 report, for the sample studied, I have calculated that chance as approximately 1 in 357 for smokers and 1 in 3807 for nonsmokers.[8] From the standpoint of the total nation that difference in risk is very important. In a large population it adds up to a magnitude of considerable importance. From the standpoint of the individual its significance is less clear (Beauchamp 1988, Ch. 5). Will he or she be that one person who comprise all the elements, known and unknown, that determine who will contract lung cancer? Smoking is a significant addition to those elements, to be sure, but its importance is accentuated from the perspective of the total population. It is the public character of the risk rather than its application to specific persons that forms the basis for environmental control and individual advice.

The contemporary place of the cigarette in American life is a distant shout from its accepted position in the 1950s. Despite the opposition of the tobacco industry, the public health campaigns of the past three decades have brought about a remarkable change in attitudes and meanings toward smoking. The health movement has produced a cultural shift in the meaning of health and patterns of living that would have seemed impossible 30 years ago. A new medical reality conflicts with an older one. The current meaning of smoking is by no means a mirror image of the early twentieth-century antismoking movement in the United States, nor is it a complete contrast to the 1950s. But it now includes some important similarities. Although in the 1960s the findings of medical science reversed the accepted place of smoking in American life, by the 1990s smoking has become a moral as well as a medical issue.

We live in a world of symbols in which commodities can represent ourselves both to others and to ourselves; in which the measures taken to improve or ignore healthful acts occur in a society that defines the virtuous, the villainous, the foolish, and the romantic. Like most acts of human beings, smoking is not aloof from a culture where meanings dilute the boundaries of medicine, morality, and science.

Notes

1. Both Wagner and Sobel lack adequate documentation. Wagner's book has neither footnotes nor bibliographical references, although there are frequent quotations. Sobel's has a bibliographical note but does not document specific assertions or quotations.

2. Virtually all material on smoking listed in the *Reader's Guide* and in the *Index Medica* before 1945 and available in the University of California, San Diego, library was read for this

article. Figures on tobacco production, voting on anticigarette bills in state legislatures, letters to the editors, and articles about other uses of tobacco (e.g., nicotine as a natural insecticide) were excluded. After 1930, the "evils" of tobacco were discounted and almost no information was listed in the *Reader's Guide*.

3. I am indebted to Milton Silverman, formerly of the *San Francisco Chronicle*, and to David Perlman, currently Science Reporter for the *Chronicle*, for informative conversations on the history and current functioning of science reporters.

4. "In sum, *any scientific estimate is likely to be based on incomplete knowledge combined with assumptions, each of which is a source of uncertainty that limits the accuracy that should be assigned to the estimate*" (National Research Council 1986, p. 44).

5. As David Perlman, science reporter for the *San Francisco Chronicle* put it in an interview: "If I write an article about AIDS most everyone in the gay community will read it but very few drug users will do so."

6. City of Los Angeles Dept. of Water and Power v. Manhart, 435 U.S. 702, 710 (1978).

7. This chapter was completed and in press before the appearance of the widely publicized report on passive smoking of the U.S. Environmental Protection Agency in December 1992 (U.S. EPA 1992). Its general conclusion, that "environmental tobacco smoke in the United States presents a serious and substantial health impact" (p. 1-1), rests chiefly on sources also reviewed for this chapter. The report appears to have already increased support for restrictions on smoking in public places.

8. This figure of absolute risks differs from that of Viscusi, who reported the risk of lung cancer death for smokers in a range of .05-.10. He used lung cancer rates per year and thus a much longer period of time in which outcomes of smoking were manifest. He also assumed that 85 percent of lung cancer deaths were due to smoking. He does not report the absolute rate of lung cancer deaths over the same period for nonsmokers. The research reported in the 1964 Surgeon General's report referred to a specific population over a period of approximately 10–15 years (Viscusi 1990). My point is not the 'true' rate but the significance of the difference between absolute and relative measurements.

4

Banning Smoking: Compliance Without Enforcement

Robert A. Kagan and Jerome H. Skolnick

The Scene: Corner of 45th Street and Lexington Avenue
The Time: Lunch Hour
Dramatis Personae: Hard Hat; Business Man; Paul Rochlin, who observes the players. The Hard Hat is sitting atop metal newspaper vending container. The Business Man is waiting for the light to change. He is smoking.
Hard Hat, sternly, reprimandingly: Hey, this is a no-smoking corner!
Business Man, very sheepishly: Sorry. [He puts out the cigarette.]
Curtain.

> Ron Alexander, "Metropolitan Diary"
> *New York Times*, May 26, 1991

A mistrial was declared in federal court after jurors deadlocked 7 to 5 in favor of convicting a suburban man of roughing up a flight attendant who asked him to put out his cigarette on a [September 1988] no-smoking flight. . . .Smokers revolted on [the] flight because it was overbooked and designated nonsmoking at the last minute. . . . Attendants testified that many passengers yelled and booed in objection to the smoking ban.

> *San Francisco Chronicle*, July 27, 1991

In recent years, nineteen American states have enacted laws restricting smoking in government buildings and health facilities, bringing the total to forty-one states plus the District of Columbia. Several state laws demand protection for nonsmokers' rights in private workplaces.[1] An estimated 450 municipalities (five times as many as in 1986) have enacted ordinances restricting smoking in restaurants, stores, and offices. Thousands of private enterprises and organizations—including a majority of large corporations—have instituted no-smoking policies covering parts and sometimes all of their facilities. By federal regulation, one can no longer smoke on Greyhound buses or on any domestic airline flights. Smokers have been banned from the seats of the Oakland Coliseum, an open-air baseball park, as well from the domed arena of the Minnesota Twins and the University of Texas outdoor football stadium. "In a relatively short time," writes Allen M. Brandt (1990, p. 171), "public space has been subdivided; cigarette smoking has become the most rigorously defined of all public behaviors."

Do Americans automatically comply with no-smoking laws and rules? Do smokers usually respond obediently, like the businessman in our opening vignette? Or is their response more often defiance, as in our second vignette? If compliance is the typical reaction, as our research indicates, why has the legal control of cigarette smoking been relatively successful—in contrast to the troubled attempts to prohibit or regulate the distribution and use of marijuana, cocaine, heroin, handguns, and (in the 1920s) alcoholic beverages? Those are the questions this chapter attempts to answer.

Research Strategy

Is the implementation of nonsmoking rules as unproblematic as the Manhattan streetcorner vignette implies? Some readers, we suspect, will recall having observed people smoking, perhaps defiantly, in no-smoking spaces. But few norms, especially those whose breach does not inflict immediate harm on others, meet with perfect compliance. And as in the case of litterbugs and subway graffiti scrawlers, a small deviant population often can create a misleading impression of widespread disregard of the law.

Ideally, therefore, one would like to know *rates* of noncompliance or resistance. Unlike robberies, however, violations of no-smoking rules are not regularly reported to enforcement officials. Nor do we have the benefit of "victimization" surveys in which a random sample of the population is asked how often they have been exposed to cigarette smoke in posted no-smoking areas. How, then, can we tell to what extent no-smoking rules have met with resistance? Lacking any easily accessible body of systematic data, we have followed a variety of research strategies.

First, we started at the top of the enforcement pyramid, asking police and other officials in three California municipalities how often disputes over noncompliance with no-smoking rules have been brought to their attention or resulted in formal legal action against violators.

Second, we interviewed managers in organizations where laws required them to ban smoking entirely or partly, or which voluntarily imposed restrictions on smoking. We selected settings where enforcement might be expected to be problematic. Thus, we interviewed principals of three urban high schools; security personnel at the Oakland Coliseum and at a predominantly working-class shopping mall; managing editors of newspapers (about banning smoking from the newsroom); and managers of McDonald's and Sizzler restaurants in a variety of midsize cities.

Third, we searched newspaper files and academic references for stories and studies concerning enforcement of or resistance to smoking bans.

All of this falls short of systematic observation of the behavior of smokers (and nonsmokers) in workplaces, train stations, shopping malls, and restaurants. School principals and restaurant managers may be inclined to minimize noncompliance. A shopping mall security chief said he was not conscious of any problems, but a police official in that city said "Some days I walk the mall and everybody's smoking." Nevertheless our interviews do indicate how often smoking in no smoking zones results in *conflict* that evokes official attention.

What We Learned

A Tale of Three Cities

Berkeley, Richmond, and Oakland lie adjacent to each other on the east side of San Francisco Bay. Each of the three cities has substantial minority populations and pockets of poverty and wealth. Oakland, with a population of about 350,000, is three and four times as big as Berkeley and Richmond, respectively. Berkeley enacted one of the first smoking ordinances in the nation, in 1977. Richmond passed its ordinance in 1985; Oakland followed suit in 1986.

Based on model laws disseminated by antismoking activist organizations, all three ordinances prohibit or restrict smoking in nearly all public places.[2] Restaurants must designate a portion of their seats as nonsmoking and post signs to that effect.[3] Employers are required to establish and make known their smoking policies. Employees have the right to designate their immediate work areas as nonsmoking, and smoking is banned in hallways, elevators, meeting rooms, and restrooms. Employee cafeterias and lounges must have nonsmoking sections.[4] In disputes about workplace smoking policy, all three ordinances state that "the rights of the nonsmoker shall be given precedence."

In Berkeley, the responsible city health department official estimates receiving only ten complaints or so a year. He responds either by telephone or by dispatching an inspector. When interviewed in 1990, he could not recall a single instance in which an additional compliance letter or investigation was deemed necessary. In the past ten years, no formal citations have been issued, and no cases (against noncomplying businesses or recalcitrant patrons) have been referred for prosecution. Neither the community relations office of the Berkeley Police Department nor the district attorney currently in charge of misdemeanor prosecutions could recall any arrest or prosecution for a smoking-connected incident, such as a physical or verbal assault arising out of a dispute with a smoker.

The same has been true in Richmond. Complaints[5] usually involve workplaces and invariably are resolved through negotiation. Municipal officials, chamber of commerce representatives, and nonsmokers' advocates in Berkeley and Richmond agree in estimating that compliance with the ordinances is very high. Restaurant compliance, they say, is close to 100 percent, workplace compliance around 75–85 percent.

In Oakland, the single enforcement official in the city manager's office told us that although he occasionally spot-checks restaurants and stores, enforcement activities usually arise from complaints. In 1990, the city received fifty-seven complaints; the year before, seventy-four.[6] When complaints arrive, the official sends a letter; if the business fails to answer, a second letter is sent. The official says he has had to send out a second letter on only two occasions, and the city has never cited anyone for a violation.

Conflicts arising from smoking-control ordinances are usually handled in a conciliatory manner. The Oakland enforcement official told us he has some problems with certain restaurants in the Asian community where nearly all the patrons are smokers. But to cite the owner, he thinks, would be wrong because "We're not trying to put this guy out of business." The Oakland official also thought that violations occurred frequently in the indoor Oakland Arena, not so much during basketball games but during the rock concerts often held there, when "just about everything is smoked." As in the case of the Asian restaurants, when he saw a large gap between the nonsmoking law and subcultural patterns, he was not inclined to take legal action.

The Richmond official recalled only three cases in which a letter from the city did not quickly result in a promise to comply. After a complaint about smoking in a municipally owned nursing home, the official held three meetings with residents over the course of a year in order to develop a policy that both smokers and nonsmokers could abide.[7] When agreement proved elusive, the city banned smoking in the facility entirely. Management at a large enclosed shopping mall, reluctant to alienate customers, refused to instruct its security guards to enforce the ordinance against noncomplying shoppers. The assistant city manager said, "I did not want to come down in a heavy-handed manner" because "the publicity that could result from that could hurt both the mall and the city." He approached the local chamber of commerce to mediate; after three years an agreement was reached. Today, the mall's security chief says that he has had no incidents of resistance by smokers, but acknowledged that enforcing no-smoking rules is not high on his agenda of worries.[8]

Studies of other municipalities report similar results. In March 1987, a Cambridge, Massachusetts, ordinance banned smoking in a variety of public places and required employers to guarantee smoke-free work areas. Researchers observed smoking in stores and surveyed businesses and residents before and after the ordinance went into effect. Enforcement in Cambridge was gentle: no one had been cited for violations or fined. After an initial rush of telephone calls, the city health department official responsible for implementation handled a declining number of complaints, averaging three or four a week for the next two months. The researchers observed fewer incidents of smoking in stores. Thirty-two percent of survey respondents said they had witnessed a violation, but none had filed a complaint; the most common response to observed violations was to do nothing. But overall, the researchers concluded that "compliance was high, especially given the low-key approach to enforcement" (Rigotti et al. 1987).[9] The source of compliance was public support. Knowledge of the ordinance climbed from 57 percent to 80 percent in the first three months after enactment, and 78 percent (90 percent of nonsmokers, 41 percent of smokers) approved of the law.

Similar results emerged from a 1986 survey of shops and restaurants in Winnipeg, Manitoba, three years after a "clear indoor air" law banned smoking in all retail stores and required restaurants to provide nonsmoking sections. Shopkeepers seemed either more ignorant of the rules or more hesitant to enforce the law than restaurant personnel, but based on this survey and a review of studies in other Canadian cities, the authors concluded that antismoking bylaws are "self-enforcing" when (1) signs are conspicuously posted and (2) officials engage in a periodic program of reminders (Stanwick et al. 1988, pp. 229, 230).

McDonald's

McDonald's restaurants cater to a cross-section of the American population but draw heavily on the working class and teenagers—population groups with higher-than-average smoking rates. McDonald's corporate headquarters told us that all franchise owners are instructed to have smoking and nonsmoking sections, but have discretion to determine their relative size. Picking at random from a list of American cities between 100,000 and 500,000 in population, we called the first-listed McDonald's in the telephone directory, and spoke to the manager on duty. We also added several McDonald's restaurants located in cities which by municipal ordinance had banned *all* restaurant smoking.

As indicated in Appendix 1, the reports were virtually uniform. In Savannah, Georgia, the one deviant case, management had not obtained signs and officially designated an area as nonsmoking. In all other cities, management had posted such signs. Relatively few customers, managers said, violated the posted rules. When detected violators were asked to comply, they did so readily. This pattern also held in most cities (Lodi, Paradise, and San Luis Obispo, California; Aspen, Colorado) where ordinances mandated no smoking at all in restaurants, and hence the customers could not simply move to a "smoking area." The one exception we encountered was in Oroville, California, where a number of patrons reacted very angrily when told they could not smoke at all.

Sizzler

Sizzlers are franchised low-price steak and salad bar restaurants. We wondered if they presented a "harder case" than McDonald's, for Sizzler diners probably linger more, and hence smokers may resent the restrictions more. However, our interviews with Sizzler managers, as Appendix 2 indicates, offered no indication of resistance by smokers.

Newspapers

It might be more difficult to institutionalize nonsmokers' rights in workplaces than in restaurants. Smokers typically spend more time at work and hence may find it more difficult to abstain. They may resent enforced separation (when they do smoke) from nonsmoking fellow workers. Assuming that high rates of smoking traditionally prevailed among deadline-combatting journalists and pressmen, we called newspapers in the same medium-sized cities that we used for interviewing fast-food restaurant managers. We also interviewed in Sacramento, Lodi, Oroville, and San Luis Obispo, cities where ordinances forbid smoking entirely in all workplaces, or give strong precedence to nonsmokers' preferences. As indicated by Appendix 3, however, implementation of nonsmoking rules in the newsroom does not seem to have been difficult. One reason, perhaps, is that, as one managing editor told us, "The image of hard-drinking, hard-smoking newspaper people is a thing of the past. Now it's yuppies who like to write . . . not yuppie, really, just healthy."

Out of a newsroom staff of 100–125 at a Baton Rouge, Louisiana paper, we were told, there were only ten to fifteen smokers, and nobody has tried "to stretch the rules" against smoking in the newsroom, "even at night. It's working fine." Every paper we called had similar restrictions, and a few banned smoking "in the whole building," but in each case high levels of compliance and virtually no resistance was reported.

Three Urban High Schools in California

Under the Education Code of the State of California, smoking or possession of cigarettes at school are grounds for suspension. We speculated, however, that implementation of "no-smoking" rules in high schools would present problems. Teenage smoking is thought to remain significant, and teenagers often try to evade official rules. Given norms against "snitching," they are also less likely to complain to authorities about violators than are restaurant patrons or coworkers. Since a full-scale study of high schools was beyond our research means, we settled for interviewing principals or assistant principals in three urban high schools, two in Oakland and one in Berkeley.

Oakland High School's student body is drawn primarily from working and lower classes and is 70 percent bilingual. Assistant Principal Wayne Young told us that compared with tardiness, truancy, and interpersonal conflict, smoking has become almost a "nonissue." Because of routine patrolling of the school campus for truants and class cutters, smokers are at risk of being seen. That is not to say violations don't occur. On the day we interviewed him, Mr. Young acknowledged finding a group of Asian students smoking behind the school, and he reported a similar encounter some time earlier. But formal sanctions, such as suspension, he said, would not eliminate smoking and would harm students more than smoking. His style? The last time he saw students smoking, he reported, he made sure they took notice of him and said, "I think I heard the class bell ring. Why don't you go to your next class?"[10]

Castlemont High School serves Oakland's poorest community. Principal Reuben Trinidad reported that his two biggest discipline problems are tardiness and student conflict. Smoking, comparatively, "is not a problem." Students model themselves, he said, after body-conscious athletes and entertainers who don't smoke. He recalled seeing a student smoking a cigarette only once in the academic year, and simply issued a reprimand. Even if noncompliance at Castlemont is higher than Principal Trinidad suggested, his statement that smoking violations don't constitute a *significant* problem seems credible, as is the paucity of enforcement activity. [11]

Berkeley High School has twenty-five hundred students, spanning a wide range of socioeconomic and ethnic/racial categories. Ed Randolf, dean of students for eleventh and twelfth grades, told us student cigarette use was not a problem. Smoking is simply not a "cool" thing to do anymore, he said. Students chastise others they see smoking. He himself found only two students smoking in the school yard this year; he told them to put out the cigarettes and warned them it would be really stupid of them to mar their school records with a smoking citation. Dean Randolf says he has never caught a repeat offender whom he had to discipline.[12]

Dean Randolf, it seems, is not particularly observant—or more likely, doesn't want to be. Our research assistant, walking through the courtyard at lunchtime, counted over twenty cigarette butts near the steps leading to the school theater and observed two students on a somewhat secluded outdoor staircase smoking rather nonchalantly; two teachers walked by and didn't seem to notice. A guidance counselor, talking to our research assistant, pointed out two gathering spots on campus where students smoke. When this observation was reported to Dean Randolf, he acknowledged that he notices smoking, but doesn't see it as so major a problem as to warrant raiding the area to stop the smoking.

The inference we draw from these accounts is that some high school students, now as ever, evade no-smoking rules. The incidence of smoking among students, however, has declined so significantly that administrators regard it as a low-level problem, not meriting strong deterrent measures.

Oakland Coliseum

The Oakland Athletics baseball team prohibited smoking in seats in its open-air ballpark, the Coliseum, beginning in the spring of 1991. To smoke, patrons in reserved seating areas are directed to an area partway down the stadium ramps, where they may watch the game on a television screen. In the bleachers, one can smoke standing on a walkway behind the seats, in full, but exceedingly distant, view of the field.

Despite the inconvenience and the novelty of banning smoking in an outdoor space, compliance was high and relatively conflict free. Security guards patrolling the bleachers told us they had to enforce the rule, on average, less than once each game, and fans caught smoking typically comply immediately when guards ask them to move; only a few ask questions or grumble. According to Athletics vice president Andy Dolich, as of August 5, 1991, only three people had been ejected for violating the smoking policy, out of an attendance of more than 1,800,000. Based on his mail, which runs about 70 percent in favor of the no-smoking policy, Dolich estimates that about twenty season ticket holders have cancelled, but just as many have signed up because of the policy (Dickey 1991). During a well-attended midsummer night game, one could observe hundreds of smokers meekly leaving their seats in the bleachers to smoke a cigarette in the designated area.

Other Settings

Published studies suggest a lack of resistance to smoking bans in a variety of other settings. Some experimental studies in the late 1970s and early 1980s found that the posting of no-smoking signs, if accompanied by polite reminders from nonsmokers, resulted in high compliance in supermarkets and elevators (Jason et al. 1979–80), a university cafeteria (Jason and Liotta 1982), and a barber shop (Jason and Clay 1978), although no-smoking signs by themselves, if not supported by reminders from nonsmokers, had only minimal effects on smoking levels (see also Dawley et al. 1980).

A smoking ban was found to be reasonably effective in an American hospital (Dawley and Burton 1985; Dawley and Baldwin 1983). At a large Australian tele-communications company that banned smoking, after eighteen months only 10 percent of employees surveyed reported regular violations, although 31 percent noted that a de facto smoking room (contrary to company policy) had been established in the building (Hocking et al. 1991). Other studies have measured employee attitudes, and with one exception (Gottlieb et al. 1990) found that as time went on, smokers and nonsmokers alike expressed increasing approval of the nonsmoking policy (Rosenstock et al. 1986; Millar 1988; Hudzinski and Frohlich 1990). In no case did a smoker rebellion develop.[13]

In 1991, the Bureau of National Affairs (BNA) sent questionnaires on smoking policy to 2715 American employers; 833 personnel managers, 76 percent from organizations with fewer than one thousand employees, responded (BNA 1991). Eighty-five percent of responding firms had prohibited smoking on some or all of their premises, up from 36 percent in a 1986 survey; 34 percent had *total* bans, compared with 2 percent of 1986 respondents.[14] The survey found:

> Seven out of 10 organizations with smoking policies "rarely" (50 percent) or "never" (20 percent) experience violations of their smoking restrictions. Twenty percent . . . reported "occasional" violations, while only 4 percent have observed "frequent" transgressions.

When complaints about violations are received, employers more often reported that they had stepped up efforts "to communicate their smoking policies" than that they had strengthened enforcement or disciplinary provisions. Only 2 percent said they had incurred higher enforcement or maintenance costs as a result of their smoking policy.

Explaining Compliance

Why does implementation of antismoking regulations seem to be relatively smooth, as compared with attempts to regulate narcotics use, firearms, drunk driving, and some forms of pollution? In view of the prevalence and addictive nature of cigarette smoking, why has there been so little open defiance of nonsmoking rules, at least in the United States?

Social scientists sometimes have argued that law cannot change folkways (Sumner 1959), but that surely is not always the case. As Zimring and Hawkins (1971) point out, much depends on two sets of factors: (1) the *social organization* of enforcement and (2) the *culture* of enforcement, that is, the values attached to a regulated "folkway" by the dominant culture and affected subcultures.

The Social Organization of Smoking

To understand why no-smoking rules seem to have elicited relatively little resis-tance, consider the social restrictions, risks, and incentives that are faced by "regulated" smokers. Compared with laws concerning cocaine use, to take an extreme case, no-smoking rules (if obeyed) impose relatively minor "compliance costs" on addicted users. Second, violations often are hard to conceal from nonsmokers, including potential complaints. Third, violators usually are not surrounded by a strongly supportive "deviant subculture" that will help resist potential enforcers. In short, because of the social organization of legally restricted smoking, smokers encounter a social world that to a remarkable degree *discourages* evasion and defiance.

Zoning versus Prohibition. In contrast with cocaine or marijuana, the production and sale of cigarettes, although regulated and taxed, is completely legal. With some restrictions, cigarette advertising, intended to heighten demand, is also permissible in the United States. Smoking regulations are predominantly "zoning" rules, applicable to public, not private spaces. Smokers in restaurants and workplaces retain the option of repairing to alternative sites if they wish to smoke. Smoking must be postponed, not abandoned. The costs of compliance to smokers, in sum, are relatively low.

Partly because smoking is lawful, partly because it has been such a normal aspect of social life, and partly because it is so common to cross the line, the "social distance" between smokers and nonsmokers is insignificant. Rule enforcers are often former smokers, or relatives of smokers. Not surprisingly, therefore, our research indicates that violators are treated as errant family members, not as criminals. Like the unmannerly, they are reproved, even shunned, but scarcely penalized. The gentleness of the social condemnation they encounter probably contributes to the generally gracious way in which they respond. For example, after the *Dayton* (Ohio) *Daily* established a strict no-smoking policy (except for closed editors' offices) in 1988, the newspaper's human resources director told us that she left enforcement to supervisors in each office. "I'm not going to call out the smoking police," she said. "Smokers are aware of how others feel, and they are basically courteous—so they follow the rules."

Exceptions underscore the general observation. Smokers seem inclined to complain or resist only when compliance seems especially difficult or painful, as it may to addicted smokers on six-hour transcontinental flights.[15] In the first months following the federal government's smoking ban on all domestic airline flights, police at Chicago's O'Hare Airport arrested five people for smoking aboard planes. When smokers resorted to furious puffing before boarding, airline lounges became clouded with smoke and many airlines banned smoking in the lounges. "I told one guy to stop, and he put it out on the wall," the director of the Minneapolis airport told a reporter (Dahl 1990). Several legislatures enacted smokers' rights legislation after employers began to refuse to hire employees who smoke even off the job. Off-the-job smoking rules, besides transgressing the unwritten norm that an employee's private behavior is no business of the boss, raise compliance costs for smokers to extraordinary levels, since they are faced with the choice of giving up either smoking or employment.[16]

Enforceability. In contrast to violations of laws against driving and drinking, narcotics use, and tax evasion, infractions of no-smoking rules in public places are relatively visible, not only to officials responsible for enforcing the rules, but to an almost omnipresent army of self-interested, highly motivated private enforcement agents—nonsmokers who resist exposure to tobacco smoke. Research teaches us that the likelihood of detection and complaint, even more than the severity of threatened punishment, is the most important term in the deterrence equation (Zimring and Hawkins 1973). And violations of no-smoking rules in public places, workplaces, and commercial establishments are particularly vulnerable to detection and complaint.

From that perspective, consider the primary examples of *noncompliance* we learned about. One was a shopping mall where transient shoppers are exposed to smokers only briefly, and hence have less incentive to complain than when they are exposed to the smoke of coworkers or diners. The other relatively high noncompliance sites (perhaps) were high schools, where the potential complainants, nonsmoking students, are bound by schoolyard norms not to "snitch" on fellow students. These are also places in which unwanted exposure to smoke is fleeting.

The Absence of a Socially Supportive Deviant Subculture. People will defy dominant norms or laws, despite considerable risks of punishment, when they enjoy the social support of a "deviant subculture" that continues to endorse the validity of condemned behavior. But unlike marijuana-smoking musicians (Becker 1963), police (Skolnick 1975), and tax-evading housepainters (Kagan 1989), cigarette smokers in the United States generally lack such consortiums of support. Smokers and nonsmokers do not belong to distinctive groups or occupations. Smokers, we can assume, prefer to be socially accepted. And despite efforts of tobacco companies to foster resistant smokers' rights organizations, smokers rarely, if ever, see themselves as part of a *major* cause or self-defining social movement, such as those on either side of the abortion issue.

We could find only one instance of resistance by smokers as a *group*. It happened when a cluster of smokers with airline tickets were suddenly told that they had been entirely "zoned out" of a flight. But smokers rarely find themselves in such solitary assemblies. Soon after the federal government banned cigarette smoking entirely on all domestic airline flights, a lone woman insisted on lighting up while her plane was still boarding in Pittsburgh. According to the police, when uniformed officers arrived on board:

> She pleaded with her fellow passengers. "Shouldn't I be allowed to smoke?" she asked. "No!" the passengers shot back in unison, miffed at being held up twenty minutes by the woman's tantrum. "When we led her away," recalls Lt. Norbert Kowalski of the airport police . . . "everybody was cheering." (Dahl 1990)

A majority of smokers don't even approve of their own smoking. Surveys show that a majority of adult smokers say they want to quit, and have tried and failed several times. Some say they are grateful for workplace restrictions, or for restrictions on airlines, because the added inconvenience might help them try once again to quit.

Culture

Not many years ago, the imposition of restrictions on smoking probably would have resulted in widespread evasion, and enforcement efforts would have encountered considerable defiance. Nonsmokers would have been reluctant to complain to or about smokers who violated the rules. That is still true in parts of Europe and in the Third World. In Milan, Italy, for example, porters in the arrival section of Linate Airport smoked cigarettes in the summer of 1991 in violation of the no-smoking signs.[17] A couple who politely asked nearby diners in a London restaurant "if they would mind not smoking" was bluntly told "to mind their own business" (Schmidt 1991). A Dutch journalist and former managing editor we spoke with recently expressed amazement at the ease with which smoking bans have been imposed in American newsrooms. "We could never get away with it," he said. American compliance with nonsmoking rules thus cannot be explained solely by such factors as relative ease of detection and low cost of compliance.

Throughout the United States, in universities, in other workplaces, in restaurants, there has been a dramatic change in the social acceptability of tobacco smoking. Smokers feel condemned, isolated, disenfranchised, alienated.[18] There appears to have been, in the United States, nothing short of a transformation of the rules governing the *civility* of smoking, which, we suggest, is what ultimately quells resistance by smokers. Why that should have occurred primarily in the United States is not entirely clear, but it seems related to several aspects of American civic culture. First, the emerging civility norm—"don't smoke where others may object"—developed as cigarette smoking declined among publicly visible American elites. Second, the norm was given a huge boost by the 1986 U.S. Surgeon General's report concerning the hazards of exposure to "secondary smoke." More fundamentally, however, these messages fell on receptive ears; for a variety of reasons, American popular culture has come to emphasize concern about personal health, and especially about exposure to carcinogens. Finally, we suggest that as long as communities enact no-smoking ordinances only when and where support for the informal no-smoking norm has been growing, the embodiment of the norm in law strengthens the position of nonsmokers, further legitimates the norm, and helps ensure that defiance will be minimal.

Changing Norms of Civility. Most human beings seek to conform rather than to rebel, to be accepted in a group rather than to be ostracized. Even the most symbolically rebellious of us, the adolescent, is defiant only with respect to the older generation. Among their peers, adolescents are hugely conformist, among the most compliant beings in the entire spectrum of human associations. Thus, most smokers initiate the activity during adolescence. Those who begin to smoke cigarettes usually do not experience, as do initiates of other drugs, feelings of pleasure. On the contrary, they feel sick or at least discomfited. That they continue to inhale smoke is a measure of the power of peer group understandings as to what renders one an "adult" woman or man. Once smoking is regularized, smoking becomes pleasurable, even addicting. Addicted smokers who run out of cigarettes are palpably uneasy, and will say that they are "dying" for a cigarette. When they get one, and smoke it, they smile. But initiation is unpleasant, and has to be understood as a profoundly social phenomenon rather than as a physiologically or psychologically generated experience.

Peer influence may be less involved in the cessation of smoking. Stopping, it could be argued, is simply a rational response, since smoking has been shown to impose high risks on the smoker and under some circumstances on others. There are no excuses for continuing to smoke, save one: "I am an addict." And that excuse has become increasingly unacceptable in the United States (but not in Europe, Africa, or Asia), for here 75 percent of adults no longer smoke, twice the percentage of thirty years ago. Nevertheless, fifty million Americans still smoke, some defiantly, some because they enjoy smoking, some because they are strongly addicted. Most would prefer to stop, their families and friends urge them to, but they have become psychologically and physiologically dependent.

Hence the question remains: why is there so much compliance with nonsmoking rules among those who *continue* to smoke and find it difficult to do otherwise? The answer, we suggest, cannot be grounded primarily in a theory of deterrence through fear of punishment. In many nonsmoking areas, one could sneak a cigarette and not be caught. Or, if caught, the offender is more likely to be admonished than brought to trial.

The answer, we believe, is predicated on the social and psychological power of what Norbert Elias, in *The History of Manners*, calls civility norms (Elias 1978, p. 159). In a Hobbesian world, human beings strain toward conflict. Each individual seeks to gratify his or her desires and impulses, regardless of their effect on others. Life is nasty, brutal, and by implication, inconsiderate. In Norbert Elias' world of manners, there is a strong need to achieve acceptance in face-to-face interaction, primarily by our friends, lovers, and spouses—but also by strangers, whom we wish to have view us as significant persons. People comply with norms of propriety. Thus, lawyers do not wear their legendary three-piece suits to baseball games or wear a baseball cap and shorts in the courtroom.

Elias does not present a well-developed theory of how behaviors become defined as socially unacceptable irrespective of an enforcement apparatus. What he does do brilliantly, however, is to show the power of civility norms, and how conceptions of "civilized" behavior have shifted through time without apparent reason or logic. In medieval society, for example, people ate with their hands and also blew their noses into their hands. Doing both with the same hand, however, came to be considered to be impolite. It was advised, rather, to eat with the right hand, and to reserve one's nose blowing for the left. But this restriction applied only at the table. "The distasteful feeling frequently aroused today by the mere thought of soiling the fingers in this way was entirely absent" (Elias 1978, p. 148). Similarly, spitting, Elias maintains, was quite common as late as the eighteenth century.[19]

If smoking in the presence of objecting nonsmokers—like spitting at a dinner party—is emerging, as we maintain, as a violation of a civility norm, it is relevant to consider how and why civility norms change. Social stratification and the search for upward mobility always have had a catalytic effect on manners. "Courtesy" derives its name from the court and court life. "The courts of great lords," Elias wrote, "are a theater where everyone wants to make his fortune. This can only be done by winning the favor of the prince and the most important people of the court." Courtin, writing in 1672, tells his readers in his *Nouveau traite de civilite* that it is no longer permissible, before people of rank, to spit on the ground and cover the sputum with one's foot (Elias 1978, p. 154).[20] As wealth increased in the eighteenth century and the bourgeoisie sought inclusion in court society, pressures to conform to the manners of the nobility spread through the ranks of the growing middle class.

Sometimes royal authority could "upgrade" social practices in a relatively short time. In seventeenth-century France, according to the historian W. H. Lewis (1957, p. 174), visitors in the Louvre, the royal palace, would relieve themselves "not only in the courtyards, but on the balconies, and staircases, and behind doors," despite repeated complaints about the consequences. But when the court moved to Versailles in the 1680s, visitors discovered "that the King there insisted on the same degree of decency and cleanliness which was to be found in a private house." Compliance at Versailles was high because failure to abide by the elaborate code of etiquette was sure to lead to gossip, rumors of royal disfavor, and a lower credit rating.[21]

Highly visible elites likewise have contributed to the rapid social redefinition of cigarette smoking. Only a generation ago, Franklin Delano Roosevelt's jauntily tilted cigarette holder provided an indelible public symbol of feisty political leadership. Humphrey Bogart's hard-bitten heroes, blowing cigarette smoke into the faces of threatening villains, symbolized masculine courage and decency. Edward R. Murrow, thoughtfully puffing his cigarettes on television, epitomized journalistic intelligence and integrity. A few decades later, American talk show hosts, movie stars, and even outwardly antiestablishment pop singers are *never* seen smoking cigarettes. The Clinton White House has banned smoking entirely. It seems clear that a rapid decline of smoking among publicly visible elites has painted smoking in negative colors and nonsmoking in affirmative ones.

Health Risks and Civility Norms. Why has smoking declined among American elites? One obvious factor would seem to be the dissemination of research documenting the link between cigarette smoking and high risks of death from lung cancer and heart disease. As in the case of defecation in public places and sharing of utensils, shifts in manners often seem related to concerns about the adverse health effects of common social practices. Elias observes, however, that while it became impolite to spit by the late eighteenth century, the dangers to public health of spitting were not known until the late nineteenth century. "It is well to establish once and for all," Elias maintains (1978, p. 158), "that something which we know to be harmful to health by no means necessarily arouses feelings of distaste and shame. And conversely, something that arouses these feelings need not be at all detrimental to health."

Similarly, discussing cross-cultural differences in the practices that are considered polluting, Douglas and Wildavsky say "ideas about pollution are not sufficiently explained by the physical dangers." While recognizing that some perceived dangers, as in the links between lung cancer and smoking, can be genuine, they add that the connections between "a certain selection of troubles" and a "particular set of moral faults" are always socially constructed and are not necessarily rational (Douglas and Wildavsky 1982, p. 38).

Thus, even as American workplace norms are changing to give nonsmokers' preferences clear priority, the American Smokers' Association News (a tobacco-industry newsletter) reported in 1990:

> In Cologne [Germany], when a department store clerk complained about having to share a small office with a heavy smoker, she was asked to sign a paper declaring herself willing to live with existing conditions. When she refused she was sacked.

Some German courts, the publication added, have ruled that mandatory no-smoking sections in restaurants infringe on smokers' rights to sit where they choose. And Lufthansa dropped plans to ban smoking on domestic flights because "We feared trouble on board." In Japan, where information on the carcinogenic effects of smoking is widely available, smoking rates among women *rose* in the 1970s and 1980s. There are few *non-fumeur* sections in expensive restaurants in France. When the management of a Hewlitt-Packard branch in France tried to impose smoking restrictions, Gooding reports (1992, p. 54), "staff members threatened to barricade the company restaurant and keep fat people out, on the grounds that more food would be bad for their health." Cross-cultural evidence thus suggests that the dissemination of epidemiological knowledge alone has not yet produced changes in civility norms as dramatic as those that have emerged in the United States.

Similarly, although cigarette smoking has been proven to create elevated risks of cancer and heart disease for nonsmoking relatives who are pervasively exposed to family members' tobacco smoke, the published scientific studies provide no compelling evidence of comparable danger to fellow diners intermittently exposed in restaurants, to fellow workers in reasonably well-ventilated buildings, or to fellow patrons at baseball games. The emerging hegemony in the United States of the civility norm—"don't smoke where nonsmokers object"—cannot be explained entirely by demonstrated danger.

The Risks of Secondary Smoke. It remains true, however, that the authority of science has been enormously important in stimulating the cultural redefinition of smoking in the United States. Few scientific reports have received as much publicity and have been accorded as much legitimacy as the U.S. Surgeon General's report in January 1964, asserting that smoking was unquestionably very harmful to human health. Public health elites seized upon it to mount a steady propaganda campaign against smoking. By 1965, Congress had mandated warning labels on cigarette packages, and in 1970 it banned broadcast advertising for tobacco products. By the time laws and corporate policies designed to protect *nonsmokers* were implemented, in the mid-to-late 1980s, nonsmokers had become a majority in many settings, and the foundations of an antismoking civility norm had already been laid.

Even in 1980, however, those who continued to smoke often felt free to do so in the presence of nonsmokers. Restaurants, bars, and hotel rooms routinely provided ashtrays. Gaming casinos in Nevada provided free cigarettes to bettors. Nonsmokers' "rights" enjoyed little official recognition. If cigarette smoking was disagreeable, its unpleasantness was supposed to be accepted amiably by the nonsmoker. Nonsmokers often spoke up, but they had to be somewhat bold, and might be regarded as contentious whiners.

Nonsmokers, year by year a larger majority, were not happy with a norm requiring them to defer to smokers' preferences. In 1982, 82 percent of nonsmokers polled by Gallup said "Yes" to the question, "Should smokers refrain from smoking in the presence of nonsmokers?" Asked again in 1985, 85 percent answered affirmatively. More significantly, a majority of *smokers* agreed—55 percent in 1983 and 62 percent in 1985. And most adults surveyed also supported workplace restrictions. In 1983, Gallup found that 79 percent of adults thought companies should restrict smoking at work, assigning it to certain areas; 76 percent of current smokers agreed, as did 80 percent of former smokers (Rigotti 1989, p. 20).

The release of the Surgeon General's 1986 report, with its data on "involuntary" smoking, gave nonsmokers' rights activists the ammunition to turn their preferences into a civility norm and the civility norm into law. The establishment of the detrimental health consequences of secondary smoke, Allen Brandt (1990) points out, made it difficult for smokers to take refuge in a libertarian ethic, claiming that cigarette smoking affected only themselves. In 1985 only ninety municipalities had adopted nonsmokers' rights laws; by 1988, 320 local communities had adopted laws restricting smoking, and smoking was banned on all domestic airline flights and interstate buses by 1990.

American Health Values and Civility. Yet not every municipality or employer adopted such a policy; far from it. And more significantly, the same epidemiological information has not led to similar nonsmokers' rights rules in Japan (where some of the most important research was done) or in Germany or in Great Britain—at least not nearly to the same extent as in the United States. In countries that have enacted restrictions on smoking in public places, such as France and the Netherlands, compliance appears to be much lower than in the United States. It would seem, therefore, that there is an intervening variable between medical finding and social response, one that is strongly present in substantial segments of American life, weaker in many other societies. The mediating factor in the United States, we suggest, is a cultural disposition, strongest in the educated classes but with wide support throughout the middle and working classes, to decry the ingestion or inhalation of chemical substances that are thought to be causes of disease, especially if carcinogenic, and especially when people are involuntarily exposed to those substances.

The roots of this particular disposition are not entirely clear but several features of American culture seem to tie together here. Americans have long had a rural *ascetic Protestant tradition*, which was once ascendant in American society, and was validated by the Eighteenth Amendment prohibiting the sale of alcoholic beverages. This tradition has always eschewed smoking, as well as alcohol. But America also has an urban *immigrant tradition*, which in the past was more accepting of drinking and smoking. Yet many observers have also noted that Americans—the children of immigrants, less beaten down by cycles of war and despotism—are on average less fatalistic, more optimistic than "Old World" peoples. Hence they may be more inclined to think it possible to ban disease from their world if they are sufficiently vigilant against chemical "risk factors." There is also a *populist* strain in American culture, which leads Americans to mistrust "big business" and its intentions. Finally, America has an *individualist* tradition which tends to mistrust government and its capacity and willingness to protect citizens from chemical risks (Vogel 1986).

Whatever the background reasons, fears of toxic chemicals were enough to produce successful demands for abandonment of Times Beach, Missouri, and neighborhoods near Love Canal in Niagara Falls, New York, although subsequent studies indicated the dangers posed were exaggerated (Irvine 1991; Verhovek 1990).

Countless schools were closed to remove asbestos ceiling tiles, even though the cleanup effort itself seems to have caused far more risk (Stevens 1990).[22] Multinational corporations that successfully market packaged foods in the United States as low-in-cholesterol find they have to change their pitch entirely to succeed in the Common Market.

In short, it appears that American popular culture incorporates special receptors that could *amplify* the Surgeon General's message about the dangers of secondary smoke, transforming it not only into law but also into a nonsmokers' rights norm that even smokers could interpret as being legitimate. It seemed to matter little that the Surgeon General's report did not indicate exactly how much exposure to secondary smoke would increase the risk of disease. American society's traditions and health values turned "carcinogenic"—a taboo word—into a trump card with which a nonsmoker could parry the smoker's claim that "a little smoke once in a while won't hurt you." Indeed, our interviews indicate that most smokers have not detected the scientific vacuum concerning the threshold level at which secondary harm poses a significant risk; many seem to accept uncritically the idea that their smoke invariably poses an unreasonable risk of harm on others (Viscusi 1990).

More important, our research suggests that *certified harm* does not mark the bright line where civility begins. Rather, smokers seem to accept that if nonsmokers find smoke annoying or unpleasant, and *possibly harmful*, that alone is sufficient justification for mandating nonsmoking areas. Thus, a spokesman for the Oakland Athletics baseball team, explaining the team's decision to ban smoking in stadium seats, told us "it was more of a social decision than a medical one. We did not consult a panel of seventeen experts about the dangers of secondhand smoke." He continued, "Our goal was to be the most affordable, safe, clean family attraction in Northern California."

From the perspective of the development of civility norms, the most important word in that statement is "clean." Once smoking is labelled "dirty," as well as unpleasant, to nonsmokers, smokers are *obliged* to take their dirty habit somewhere else. This seems especially true among the affluent, who doubtless have a strong affinity to health values. The smoker is now obligated, under the developing norms of politeness, to ask the permission of the nonsmoker before lighting up, and is expected to extinguish the cigarette if asked. Dinner party hosts and hostesses feel entitled to refuse permission to smoke, even to guests who ask politely if they may.

The deference of the smoker to the rights of the nonsmoker, however, seems to prevail in every social class. The McDonald's in Savannah, Georgia, for example, is one of the few that in June 1991 had not designated a nonsmoking section. Nevertheless, when people smoke in the lines, waiting for service, they may be asked by other customers to abstain. "The smoking customers hold the cigarette off to the side, or put it out," reported Annette, the manager. "Most people are polite," she said. Similarly, the manager of a McDonald's in Lodi, California, told us, "It used to be that the nonsmoking workers would take their break in the lobby or out-of-doors if they needed to get away from the smoke." Now everything has changed. "Most of the crew are nonsmokers," he observed. "If anything, now the smokers make themselves scarce by smoking out-of-doors."

As a social process, the institutionalization of the civility norm is bound to proceed in fits and starts. Smoking has not yet, like blowing one's nose in one's hands, or spitting, or eating with the fingers, been stigmatized as "disgusting." But when smokers are *segregated* a powerful message is conveyed: their conduct has formally been recognized to be so harmful that it defiles others, with whom the law forbids them to congregate. American smokers—in fast food restaurants, in baseball parks, in universities, in police departments—have largely come to understand that it is the nonsmokers, not the smokers, who enjoy the moral superiority conferred by civility rules.

The Role of Law

In a society where elites visibly engage in aerobic exercise, teach their children to drink nonfat milk, and denounce nuclear power, it is not surprising that smoking rates have declined and smokers are regarded as somewhat weak-willed or self-destructive. But what about smokers in McDonald's and the Sizzler—more likely to be the Hard Hat in our opening vignette than the Business Man—who meekly extinguish their cigarette when asked? Why has the civility norm spread to the fast food restaurant, the ballpark, and the high-pressure pressroom? Another, even major, part of the answer, is traceable to the role of law as a form of symbolic authority.

Anthropologist Paul Bohannan (1967) saw law as a body of norms "restated in such a way that they can be 'applied' by an institution designed . . . for that purpose." The idea of "double institutionalization" suggests that the law reinforces an already existing normative order. The American experience with laws restricting smoking suggests that in a rapidly changing society, legal enactments can transform norms that are only partly or tentatively institutionalized at the social level into more authoritative and widely institutionalized social norms.

Although smoking was declining and opinion polls indicated majority acceptance of the idea of smoking controls, social norms regulating smoking changed slowly until the 1986 Surgeon General's report emphasizing that cigarette smoke contained carcinogens harmful to nonsmokers. In the years following the report, hundreds of new ordinances and corporate policies subdivided public space, segregating smokers (Rigotti 1989). These laws and corporate regulations, we believe, articulated and legitimated the inchoate norms concerning nonsmokers' "right" to breathe "clean" air, and thereby, accelerated the acceptance of "no smoking among nonsmokers" as a civility norm.

Law, of course, cannot do this alone. The same regulations, if promulgated twenty-five years ago, might have been flouted and contested. Like surfers, legislators and corporate officials who wish to change everyday social norms must wait for signs of a rising wave of cultural support, catching it at just the right time. Legislate too soon and they will be swamped by the swells of popular resistance. Legislate too late and they will be irrelevant. Legislate at the right moment and an emerging cultural norm, still tentatively struggling for authority—such as that condemning involuntary exposure to tobacco smoke—acquires much greater moral force.

There used to be no clear smoking norms at the Lodi (California) *News-Sentinel*, according to Toni Matta, a reporter. Smoking policy changed, she said, with whoever was in the majority, smokers or nonsmokers, and with the attitudes of the editor. Due to turnover in the newsroom, policy changed frequently. In other sections of the paper, where turnover was lower, the nonsmokers were more vocal in demanding a no-smoking policy and there was "a constant battle." Then, in 1990, Lodi enacted a municipal nonsmokers' rights law. After the enactment, which gave nonsmokers preference in the designation of smoke-free areas in workplaces, the paper banned smoking entirely except in closed editors' offices—including the newsroom and the cafeteria. Despite the earlier conflict, says Matta, when the new policy went into effect, "nobody flouted it." Asked to explain why, she speculated it was because (a) smokers were in the minority; (b) they realized it was "not a rights issue, but a health issue"; (c) the policy was a reasonable compromise; and (d) "common courtesy." But all those factors, it might be pointed out, were present before the law was enacted.

The change was in the *official* endorsement of the validity of the nonsmokers' claims based on health and "common courtesy." The articulation of emerging norms in formal rules appears to have four effects. First, formal rules serve an important *communication* function, overcoming the familiar problem of pluralistic ignorance and inaction. Even if, in 1983, most nonsmokers (and many smokers) favored restrictions on smoking in the workplace (Rigotti 1989), individual nonsmokers may not have realized the *extent* of support for such rules, and hence may not have felt emboldened to complain directly to smokers. The enactment of ordinances and workplace rules told nonsmokers that they had a *right* to breathe air that was free of smoke. Signs were posted. Memos were circulated. Smokers were confronted unambiguously with indicators of their social undesirability, underscored by spatial banishment and by the cheers of nonsmokers who openly expressed gratitude for the new regime.

Second, formal rules have what Joseph Raz (1979) has called *practical authority*, that is, rules tend to be obeyed because people generally believe that they are supposed to obey rules. Most drivers, when confronted with a red light on a deserted but well-lit street at three o'clock in the morning, will wait for the light to change even when there is no apparent reason for doing so. Most smokers will similarly obey no-smoking rules. Even when they do not, however, formal rules permit the nonsmoker to rely on the authority of the rule itself to justify asking the smoker to stop smoking. In effect, the smoker is now empowered to say "I am not asking you to stop smoking as a favor to me. The rule requires that you stop."

If the violator refuses to comply, the "victim" of the rule-breaking can invoke the third feature of rules, namely, *enforcement authority*. Now, the tasks of posting no-smoking signs, checking to see that they are not widely flouted, and dealing with complaints all have been incorporated into the everyday work of restaurant hostesses, managing editors, flight attendants, and hospital administrators. The nonsmoker, instead of having to confront directly a forbidding-looking stranger or a prickly coworker, can appeal to a third party—a security guard at a ballpark, an office manager, or whoever has been designated to enforce the rule. That only three persons have been ejected from the Oakland Coliseum for violating the "no-smoking in the seats" rule may be attributable in good part to the visible presence of a platoon of ushers and security personnel responsible for enforcing rules.

Finally, the legal subdivision of public space into smoking and nonsmoking areas adds *moral authority* to emergent civility norms concerning the deference smokers owe to nonsmokers. The laws influence attitudes even in settings where there are as yet no such formal rules. For in the course of a day, smokers (and nonsmokers) now often encounter *some* legally segregated places, amplifying the basic message and further relegating smokers to the demeaning social territory of the deviant and faintly unrespectable.

This is not true everywhere in the country. Casinos in Las Vegas, while willing to provide a few nonsmoking tables, are still not inclined to restrict smoking in general. Whereas the California Restaurant Association endorsed a state law banning smoking entirely in restaurants, Nevada casinos lobbied successfully to exempt themselves from a state nonsmokers' rights law. California, like most of the rest of the United States, is responsive to emerging concerns about health values. Nevada, by contrast, advertises itself as an oasis of hedonism (Skolnick 1978, pp. 35–46).

Yet most of America is not Las Vegas or Atlantic City. Fewer and fewer public spaces remain open to the smoker. Cigarette machines are harder to find. As this chapter was being written the Veterans Administration banned the sale of cigarettes in its hospitals. In ever-increasing numbers, smokers are ceasing to smoke, joining the ranks of the nonsmokers, and affirming their standing as responsible champions of health values and the Puritan tradition. When former smokers implicitly condemn smoking by stopping the practice, when they support the subdivision of public space into ever-shrinking areas for smokers, they slowly but inevitably push the *idea* of cigar and cigarette smoke, ash, and butt—like the spittle and nasal drippings of the seventeenth and eighteenth century—toward the "disgusting" end of the civility continuum.

As long as new legal controls do not leap too far ahead of the spreading social norm—which seems unlikely—then enforcement of the rules should remain unproblematic. Resistance is likely to arise only if and when smoking becomes so confined to particular subcultures or deviant communities that it comes to be regarded as a badge of defiance or dissent, and enforcement becomes less civil, more intolerant, and more coercive.

Appendix 1. Responses of McDonald's Managers

City	Proportion of Nonsmoking Area (%)	Problem Involving Violators?
Corpus Christi, TX	25	Never had a problem. Never had to say anything. One staff member smokes in crew room, rather than outside, and "We all think he's pretty rude."
Dayton, OH	50	No real problem. Usually they just move to designated area.
Fort Wayne, IN	33	No. Detected violators are "always pretty agreeable." "We spend a lot of time sweeping up butts by the front door."

(*continued*)

Appendix 1. (Continued)

City	Proportion of Nonsmoking Area (%)	Problem Involving Violators?
Kansas City, KS	60	Two weeks ago customer was smoking in nonsmoking section. When manager asked him not to smoke, he said "No problem." Even that is fairly rare.
Pittsburgh, PA	50	Normally, no problem. Once in a while, someone makes a mistake and smokes in wrong area.
Portland, OR	50	No problem at all.
San Bernardino, CA	30	Never had any problem with someone smoking in nonsmoking section.
Savannah, GA	none (plan to make 25% nonsmoking)	People smoke at tables with ashtrays and in line "all the time." Most smokers are polite about complying with neighbors' request not to smoke. Management reluctant to intervene until they post "no smoking" signs.
Stockton, CA	66	Someone smoked in the wrong section "maybe once in the last 2 months." Customer apologized and moved. Even in the evening, no problem.
Auburn, CA	50	About once a month someone found smoking in nonsmoking section; they always comply without trouble after being asked to move.
Bell, CA	50 (by law)	Three to four weeks ago, smoker in wrong section; immediately moved when asked. "The rule doesn't bother people in this area; they don't mind."
Aspen, CO	100 (by law)	Two or three violations a month. When manager tells them, they put it out, usually apologizing. Sometimes they then smoke outside. Never any resistance, never had to call police.
Bellflower, CA	100 (by law)	Almost every day, 1 or 2 violators. When manager mentions it, "they just step outside and finish cigarette. Some get mad, but vast majority say, "I'm sorry, I didn't know."
Lodi, CA	100 (by law)	Some grumbling, but no real complaints or recalcitrant violations.
Oroville, CA	100 (by law)[23]	In first month of total ban rule, manager had to remind people five times. All got angry. One dumped food on floor and left, another dumped ashes on floor.[24]
Paradise, CA	100 (by law)	Management allowed grace period. Since management started "seriously enforcing

(continued)

Appendix 1. (Continued)

City	Proportion of Nonsmoking Area (%)	Problem Involving Violators?
		it" (2 months ago) they "had a problem two times." Both times "they were nice" and put out the cigarette.
San Luis Obispo, CA	100 (by law)	Violations very infrequent, by out-of-towners. They respond politely, usually go and smoke outside. Never any problem.

Appendix 2. Responses of Sizzler Managers

City	Proportion of Nonsmoking Area (%)	Problem with Violators?
Auburn, CA[25]	80	Only one violation in last 6 months—an elderly couple who, when asked by management, moved to smoking area without complaint. Some smokers complain because seats with best views are nonsmoking.
Baton Rouge, LA	50[26]	One "problem" in last 6 months. Smoker sat in nonsmoking section because no clean, set tables in smoking section. "We had to run and clean up."
Bellflower, CA	100 (by law)	One confrontation with a "kind of drunk" patron who continued to smoke. Finally manager cajoled him into stopping, emphasizing legal obligation to do so. All other violators (about 2 a week) comply immediately when approached.
Corpus Christi, TX	60	"Rare to never. There might have been a couple of problems six years ago but none that are really memorable." "Smokers ask where the smoking section is; nonsmokers never ask."
Dayton, OH	50	About once a month someone smoking in nonsmoking section. Manager asks them to move and 99 times out of 100 there's no problem. Occasionally they complain.
Fort Wayne, IN	75[27]	Sometimes smokers sit in wrong section (or "complain if you can't find smoking spaces for them"). But most people will get up and move if told they're in wrong section.
Portland, OR	50	Doesn't happen very often. The server occasionally will remind someone. No one

(continued)

Appendix 2. (Continued)

City	Proportion of Nonsmoking Area (%)	Problem with Violators?
		ever puts up an argument. "Smokers feel pretty persecuted anyway . . . They don't want to get into a hassle."
San Bernardino, CA	50	Violations don't happen often. "Maybe 2 times in 3 years." Can't remember any difficult incidents.
San Luis Obispo, CA	100 (by law)	People from town comply fully. About once a month, out-of-towners found smoking; 90 percent comply with no trouble, some complain. Once in a while gives them their money back.
Savannah, GA	12[28]	Never a problem.
Stockton, CA	100[29]	Never had to tell someone to stop smoking, although some people complain. Many signs on buffet line make no-smoking policy very clear.
Walnut Creek, CA	60	Saw only one violation in last year and a half, heard of one other. Customer immediately extinguished cigarette when violation pointed out.

Appendix 3. Newspaper Editors' Responses

City	No-smoking Areas	Enforcement Problematic?
Baton Rouge, LA	No smoking everywhere except designated room, segment of coffee shop, & individual exec. offices.	Out of newsroom staff of 100–125, only 10–15 smokers. Nobody has tried to stretch the rules even at night. "It's working fine."
Dayton, OH	No smoking everywhere except in a few hallways, staircase, editors' offices. None in cafeteria.	In first few months, some complaints about violations; now only 3 or 4 a year, and "It's not a problem. People have handled it."[30]
Fort Wayne, IN	No smoking in whole bldg, or sidewalks around bldg (500 employees).	Only small percentage of newsroom staff smoked. "We had one or two people who tried to stretch the rules, but when they saw that didn't work, they stopped."
Kansas City, KS	No smoking control policies at all[31]	Not applicable
Portland, OR	Smoking only in small designated room off newsroom, part	No recollection of resistance. Nobody disobeys. "When they

(*continued*)

Appendix 3. (Continued)

City	No-smoking Areas	Enforcement Problematic?
	of cafeteria, & closed editors' offices (300 employees).[32]	put this in, there were two assistant managers who smoked. Once we complied, that didn't leave the writers much choice."
Savannah, GA	No smoking (since 6 months ago) except for small designated room and editors' closed offices.	When policy instituted by new antismoking managing editor, some surreptitious violations. Some still occurs, but generally it works. One editor quit when staff complained.[33]
Sacramento, CA	No smoking except in 3 outdoor areas.	For the most part, people follow the rules. Last complaint was someone smoking in bathroom, a year ago. Smokers were in minority, and weren't happy about it, but didn't fight it. "They could read the ordinance and see the handwriting on the wall."
San Bernardino, CA	No smoking except in designated areas—hall, half of lunchroom. No smoking in editors' offices. Preference for nonsmokers in disputes.	No problems except late evenings, when people smoke at their desk. Frequent complaints by nonsmokers about smoke wafting from designated smoking areas.
San Luis Obispo, CA	Since enactment of strong municipal law, no smoking in bldg.	No trouble, never seen or heard of violation (staff of 125). "In this town . . . you're practically an outcast if you smoke."
Lodi, CA	No smoking except in closed editors' offices, pursuant to strong local ordinance.	At first some friction about ordinance, but "nobody flouted it." (4 of 16 newsroom employees smoke; they realize it is "not a rights issue, but a health issue."
Oroville, CA	No smoking except in small break rm.	Few violations (except perhaps in bathroom) or complaints. No conflict. (Only 5–6 of 52 staff members are smokers.)

Notes

1. *Congressional Record*. 5 March 1991. S2675.

2. Traditional smoker havens such as bars and tobacco shops are exempted.

3. In Berkeley, 50 percent nonsmoking is required; in Oakland and Richmond, it is 40 percent. Oakland exempts restaurants with fewer than 30 seats; Richmond exempts those with fewer than 50.

4. Oakland's ordinance does not specify a set amount of nonsmoking space in lounges and cafeterias, but guarantees employees a "smoke-free environment."

5. During the first 90 days after enactment, the Richmond enforcement official estimated, 15 percent of his time was taken up with implementing the ordinance; since then, enforcement has required no more than 5 percent.

6. In 1990, nine of the complaints were filed against private employers, two against the city, seventeen against public businesses, and nineteen against restaurants (ten other complaints were apparently not categorized). In 1989, fifteen complaints were against employers, seven against the city, thirty against businesses and twenty-four against restaurants (Office of the City Manager, 1989, 1990 Annual Reports).

7. Depriving the elderly, disabled, and ill smokers of opportunities to smoke raises difficult questions, even for some advocates of nonsmokers' rights. Speaking of two Florida hospitals that banned smoking entirely in the building, Hewitt (1991) noted:

> My mother, at age 77, still enjoys a couple of cigarettes a day. This lady survived the catastrophic flu epidemic of 1918, the Depression, and two husbands. . . . Anyone who believes she is to be told that . . . she may not smoke is in for a tangle. . . . And if she were again immobilized with a fracture and lying in a hospital bed, she'd prove it. . . . Will each room be equipped with a fire extinguisher to handle the blazing beds ignited when patients . . . light up under their sheets? Are staff members going to tell dying patients . . . that smoking is bad for their health?

8. A Richmond patrolman, referred to earlier, told us that sometimes he goes into the mall and sees a fair number of people smoking, including shop personnel on break. Moreover, the mall is a very large space; encounters between smokers and nonsmokers usually are transient. Consequently one might expect that complaints by nonsmokers would be infrequent.

9. Rigotti et al. (1992) reached the same conclusion after conducting a similar survey of compliance with a 1987 Brookline, Massachusetts, smoking control ordinance. Researchers saw a customer smoking, in apparent violation of the law, in 36 percent of businesses visited, and an employee in 14 percent. But overall, the researchers found that businesses complied willingly, reporting few implementation problems, and that "the law achieved much of its intent—reducing exposure to passive smoke."

10. High schools, of course, are also workplaces. Ten years ago, when Oakland High moved to a new building, it adopted a no-smoking policy for faculty and staff. There is no smoking in the faculty lounge, and Mr. Young says conflict over violations is unheard of. However, social studies teachers, most of whom smoke, use the social studies work room (a supply and copy machine room) as an informal smoking area.

11. Officially, Castlemont faculty and staff are not supposed to smoke on school grounds, for there are no designated smoking areas (as would be allowed under Oakland's ordinance). But informally, Mr. Trinidad acknowledges, smoking is allowed in the faculty lounge in off-peak hours; it is prohibited during lunch period and before classes begin. Arguably, this laxity should be read to color the principal's statement that there is no significant smoking problem among the student body. Still, Mr. Trinidad claims he twice wrote letters to faculty/staff members during the past year for violating no-smoking rules.

12. Dean Randolf says smoking is prohibited in Berkeley High School's faculty lounge, but some teachers occasionally smoke there. Twice, violations by older teachers were called to his attention, and he did tell them "in a friendly manner" not to smoke there. Now, he claims, there is no problem. To Randolf, as to the other school administrators we spoke to, "problem" does not mean that there are no violations of no-smoking rules, but that violations are neither epidemic nor endemic, but infrequent and not increasing.

13. The 1989 U.S. Surgeon General's Report (U.S. DHHS, Surgeon General 1989, pp. 590–91) summarizes additional studies reaching the same results.

14. About 60 percent of respondents reported prohibitions against smoking in employee lounges, cafeterias, and even private offices, compared with 27–33 percent in a 1987 BNA survey.

15. In fact, the resistance of the smokers mentioned in the vignette at the beginning of this article arose not only because they were prohibited from smoking, but because they had no advance warning of that restriction; they were informed only at the last minute that the "smoking" seats they had booked would be eliminated.

16. By one account, however, "at least 6,000 U.S. companies, including Atlanta-based Turner Broadcasting, refuse to hire smokers," presumably to help control health-care costs (Elson 1991). Another survey found that in a sample of 833 firms, 17 percent accorded hiring preferences to nonsmokers (BNA 1991).

17. Personal observation by one of the authors.

18. Yvonne Hester, a Belmont, California, woman who works as a ballroom dance instructor, has smoked two packs a day for forty years. But she feels condemned, lonely, and angry in the society of nonsmokers. "I used to be in the mainstream," Hester laments. "Now I'm out of it" (DelVecchio 1991).

19. For centuries earlier, it had been believed that the retention of spittle was harmful. As late as 1729, medical writers advised that, for reasons of personal health, spittle should not be withheld in the body. There was not the faintest suggestion that spitting might be unhygienic, although admonitions about how and where to spit are found in the late seventeenth to early eighteenth century.

20. Similarly, La Salle in 1774 advises that "It is even good manners for everyone to get used to spitting into a handkerchief when in the houses of the great and in all places with waxed or parquet floors" (Elias 1978, p. 155).

21. Lewis (1957, p. 205) provides another example of very rapid change among the elite regarding table manners: "In the earlier part of [Louis XIV's] reign, soup was not served in plates but in a two-handled porringer, from which each guest drank in turn; and even when tureen and soup plates came into existence, everyone dipped into the tureen with his own soup spoon. 1695 seems to have been a revolutionary year in matters of table deportment; Coulanges then expresses his disgust at a lady helping him to sauce with a spoon which she has just removed from her own mouth . . . and the Duc de Montaurier, who was held to carry cleanliness to the point of absurdity, invented the soup ladle."

22. Similarly, when an environmental group publicized research suggesting that Alar, a chemical used to treat apples, was unsafe, school boards across the country removed apples from school cafeterias, even though, according to the EPA, 95 percent of American apples were Alar-free and many researchers thought the risks posed by the chemical were low (Shabecoff 1989). The FDA banned saccharin with only minimal evidence of risk, discounting the health benefits of the sugar substitute for diabetics and dieters (Havender 1982a, 1982b).

23. Before the Oroville ordinance, which took effect July 1, 1991, the Oroville McDonald's was 65 percent nonsmoking, but at times smokers were allowed to smoke in the nonsmoking section if it wasn't obviously bothering anybody. ("We're a people business.")

24. Oroville is a working-class northern California community with a high unemployment rate. The McDonald's also gets many patrons who stop off from a major highway and are unaware of the ordinance.

25. We called the Sizzler in Auburn because that city had enacted an ordinance banning smoking in restaurants completely. We wondered if compliance would be more problematic

where there was no "smoking section" at all. It turned out, however, that the Sizzler was just outside the city limits and was not covered by the ordinance.

26. Baton Rouge Sizzler increased nonsmoking area from 20 percent six months before our interview because the smoking section often remained largely empty while patrons waited for nonsmoking tables.

27. Increased from 50 percent nine months before our interview, following agreement among nine Sizzler owners in Indiana. "Now, during busy times, we often run out of smoking seats"—which suggests that 75 percent nonsmoking runs ahead of social patterns. But manager claims he has received more praise from nonsmokers than complaints from smokers.

28. Considering expanding nonsmoking to 50 percent. Sunday lunch is the only time that smoking section fills up first.

29. Since July 1, 1991, by company decision for the region. Previously, 75 percent nonsmoking.

30. A copy-desk employee at the *Dayton Daily* (staff of over one thousand) who is a smoker told us, "We still cut a butt in the toilet," and that he sometimes smokes at his desk if there are few people (and no nonsmokers) around. But he accepted the restrictions as legitimate (nonsmokers have a legitimate complaint about secondhand smoke).

31. According to the circulation manager of the Kansas City *Kansan*, the paper (employer of about sixty people) has no restrictive policies concerning smoking because (1) five out of the seven department heads smoke ("What are they [nonsmokers] going to do if they want to complain? The bosses all smoke, too") and (2) "The newspaper business is 'pressure city' so we pretty much let them do want they want." The experience of other papers suggests that (2) is not universally accepted as a justification.

32. Assistant managing editor of Portland *Oregonian*: "When I started here over twenty years ago, half the people smoked. We're down to . . . at most a couple dozen [out of 300], that's at most."

33. Managing editor, Savannah *Morning News*: When she first arrived, only a few of the day staff smoked, but at night the newsroom was full of smoke. Maybe 30 percent of night staff smoked. After new restrictions were announced, nonsmokers on staff expressed great appreciation.

5

Comparing Cigarette Policy and Illicit Drug and Alcohol Control

Franklin E. Zimring

Tobacco is not the only habit-forming psychoactive substance that is regarded as a special problem for public policy in modern American life. Alcohol, prescription drugs, and a variety of currently illicit substances, including marijuana, heroin, and cocaine, are judged to pose significant challenges to public health and public order, and these substances are associated with a variety of public law strategies to minimize the damage they inflict.

The variety of substances and the range of regulatory strategies associated with them invite comparative study. While the various components of modern society's psychoactive cornucopia differ from each other in important ways, the lessons we learn in regulating one substance should prove helpful in assessing the costs and benefits of strategies to regulate others. The question of the moment is, what insight into the social and governmental dynamics of cigarette regulation can be gained from comparing public policy toward cigarettes with policy toward drugs and alcohol?

The first section of the chapter discusses three respects in which patterns of drug, alcohol, and cigarette use have been parallel despite contrasting legal regimes. I argue that, rather than changes in legal regulation causing changes in levels of substance use, often it is the other way around. Socially caused decreases in drug and tobacco use, particularly those that remove large numbers of high-status users, prepare the way for the adoption of get-tough programs by government.

The second section of the chapter examines the distinction between the general criminal prohibition of some drugs and the kind of regulation without prohibition that currently governs alcohol and tobacco. What is thought to be the distinctive attribute of criminal prohibition is the capacity to convey stigma, yet not all criminal prohibitions generate strong social stigma and some forms of noncriminal government policy may still convey disapproval effectively.

This leads to the final section of the chapter, where I suggest that the late twentieth-century tobacco policy seems increasingly like a stringent but nonprohibitionist policy that facilitates, if it does not cause, a substantial level of social stigma against cigarette smoking. If this combination works well with cigarettes, it might become a model for control of other substances.

Three Parallels

The most significant lesson in the recent history of drinking, drug taking, and smoking concerns the variability in use rates arising from social change. Recognizing how much variations in behavior originate in social changes helps us guard against assuming that any changes in smoking rates that occur after government action were caused by that action. Three parallel patterns in the social history of cigarettes and of other drugs merit special attention from students of public policy: (a) the degree to which smoking and drug-taking behaviors change over time as a result of nongovernmental processes; (b) the "trickle-down" pattern of desistance that has characterized both cigarette smoking and cocaine use in recent years; and (c) the extent to which shifts in public policy have often resulted from socially motivated desistance from cigarettes and drugs rather than causing them. When social support for a substance drops off, and when smaller proportions of the middle class use the substance in question, the conditions become more favorable for stringent governmental controls in a democracy. This pattern can be observed in the history of a variety of substances.

Desistance as Social Change

With respect to alcohol, per capita consumption in the United States varied by a factor of three and one-half over the nineteenth century and has varied by a factor of two over the twentieth century (Lender and Martin 1987). The use of other drugs has probably fluctuated even more than has alcohol use, which has a settled institutional base that contributes to lower volatility.

One of the principal lessons from the period before the first alcohol prohibition periods in the 1850s is that wide fluctuations in alcohol use occurred independently of legislative or law enforcement action. Nationally, per capita consumption of alcohol is reported to have dropped by 70 percent in the thirty years before the first state-level prohibition statute. Thus, it should not be assumed that any change in the folkways of drug use must be attributed to some prior shift in "stateways."

This appears true for illicit drug use as well as alcohol. Although we are only beginning to use multiple measures to assess shifts in the consumption of a wide variety of drugs, including marijuana, cocaine, and amphetamines, what we have learned to date about the consumption patterns of those drugs is consistent with the historical data on alcohol consumption. The use of particular illicit drugs often follows cyclical patterns, where upward and downward shifts in the incidence of use occur that are not related to changes in government policy (see Zimring and Hawkins 1992, pp. 74–75).

Patterns of cigarette consumption have also varied substantially with changing social conditions. The twentieth century has witnessed a huge upswing in tobacco consumption that was a product of social and marketing shifts, an increase that occurred in different eras and with different intensities for men and women. But in the past two decades, the United States has experienced a decreasing prevalence in cigarette smoking, resulting from individual and group reactions to cigarettes and health.

There is no disputing that the tremendous upsurge in smoking in the first half of the twentieth century was a social phenomenon. But some observers may be tempted to assume a cause-and-effect relationship between government antismoking measures over the past two decades and the decline in smoking prevalence. Yet the broad international character of the decline and the temporal sequence of both the trends in smoking and most government countermeasures suggest that social change is the major explanation of changes to date in cigarette smoking in the United States.

The Multinational Pattern. The downward trend in smoking extends well beyond the borders of the United States, and the international breadth of the pattern is further evidence against assuming that the decreasing prevalence of cigarette consumption is mainly a function of the acts of particular governments at specific times. Since mid-century, information on the health dangers of cigarettes has been disseminated and digested in social systems all over the industrial world. It is likely that this change in perceptions about cigarettes is most responsible for the broad pattern of desistance.

Figure 5.1 is reproduced from a World Health Organization report and gives trends in the prevalence of cigarette smoking by males for the period from 1970 through 1985.

The pattern of decline documented in this figure extends across the majority of western industrial countries and is similar in timing, if not in magnitude. No national government can be the principal architect of this broad temporal trend.

The most plausible explanation for a broad multinational trend of the magnitude and character of figure 5.1 is the adjustment of social attitudes and systems to definite information on the health risk posed by smoking. Widespread discussion of smoking risks begins after 1950 and receives particular focus after the 1964 Surgeon General's report. This new information begins to have noticeable impact on individual perceptions and social attitudes in the late 1960s. As individuals modify their behaviors, the conditions for social change can occur with little or no further government intervention. The broader the transnational change, the more likely that voluntary adjustments to new information is a major explanation for the shift.

Yet observing a trend over time in only one jurisdiction without knowledge of the breadth of the downturn could invite the conclusion that particular actions of government in the jurisdiction under study were responsible for more of the observed change than was in fact the case. So figure 5.1 serves notice both of the value of comparative study when trend over time is a significant issue and of the dangers of attributing shifts over time to policy changes in particular jurisdictions.

The Trickle-Down Pattern of Behavior Change. The decline in the social status of smoking in the United States involves more than just the number of persons who have quit smoking. There is a qualitative dimension to the decreasing prevalence of smoking that explains why smoking and smokers have lost status so quickly in American society. The first generation of those who quit smoking cigarettes was made up of disproportionate numbers of high-status persons, and the leadership of these persons makes a special contribution to the erosion of popular sympathy for smoking and smokers (Pierce 1991).

I will call this pattern of desistance a "trickle-down" process, because older and higher status groups are trendsetters. The move away from smoking thus started at

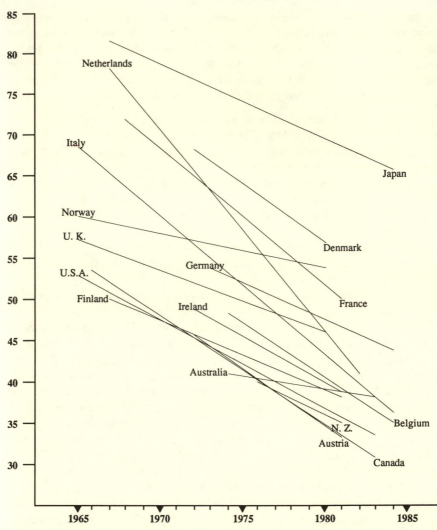

Figure 5.1. Trends in Smoking Prevalence by Men. Source: Reproduced, by permission, from Marsh, The Dying of the Light: Why People Smoked and Why They are Stopping (Smoke-free Europa Series No. 7). Copenhagen, WHO Regional Office for Europe, 1987.

the top of the social distribution in the 1960s and 1970s while lower-status segments of the population lagged behind. "One hundred thousand doctors have quit smoking" was an advertising slogan in the anticigarette campaign long before similarly significant proportions of young persons had quit. Just as trickle-down economic theories hope that the economic lot of the poor will improve after the well-off gain more wealth, it is hoped that the behavior of high-status groups will be later reflected across class, age, and ethnic categories.

The sharp trickle-down pattern present in the declining prevalence of smoking in the United States is consistent with the conclusion that the decline is in response to health information. That is, because the middle-class and middle-aged are more likely to respond to health appeals than younger and lower-status groups, the social shape of the trend toward desistance lends credibility to the theory that this social change is largely information-based.

A parallel example of a trickle-down pattern was observed in the 1980s with respect to cocaine use. Cocaine began that decade with a reputation as a relatively benign illegal drug, one possessing a user population that contained relatively high proportions of high-status and high-income adults, at least when the cocaine-using population was compared with user populations of some other illegal drugs. But the older and higher-status users fell away quickly in the 1980s as the anticocaine campaigns heated up in the United States and the social reputation of cocaine declined. By 1988 cocaine use was said to be concentrated among young, low-status, and minority populations, by then consisting increasingly of persons smoking crack (Roehrich and Gold 1988).

The qualitative shift in user populations that characterizes a trickle-down pattern helps to explain how the social status of a substance can decline more rapidly than the proportion of the population using it. When the residual population of users is disproportionately low-status, young, or marginal in other respects, desistance patterns that reduce the population of users by only 30 or 40 percent can still be associated with sharp declines in the social status of use. Whether the trickle-down pattern is only a symptom of declining social reputation (and that is why high-status individuals abandon use) or whether the qualitative shift in who is using a substance can independently influence the social reputation of substance use for others in society is hard to say on present evidence. My guess is that both influences are at work in the recent change in cigarette smoking.

In either case, however, a trickle-down pattern of desistance invites the attachment of moral stigma to the residue of the population that continues to use a substance. I shall argue later that there is a current shift toward perceiving cigarette smokers as morally blameworthy individuals. If this is so, it would be much more difficult to imagine such a stigmatization if the legendary 100,000 doctors (and millions of other agents of social leadership) had not been disproportionately represented in the vanguard of former smokers created in the United States during the 1970s and 1980s.

The Social Causes of Policy Shifts

Students of the social impact of legislation tend to focus on changes in law as a cause of changes in behavior. Yet it may also be important to study the extent to which changes in social behavior create a climate in which legal change can take place. A decline in the number of persons using a substance narrows the support for the use of that substance among the general public, and the trickle-down pattern in which high-status persons differentially decrease use may narrow the base of support for a substance more quickly than a decline in use that is evenly spread across social classes. In our drug policy study, Gordon Hawkins and I found that not infrequently in U.S. history declines in the use of drugs and alcohol helped to create a climate favorable to the passage of restrictive laws (Zimring and Hawkins 1992, Ch. 3). This seems the pattern as well with cigarette smoking in the 1970s and 1980s.

Both episodes of alcohol prohibition in the United States occurred after periods of decline in per capita consumption of alcohol. While less is known about the extent of opiate and cocaine consumption on the eve of World War I, it appears to have been neither particularly widespread nor sharply on the increase. Indeed, it is notable that there has never been sharply increased use of a psychoactive drug among broad segments of the population as a precursor to prohibition. Instead, declining use and restrictive laws are often both symptoms of the lower social status of particular drugs, and declining use often precedes official public acts restricting drug use.

The sequence of events in the recent public policy career of tobacco is typical of the general pattern. The official antismoking campaign was confined to exhortation and information for over a decade before strong pressures to eliminate cigarette smoke from work areas, public places, and airplanes produced negative zoning legislation in the late 1970s and 1980s. Measured as a percentage of the total adult population, the share of smokers had declined for at least a decade by the time the zoned prohibitions became popular, and the social status of smokers had also declined. Thus, while governmental persuasion in the form of the 1964 Surgeon General's report no doubt helped launch the social shift away from smoking, most of the coercive governmental action came well after the downward trend had started. The regulatory bite of government smoking policy in the United States happened well after the desistance pattern had become pronounced.

I am not arguing that the only plausible causal sequence is declining use, yielding lower social status, leading to restrictive legislation. Rather, my position is that the relationship between declining use and restrictive laws over time is a complicated two-way street in which governmental initiatives may both be caused by and cause declines in use. Frequently, however, the complexity of this relationship is missed when observers speak of the trade-off between various different regimes of regulation and their public health impacts.

It has been said, for instance, that criminal prohibition of substances produces much lower use rates than do legal regimes that regulate but do not prohibit. But if regimes of prohibition are usually initiated and maintained only under conditions of low social usage, it is highly misleading to compare the two strategies in terms of the use rates associated with them. In other words, a large part of the difference in usage that we find associated with prohibited drugs is the condition that made the prohibition possible rather than the result of the legal status. Crediting the criminal law for the low usage levels of prohibited substances is a bit like congratulating children for the fine job they did of raising their parents.

Prohibition Versus Regulation

The basic contrast between government response to tobacco and to illicit drugs is the obvious point that the use of tobacco is not prohibited to all citizens by the criminal law while illicit drugs are the subject of a general criminal prohibition. Comparing the way tobacco and illicit drug policies are carried out helps to define the real-world differences that prohibition and regulation produce. This section first discusses the complex of choices that lie behind the labels of prohibition and regulation for psychoactive substances, a choice between giving the criminal law total control of substance regulation and using the criminal law as a backup to other forms of primary regulation. That is followed by a discussion of the relationship between the type of government regulation used for a substance and the moral view about the substance on the part of citizens. While the principal advantage of a general criminal prohibition is that it facilitates the attachments of moral stigma to behavior, the recent history of tobacco use suggests that this can happen without general prohibition as well.

Contrasting Mechanisms

There are two distinct ways one can ask about the difference between prohibition and regulation as a governmental strategy:

1. What difference does the criminal law make in state regulation of psychoactive substances?
2. What are the characteristic elements of state regulation of psychoactive substances when the government does not seek to prohibit substance use by citizens?

The first question emphasizes the distinctive elements of the criminal law and the criminal process. This is the conventional way in which scholars, particularly legal academics, have structured comparisons of criminal and noncriminal regulatory processes. Further, the distinctive processes of the criminal law have preoccupied comparative discussion of regulatory options for drugs (see Nadelmann 1989; Packer 1968).

If the question is asked in the second way, the emphasis shifts from centering attention on the criminal process to examining the wide variety of elements of governmental efforts to limit and channel uses of psychoactive substances short of general prohibition. In the 1990s, a strong argument can be made for the value of the second phrasing of the question. The last half century has seen a substantial increase in the instances where the government has an interest in limiting or discouraging behaviors or substances for public health and safety reasons, but pursues these ends through policies other than criminal prohibition.

Indeed, most psychoactive substances susceptible to abuse are governed by methods other than general prohibition, such as regulatory schemes that attempt to control the time, place, manner, and extent to which substances can be ingested. Furthermore, government policy seeks to either discourage or restrictively regulate not only alcohol and tobacco, but substances ranging from dietary fat to prescription tranquilizers (see, e.g., Code of Federal Regulations 21: 70–800). Thus, the distinctive institutional patterns and tensions associated with regimes of regulation without prohibition raise questions that are both theoretically interesting and practically important in modern societies, where increasing numbers of behaviors and substances are seen to affect the public welfare but where the use of general prohibition is restricted to a few consensus public harms.

Of course, it is far from the case that alcohol and tobacco are unregulated by the criminal law. There are more laws—including more criminal laws—regulating tobacco and alcohol than there are laws concerning most substances covered by general criminal prohibitions. Criminal laws prohibit selling and distributing tobacco to minors, smoking in designated places, and many other aspects of cigarette use (see, e.g., California Penal Code Section 308 [sales to minors]). And alcohol has spawned its own distinct criminal jurisprudence as well as manifold laws regarding its use, sale, and effects (see, e.g., California Business and Professions Code Sections 23000–25762). Yet while a great number of criminal laws support the regulation of alcohol and tobacco, this sort of regulatory enforcement has a low priority in general jurisdiction policing, and law enforcement perspectives are less dominant in the construction of policy for regulated substances than is the case for prohibited substances.

The contrast between regulation and criminal prohibition concerns not just the kind of policy that is made, but the people and the institutions that make policy. For prohibited substances, law enforcement is the dominant expertise consulted in the policy process. The great majority of governmental experts on heroin and cocaine are police officials (see, e.g., Select Committee on Narcotics Abuse and Control 1990b [seven of eight professionals on the witness list from law enforcement], 1987 [six of seven witnesses with professional backgrounds from law enforcement], and 1990a [seven of eleven witnesses from law enforcement]). The range of disciplines and locations of government responsibility that have influenced policy toward tobacco, alcohol, and prescription drugs are much larger. While medicine and public health are consulted to some extent in policy toward prohibited substances, the influence of these disciplines on policy seems much larger for regulated substances, and their influence extends well beyond medicinal claims and applications (see, e.g., U.S. DHHS 1980a, pp. xiii–xxii).

The dominance of law enforcement with respect to prohibited drugs extends well beyond the boundaries where the comparative advantage of police would follow logically from the status of the substances prohibited. Law enforcement personnel are considered authorities not only on methods of interdiction and apprehension but also on patterns of prohibited drug use, drug effects, and other matters that are not closely connected to police training and expertise. Police are also regarded as experts on illicit drug prevention and education programs. It is as if the classification of behavior as criminal provides police with a special province for understanding every aspect of that behavior. In fact, criminal prohibition does make access to information about the use of prohibited drugs harder for public health, education, and welfare professionals to obtain. Still, it is by no means clear that the comparative advantage in relation to illegal substances lies with police authority on questions that range from pharmacology to pedagogy.

Enforcement of criminal law seems always to be a higher priority for law enforcement if a substance is subject to a general prohibition rather than only regulated as to the time, place, and extent of use. The operative distinction is probably that general prohibitions are easier to imagine as clear-cut conflicts between good and evil. Whatever the reason, however, it understates matters to say that searching for the French Connection constitutes a higher priority for police agencies than enforcing the criminal prohibition against serving liquor to minors or ensuring compliance with regulations governing prescription medicines. Absent the creation of special-purpose law-enforcement agencies that are devoted to supporting regulation of licit drugs, the enforcement of regulatory support functions for licit substances can drift very close to the absolute lowest priority for general jurisdiction police (see Wilson 1968, pp. 118–21). Thus, it should come as no surprise that general jurisdiction police place very low priority on both the enforcement of tax laws in relation to cigarettes and the enforcement of age-specific prohibitions. The same is true for juvenile and criminal courts. Indeed, no police agency at any level of government gives policy attention or priority to criminal laws regarding sale or access to cigarettes.

Just as the institutions and styles of enforcement vary for regulated and prohibited substances, there is substantial variation in the structure and intensity of law enforcement activity for different regulated substances. As an aftermath to Prohibition and its repeal, those who play key roles in the regulation of alcohol are special-purpose personnel who are very close to and identify with the alcoholic beverage industry. Tax and production control authorities are close to the producers of alcohol and identify with that segment of the industry. State and local beverage control authorities also tend to identify positively with the legitimate production and distribution segments of the industry (see Zimring 1975).

The tobacco story is more complex. Policy has been made in different branches and levels of government by a variety of different policy communities. In state and local government, there is no natural center for policy analysis of cigarette policy. At the federal level, tobacco's constituency in the Department of Agriculture has less in common with tobacco policy groups in the Surgeon General's office than it does with other special-purpose constituencies in the Department of Agriculture. And the public health groups that have been increasingly influential on federal policy statements toward tobacco do not seem to have been closely connected with any regulatory agencies other than the Surgeon General's office.

For some time then, tobacco policy has primarily been discussed at a federal level, where the policy community has been abstracted from both commerce in cigarettes and criminal law enforcement. Coordinating the design, enforcement, and evaluation of legal controls on cigarettes has been almost literally nobody's business in the patchwork of federal, state, and local responsibilities that has evolved. This lack of policy planning may not be destructive where regulations about smoking are costless and self-executing (see Kagan and Skolnick, this volume), but the usual results of anarchy in the policy planning process are lack of focus and priority.

A further contrast between government campaigns to regulate and to prohibit substances relates to the prominence of persuasive appeals in the total government effort. When mind-altering chemicals are not illegal, persuasion campaigns in the general media and in school settings are frequently used as high-priority elements in efforts to moderate abuse. For a quarter-century, the quit-smoking campaigns have been emulated by antialcohol and antidrunk-driving persuasive messages, created with governmental participation and approval.

Persuasion aimed at users and potential users was for a long time less frequently and less prominently used in governmental campaigns against illegal substances. Perhaps persuasive messages to illegal drug users were believed to confer too much autonomy on the user. Or perhaps persuasive appeals were considered necessary for the licit drug campaigns, but inferior to punishment threats when dealing with illegal substances.

However, apparently inspired by the anticigarette appeals to adolescents and adults of the 1970s and 1980s (see Polich et al. 1984), this reluctance has been overcome. At least since the mid-1980s, publicly sponsored and encouraged illicit drug control campaigns have been designed for general media programming to adult audiences and school and mass-media prevention programs aimed at the young (see Levine 1991). Whether or not the anticigarette campaigns were regarded as successful by tobacco policy insiders, they seem to have produced a rare instance of technology transfer in substance policy from cigarettes to drugs.

The Moral Dimension of Policy Alternatives

Whatever the problems with criminal law controls, the advantage of general prohibition is moral simplicity. The message the government transmits is that the use of the substance is wrong and the people who use it are bad. Whatever the gaps between the message sent and the message received by many different social audiences, the moral force of criminal prohibition is not hampered by internal inconsistencies.

Regulation of substances that falls short of criminal prohibition frequently sends mixed messages that might compromise government's ability to condemn substance use and to morally isolate those who violate regulatory prohibitions concerning a substance. The government has said that all use of heroin by all persons is a serious offense. And it is hard for individuals who contemplate the use of heroin to imagine that government policies see them as anything less than moral miscreants. They may not care much, but they know.

The moral message of nonprohibition policies is less clear. Cigarette smokers who are under eighteen may knowingly violate the law, but it is easy for them to reason that state policy does not see them as engaging in morally offensive behavior. How can one characterize those under eighteen who smoke as immoral when the government taxes rather than condemns the same behavior by an adult? The law may wish to brand the underage smoker as immature, but smoking itself is sufficiently sanctioned for fifty million American adults that the government's attempt to define the behavior by young smokers as morally offensive is substantially undermined.

The circumstances surrounding the moral status of those adults who supply cigarettes to young smokers is a more complicated matter, but the messages provided by regulatory enforcement allow enough room for confusion to mitigate the moral harm of this offense. Adults supplying cigarettes to minors are engaging in predatory behavior, exploiting the immaturity of their customers for personal gain. Under these circumstances, determined state enforcement machinery could probably push for penalties attached to such behavior that were substantial if still short of jailing.

But even this is far short of the moral fury the public attaches to the people who sell illicit drugs to children, where it is hard to think of criminal punishments that are not regarded as too good for the guilty. The similarity of these two cases is the corruption of minors, but the social meaning of the substances is quite different because the state does not condemn the use of tobacco by adults. This limits the moral condemnation even of those who corrupt the young by moderating the negative image of the substance that is the source of corruption.

The contrasting moral accounts of heroin and cigarette smoking would have served as textbook examples of the difference in stigma between licit and illicit drugs until quite recently. Heroin was projected as antisocial as well as self-destructive in all public depictions of its use. The cigarette smoker, by contrast, was regarded as victim rather than offender in the anticigarette propaganda of the 1960s and 1970s in the United States. Youthful foolishness was as close to sin as these portrayals would come in relation to the smoker, while the moral fury of the antismoking crusaders was reserved for tobacco companies. These corporate entities, treated much as the armament manufacturers who were labeled as "merchants of death" in earlier days, were the only embodiment of evil in the private-sector antismoking crusades (see Whiteside 1971). And government campaigns proceeded for two decades without any moral villain. But all of this may be changing in ways that may instruct us in the possibility of stigma without criminal prohibition. This important possibility is discussed in the next section.

The existence of large categories of nonprohibited use is conventionally thought to undermine the moral force behind criminal law regulation of the use of mind-altering substances. The limited capacity to condemn and stigmatize the use of drugs permitted by law suggests the slogan, "It is impossible to prohibit what you regulate." This is a corollary, if you like, to the slogan, "It is impossible to regulate behavior that is prohibited" coined by my colleagues Norval Morris and Gordon Hawkins concerning the regulatory inflexibility of criminal prohibitions (Morris and Hawkins 1977, p. 21).

However, general laws about the moral messages of prohibitory and regulatory regimes are not easy to derive from historical experience. It has long been suspected that criminal prohibition is not a sufficient condition for stigma to result. That was demonstrated by the moral career of alcohol prohibition from 1919 to 1933. Even longer-term prohibitions are not inevitably bulwarks against the social acceptance of particular forms of drug use, as shown by the growth of a relatively benign reputation for marijuana in some parts of the United States in the 1960s and 1970s after thirty years of criminal prohibition (Zimring and Hawkins 1992, Ch. 3). So identifying the criminal prohibition as less than a sufficient cause for moral stigma is not controversial.

There is more novelty in the suggestion that criminal law may not be the only means of government policy capable of conveying and reinforcing stigma. While there are limits to the government's capacity to stigmatize short of prohibition, a mix of social attitudes and noncriminal governmental regulations may produce substantial changes in the social reputation of a drug, changes that both promote desistance and prevent the onset of drug-taking behavior on the part of socialized groups. Indeed, one way of reconceptualizing the last twenty years' experience of social attitudes and government policy toward cigarette smoking is as a case study on the development of stigma without criminal prohibition. This thesis is argued in the next section.

The Moral Transformation of Smoking

For some years now, we have been witnessing what amounts to a social transformation of cigarette smoking in modern American life, a process in which the image of the cigarette smoker is changing from that of victim to that of one who offends against the interests of innocent persons. The most significant shift in social attitudes toward smoking in the United States in the 1980s and 1990s is the developing tendency in many segments of public opinion and government to view cigarette smoking as socially deviant and morally wrong. If social stigma can be maintained with policies other than general prohibition, it may significantly expand the options that many citizens are willing to entertain for control of other drugs.

The antismoking campaigns in the United States in the fifteen or so years after 1964 portrayed the cigarette smoker as self-harming, either an innocent or a foolish victim of tobacco's ill effects but clearly the primary victim of a tobacco habit. As previously mentioned, to the extent that private antismoking crusades required villains during this period, the black hats were almost exclusively worn by tobacco companies.

Three related developments have altered the portrait of cigarette smoker as victim. First, declines in smoking behavior have made smokers and smoking more vulnerable to negative social evaluations. In many middle- and upper-middle-class gatherings of the 1990s, cigarette smoking is already a socially deviant act. As smokers, the group most interested in defending the moral position of the cigarette smoker, become both less numerous and less influential, smoking behavior and the people who engage in it become more vulnerable to social reinterpretation.

Probably related to the declining social influence of cigarette smokers is the fact that nonsmokers who object to or feel themselves harmed by smoking began to organize and publicize complaints about smoking as a harm to others. The phenomenon of nonsmokers' rights is more significant than the limited numbers in such interest groups might suggest, because the existence of these groups is a symptom of the increased vulnerability of smokers and because the antismoking information and appeals generated by these groups can have a significant impact on the attitudes of many citizens not directly involved in such activities.

A third force behind the shift in emphasis from self-harm to harm to others has been the reorientation in both the patterns of investigation and the patterns of emphasis among the scientists who do research on the health effects of smoking and interpret such research to policy bodies. During the 1980s, the scientific community paid much more attention to morbidity and mortality among a diverse assortment of nonsmokers exposed to smoking, including children of smoking parents, nonsmoking spouses, nonsmoking airline passengers and flight personnel, and nonsmoking office workers. The number of articles dealing with the impact of "passive smoking" on health started as a trickle in the late 1970s and soared from 28 studies in 1981 to 213 in 1989 (National Library of Medicine 1975–1991). That the National Library of Medicine in 1982 created the separate category "Tobacco Smoke Pollution" in which to compile passive smoking studies in its *Index Medicus* is further evidence of the increased attention and importance ascribed to these studies. Second-party harms were the focus of the new research in the late 1980s just as certainly as the risks run by smokers was a central concern of the 1960s and the 1970s. The shift in emphasis is dramatic when the Surgeon General's Report of 1986 is compared with the 1964 original (U.S. DHEW 1964a; U.S. DHHS, Surgeon General 1986).

The causal sequence involved in the processes of social transformation is not easy to specify. Each of the three factors mentioned is a plausible candidate as both an outcome of and a cause contributing to the other two features. A decreasing base of smokers can be a result of medical information focusing on smoking harms and of increased agitation by nonsmoking groups. But this shrinking base of smoking behavior can also embolden nonsmokers and leave the individual cigarette smoker as a more identifiable target for nonsmokers' ire. In a room where seven people are smoking, no one of them easily becomes a target for particular blame. When all tobacco clouds in that room are traceable to one or two participants, the finger of blame is more easily pointed.

A similar ambiguity exists about the role of the new scientific concern about passive smoking as both a cause and a consequence of the moral transformation process. A rationalist account would emphasize the new scientific data and concern as a cause of the reorientation. Once some scientists estimate that upwards of sixty thousand nonsmokers are killed each year as a consequence of the smoking behavior of others (see Kleiman 1992), the moral focus of attitudes toward smoking will of course shift from an emphasis on self-harm to the risk of harm to others. But it is equally plausible to see this new focus as a consequence of the concern about smoking as a threatening behavior rather than a cause of the reorientation.

American history has been a repeated witness to dramatic changes in the social reputation of psychoactive substances that were not importantly related to new medical or scientific evidence. The progress of marijuana from the villain of *Reefer Madness* of the 1930s to the harmless universal solvent of early 1970s youth culture is one example. The benign health reputation of cocaine in the 1970s followed by its emergence as a killer drug in the 1980s is a second example (Zimring and Hawkins 1992, Ch. 3).

The first shift during the 1960s in the U.S. policy toward cigarettes is the clear exception to this usual pattern. The Surgeon General's report of 1964 was both prompted by and predominantly influenced by medical research on cigarettes and lung cancer. Most of the social change since 1964 can legitimately be regarded as the progeny of that scientific research and the information campaigns that resulted from the findings of that research.

In timing, at least, the new emphasis in medical research and policy literature on passive smoking appears to be as much an effect of shifting attitudes toward smoking as a cause (see Garfinkel 1981; Gilles et al. 1984; Akiba et al. 1986). The credibility of these estimates among policy audiences and the immediate use of passive smoking harm estimates in legislative proposals and rule-making probably owe much to the decline in smoking that preceded the arrival of these data and the increase in antismoking concern and activism. By the time the passive-smoking research of the late 1980s was made public, a ready-made market was waiting to receive the news; no parallel market existed for the news in the Surgeon General's 1964 report.

There are two plausible ways to interpret the coincidence of the passive-smoking research and the social conditions to support it in the late 1980s. One is that the appetite for policy applications that portray smokers as dangerous created an overly enthusiastic reception for data implicating passive smoking in the 1980s— parallel to the inappropriately broad embrace of "crack baby" scare stories during that period (see, e.g., Barol 1986). Equally plausible is that the passive-smoking harm hypotheses were stifled due to a lack of funding in the scientific and policy communities until the 1980s. In this telling, the role of the social change in attitudes toward smoking was to finally provide a level playing field in which the merits of the theory could be demonstrated.

Which of these stories comes closer to truth may not be known for many years. Both of these accounts, however, recognize the important influence of social forces on the kind of research conducted and the policy changes that are announced in the name of research. In this sense, very few would assert that the change in smoking attitudes and the shift in focus of the medical research of the 1980s were purely coincidental.

Where will the social transformation of smoking lead the United States in the 1990s and beyond? There are no indications of a smoking renaissance in the United States or anywhere else in the industrial West. The progressive social processes that have been isolating smokers do not seem cyclical; a resurgence in smoking resulting from a change of fashion now seems highly unlikely because of the harms risked by smokers. Unless a socially credible version of a safe cigarette appears, the social consensus around the risks of smoking does not seem imperiled by cyclical patterns.

But legal policy will most probably stop well short of making adult cigarette smoking into a criminal offense. There is some parallel between the growing anti-smoking fervor and the drive toward alcohol prohibition, but there are differences as well. In the temperance rhetoric that is the backdrop to drug and alcohol prohibition (see Wilson 1990), the intoxication of drinkers and drug takers is itself a threat to morality and productivity. By contrast, smoking itself does not threaten the social order in the world view of most citizens. The moral fault of cigarette smokers is limited in the antismoking account to the harm their smoke does to others. This means that legislation that protects only nonsmokers is a viable alterative to prohibition.

A second difference between the drive to alcohol prohibition and the current antismoking campaigns is the enduring lesson of the prohibition experiment. The consensus that Prohibition failed seems a strong bulwark against attempts to legislate out of existence a bad habit maintained by fifty million adults, or twenty-five million, or even ten million. Much stronger prohibitions for the underage, differential health insurance and life insurance rates for smokers, and legal recognition of employer antismoking sanctions are likely in the coming years. Intensified propaganda wars and tax rates that will seem prohibitive to smokers are almost guaranteed. But more than lip service will be paid to adult liberty in this version of the coming decades.

So the midterm policy future for cigarettes will probably be one that builds on and attempts to reinforce stigma but stops short of criminal prohibition for adults. This same pattern has evolved de jure in regulation of pornography in public and de facto for gambling and many other vice behaviors. Given the enormous health costs of cigarette smoking, the pace at which smoking consumption will decline will seem painfully slow. But an almost smoke-free country will be an even more remarkable achievement if its evolution takes place in an atmosphere of government restraint.

6

Institutional and Historical Perspectives on Tobacco Tort Liability

Robert L. Rabin

The 1950s are generally regarded as the last decade of America's innocence—a period of relative quiescence in which political activism was at a low ebb. Postwar industrial growth had brought unprecedented economic prosperity, but misgivings about the costs of the new affluence—the development of a refined sensitivity to health and safety concerns that would strongly influence popular attitudes beginning in the next decade—had yet to arise.

Tort law, on the whole, mirrored these cultural themes. By the late 1960s, what would be heralded as a revolution in products liability law had begun, reflected in the adoption of "strict liability" for defective products (Priest 1985). Spurred on by a newly emerging concern about toxic exposures and a broader-based rise in the public's claims consciousness, tort awards and tort doctrine were swept up in a period of legal turbulence that has yet to abate. In sharp contrast, the 1950s had been something of a dormant period in tort law, with products liability no exception (Rabin 1988). The principle of responsibility for unreasonably dangerous products, articulated by Judge Benjamin Cardozo forty years earlier, held sway.[1] An effort by another notable common law judge, Justice Roger Traynor, to shift the focus of products liability from unreasonableness to defect per se, had been soundly rebuffed a decade earlier.[2] It was a period of calm before the storm.

While few noticed, a first wave of tobacco litigation arose at the end of this tranquil period. By the time this litigation had subsided in the mid-1960s, without any noteworthy successes, the products liability revolution was under way. Following a twenty-year hiatus, a second wave of tobacco litigation arose in the 1980s. By this point, many observers viewed the tort system with a jaundiced eye; it appeared to be in disarray from rising costs and award levels, with products liability law regarded as a prime villain. This time, the tobacco cases received greater attention. But for all the twists and turns in the quarter-century development of tort law, the disposition of the new wave of contemporary tobacco litigation bore many similarities to its less prominent predecessor. Once again, cigarette smokers who had contracted lung cancer failed to gain a single clear-cut victory.[3]

This essay surveys the period of roughly thirty-five years in which litigation twice came to be regarded as an attack threatening the very existence of the tobacco industry, and yet, in each instance, was ultimately repulsed. First, I will explore why the litigation arose when it did—in other words, the characteristics of each period that inspired tort claimants and litigators to seek redress in the courts.

Next, I will shift my focus to the contesting parties and their litigation strategies. The success of tort litigation turns on many factors, only one of which is formal rules of liability. I will look at the nature of the underlying claims and the adversarial techniques employed by the contesting parties, as well as doctrinal issues. In chapter 7, Professor Gary Schwartz systematically examines the doctrinal issues in greater detail in the broader context of product liability rules.

Because an overall assessment of the efficacy of tort litigation as a strategy for redressing harm is an underlying purpose of this essay, in a final section I will take a broader view of the relative promise of other political initiatives. From this comparative institutional vantage point, I will indicate why one might have expected the developments that, in fact, have taken place: the far greater success of legislative initiatives that focus on a public health perspective, in contrast to the individual rights perspective that has characterized the tort litigation.

Early Efforts

Today, it is difficult to recapture fully the allure of smoking in American life at mid-century. Numbers tell part of the story. Nearly one out of two Americans could be counted as a regular smoker in 1950 (U.S. DHEW 1964a, p. 26). But raw numbers fail to convey the mystique attached to the cigarette. Observers of popular culture remind us of the dramatic impact of cigarettes in the movies: Paul Hendreid, in *Now Voyager*, lighting two cigarettes at once to seal his relationship with Bette Davis; Lauren Bacall asking for a smoke in *To Have and Have Not*, to ignite not just her cigarette but her larger-than-life romance with Humphrey Bogart; legions of *film noir* heroes lighting up the only companion they could trust in a pinch (Allen 1988, p. C1; see, generally, Sobel 1978). Then there was the ubiquitous advertising presence of athletes, high-society and professional figures, as well as celebrities from the entertainment world, endorsing smoking on billboards, in magazines, and over the radio (Warner 1986, pp. 46–48). It seems no exaggeration to say that Americans loved the cigarette almost as much as the automobile.

In these early days, there was hardly a trace of the risk-sensitivity that has fueled the products liability litigation of the past twenty-five years. Product injury lawsuits in 1950 almost invariably were based on a deviation from the product norm—the occasional exploding soda bottle, pin in a bread loaf, or crumbling wheel base. Standardized product lines, especially those involving widely accepted consumer goods, simply did not generate litigation questioning the reasonableness of the intended version of the product. Looking back, we realize that an entire generation of future litigants—asbestos workers, DES mothers, radiation victims—went about their daily lives, not realizing that they had already been exposed to a substance that would one day enlist them in the ranks of tort claimants. At the time, however, long-term exposure claims were virtually unknown.

In this context, even though cigarettes had long been regarded as less than wholesome—coffin nails, as some called them—tobacco use would hardly have seemed a likely candidate for the bitter and protracted litigation in the tort system that was about to commence. But the tort system is an unusually sensitive barometer to health and safety-related events. And 1953 brought news of specific health risks—scientific findings establishing a relationship between smoking and lung cancer—that would generate an unprecedented assault on tobacco use.[4]

These findings were first published in journals that were not widely read by the general public, such as the *Journal of the American Medical Association*.[5] But in a critical development, the most widely read magazine of the day, the *Reader's Digest*, long a foe of the tobacco industry, published a series of articles vividly translating the risks of smoking into terms everyone could understand. Interestingly, the first of these, appearing in December 1952 under the suitably alarming title "Cancer by the Carton," was only two pages long—a wholesale condensation of a longer article written for the *Christian Herald* by an antismoking crusader of the time (Norr 1952). The article was to the point, however: based on a projection from a new study of the steady rise in the incidence of lung cancer in the U.S. population—and assuming a corresponding continued growth in the size of the smoking population—Norr asserted that the number of future deaths attributable to tobacco use might well reach mass-epidemic proportions.

The public response was swift. In 1953 and 1954, for the first time in the twentieth century, adult per capita cigarette consumption fell two years in a row (Warner 1986, pp. 22–23). The great cancer scare of the 1950s had begun. The industry had its response, however, which was effective in reversing the flight from tobacco use—vigorous marketing of the filter-tip cigarette. But the critics did not let up; in July 1954, by way of illustration, the *Reader's Digest* published an article by Lois Mattox Miller and James Monahan, "The Facts Behind the Cigarette Contro-versy," which carefully detailed—in easily understandable prose—the major epidemiological and laboratory studies (painting cigarette tar on the backs of mice) of smoking-related cancers, and questioned the efficacy of filters as a protective device (Miller and Monahan 1954). In the same year, Edward R. Murrow, whose "See It Now" television program had much the same widespread appeal as the *Reader's Digest*, aired widely noted programs devoted to the health risks of smoking.

Not by chance, the first wave of cigarette litigation was launched as well, in 1954, with the filing of *Lowe v. R. J. Reynolds*[6] in St. Louis. This case was followed by a succession of lawsuits before the first wave exhausted itself: at least eleven judicial opinions were written, and an estimated 100–150 others, like *Lowe*, were simply dropped at some point without formal disposition.[7] The early years, in particular, were critical. Personal injury lawyers, then and now, see themselves as the last frontiersmen: ready to take high risks to engage the organized forces of wrongdoing. Encouraged by a contingency fee system which provided relatively easy access to these attorneys, smokers with lung cancer found not just a rationale for what had befallen them, but a means of seeking redress for their sense of victimization. The reservoir of goodwill toward the tobacco industry was swiftly depleted.

Whatever optimism plaintiffs might have had at the outset about the prospect of a landmark victory in court or an early settlement to avoid protracted litigation was quickly extinguished, however, by the strategy adopted by the defense in the earliest tobacco cases—one that has been maintained, without exception, throughout both waves of smoking cases. From the beginning, the cigarette companies decided that they would defend every claim, no matter what the cost, through trial and any possible appeals. Concomitantly, the companies decided that they would, as a first line of defense, spare no cost in exhausting their adversaries' resources short of the courthouse door.

This no-compromise strategy warrants special consideration. In the first place, it is unique in the annals of tort litigation. As a general proposition, personal injury lawyers estimate that more than 90 percent of accident claims result in settlement (Norton 1981, p. 267). More specifically, in mass tort litigation—that is, litigation involving a huge number of claims arising out of a single hazardous course of conduct or event, such as the asbestos, Dalkon Shield, and DES cases—there has always come a point when the beleaguered defense has decided that at least some of the persistently arising claims are worth settling. By contrast, over a period exceeding thirty-five years, the tobacco industry never offered to settle a single case.

The cigarette companies' intransigence is simply explained by the size of the projected financial stakes as the initial cases arose in the mid-1950s. The industry was well aware of published figures indicating that in 1954 there were some twenty-five thousand deaths reported from lung cancer, and the annual mortality was rising steadily (U.S. DHEW 1954, vol. II, p. 38). Studies indicated that more than 60 percent of these deaths among males were attributable to cigarette smoking (U.S. DHHS, Surgeon General 1989, p. 122). It took no great mathematical sophistication to project the number of claims that might be brought against the industry each year if stricken smokers and personal injury lawyers came to believe that tort suits had a good chance of settling for a decent sum of money. The industry saw its very existence threatened and responded in an uncompromising fashion.

The litigation process was, in fact, made to order for a stonewall defense in cigarette cases—as the industry and its attorneys well understood. Personal injury lawyers were, for the most part, lone wolves. They practiced alone or in very small firms, and relied on quick disposition of a high turnover caseload to survive—in some instances, to flourish—in a contingency fee system. Heavy front-end costs, which cannot realistically be recouped in a losing case from an impecunious client, are a major disincentive to involvement in high-risk cases. So, too, are lengthy pretrial delays without prospect of settlement; cash-flow concerns are endemic to contingency fee representation.

The cigarette cases provided ample opportunity to exploit these defense advantages. To begin with, there was the necessity of relying on expert witnesses. From the outset, the industry hotly contested the causal linkage between smoking and lung cancer. Typically, the treating surgeon and various pathologists would be required to testify as to when the claimant contracted the disease, whether the claimant had the type of disease normally associated with smoking, and when the scientific literature first clearly indicated the risks of smoking. While some scientists were willing to volunteer their services on the plaintiffs' behalf in the early smoking cases, expert testimony is nonetheless costly; apart from witness fees, there are the travel and time-related costs associated with pretrial depositions of experts on both sides of the case. Moreover, marketing and advertising experts—and, in the second wave, addiction specialists as well—were essential witnesses if a comprehensive case was to be presented (Townsley and Hanks 1989, p. 291).

More generally, pretrial deposing offered massive leverage to the defense. Relevant litigation issues, such as how much the plaintiff knew about the risks of smoking and whether the plaintiff was generally indifferent to personal risk—issues that have remained salient through both waves of tobacco litigation—created an opening for, in effect, examining every dimension of the claimant's earlier conduct. And the tobacco defense was quick to seize on this opportunity by engaging in seemingly endless pretrial interrogation.

But there were also more subtle aspects to the apparent juggernaut that the personal injury lawyer confronted in these cases, ranging beyond a continuing onslaught of pretrial motions, procedural challenges, and deposition-taking. Beginning with the earliest cases, the tobacco companies retained counsel from the most prestigious law firms in the country. Those firms, in turn, closely coordinated their litigation efforts. Indeed, in some cases, where the plaintiff had switched brands, the companies were jointly sued and regularly retained local counsel to handle some aspects of the case (with an eye to the courthouse benefits of local counsel if it became necessary to try the case before a local jury). As a consequence, from the earliest pretrial stages, the plaintiff's lawyer, and perhaps an associate, might find ten or fifteen defense attorneys on the other side during the proceedings.

It should not be surprising, then, that only a handful of the first wave cases actually came to trial. That none resulted in a plaintiff's victory, however, is another matter. Although the courts recognized strict liability for defective products only at the very end of the first wave, the mid-1950s cigarette litigant could rely on negligence and warranty theories. And, at first blush, the persistent personal injury lawyer, who had surmounted all of the pretrial obstacles that the defense could devise, appeared to have a respectable shot at prevailing.

The mid-1950s litigant did not have to confront the powerful freedom-of-choice argument that came to dominate the later litigation; in the period when he fell victim to the consequences of his smoking, the public was unaware of the risks of lung cancer. At the same time, the lung cancer victim could argue, under a negligence theory, that the tobacco industry had sufficient information about the possibility of harm to engage in research on the issue, adopt warnings, or, at a minimum, refrain from advertising that suggested the absence of any health concerns. Moreover, if the claimant were to proceed under a warranty theory, it might not even be necessary to show unreasonable failure to take protective action on the part of the cigarette company; the marketing of a product that was not of merchantable quality or reasonably fit for use, might suffice.

Yet, armed with these offensive weapons, the plaintiffs without exception failed to realize a successful outcome. One reason is that they continued to be overmatched throughout the litigation process. This underlying reality of the litigation is perhaps most revealingly illustrated in an unpublished opinion, *Thayer v. Liggett & Myers Tobacco Co.*,[8] where the trial judge, stung by defense allegations of personal bias, catalogued in great detail the manner in which the tobacco company lawyers simply wore down the opposition through reliance on protective orders (isolating the plaintiffs from opportunities to collaborate or realize economies of work-product), mass deposing, multiple lawyering, intransigence, and delay. The case was ultimately dropped at the point when the court was about to grant a new trial (after a defense verdict), due to, in the plaintiff's words, "prohibitive costs." Among the other first-wave cases that managed to survive to trial, at least four of the ten were abandoned at some point during the litigation process (Garner 1980, p. 1426).

Nor were the plaintiffs' attorneys overmatched only in resources. The cases reveal many instances of dubious lawyering. In *Albright v. R. J. Reynolds Tobacco Co.*,[9] the court dismissed the plaintiff's suit for failure to reserve the claim when settling a related action for damages against the city of Pittsburgh (plaintiff had argued that his lung cancer was exacerbated by an auto accident caused by the city's negligence). In *Cooper v. R. J. Reynolds Tobacco Co.*,[10] the claimant's allegation of deceptive advertising was based on a purported ad that, in response to interrogatories, the plaintiff could not produce. In *Pritchard v. Liggett & Myers Tobacco Co.*[11] and *Padovani v. Liggett & Myers Tobacco Co.*,[12] both of which were subsequently dropped, the court went on record to comment on the attorneys' incompetence in handling various procedural aspects of the claims. A fairly clear picture emerges of a claimant group both outmanned and outgunned.

Interestingly, in the handful of cases that successfully ran the gauntlet of potential pitfalls and presented the negligence and warranty claims in serious fashion, the central issue in public debate—causation—played a relatively minor role. While the industry never has conceded a causal link between smoking and lung cancer, this refusal worked to their advantage principally in imposing an enormous cost burden on their adversaries in waging a battle of the experts. From the outset, juries seemed to accept the evidence of a generic link between smoking and cancer. The defense efforts to sever the link in the individual case, by arguing that the particular claimant contracted the disease from other sources, often failed to carry the day as well.

Foreseeability, rather than causation, emerged as the central doctrinal theme in the early cases. This could be regarded as somewhat surprising, since a principal theory relied upon was implied warranty. Why, one might ask, should it have mattered whether the cigarette companies could foresee the risks of smoking so long as they were supplying a product that in fact was not of merchantable quality or fit for use? But the courts of the era had no taste for truly strict liability, whether it came packaged as tort or warranty. Instead, as the court announced in one of the leading cases, *Lartigue v. R. J. Reynolds Tobacco Co.*,[13] the manufacturer "is an insurer against foreseeable risks—but not against unknowable risks" or "the harmful effects of which no developed skill or foresight can avoid."

Lartigue was followed in other cases.[14] Its impact, of course, rested on the premise that there was no risk of harm that the industry should have foreseen—with hindsight, anything but a self-evident proposition. At the time, however, the legal conception of foreseeability was far more constrained than it is today. Where a modern court might well find an affirmative obligation to have engaged in research simply on the basis of the kinds of questions that independent scientists were raising and exploring in the 1940s (and even earlier), most mid-century jurists resisted such expansive tendencies; the first wave cigarette claimants were a generation ahead of their time.

Even so, the personal injury bar scored two near misses. In *Green v. American Tobacco Co.*,[15] the plaintiff managed to persist through twelve years of litigation, including four trips to the Fifth Circuit Court of Appeals and one to the Florida Supreme Court. The Fifth Circuit initially held, as in *Lartigue*, that foreseeability was a prerequisite to a warranty claim.[16] But on certification to ensure correct interpretation of state law, the Florida Supreme Court decided that the state in fact did not require foreseeability in a personal injury case based on implied warranty.[17] Victory appeared within the plaintiff's grasp. It was not to occur, however. After still another round of trial and appeal, the Fifth Circuit, sitting *en banc*, eventually held—in singularly premodern fashion—that the alleged unwholesomeness of a standardized product line, as distinguished from an aberrant instance of adulteration, was not the occasion for a breach of warranty claim.[18]

The second near miss, *Pritchard v. Liggett & Myers Tobacco Co.*,[19] is perhaps the most interesting of the first-wave cases because it provides a bridge to the litigation that would recur twenty years later. Once again, the case dragged on for over a decade with multiple appeals. This time, however, the focal points were negligent failure to warn and breach of express warranty based on misleading advertising claims—theories that were relied on in many of the other first-wave cases, as well.

The deception claim was a natural. For years, the cigarette companies had run ads suggesting the harmless nature of the product. By way of illustration, one famous ad, at issue in *Pritchard*, proclaimed "nose, throat, and accessory organs not adversely affected by smoking Chesterfields." As the case progressed, the question became whether the plaintiff had to show reliance on the ad in order to prevail, and the court of appeals—reversing a jury finding of no explicit reliance— took the liberal position that a "natural tendency to inducement" would suffice.[20]

On the failure-to-warn issue, the court of appeals took a similarly bold proplaintiff stance, foreshadowing the modern duty-to-warn cases. The court held that the medical science of the 1940s was sufficient to raise a jury issue regarding whether the cigarette company *should have known*—not whether it actually knew—enough to warn. On this count, too, the district court, which had directed a verdict for the defendant, was reversed. Undaunted, however, the defense succeeded in convincing the jury, on retrial, that the plaintiff had assumed the risk of contracting lung cancer. By the time the plaintiff managed to overturn on appeal this rather paradoxical holding—recall that the principal defense argument throughout this series of cases was that the cigarette company (let alone the smokers) had no knowledge of lung cancer risk associated with smoking—the claimant's resources were nearly exhausted and the case was later abandoned.

But the *Pritchard* case did not vanish without a trace. Ironically, in light of its expansive view of the applicable law, it came to be remembered, and cited, for the concurring opinion of Judge Goodrich on the duty-to-warn issue. Troubled by the court's broad view, he was unwilling to find a negligent misrepresentation unless the cigarette company had asserted in its ads that cigarettes do not cause cancer and now claimed that no one knew whether a causal link existed. If, however, the dangers of smoking were commonly known, that would be another matter. In a much-cited passage, Goodrich compared cigarettes to whiskey, butter, and salted peanuts and suggested that in each case there would be no liability unless the manufacturer either told the consumer that there would be no harm or adulterated the product. After all, he added, "there was no claim that Chesterfields are not made of commercially satisfactory tobacco."[21] The point seems to be that consumers must bear the generally recognized risks of a standardized product.

This seems an odd point to have been pressing in a case involving a pre-1950s smoker,[22] but Judge Goodrich may have been looking to a future time when the risks of smoking would be well known—indeed, writing in 1961 he may have thought the future had arrived. Clearly, he was not alone in his concern. As it happened, the case came before the court at precisely the same time that the American Law Institute (ALI) was debating the comments to its pathbreaking new Section 402A of the Restatement, Second of Torts, dealing with strict liability for defective products.[23] Dean Prosser, the drafter of 402A, had provided that liability should attach to products in a "defective condition unreasonably dangerous" to the user (American Law Institute 1961, pp. 87–88). Professor Dickerson asked why it was necessary to add "defective" when "unreasonably dangerous" seemed to cover the same territory. In response, Prosser noted that products such as whiskey and cigarettes might be regarded as "unreasonably dangerous" even though it seemed clear to him that they were not "defective"; thus the additional term was necessary to preclude ill-advised claims.

And so, with apparent common assent to this proposition, the final version of Section 402A, comment i, incorporated language and thinking strikingly similar to Judge Goodrich's concurrence in *Pritchard*:

> The article sold must be dangerous to an extent beyond that which would be contemplated by the ordinary consumer who purchases it, with the ordinary knowledge common to the community as to its characteristics. Good whiskey is not unreasonably dangerous merely because it will make some people drunk, and is especially dangerous to alcoholics; but bad whiskey, containing a dangerous amount of fusel oil, is unreasonably dangerous. Good tobacco is not unreasonably dangerous merely because the effects of smoking may be harmful; but tobacco containing something like marijuana may be unreasonably dangerous. Good butter is not unreasonably dangerous merely because, if such be the case, it deposits cholesterol in the arteries and leads to heart attacks; but bad butter, contaminated with poisonous fish oil, is unreasonably dangerous. (ALI 1965, Section 402A, comment i)

To close the circle, it should be added that the director of the ALI at the time of these proceedings was none other than Judge Herbert Goodrich.

In a sense, the Restatement proviso sounded the death knell for the first wave of tobacco litigation. Bringing their claims in a period of comparative consumer innocence, smoking/lung cancer victims of the 1950s had been unable to register a single victory in their struggles with the tobacco industry. Now, as a period of relative enlightenment about risk was dawning, the most prestigious association of lawyers, judges, and academics in the country "restated" the law with an eye to the future, and it did not augur well for the knowledgeable—by ALI lights—smoker. Small wonder, perhaps, that tobacco litigation was virtually to disappear from the dockets of American courts for the next twenty years.

A Resurgence

By 1983, the era of first-wave litigation seemed light-years in the past. In the interim, the landmark Surgeon General's report of 1964 was published, followed by the enactment of major legislation requiring warning labels on cigarette packages and banning broadcast advertising of tobacco products (Rabin 1991, p. 478). Smoking, which had seemed such a natural accoutrement of the good life, now was regarded with disdain by many—as an unhealthful sign of weak character.

But more than attitudes toward smoking had undergone wholesale upheaval. Beginning in the mid-1960s, American society had developed an unprecedented level of concern about health and safety, with particular emphasis on exposure to the unseen dangers posed by toxic substances. One result was an outpouring of consumer and environmental legislation aimed at regulating air and water quality as well as hazardous wastes. Still another sign of the rising sensitivity to toxic risk was a growing recourse to the courts in what came to be a new branch of tort litigation: the toxic harm cases. By the early 1980s, anyone who followed the news in even cursory fashion had heard of Agent Orange, DES, Dalkon Shields, and Bendectin. As cigarette claims continued their long slumber, products liability law came alive with possibilities for injury victims contending that past exposure to toxic substances had culminated in unanticipated disease.

Nowhere had those possibilities been exploited with greater impact on the tort system than in the asbestos litigation. In 1966, just as the curtain was falling on the first wave of tobacco claims, the initial filing occurred in what would become the single heaviest onslaught of cases ever experienced by the American tort system. From the outset, the contrast to the cigarette cases is illuminating. While the plaintiff in the initial asbestos case, *Tomplait v. Fibreboard*, would eventually lose in court, five codefendants chose the route steadfastly avoided by the tobacco industry—settlement (see generally Brodeur 1985). And that was a sufficient signal to asbestos victims to create, overnight, an area of specialization for Tomplait's lawyer; fellow asbestos installers, as they fell ill, sought out his services. Eventually, in the landmark 1973 case of *Borel v. Fibreboard Paper Products Corp.*,[24] one of those cases resoundingly succeeded: the Fifth Circuit Court of Appeals held asbestos manufacturers to the standard of experts, obliged to have warned on the basis of the medical evidence, and affirmed a jury verdict for the plaintiff. Asbestos claimants had achieved the breakthrough that eluded tobacco plaintiffs throughout the first wave, and an avalanche ensued—in the next decade some twenty-five thousand cases were filed (Hensler et al. 1985).

The asbestos litigation serves as the most immediate link to the second wave of smoking cases. Indeed, the most celebrated of second-wave cases, *Cipollone v. Liggett Group, Inc.*,[25] was actually handled by a team of attorneys who had developed their expertise on the scientific/epidemiological link between cigarette smoking and lung cancer in decoupling the synergistic relationship between asbestos exposure and cigarette smoking in a series of asbestos cases. In these cases, the tobacco companies in fact were most notable for their absence. The so-called empty-chair defense of the asbestos defendants reflected the fear shared by asbestos claimants and the industry that naming the tobacco companies as a party would be an invitation to the all-out blitz suffered by the cigarette litigants in the past. Nonetheless, the parties routinely contested the causal contribution of smoking in the asbestos cases. And, having examined the evidence, none of the lawyers doubted that smoking, taken alone, was a principal source of lung cancer.

Still, even a casual observer of the earlier tobacco litigation recognized that far more than a strong claim of causation was required to launch a cigarette/lung cancer case with any hope for success. First, how could one withstand the staggering resource commitment that the defense would impose? And second, even if a litigator persevered on the first score, what legal theory might prove more viable than those which had ultimately failed earlier?

The first obstacle was addressed by efforts to pool resources. Thus, in the two most prominent second-wave cases, *Cipollone* and *Horton v. American Tobacco Co.*,[26] plaintiffs' lawyers sought to join ranks with colleagues in order to respond effectively to the anticipated blizzard of pretrial motions, depositions, and other procedural moves.[27]

The second obstacle—finding an effective legal theory—appeared somewhat less formidable by the early 1980s, in light of the continuing evolution of products liability law. Two developments, in particular, stand out. To begin with, plaintiffs' lawyers had reason to believe that the shift in focal point from warranty to tort, which had then been fully effected under the influence of Section 402A, would bring to fruition a version of strict liability that focused on the intrinsically dangerous nature of the product, rather than on the foreseeability-based approach of the 1950s. In New Jersey, for example, where *Cipollone* would be brought, the state Supreme Court in 1983 decided the much-noted *O'Brien v. Muskin*,[28] involving the liability of an above-ground swimming pool manufacturer. Treating the pool as a "luxury item" under a broadly defined risk/utility analysis, the court suggested that the manufacturer might appropriately bear the cost of such an item, even if it could not be made any safer—and indeed, even if it bore a warning of its dangers.

While other states were perhaps less bold than New Jersey, the emerging emphasis on risk/utility analysis, however vaguely defined, was a powerful incentive to potential tobacco litigators seeking assurance that a *prima facie* case could be established.[29] After all, reputable studies indicated that cigarettes were killing tens of thousands annually and the intangible benefits of smoking would not be similarly quantifiable.[30]

Strict liability had a second, equally important attraction. Despite the adverse language in Restatement (Second) Section 402A, comment i, it was not at all clear that a fault-based defense would apply to a claim based on risk/utility analysis. Admittedly, a court attracted by the growing influence of economic analysis might find a risk-conscious smoker the "cheapest cost-avoider" (Calabresi 1970). But it seemed at least as likely that a court would subscribe to the alternative "best cost-spreader" rationale and eschew a version of assumed risk that barred a smoker from recovering. Nor was it necessary to lift the bar entirely. In the early 1980s the courts began applying the comparative fault principle to strict liability defective product cases; as a consequence, potential tobacco litigators could pin their hopes on a retreat from the harsh total bar of comment i to a battlefield where partial victory—a reduced, comparative award—was a distinct possibility.

And so, the second-wave cases began to be filed.[31] The defense was poised for the assault, however, and once again relied on the singular features of tobacco litigation to press the plaintiffs' attorneys to, and in most cases beyond, their limits. In the words of a leading tobacco litigator:

> They have done this by resisting all discovery aimed at them, thus requiring a court hearing and order before plaintiffs can obtain even the most rudimentary discovery. They have done it by getting confidentiality orders attached to the discovery materials they finally produce, thus preventing plaintiffs' counsel from sharing the fruits of discovery and forcing each plaintiff to reinvent the wheel. They have done it by taking exceedingly lengthy oral depositions of plaintiffs and by gathering, through written deposition, every scrap of paper ever generated about a plaintiff, from cradle to grave. And they have done it by taking endless depositions of plaintiffs, expert witnesses, and by naming multiple experts of their own for each specialty, such as pathology, thereby putting plaintiffs' counsel in the dilemma of taking numerous expensive depositions or else not knowing what the witness intends to testify to at trial. And they have done it by taking dozens and dozens of oral depositions, all across the country, of trivial fact witnesses, particularly in the final days before trial. (Townsley and Hanks 1989, p. 277)

Once again, the defense was able to wear down the tobacco litigants through a seemingly inexhaustible expenditure of resources,[32] occasioned by the convergence of two circumstances. Had the tobacco cases hinged on issues of law or factual determinations generally resolvable by summary judgment, the courts might have provided the tobacco victims a level playing field similar to the classic instances in which civil rights, civil liberties, and public interest groups effectively waged battle against far more powerful economic interests. In fact, however, the tobacco cases lie on the other extreme of the law-fact continuum. Since lung cancer may gestate over most of an adult life, the investigation of a claimant's habits may cover an exceedingly long period of years. The companies could legitimately argue the relevance of questions such as which brand the plaintiff used at various times, how heavily the victim smoked, what level of awareness the claimant had about risk, how much of a taste for risk he or she had, and what other toxics the victim had encountered. Each of these questions was salient to some aspect of the causation issue. While the character investigation of the plaintiff was intimidatingly detailed and extraordinarily exhaustive, no trial court judge was impelled to find that the defense created any impropriety.

This massive resource expenditure by the tobacco industry was occasioned by another factor, perceived necessity, as well as by the simple fact that the opportunity presented itself. Thirty years earlier, simple arithmetic had persuaded the industry that a no-holds-barred defense of every claim was in its economic self-interest. In 1983, the tobacco companies had more than arithmetic to fuel their sense of resolve.

The spectacle of the asbestos industry under siege, most vividly apparent in the Manville bankruptcy just one year earlier, was convincing evidence that the very existence of the industry was at stake in the litigation.

It was, then, in the first instance the lawyers' litigation strategies rather than their legal arguments that once again constituted the first line of defense. As a tobacco industry lawyer would put it, in a leak later published in the Los Angeles *Times*, the industry's hardball tactics made the litigation "extremely burdensome and expensive for plaintiffs' lawyers. . . . To paraphrase General George Patton, the way we won these cases was not by spending all of Reynolds' money, but by making (the enemy) spend all his" (Levin 1989, p. A41).

As before, however, a handful of resolute tobacco litigators and their clients reached the courthouse door, putting the defense to the test in the new era of strict liability for defective products. And at first, there were reasons for optimism among tobacco activists. Two cases, filed almost simultaneously in 1983, seemed especially noteworthy. In California, amid much fanfare, Melvin Belli had filed *Galbraith v. R. J. Reynolds* and predicted the downfall of the industry (Roberts and Scardino 1985, p. 8E). In New Jersey, a team of experienced asbestos litigators had filed *Cipollone*, confident that they could pool their resources and win the war of attrition. A breakthrough, at long last, seemed a real possibility, particularly after Judge Sarokin issued a lengthy opinion in September 1984 disposing of the defense arguments that the 1965 Labeling Act had preempted tort claims and clearing the way for trial on the merits.[33]

But a counterattack was in the offing, and it proved to be especially devastating. In April 1986, the Third Circuit Court of Appeals reversed Judge Sarokin, declaring that all adequacy of warning and advertising and promotion claims based on industry conduct after January 1, 1966 (the effective date of the Labeling Act), were preempted.[34] The court based its decision on the dubious ground that, in light of Congress' desire to "balance" warnings of health hazards with the interests of the nation's economy, an intent to preempt state tort claims—rather than just regulatory initiatives—could be implied in the statutory language proscribing any "requirement or prohibition based on smoking and health . . . imposed under State law with respect to the advertising or promotion of any cigarettes the packages of which [conformed to the statute]."[35] The court's reading of "requirement or prohibition" as a preclusive reference to state *tort* suits can most charitably be regarded as an unconventional way of identifying tort compensation awards. It is a reading that is even more suspect in view of the rather strong tradition of federal deference to competing state interests in compensating injury victims. Nonetheless, in the succeeding three years, four federal courts of appeals followed the lead of *Cipollone*, in varying measure.[36] The effect was to severely truncate the litigation by relegating the plaintiff to pre-1966 claims of duty to warn and overpromotion.[37]

Just four months before the *Cipollone* setback, the second-wave offensive was routed on its other flank by a jury verdict for the defense in the *Galbraith* case. Highly refined legal theory played no part here. In his eagerness to reenter the tobacco fray, Melvin Belli had selected a seventy-year-old lung-cancer victim who had smoked for fifty-five years, suffered from a variety of noncigarette maladies, including heart disease and pulmonary fibrosis, died without an autopsy, and was attended by a physician who could not say that smoking was directly related to his death. A solid majority of jurors expressed the conviction that causation had not been established (Jenkins 1989, p. 182; Gidmark 1986).

Once again, the contrast to public interest litigation is interesting to note. Thoughtful case selection might well have weeded out a *Galbraith* case, or at least put it on the back burner at the outset of the second wave. And *Galbraith* is no isolated example of dubious litigation priorities. In *Marsee v. U.S. Tobacco Co.*,[38] a smokeless tobacco case, a jury came to a quick verdict in finding that a nineteen-year-old's death from tongue cancer had not been clearly linked to his use of snuff; in *Roysdon v. R. J. Reynolds Tobacco Co.*,[39] post-trial interviews brought out that the jurors thought complications arising from bunion surgery rather than smoking were probably responsible for the plaintiff's condition (Gidmark 1987b).

Given the staggering obstacles to successful litigation of a tobacco case, and the symbolic importance of an early victory, one might have expected careful attention to be given to the prospective plaintiff's medical profile. But coordinated efforts in the tobacco cases have been, at most, limited to modest pooling of resources in individual cases. Strategies of refined test case selection are not consonant with the structure of the personal injury bar—no matter how sincere the conviction of some participants that tobacco litigation is motivated, at least in part, by its potential contribution to a critical public health goal.

As crucial as issues of preemption and causation have been, the most salient theme in the second-wave litigation has been freedom of choice. The centrality of this theme creates a striking anomaly. Increasingly, late-twentieth-century accident law has come to be defined by impersonal, bureaucratic norms: mass tort cases are relegated to the bankruptcy system (Dalkon Shield, asbestos), settled through damage-scheduling approaches (Agent Orange, airline cases), and adjudicated on quasi-legislative liability apportionment principles (DES). High-stakes medical malpractice and product liability suits are decided with reference to social utility goals of risk-spreading and proper cost allocation. Even auto accident cases are handled through routinized patterns of disposition that deemphasize individualized treatment. By contrast, tobacco litigation is a last vestige of a vision of nineteenth-century tort law as an interpersonal morality play.

The sophisticated tobacco plaintiffs' lawyers, attuned to the role of comment i in the final stages of the earlier wave, recognized that consumer awareness would be a linchpin of defense strategy in the post–Labeling Act era. But they counted on the advent of comparative fault, buttressed by their ability to depict a socially irresponsible industry overpromoting a highly dangerous product, to counter—or at least blunt—the personal choice argument.

In doing so, they underestimated the force of the defense strategy in two distinct ways. First, and, with the benefit of hindsight, most obvious, they simply failed to grasp how intensely most jurors would react to damage claims by individuals who were aware of the risks associated with smoking, and nonetheless chose to continue the activity over a long time period. When *Cipollone* eventually went to trial on the pre-1966 (nonpreempted) claims, plaintiff's attorneys, armed with the most extensive array of discovery documents and promotional revelations ever brought to bear against the industry, succeeded only in convincing the jury that the defendant was

20 percent at fault, as compared with the plaintiff's 80 percent responsibility. This apportionment fell considerably short of the 50 percent or less victim-responsibility necessary to support a damage claim under New Jersey tort law.[40] Even more dramatically, in *Horton*—decided under the Mississippi "pure" comparative fault law where even a 99 percent allocation of responsibility to the plaintiff would support a 1 percent recovery—the jury took the virtually unprecedented step of finding the defendant at fault but refusing to award any damages.

The obvious tactic for countering the freedom-of-choice defense is a head-on rebuttal based on the addictive character of tobacco—a tactic that has come to be a central feature of the second-wave litigation. But the claim is confounded by common observation. Notwithstanding extensive expert testimony available on the physiological and psychological effects of nicotine, everyone knows some number of ex-smokers, and the data indicate that about one-half of all long-term smokers have managed to quit (U.S. DHHS, Surgeon General 1989, p. 286).

Moreover, the data on nicotine addiction are not dispositive from a tort perspective. There is general scientific agreement that a chemical is addictive if (a) it is psychoactive (i.e., it has intrinsic effects on mood or performance); (b) it is reinforcing (i.e., it initiates "searching" behavior that is determined by a need for the substance); and (c) it triggers compulsive use (and, concomitantly, withdrawal symptoms associated with nonuse) (U.S. DHHS, Surgeon General 1989, p. 341). Smokers become addicted to nicotine in the sense that they derive positive benefits from its use, such as relief from stress or depression, and they avoid the negative costs of nonuse, such as irritability or worse. As the nicotine level in the body falls, withdrawal begins and a person smokes to initiate a new cycle of pleasure—including conditioned response to a variety of "situational" factors, such as finishing a meal or beginning a work assignment—and to avoid the emerging symptoms of nonuse.

This patterned behavior can be labeled "addictive," but it does not follow, obviously, that an addicted smoker cannot quit. Indeed, there is commonly observed evidence to the contrary—and not just with tobacco. One study indicates, for example, that the majority of Vietnam veterans who were "addicted" to heroin during the war discontinued the habit when they returned from active service (Sonnenberg et al. 1985, p. 329). Like tobacco, heroin addiction tended to have its greatest staying power among users with lower socioeconomic status (SES). It is wildly improbable, of course, that systematic differences in genetic predisposition to addiction exist between high and low SES individuals. Nor is there good reason to think that significant differences exist in their access to risk information, as distinguished from risk processing, at the relevant level of knowledge about the hazards of smoking (U.S. DHHS, Surgeon General 1989, pp. 190, 222–23, 344–45).

This is not to diminish in the least the difficulties in quitting smoking; nor is it to ignore potential differences in time-horizon and stress among social classes. Rather, the point is that, in court, the addiction expert can say at most only that quitting is often extremely hard to do. If the jury believes that a gap remains between commitment to a difficult personal sacrifice and extinction of free choice, there is little that the expert can offer in rebuttal.

Moreover, in the courtroom, the addiction expert's translation of scientific data on reinforcement, withdrawal, reactive effects, and other esoteric phenomena into terms that make some sense to the jury remains a rather abstract undertaking. The expert is in no position to say anything about the individual smoker—in fact, the lung cancer victim is usually dead by the time of trial. By contrast, the defense on the addiction issue is grounded in particulars: the claimant could have quit, knew the risks, evinced a life-long taste for dangerous activities, and so forth. The painstaking pretrial investigation of the plaintiff's life pays additional dividends at this stage, underscoring the tobacco litigator's miscalculation of the intensity with which jurors embrace the freedom-of-choice argument.

In a second, somewhat less direct sense, the plaintiffs' lawyers underestimated the resonance of the freedom-of-choice strategy. Drawing on its wide-ranging pretrial inquiry into the claimant's lifestyle, the defense appears to have had considerable success in trying not just the plaintiff's decision to smoke but his or her character more generally. In *Horton*, for example, plaintiff's attorney complained that the defense "portrayed the claimant 'as an unattractive person for Bible Belt jurors' by introducing evidence of his gambling and drinking" (Ramirez 1990, p. B4). In *Gunsalus v. Celotex Corp.*,[41] the defense was allowed to introduce evidence that the plaintiff was a heavy drinker, lived with other women while he was married, had trouble holding a job, and had suffered multiple stab wounds. After interviewing the *Cipollone* jurors, a reporter remarked:

> Not only did most of the jurors feel that [Rose Cipollone] knew what she was doing but they also regarded her as stubborn and domineering. She was so difficult, they say, she had even sent her husband—a sympathetic figure—out late at night to fetch her cigarettes. When he came back with the wrong brand she insisted he go again. The defense emphasis on Rose Cipollone's strength and independence had made a deep impression. "He was madly in love with her and she drove him into the ground" says one juror. (Singer 1988, p. 35)

While one can only speculate on the weight attached to such revelations, they certainly add to the sense of the cigarette litigation as a full-dress morality play.

Remarkably, then, twenty-five years after the first Surgeon General's report triggered a steadily rising level of concern and publicity about the health risks of smoking, the tobacco defense had refined a highly successful strategy of assigning wholesale responsibility for harm to allegedly informed users, rather than the industry—while, at the same time, adamantly denying that any risk from smoking had been established.

There remained, as mentioned earlier, one possible tort strategy for circumventing the lifestyle defense—a risk/utility or design defect theory, rather than a failure-to-warn approach. Success has not been forthcoming so far. To some extent, Judge Goodrich's heritage lives on. A number of second-wave cases in which opinions have been written indicate continuing allegiance to the comment i proposition that "good" tobacco is not defective.[42] And risk/utility analysis has had no talismanic effect; where not rejected outright as a separate head of liability,[43] one approach has been to read in a required showing of a safer alternative way of making the product[44]—a requirement that has yet to be satisfied in the tobacco litigation.[45]

Finally, in a demonstration of their continuing ingenuity on all fronts, once the second wave emerged, the industry lobbied in a number of states for legislation creating a common-knowledge defense in litigation involving products that are inherently unsafe.[46] This legislation has effectively eliminated tobacco litigation in California,[47] where tobacco product is mentioned by name in the statute, and, barring heroic statutory construction, cut off the prospect of future lung cancer claims in the other states as well.

Thus, after thirty-five years of litigation, the tobacco industry could still maintain the notable claim that it had not paid out a cent in tort awards. On March 25, 1991, when the Supreme Court of the United States agreed to review the preemption issue in *Cipollone*, the second wave of tobacco tort litigation effectively ended.[48] Subsequently, the Supreme Court decided that only the tort claims based upon either failure to warn in advertising and promotion or misrepresentation through over-promotion were preempted by the warning legislation.[49] As a practical matter, this leaves open the possibility of tort claims for intentional misrepresentation or concealment of material facts (and possibly failure to warn through some means other than advertising and promotion). In all likelihood, some venturesome personal injury lawyers will test the industry's resolve under the revised ground rules—a third wave of litigation, in other words, is likely to follow, focusing on the industry's conduct after the enactment of the warning legislation.

By no means is success ensured. Undoubtedly, the tobacco defense will be conducted as skillfully and vigorously as it has been until now. In sharp contrast to the asbestos litigation, extensive discovery in *Cipollone* and *Palmer* failed to yield "smoking gun" revelations from the internal files of the industry and its consultants.[50] While it is possible that a new wave of lawsuits will unearth egregious evidence of a cover-up, it is far from certain.[51] Even if industry efforts fell short of affirmatively suppressing damaging scientific studies, a case for fraud could rest on knowing misrepresentations by industry spokespersons, such as the supposedly independent Council for Tobacco Research, which were likely to be relied upon by smokers. But the reliance issue would, once again, be problematic in light of the growing public awareness in the last two decades of the risks associated with smoking.

Whatever the outcome, it seems clear that an augmented time frame will give new meaning to cigarette litigation as a morality play. But a more fundamental question remains about the long-term efficacy of viewing the problem of smoking-related harm from a tort perspective.

A Broader Institutional Perspective

In thinking about the larger meaning of the tobacco litigation, it may be helpful to consider two vantage points from which the harm attributed to smoking might be viewed: an individual-rights perspective and a public-health perspective. Clearly, these contrasting perspectives lead to different lines of inquiry. Take the question of addiction. From an individual-rights perspective, which has characterized the tobacco tort litigation, defendants have had success in arguing that the loss of individual autonomy associated with nicotine consumption is too weak to support a claim to compensation—that claimants do not qualify as "deserving" victims. Even if this is regarded as a persuasive position, the aggregate evidence of 400,000 annual deaths and millions of "hooked" individuals going through recurring cycles of regret and remorse could well be sufficient, from a public-health perspective, to support a variety of regulatory controls.[52]

And such has been the case. The issue of personal blame, which has stymied the tort claimant, has had very limited appeal in the political arena. During the twenty-five year period following the initial Surgeon General's report, as the tort claims continued to flounder, tobacco activists achieved dramatic successes in legislative and regulatory forums. Many of these victories simply underscore the limitations of the tort remedy: prohibitions on smoking in the workplace, on public transport, and in recreational and shopping facilities reflect a concern about secondhand smoke that is difficult to frame effectively in a tort suit, given the causal identification problems.[53] Other initiatives, such as restricting advertising and compelling information about risk, could only be implemented through injunctive relief—an unavailable remedy in an action for tort damages.[54]

The case for these strategies turns not on whether the individual smoker, now disabled, deserves monetary redress, but on a collective perception that the social costs of smoking are intolerably high. In fact, the secondhand smoke restrictions once again label smokers as a less deserving class—in this case through locational segregation—rather than directly sanctioning the tobacco industry. And the panoply of regulatory strategies aimed at the industry evince a neutral stance, at best, toward the confirmed smoker: advertising and labeling requirements in no way express sympathy for those who choose to ignore them, and tax initiatives raise the cost of smoking without offering direct benefits to the smoker. There is, then, a sharp divergence between the regulatory and litigation perspectives. The former, based on public health considerations, is largely indifferent to the merits of individual claims for redress of injury.

Tort litigation can serve ends other than awarding damages and creating safety incentives in individual cases. Often, as in the asbestos and other mass tort episodes, litigation can play an educational role, informing the public about the magnitude of health risks that might otherwise be less clearly perceived. Analogously, many of the great early successes in the public interest law movement were symbolic educational victories, in which there was no clear-cut courthouse victory (Rabin 1976).

It seems doubtful, however, that much of a case can be made for the educational effects of tobacco litigation. The scientific findings linking smoking to lung cancer have been widely reported in popular journals and the mass media, with the Surgeon General's annual reports playing a particularly pivotal role since the mid-1960s. Health information, of course, is not the only important educational perspective; the tobacco industry, as well as its product, is of public concern. But internal industry advertising and "risk-management" strategies until recently have been hidden behind protective orders in the litigation. It remains uncertain whether startling revelations of corporate venality will be uncovered.

There persists a sense among tort activists that the cigarette litigation can independently contribute to the social control of a product that is responsible for such widespread harm. This perception may run counter, however, to the effective limits of tort law. While tort litigation has often served a distinctive dual role in awarding compensation and sanctioning wrongdoing in cases involving larger issues of public concern, it has been most effective in this regard when the plaintiff's claim crystallizes an unsatisfied demand for political action. The Agent Orange settlement is a classic illustration: the veterans' claims took on symbolic significance tied to assuring them their just deserts in return for their service to the country. Likewise, the major mass tort cases of the 1980s—asbestos, Dalkon Shield, DES, and such— were strongly colored by the evocative specter of innocent exposure to unseen toxics. In these cases, victimization again was fraught with symbolic significance. Any of us, taken unaware, might have suffered such misfortune. If there is a responsible party in such cases—where the victim has "clean hands"—the intuition is that he or she should be held to account.

Moral judgment seems alive and well, then, in the tort system, and not just in mass claims cases. Auto accident victims have recovered against the social host who served the intoxicated errant driver; by contrast, however, it seems highly unlikely that the drunken driver would himself be allowed recovery—indeed, the courts invoke no-duty rules to prevent such cases from even being heard by (probably unsympathetic) juries. Conscious risk-taking has not fared very well in tort litigation, harking back to Judge Cardozo's famous remark, in a fun-house slip-and-fall case, that "[t]he timorous may stay at home."[55]

Tort law and tort process seem to conspire against any effective role for the tobacco litigant. Nonetheless, in an era of comparative fault, it must be regarded as a remarkable feat that an industry claimed to be responsible for the highest toll of premature death in human history could withstand almost four decades of litigation without paying a single adverse monetary award. Whatever happens in the future, this record stands as an instructive lesson in the limits of social control through the tort system.

Notes

1. See MacPherson v. Buick Motor Co., 217 N.Y. 382, 111 N.E. 1050 (1916).

2. Escola v. Coca Cola Bottling Co. of Fresno, 24 Cal.2d 453, 461, 150 P.2d 436 (1944) (concurring opinion).

3. Two cases involved close misses. In Cipollone v. Liggett Group, Inc., 693 F. Supp. 208 (D.N.J. 1988), a $400,0000 judgment for plaintiff was entered, but it was overturned on appeal, 893 F.2d 541 (3d Cir. 1990), aff'd in part and rev'd in part, 112 S. Ct. 2608 (1992). In Horton v. American Tobacco Co. (Miss. 1990) (unreported case), the jury returned a verdict finding defendant liable but refused to award damages.

4. In fact, scientific studies that spanned the previous half-century had documented the incidence of cancer among smokers (Sobel 1978, p. 164).

5. See, e.g., Doll and Hill (1952); Wynder and Graham (1950).

6. No. 9673(C) (E.D. Mo. filed Mar. 10, 1954). The case was subsequently dropped.

7. The claims estimate comes from a defense lawyer who was intimately involved in the first wave of litigation. He has asked that I respect his anonymity.

8. Civ. Action no. 5314, U.S. District Court for the Western District of Michigan (filed February 20, 1970).

9. 350 F. Supp. 341 (W.D. Pa. 1972), aff'd, 485 F.2nd 678 (3d Cir. 1973), cert. denied, 416 U.S. 951 (1974).

10. 234 F.2d 170 (1st Cir. 1956).

11. 350 F.2d 479, 486 (3d Cir. 1965), cert. denied, 382 U.S. 987 (1966).

12. 27 F.R.D. 37, 37–38 (E.D.N.Y. 1961).

13. 317 F.2d 19 (5th Cir. 1963), *cert. denied*, 375 U.S. 865 (1963).

14. See, e.g., Hudson v. R. J. Reynolds Tobacco Co., 427 F.2d 541, 542 (5th Cir. 1970); Ross v. Phillip Morris and Co., 328 F.2d 3, 11 (8th Cir. 1964).

15. 409 F.2d 1166 (5th Cir. 1969) (en banc), cert. denied, 397 U.S. 911 (1970).

16. Green v. American Tobacco Co., 304 F.2d 70, 76 (5th Cir. 1962).

17. Green v. American Tobacco Co., 154 So. 2d 169, 170–71 (Fla. 1963).

18. Green v. American Tobacco Co., 409 F.2d 1166 (5th Cir. 1969) (en banc), cert. denied, 397 U.S. 911 (1970).

19. 370 F.2d 95 (3d Cir. 1966), cert. denied, 386 U.S. 1009 (1967).

20. See Pritchard v. Liggett & Myers Tobacco Co., 295 F.2d 292, 297, 301 (3d Cir. 1961).

21. Id. at 302.

22. Pritchard smoked from 1921–53. Id. at 294.

23. The correspondence in time is remarkable. *Pritchard* was argued on May 5, 1961, and decided on October 12, 1961; the ALI debated the issue on May 17, 1961.

24. 493 F.2d 1076 (5th Cir. 1973), cert. denied, 419 U.S. 869 (1974).

25. 593 F. Supp. 1146 (D.N.J. 1984).

26. No. 9050 (Miss. Cir. Ct. Feb. 8, 1988).

27. Since 1985, the Tobacco Products Liability Project, headed by Prof. Richard Daynard, has published the *Tobacco Products Liability Reporter* and a monthly newsletter, held annual conferences, established a communications network among tobacco plaintiffs' lawyers, and generally spearheaded an effort to achieve greater coordination in the handling of the litigation.

28. 94 N.J. 169, 463 A.2d 298 (1983).

29. The California case of Barker v. Lull Engineering Co., 20 Cal. 3d 413, 573 P.2d 443, 143 Cal. Rptr. 225 (1978), was another highly influential precedent establishing risk-utility analysis—in this case, as an alternative governing standard when a consumer expectations test is inapplicable. In succceeding decades it has become evident that risk-utility analysis is often indistinguishable from a negligence approach, but in the early 1980s this development was far from apparent. See, in particular, Beshada v. Johns-Manville Products Corp., 90 N.J. 191, 447 A.2d 539 (1982), another case that exerted a powerful influence on plaintiffs' attorneys, in which the New Jersey Supreme Court held that a product manufacturer could be held responsible for failure to warn about risks that only became apparent after the product was marketed. This "ex post" liability for failure to warn was subsequently limited to asbestos cases in Feldman v. Lederle Laboratories, 97 N.J. 429, 479 A.2d 374 (1984).

30. The estimated number of deaths from lung cancer in the early 1980s was 90,000 per year (U.S. DHHS, Surgeon General 1989, p. 131).

31. My best estimate, from interviews with attorneys who have been extensively involved in the litigation, is that 175–200 cases were filed from 1983 to 1991.

32. Cost estimates must be taken with a great deal of caution. Since the tobacco defense has never indicated its expenses, I will cite no figure. The plaintiffs' lawyers have been more forthcoming in interviews. Jenkins reports that Edell and his partners spent "upward of $1 million out-of-pocket for depositions, travel, medical experts and so on" in preparing the

Cipollone case for litigation. In addition, if they had been billing at their customary rates (between $100 and $200 per hour), they would have charged another $2 million in fees (although tort cases are customarily handled on a contingent fee basis) (Jenkins 1989, p. 129). David Gidmark reports an estimate of $100,000 out-of-pocket expense in the *Galbraith* case (Gidmark 1987a). Gidmark also reports an estimate of $260,000 out-of-pocket expense and $2 million in billable hours in preparing the first *Horton* trial (Gidmark 1988).

It can be safely assumed that the defense costs considerably exceeded the plaintiffs' spending, both in out-of-pocket expenditures, and, particularly, in billable hours.

33. Cipollone v. Liggett Group, Inc., 593 F. Supp. 1146 (D.N.J. 1984).

34. Cipollone v. Liggett Group, Inc., 789 F.2d 181 (3d Cir. 1986), cert. denied, 479 U.S. 1043 (1987).

35. 15 U.S.C. sec. 1334 (1988); see *Cipollone*, 789 F.2d at 187.

36. See Pennington v. Vistron Corp., 876 F.2d 414 (5th Cir. 1989); Roysdon v. R. J. Reynolds Tobacco Co., 849 F.2d 230 (6th Cir. 1988); Stephen v. American Brands, Inc., 825 F.2d 312 (11th Cir. 1987); Palmer v. Liggett Group, Inc., 825 F.2d 620 (1st Cir. 1987).

37. The position of the federal appellate courts was subsequently rejected by the New Jersey Supreme Court in Dewey v. R. J. Reynolds Tobacco Co., 121 N.J. 69, 85–94, 577 A.2d 1239, 1247–51 (1990), after which the Supreme Court of the United States granted certiorari to resolve the conflict. Cipollone v. Liggett Group, Inc., 111 S. Ct. 1386 (1991). See also Carlisle v. Philip Morris, Inc., 805 S.W.2d 498, 517 (Tex. Ct. App. 1991) (court adopts the *Dewey* position). The Supreme Court subsequently reversed the Third Circuit Court of Appeals, 112 S. Ct. 2608 (1992), partially lifting the preemption bar. See discussion in text accompanying note 49 *infra*.

38. 866 F.2d 319 (10th Cir. 1988).

39. 849 F.2d 230 (6th Cir. 1989).

40. Rose Cipollone's husband, however, was awarded $400,000 in his wrongful death claim. That award was overturned on appeal. See Cipollone v. Liggett Group, Inc., 893 F.2d 541 (3d Cir. 1990), aff'd in part and rev'd in part, 112 S. Ct. 2608 (1992). Subsequently, the plaintiffs voluntarily dropped the case. See note 51, *infra*.

41. 674 F. Supp. 1149 (E.D. Pa. 1987).

42. See Roysdon v. R. J. Reynolds Tobacco Co., 849 F.2d 230, 236 (6th Cir.1988); *Gunsalus*, 674 F. Supp. at 1158; cf. Rogers v. R. J. Reynolds Tobacco Co., 557 N.E.2d 1045, 1053 (Ind. Ct. App. 1990) (leaving open the possibility that the "addictive" qualities of tobacco may not be common knowledge).

43. See *Gunsalus*, 674 F. Supp. at 1159.

44. See Kotler v. American Tobacco Co., 926 F.2d 1217, 1225 (1st Cir. 1990), petition for cert. filed, 60 U.S.L.W. 3014 (U.S. Mar. 19, 1991) (No. 90–1473); Semowich v. R. J. Reynolds Tobacco Co., No. 86-CV-118, 1988 U.S. Dist. LEXIS 9102, at *17 (N.D.N.Y. Aug. 18, 1988).

45. But cf. Dewey v. R. J. Reynolds Tobacco Co., 121 N.J. 69, 94–96, 577 A.2d 1239, 1251–53 (1990) (holding that until New Jersey legislature changed state law, risk/utility analysis applied to tobacco cases); Gilboy v. American Tobacco Co., Sup. Ct. of Louisiana, June 21, l99l (until Louisiana legislature changed state law, cigarettes could be found "unreasonably dangerous per se").

46. The tobacco industry scored legislative victories in several states, including California, New Jersey, and Louisiana. See Cal. Civ. Code sec. 1714.45 (West Supp. 1991); N.J. Stat. Ann. sec. 2A:58C-3(a)(2) (West 1987); Louisiana Products Liability Act, LSA-R.S. 9–2800.51, et seq. See also Rushford (1990).

47. See American Tobacco Co. v. Superior Court, 208 Cal. App. 3d 480, 255 Cal. Rptr. 280 (1989) (upholding the statutory bar on cigarette products litigation).

48. Cipollone v. Liggett Group, Inc., 111 S. Ct. 1386 (1991). It has been estimated that about forty-five lawsuits were pending at the time *Cipollone* was finally decided in June 1992, awaiting the outcome of that case (Barrett 1992).

In a handful of recent claims, plaintiffs have alleged that the smoking of Kent cigarettes, which had "Micronite" filters containing asbestos in the early 1950s, caused the contraction of mesothelioma (Geyelin and Lambert 1991). In the first case to go to trial, plaintiff failed to present sufficient evidence that the decedent had smoked Kents during the relevant period. See Id. But it is conceivable that causation might be established in a subsequent case, and plaintiffs would almost certainly avoid the common-knowledge bar, since smokers were unaware that an asbestos product was in the filter. At the same time, the precedential value of a favorable outcome would obviously be limited.

49. Cipollone v. Liggett Group, Inc., 112 S. Ct. 2608 (1992).

50. For the most part, discovery in the tobacco cases confirmed widely held suspicions— that the tobacco companies made a systematic effort to disregard the experiments and conclusions of independent scientists, and sometimes their own, who posited a connection between smoking and cancer; and that the companies sought to discredit those findings through a public relations blitz (TPLP 1988). By contrast, discovery in the asbestos cases revealed that the industry was actually aware of the risks from experience with their own workers, long before the landmark Selikoff studies appeared in 1964 (Brodeur 1985, pp. 98–153).

51. In Haines v. Liggett Group, Inc., 140 F.R.D. 681 (D.N.J. 1992), the question of industry concealment arose once again. Plaintiff sought review of fifteen hundred documents related to an alleged "special project" relationship between the industry-established Council for Tobacco Research and the tobacco defense lawyers, arguing that the documents would establish evidence of fraud on the part of the industry in holding out the council as an independent health research organization. Judge Sarokin, who was also the trial judge in *Cipollone*, ruled that plaintiff presented sufficient evidence of fraud to overcome defendants' attorney-client privilege claim to confidentiality of the documents, and appointed a special master to review the documents. It remains unclear whether the documents will reveal more than a continuing effort on the part of the industry to cast doubt on the accumulating body of scientific research on the health risks of smoking. See Freedman and Cohen (1993).

The plaintiff's case suffered a dramatic setback on appeal when the Third Circuit Court of Appeals removed Judge Sarokin from the case for failure to maintain the appearance of impartiality, and vacated his decision ordering review of the documents. Haines v. Liggett Group, Inc., 975 F.2d 81 (3d Cir. 1992)

52. There is also the related point that most smokers are "hooked" at an early age, before they may have the judgment to make a fully informed choice.

53. Litigation has had somewhat greater success against the employer or custodian of the premises (Glantz and Daynard 1991, p. 40).

Also, it should be noted that these legislative successes have been addressed primarily to "secondary smoke" problems. Legislative efforts to target tobacco sales directly, such as through prohibitions on advertising, have not been similarly successful.

54. There are judicial initiatives, apart from tort, where smoking activists have achieved some success; see, e.g., Freedman (1991), discussing a convenience chain store's settlement of a suit in which they agreed to demand proof of age from young customers. Nontort remedies generally are beyond the scope of this chapter.

55. Murphy v. Steeplechase Amusement Co., 250 N.Y. 479, 483, 166 N.E. 173, 174 (1929). Moreover, if the addiction claim is put aside, the tobacco cases have the distinctive element that they involve conscious *repetitive* risk-taking.

7

Tobacco Liability in the Courts

Gary T. Schwartz

The Surgeon General's 1989 Report avoids any discussion of tobacco companies' tort liability, explaining that "the lawsuits themselves are private matters, not public issues, and while there are public issues relevant to the lawsuits, the lack of a significant body of literature on the issues of interest precludes coverage of them" (U.S. DHHS, Surgeon General 1989, p. 472). This chapter seeks to offset the scholarly void to which the Surgeon General refers by identifying and discussing the responses of judges and juries to suits against the manufacturers of tobacco products (mainly cigarettes).

The likely causal connection between cigarette smoking and lung cancer was first publicized by the media in the early 1950s. This publicity led to a wave of suits against cigarette manufacturers. The last of this first wave of suits was not disposed of until the early 1970s. It is commonly said that in this "first round of cases . . . , the defendants scored a knockout" (Keeton et al. 1989, p. 909). During the 1970s, litigation against tobacco companies was all but nonexistent. The 1980s, however, witnessed a second wave of suits. Many of these suits were eventually dropped (for reasons described by Professor Rabin in Chapter 6); many other suits are still pending. Several suits have led to jury verdicts or final judicial rulings in favor of defendants. At least so far, plaintiffs have secured only a single award of damages, and this award—for the comparatively meager amount of $400,000—was reversed on appeal, the appellate court concluding that a new trial was needed. Furthermore, tobacco companies have refused to offer settlements in any of the cases brought against them. These companies are hence in a position to say that they have never paid a penny in modern tort cases involving claims that cigarettes have caused cancer and other diseases.

Given the general sense that since 1960 American tort law has imposed increasingly strong liabilities on product manufacturers, this result can easily seem surprising. To explain that surprise, this chapter identifies the rules deployed by courts in handling these suits and the results reached by juries in applying these rules to the cases' facts. As it happens, the tort claims of smokers whose diseases were caused by smoking before 1960 seem, as a matter of law, quite plausible; those claims have tended to fail because of the lack of sympathy displayed by juries. It is certainly true that since 1960 products liability doctrines have expanded significantly. Interestingly, however, many of these expanded doctrines—for example, strict liability for manufacturing defects and broad liability for design defects—turn out to have not much relevance in tobacco cases. Furthermore, actual changes in the character of smoking-related activities subsequent to 1960 have significantly weakened smokers' claims. For example, the cessation of cigarette advertisements making explicit health claims has gone a long way toward eliminating plaintiffs' express warranty arguments. Also, given the warnings provided by cigarette companies beginning in 1966, post-1966 smokers can no longer argue that the companies have failed to give any warning. Furthermore, in the years since 1960 smokers have become far more aware of the hazards of smoking. This awareness prevents those smokers from invoking the doctrine of implied warranty and makes it much more difficult for them to argue that the warning given by cigarette companies is legally inadequate.

This chapter closes by identifying certain broader rationales associated with products liability doctrine and considering whether those rationales apply to tobacco-induced diseases in any way that might justify the substantial broadening of current liability rules. Its assessment, however, is that these rationales do not make adequate sense in the tobacco context. Hence my conclusion is that a major expansion in liability doctrines should not be recommended. More generally, I conclude that tort law does not have a major role to play in the development of public policy for smoking in the 1990s.

Causation

The suits brought by smokers against cigarette manufacturers involve products liability; they also involve what are commonly referred to as "toxic torts." Within the area of toxic torts, questions of causation often are vexing. This discussion of the law of tobacco liability begins by considering the causation issues raised by the suits against tobacco companies. First is the question of background or general causation: are cigarettes a cause of lung cancer (or heart disease, or whatever)? Second is the question of foreground or specific causation: did cigarettes indeed cause the cancer about which the particular victim is complaining?

In many of the lung cancer cases—even cases decided before the release of the Surgeon General's Report in 1964—these causation problems, while no doubt adding to the expense that a plaintiff incurs in presenting his case, have not proved to be a final barrier to recovery. For example, in *Green v. American Tobacco Co.*, the victim had smoked Lucky Strikes every day from 1924, when he was sixteen, to 1956, when he contracted lung cancer.[1] When the *Green* case went to trial in 1960, one question was whether the victim's lung cancer had been caused by his cigarette smoking. "Eight eminent medical doctors testified on each side. They were in sharp disagreement." The jury resolved this disagreement by finding that smoking cigarettes was "one of the proximate causes" of the fatal lung cancer, and this causal finding was not seriously challenged by the tobacco company on appeal. Faced with a similar conflict in the evidence, the jury in *Pritchard v. Liggett & Myers Tobacco Co.* similarly concluded, in 1963, that smoking Chesterfields had been "the cause, or one of the causes," of the plaintiff's cancer.[2]

In other lung cancer cases, however, the causation issues have involved additional difficulties. Another first-wave case was *Lartigue v. R. J. Reynolds Tobacco Co.*[3] In this case the victim had smoked cigarettes from 1899, when he was nine years old, until he was diagnosed with lung cancer in 1954. In ways unrelated to smoking, however, his health record was dismal. Over the years, he had suffered from measles, pertussis, diphtheria, malaria, gonorrhea, syphilis, tuberculosis, rheumatism, and other maladies. Evidence offered by the defendant—though disputed by the plaintiff—suggested that most of these ailments are suspected causes of cancer. The jury returned a general verdict in favor of the tobacco company; in the trial judge's view, the best explanation for this verdict was that the jury had not been persuaded by the plaintiff on the causation question.

Among the second-wave cases, the first to be considered by a jury was *Galbraith v. R. J. Reynolds Tobacco Co.*, in Santa Barbara in late 1985. This was filed as a lung cancer case. But the victim was also suffering from heart disease, pulmonary fibrosis, and emphysema. While the case was pending, the victim died, and his family's attorney, Melvin Belli, failed to arrange an autopsy. Uncertainties surrounding the causation-of-death issue helped persuade the jury to return a defense verdict (Gidmark 1986). Another second-wave case is *Cipollone v. Liggett Group, Inc.*[4] In finding that Rose Cipollone's lung cancer was at least partly due to her smoking, the jury needed to consider defense testimony that her tumor was not a small-cell carcinoma, but rather an atypical carcinoid—an unusual form of cancer not clearly linked to cigarette smoking. In addition, *Cipollone* raised a problem of "multiple sources," which frequently complicates toxic tort litigation. Cipollone had begun smoking Chesterfields as a seventeen-year-old in 1942. In 1955, she shifted to L&M, a new brand manufactured by the same company. In 1968, however, she switched to Virginia Slims, manufactured by Phillip Morris, and she flirted with other brands until her cancerous lung was removed in 1982. Complicating the causal questions that inevitably surround the problem of multiple sources is the point that liability rules might not apply equally to each of these sources; later manufacturers, because their cigarettes carry the federal warning, may have defenses against liability that earlier manufacturers do not enjoy. In *Cipollone*, however, the plaintiff's experts were able to testify that Mrs. Cipollone's early years of smoking contributed more to her lung cancer than her later years of smoking, because the "lung injury" produced by this earlier smoking had more years in which to "develop" its cancer "potential." This testimony is rendered somewhat problematic by the medical point (set forth in current cigarette warnings) that the long-time smoker who is able to kick the habit sharply reduces the risk of subsequent disease. Nevertheless, the jury in *Cipollone* found that the victim's pre-1966 smoking was "a substantial contributing factor" in the development of her lung cancer, and the appellate court regarded this finding as acceptable.

The causation problems, difficult enough in certain lung cancer cases, become more difficult in cases involving other diseases. Something like 87 percent of all lung cancer fatalities and 82 percent of all emphysema fatalities are attributable at least in part to smoking.[5] These high general figures encourage findings of causation in specific cases. Yet for smokers, lung cancer is no more of a problem than heart disease; smoking results in about as many heart disease deaths as lung cancer deaths. Nevertheless, because heart disease is so common among the population, only 21 percent of all heart disease fatalities seem due to smoking. Similarly, about 30 percent of all instances of bladder cancer and 18 percent of all stroke deaths are thought to be the consequence of smoking. Figures this low make it more difficult for a plaintiff persuasively to show that his own heart disease (or bladder cancer, or stroke) was due to his smoking. To be sure, techniques may be available that can facilitate a retrospective assessment of the role of tobacco in the etiology of the individual victim's disease.

Both general and specific causation posed problems in *Marsee v. United States Tobacco Co.*, a suit against a manufacturer of snuff—one form of "smokeless tobacco."[6] At trial, the plaintiff brought forward what the appellate court referred to as "an impressive amount of evidence." Fourteen expert witnesses and 140 exhibits supported the idea that the throat cancer of the victim (a high school star athlete) had been caused by the high level of "nitrosamine" in the defendant's snuff. The manufacturer's evidence, however, suggested that oral cancers among teenagers are so rare as to render assessments of general causation problematic; also, though the victim had held his snuff between his cheek and his gum, the fatal cancer had begun on his tongue, thereby casting doubt on specific causation. The jury, faced with a clear conflict in the evidence on the causation issues, resolved that conflict by returning a verdict for the defendant.

The multiple-brands problem proved fatal to the plaintiff in an even more recent case, *Ierardi v. Lorrilard*. From 1952 until May 1956, the "Micronite filter" in Kent cigarettes included some asbestos. Victims of mesothelioma, a form of cancer typically caused by asbestos, have recently brought suit against the manufacturer of Kents (on account of cancers caused by asbestos rather than by tobacco). The first of these cases went to trial in November 1991. At trial, the plaintiff testified that he had begun smoking Kents in 1953, having smoked Kools until then. Yet the evidence at trial clearly showed that Kools is a brand that was itself not brought to market until 1956. The jury, obviously unpersuaded that the plaintiff had smoked Kents during its asbestos years, returned a verdict in favor of the defense (Geyelin and Lambert 1991).

Standards of Liability

Tobacco is certainly a major cause of disease in society generally; moreover, in any one case the evidence may well adequately demonstrate that tobacco was the cause of the plaintiff's specific disease. What else does a victim need to show in order to secure a recovery?[7] Liability certainly seems appropriate if the manufacturer has advertised that its product does *not* cause that disease, and if the victim has relied on these ads in buying the manufacturer's product. Express warranty claims brought by tobacco victims are considered below.

Express Warranty

In the first wave of lung cancer cases, several plaintiffs pointed to earlier company advertisements as establishing express warranties running from the companies to consumers. Express warranty is, at least in form, a legal doctrine that does not require that company negligence be shown; once an advertisement's falsity is established, the company can be liable whether or not it knew of the falsity or was negligent in figuring it out. But in a proper express warranty action, the plaintiff does need to show that the company's representation was false—not just misleading—and that there is an appropriate connection between the false advertising claim and the harm the plaintiff has suffered. *Cooper v. R. J. Reynolds Tobacco Co.* was a lung cancer case filed in 1954.[8] This case alleged that the victim had relied on 1951 advertisements stating that "Camel cigarettes are harmless to the respiratory system." In pretrial proceedings, however, the plaintiff was unable to find these advertisements; the only ads he could identify had claimed that "more doctors smoke Camels than any other cigarette" and that Camels will "agree with your throat." Noting, in part, that these latter ads did not refer at all to "the lungs or the respiratory system," a distinguished federal judge ruled in 1957 that they did not support the plaintiff's express warranty claim. Thirty years later, in *Gunsalus v. Celotex Corp.*, another lung cancer plaintiff was denied a recovery for similar reasons.[9] In this case the victim had apparently smoked Pall Malls exclusively, and 1950s Pall Mall advertisements had claimed only that Pall Malls were "mild," would "guard against throat scratch," and would "lessen throat irritation." The judge, regarding these ads as promising nothing more than immediate smoker satisfaction, ruled that they would not support an express warranty claim for lung cancer.

The express warranty evidence was more effective in the *Pritchard* case. The victim's suit identified advertisements appearing in Pittsburgh newspapers in 1934 that claimed that "a good cigarette can cause no ills and cure no ailments . . . but it gives you a lot of pleasure, peace of mind and comfort." In one ambitious advertising campaign in late 1952, Liggett and Myers publicized the results reached by "a responsible consulting organization" on the "effects of smoking Chesterfield cigarettes." (This consulting firm was Arthur D. Little, whose study had been commissioned by Liggett.) According to the ad campaign, the study concluded that "nose, throat, and accessory organs [are] not adversely affected by smoking Chesterfields." When a federal court of appeals first considered *Pritchard* in 1961, the court indicated that the plaintiff's evidence "compellingly points to an express warranty. . . ."[10] In ruling that the express warranty claim should be submitted to a jury, the court noted that the plaintiff would need to prove that he had reasonably relied on these advertisements in continuing to smoke Chesterfields.

At the end of the ensuing *Pritchard* trial, the jury returned a verdict in favor of the defendant on the express warranty issue. Evidently, the jury found that the plaintiff had not in fact relied on the defendant's advertisements in deciding to purchase its cigarettes. While the plaintiff testified at trial that he had so relied, his testimony was weakened in cross-examination and "apparently failed to impress the jury."[11] Indeed, the jury found not only a lack of reliance but also that the plaintiff had "assumed the risk of injury" by smoking cigarettes. This defense, however, requires evidence in the record that the victim had actual knowledge of the "harmfulness" of the defendant's product. Yet no such evidence had been presented in the preceding trial. Accordingly, the court ruled that the jury's finding of assumption of risk was legally erroneous. That court also gave reconsideration to whether a show-ing of reliance is indeed required in express warranty. One judge thought it sufficient that the company's representation be of the sort whose "natural tendency" is to induce purchases. But a two-judge majority reaffirmed that an express warranty claim requires proof of the individual plaintiff's reliance. Still, those judges con-cluded that confusions in the trial judge's jury instructions on express warranty made a new trial necessary.[12] At this point, however, the plaintiff dropped the lawsuit, evidently because his attorney foresaw serious problems of proof in at-tempting to establish the reliance element of the express warranty doctrine.

That doctrine has now returned to the stage in one of the leading instances of the second-wave cases: *Cipollone*. As noted, Mrs. Cipollone smoked Chesterfields from 1944 until 1955. Her 1980 suit pointed to the same early 1950s advertisements on which Pritchard relied in his suit twenty-five years before, including the adver-tisement describing the consultant's report that "nose, throat, and accessory organs [are] not adversely affected by smoking Chesterfields." This report was discussed by Arthur Godfrey on a radio program he hosted that Chesterfield sponsored:

> Now that ought to make you feel better if you've had any worries at all about it. I never did. I smoke two or three packs of these things every day. I feel pretty good. . . . I never did believe they did you any harm and now, we've got the proof. So— Chesterfields are the cigarette for you to smoke, be they regular size or king size.[13]

Mrs. Cipollone explained her shift to L&Ms in 1955 by indicating that she expected its filter to trap whatever "bad stuff" there was in cigarettes. L&M ads had claimed that its "miracle tip" would "remove the heavy particles, leaving you a Light and Mild smoke"; this miracle tip was "just what the doctor ordered."[14]

Her suit was tried by a jury in 1988. While denying that Liggett had fraudulently misrepresented the safety of its cigarettes, the jury affirmed that Liggett had made express warranties and that its cigarettes breached these warranties. And the jury also found that Liggett's cigarettes were one proximate cause of Mrs. Cipollone's lung cancer and death. When asked, however, "what damages did Mrs. Cipollone sustain" on account of her lung cancer and death, the jury answered "none." (On its face this answer is confusing; a method for resolving this confusion will be sug-gested below.) The jury did find, however, that her husband had suffered $400,000 in derivative damages; it hence granted him an award for this amount.

This is the award—the first ever against a cigarette company—that was re-versed on appeal. What vexed the appellate court was the express warranty require-ment that the defendant's representation be "part of the basis of the bargain." According to the defendant, this legal standard means that the evidence must show that the plaintiff actually relied on the defendant's ads in purchasing the defendant's brand. (Recall that this was the position that had been accepted by the *Pritchard* majority.) The plaintiff argued, however, that the legal standard is satisfied when-ever a manufacturer publishes ads whose natural tendency is to induce consumer purchases. (This was the view that had been accepted by the trial judge, who accordingly had not submitted the issue of the plaintiff's actual reliance to the jury.) The appellate court ended up steering its way to an intermediate position. It ruled that an express warranty plaintiff needs initially to prove that she has "read, seen, or heard" the advertisements in question; with this proof in, the company can escape liability if it can show that other information available to the consumer resulted in her not actually believing the ads to which she was exposed. The court thought that these factual issues should now be explored in a new trial.

To understand the social context of the reliance issue, we should briefly consider how consumers developed over time their knowledge of cigarettes' health hazards (Calfee 1986). Cigarettes were first widely marketed in the 1920s. From an early date, the public's perception of cigarettes included elements of ambivalence. Cigarettes certainly projected a glamorous image. Nevertheless, there were consumer concerns about cigarettes' adverse effect on health. "Smokers' cough" was a much discussed phenomenon, and cigarettes were frequently referred to as "coffin nails." Responding to concerns such as these, in the 1930s cigarette advertisements emphasized the "health theme." "Why risk sore throats?" asked Old Gold; "Not a cough in a carload," bragged Chesterfield; "Smoking's more fun when you're not worried by throat irritation or smoker's cough," pointed out Phillip Morris.

The possibility that cigarettes might be a carcinogen had been raised before 1949 by a limited number of scientists. Between 1949 and 1954, however, several major reports were released that strongly suggested a connection between smoking and lung cancer. In late 1953, *Business Week* reported that "few scientists seem to doubt now that some relationship does exist" between cigarette smoking and cancer ("Cigarette Scare" 1953, p. 60). The new scientific reports were much discussed in the media; *Reader's Digest*, for example, published articles discussing the cancer issue in 1952 and 1954. From my boyhood, I can personally recall the furor generated by the latter (Miller and Monahan 1954). The very extensive media coverage of the new research findings caused a public "cancer scare." This in turn led to a new emphasis on safety in cigarette advertisements. (Ads from this era were brought forward in *Pritchard* and *Cipollone*.) In the mid-1950s, cigarette companies, attempting to improve the safety of cigarettes, reduced their nicotine and tar levels and introduced a variety of filters. Advertisements then trumpeted the likely safety advantages of these product changes.

In all, then, the minds of consumers were not clean slates on which cigarette health ads could write. Rather, those ads were the companies' response to information that had already been broadly disseminated among the consumer public. This account of public opinion makes it possible to understand why the *Pritchard* jury could find no reliance and why there might be an issue of actual belief in *Cipollone*. Rose Cipollone herself alleged that she had been psychologically reassured by the company's advertising program; yet the case's evidence also showed that from the beginning of her marriage her husband had repeatedly urged her to quit smoking, "because it was unladylike and bad for her health"; in the early 1950s, he had made a special effort to bring to her attention the newspaper stories discussing the findings of new studies on the dangers of smoking.[15]

Claims of express warranty have not loomed large in the cigarette cases involving plaintiffs who smoked after 1955. One explanation for this is the concern for preemption, to be dealt with below. Another explanation is that since 1955 cigarette advertisements have simply not included the kinds of explicit health representations that can most readily be interpreted as express warranties. And this point can itself be explained, at least in part, in terms of the position taken by the Federal Trade Commission (FTC): in 1955 the FTC adopted guidelines that tended to prohibit express health claims in cigarette ads (Calfee, 1986, p. 41). Problems of express warranty will be returned to later, in the course of discussing the Supreme Court's treatment of the preemption issue in *Cipollone*.

Failure to Warn

Express warranty is a doctrine that imposes liability for the manufacturer's communication to consumers of false statements about a product's safety. Warning doctrine subjects the manufacturer to liability for its failure to communicate to consumers relevant information about the product's hazards. In the abstract, tort law's warning obligation expresses a splendid idea. The core of this warning obligation was already in the law as of 1960. During the last 30 years, however, the courts have considerably extended the scope of that obligation. Indeed, at times the obligation has been overextended in ways that run the risk of trivializing the key idea that underlies the obligation itself.

Failure to warn has been argued by plaintiffs in both waves of cigarette cases. In these cases plaintiffs have generally needed to show that the company either knew or should have known of those health hazards at the time of its alleged warning failure. Moreover, since the law does not require manufacturers to warn of hazards of which consumers are generally aware, plaintiffs have also needed to establish that most consumers did *not* know of those hazards at the times in question. Indeed, the victim cannot recover unless he himself was personally unaware of those hazards. (Had he known of them, a warning, even if given, would not have been causally effective in preventing him from buying cigarettes.) In essence, then, plaintiffs who have pleaded failure to warn in cigarette cases have needed to establish that their cases fell within a transitional period in which manufacturers knew (or should have known) of the health hazards of cigarettes even though consumers and plaintiffs themselves did not know.

Courts have expanded on the "should have known" concept in ways that have made it somewhat easier for plaintiffs to establish such a transitional period. In first-wave cases such as *Ross v. Phillip Morris & Co.*[16] and second-wave cases such as *Kotler v. American Tobacco Co.*,[17] courts have ruled that tobacco manufacturers should be deemed "experts" who hence are obliged to keep abreast of all ongoing research findings. In its first opinion in the *Pritchard* case, a federal court went even further, imposing on cigarette manufacturers a duty to conduct "tests" to determine not only the "carcinogenitic content" of their own brands but also the more general "relationship between cancer and smoking."[18] The "testing" obligation imposed on manufacturers by previous products liability cases had largely been limited to various techniques of within-the-plant quality control; *Pritchard* seems to anticipate manufacturers' researching an entire genre of products, conducting animal studies or epidemiological tests of the products' users.

When the failure-to-warn argument is advanced in second-wave cases, the argument is rendered problematic by the warning that tobacco companies have provided since 1966 in accordance with the 1965 Federal Cigarette and Advertising Act.

Questions of the preemptive effect of these statutory warnings will be discussed below. However, many second-wave cases, including *Kotler* and *Cipollone*, have involved victims who began their smoking well before 1966, and who hence are able to complain about the manufacturer's failure to warn before this date. By the 1980s almost all states had adopted a doctrine called "strict products liability." Yet even under the strict liability doctrine, the plaintiff who alleges that the product was defective because its warning was inadequate is required by most courts to prove that the hazard in question was known or knowable at the time of the product's original sale.

How, then, have juries responded to failure-to-warn claims? *Pritchard* concerned a plaintiff who had smoked from 1921 to 1953; in 1963, the jury found that the manufacturer had not been negligent in failing to warn.[19] *Kotler* concerned a man who had smoked Pall Malls from the 1940s until sometime well after 1965. In considering, in 1987, a claim that the manufacturer had failed to warn before 1966, the jury returned a verdict in favor of the defense.[20] A pre-1966 failure-to-warn claim was also considered by the jury in *Cipollone*. While the jury rejected the claim that Liggett had been guilty of fraud in concealing the health hazards of smoking, it did find that Liggett had been negligent in failing to warn before 1966, and it likewise found that this failure to warn was a "cause of all or some of Mrs. Cipollone's smoking." In the same verdict, however, the jury also concluded that Mrs. Cipollone, in smoking cigarettes, had "voluntarily and unreasonably encountered a known danger." Moreover, in considering the relative fault of the two parties, the jury apportioned 80 percent of the fault to Mrs. Cipollone and only 20 percent to Liggett for its failure to warn.[21] Under the version of comparative negligence in effect in New Jersey, a faulty victim can secure a recovery from a faulty defendant only if the victim's proportion of fault is less than 50 percent. The jury's allocation of fault in *Cipollone* hence resulted in a ruling that the company should bear no liability for its negligent failure to warn.

The jury's assessment of Mrs. Cipollone's 80 percent fault in the context of her failure-to-warn claim casts light on its otherwise confusing finding that the victim, even though dying of cancer, had sustained zero damages. The trial judge, concluding that comparative negligence is not a defense to express warranty, had excluded any reference to comparative negligence in his express warranty instruction to the jury. Yet the jury, in determining that the victim bore 80 percent of the overall responsibility, evidently believed that this preponderance of responsibility should bar her recovery under any legal theory.[22] In considering her express warranty claim, the jury evidently manipulated its calculation of damages to achieve this desired result.

The evidence in *Cipollone* as to the husband's intervention has been described above. Others in her family also urged her to give up smoking. From 1966 on, she encountered the federally mandated warning on every package of cigarettes she bought. In her deposition she seemed to acknowledge that she continued to smoke because of the pleasure she derived from smoking in many social and personal settings. Even after her cancer diagnosis in 1981, she ignored her doctors' advice and continued to smoke. (Her lawyers defended her behavior in part by claiming that she had become addicted.) The federal appellate court, noting that the company's liability for failure to warn was cut off as of 1966, ruled that for purposes of comparative negligence calculations only the victim's fault before 1966 should have been considered. The court therefore remanded the failure-to-warn claim for a new trial on the comparative negligence issue.

Even with the relevant time period having thus been narrowed, a new jury in *Cipollone* would still have needed to review the victim's beliefs and behavior over a twenty-four-year period. This point highlights why failure-to-warn claims (and also express warranty claims) are far more difficult in cigarette cases than in cases involving more ordinary products like automobiles. The latter can focus on the consumer's purchase of a single product and the extent to which that purchase was in fact affected by the manufacturer's advertisements (or might have been affected had the manufacturer afforded an appropriate warning). Smokers, by contrast, purchase cigarettes day by day (or week by week) over a very long period. Hence there are a huge number of consumer purchases over time that may or may not be influenced by the manufacturer's ads (or warning failures). When the company's alleged tort relates only to a limited portion of the plaintiff's ongoing smoking, difficult causation issues arise as to the relationship between that limited portion and the plaintiff's eventual disease. In *Pritchard*, for example, the plaintiff smoked from 1921 until 1953, yet the advertisements his suit identified primarily appeared in 1934 and the early 1950s. In *Cipollone*, the victim had begun to smoke in 1942, yet the jury evidently found that the defendant's warning failure did not begin until 1954.

Perhaps seeking to escape the complications that ensue in a case-by-case factual analysis, the plaintiff in *Cipollone* urged the jury to consider a broad and innovative argument, one suggesting something like an industry-wide failure-to-warn. According to this argument, the industry had mounted a "sophisticated conspiracy organized to . . . undermine and neutralize information coming from the . . . medical community and . . . to confuse . . . the consuming public in an effort to encourage existing smokers to continue and new persons to commence smoking." In finding this evidence sufficient to be considered by the jury, the trial judge referred to the industry's Council for Tobacco Research, set up ostensibly to search for the truth about smoking hazards, but in fact "a hoax created for public relations purposes." The court also pointed out that the industry spends "$250,000 . . . per hour 24 hours a day, 7 days a week, 365 days a year on cigarette advertising," which creates "a consistent message of purity, health, safety, reduced tars and nicotine, etc." In a technical sense, the judge ruled merely that the evidence on conspiracy was sufficient to justify submitting the issue to the jury. The rhetoric of the judge's opinion, however, made clear the judge's own view that such a conspiracy did exist: a conspiracy that he referred to as "vast in its scope, devious in its purpose, and devastating in its results."[23] If, however, the plaintiff's evidence was successful in radicalizing the judge, it was ineffective in motivating the jury. The jury's verdict included a finding that denied the existence of a tobacco-company conspiracy.[24]

Implied Warranty

The doctrine of express warranty has been discussed above. Traditional warranty law also includes an implied warranty doctrine. By the early twentieth century, most courts recognized that an implied warranty of fitness running from the product seller (usually the retailer) accompanied ordinary consumer sales. By the 1950s, many courts were beginning to affirm an implied warranty running directly from the manufacturer to the consumer. This manufacturer warranty, first endorsed in cases involving food products, was then extended to other products intended for internal human consumption. In the first-wave cases, courts did rule that cigarette manufacturers were subject to implied warranty obligations, thereby confirming this broader coverage of the implied warranty doctrine.

What is it, however, that an implied warranty covers? Sometimes it is said that implied warranty means that a product is free of "defects." This explanation, however, does not promise obvious help to plaintiffs with cigarette-induced diseases. For there rarely are defects or flaws in individual cigarettes; and it is not easy for plaintiffs to identify defects in the design of a particular brand of cigarettes. Often, however, implied warranty is given a more affirmative definition: it means that the product is "fit for ordinary use," "wholesome for human consumption." This definition made implied warranty seem quite promising to plaintiffs in the first wave of cigarette cases. Indeed, the definition seemed admirably to fit the unique circumstance of tobacco. Products like automobiles and alcohol may be highly dangerous, but those dangers usually result from the ways in which those products are abused or negligently handled. Cigarettes, by contrast, are highly dangerous even in the course of altogether "ordinary use."

There is, however, one clear limitation in warranty doctrine that should be noted here. Implied warranty theory is generally concerned with preventing a certain kind of *deception* of the consumer. Accordingly, it is clear that a consumer cannot argue implied warranty if in buying the product he was generally aware of the safety hazard it contains. As it happens, implied warranty is a doctrine that has *not* been invoked by plaintiffs in the second-wave cases. One apparent reason for this is that any implied warranty argument would be undercut by smokers' general awareness by the 1970s and 1980s of many of the hazards of smoking.

Implied warranty held promise, however, in the first-wave cases, involving plaintiffs who had smoked before 1964 and even before 1950. Yet in those cases two uncertainties in implied warranty law needed to be considered. One concerned the manufacturer's knowledge of risk. In a typical implied warranty case (involving, for example, spoiled food), implied warranty entails strict liability, in the sense that the product seller may well be innocently unaware of the problem with the particular product. However, these sellers certainly know that food *can* spoil, and they can likewise foresee that spoiled food can easily lead to instances of food poisoning. Relying on the circumstances in these typical implied warranty cases, cigarette companies advanced the argument that implied warranty should not be extended to product hazards that are entirely "unknowable" at the time of product sale. *Ross v. Philip Morris & Co.* concerned a victim who had smoked from 1930 until being diagnosed with cancer in 1952; *Green*, as noted, concerned a plaintiff who had smoked from 1930 until his cancer in 1956. In both cases, expert witnesses disagreed as to the knowability in the 1950s of the causal connection between cigarettes and cancer. In each case, the jury resolved the dispute in favor of the defendant, finding that (in *Ross*) as late as 1952, and (in *Green*) even as late as 1956, the cancer risks "could not have been anticipated by the use of any determined human skill or foresight."[25]

In light of the development of scientific understanding as described above, these jury findings of unknowability seem quite surprising. In any event, the juries' findings, once entered, required the appellate courts to consider whether un-knowability is indeed a valid limitation on implied warranty liability. The *Ross* court approved this limitation, indicating that it could not see "how the ends of justice could be served by adopting the fiction that the manufacturer of cigarettes was—as early as 1934—in a better position, except in theory, than the consumer to ascertain the now highly-publicized causative relationship between smoking and can-cer . . . ."[26] In *Green*, however, the federal court of appeals decided to "certify" this issue to the Florida Supreme Court.[27] Accepting this certification, the Florida court ruled that the manufacturer's opportunity for knowledge is "wholly irrelevant to [its] liability on the theory of implied warranty. . . ."[28] All that is relevant, the court thought, is that the manufacturer is in a better general position than consumers to know of a product's hazards. The Florida court hence accepted precisely the line of reasoning that the *Ross* court had disparaged as "theoretical."

However, while denying that unknowability serves as an implied warranty de-fense, the Florida court indicated that its opinion did not address certain questions concerning the "scope" of implied warranty in cigarette cases. In most implied warranty cases, the plaintiff is complaining about some deficiency in the individual product or at least the manufacturer's line of products. In cigarette cases, however, plaintiffs were referring to a hazard that seemed inherent in the genre of cigarettes as a product. How does implied warranty apply in cases of this sort? When *Green* returned to federal court, the plaintiff argued that these circumstances were irrele-vant to implied warranty, while the defendant argued that the circumstances should render the implied warranty doctrine entirely inapplicable. The court itself finally compromised, determining that implied warranty can be expressed in terms of whether a product is "reasonably fit and wholesome." This "reasonableness" locu-tion gives the jury a flexible opportunity to give some weight to the magnitude of cigarettes' hazards and to the point that the danger in the defendant's Lucky Strikes was evidently common to all cigarettes. At the close of the ensuing retrial, the jury, after less than two hours' deliberation, unanimously concluded that Lucky Strikes were "reasonably fit" and returned a verdict in favor of the company. On appeal, an eight-to-three majority of the federal court of appeals, sitting *en banc*, concluded that the jury had applied the concept of "reasonable fitness" in an acceptable way.[29] The dissenting judges relied on intervening opinions from the Florida court which they read as strengthening Florida's version of the implied warranty doctrine; and the dissenters vividly expressed their dissatisfaction with the implications of the majority's ruling:

> He who sells for profit a product which caused the dread disease of cancer and also caused the ultimate of all dreads, death itself, can wiggle out of [liability] by convincing a lay jury in a swearing match among super-scientists that such a product may somehow be reasonably safe for personal consumption by the general public.[30]

The scope of implied warranty in cigarette cases had previously been considered by the federal court in *Pritchard*. That court, like the court in *Green*, had concluded that implied warranty should be flexibly explained in terms of whether a product is "reasonably fit." (In the new trial that followed the court's opinion, the plaintiff for some reason declined to advance his implied warranty argument.) In *Pritchard*, a separate opinion by Judge Goodrich suggested that the majority had been too liberal in its implied warranty gloss. The Goodrich opinion looked at ordinary food products such as whiskey (which may "cause several different types of physical harm"), butter, and salted peanuts. "Surely," Judge Goodrich stated, "if the butter and peanuts are pure there is no liability if the cholesterol count rises dangerously."[31] By analogy, he suggested, cigarettes do not violate implied warranty unless the particular package of cigarettes has been in some way adulterated. As will be shown below, the position Goodrich reached was quite similar to the position that the American Law Institute was then working out as it drafted its provisions on products liability for the Restatement of Torts.

Review

The preceding discussion has focused on the results reached in both first- and second-wave cases that have dealt with pre-1960 smoking. These cases involved the doctrines of express warranty, implied warranty, and failure to warn. In these cases, one does *not* detect any systematic bias against plaintiffs by the judiciary. On issues of appellate law, plaintiffs have incurred some defeats. Yet they also have won key victories, including, for example, the rulings in *Pritchard* that manufacturers have a broad testing obligation and can be liable for falsities in their advertisements. On some issues, judges have disagreed: for example, in assessing the unknowability limitation for implied warranty liability. On other issues judges have compromised (see, for example, the courts' "reasonable fitness" gloss on implied warranty, and the *Cipollone* position on the basis-of-the-bargain requirement in express warranty). Indeed, in most cases the courts' rulings of law have been such that the issue of liability has finally been submitted to the jury. Accordingly, the eventual verdicts in favor of defendants have essentially been due to the findings that juries have chosen to render. These findings, moreover, have been "discretionary" in the sense that in each case the evidence and arguments would clearly have permitted the jury to rule in favor of the plaintiff.

It seems fair to say that juries have not seemed angry at tobacco products. In *Green*, for example, the jury denied implied warranty liability by ruling that cigarettes are "reasonably fit"; and in *Lartigue*, *Galbraith*, and *Marsee*, juries rejected liability by finding that tobacco had not caused the diseases about which the victims were complaining.

Nor have juries displayed anger at cigarette manufacturers. In *Green* and *Ross*, the juries found that cigarette companies could not have known of lung-cancer hazards as late as 1953 and 1956. In *Pritchard* and *Kotler*, the juries ruled that cigarette companies had not been negligent in failing to warn smokers prior to 1966; and in *Cipollone*, the jury refused to find that the defendant had fraudulently concealed information from consumers or that the tobacco companies were engaged in a more general conspiracy.

In addition, juries have seemed willing to place responsibility on cigarette smokers for the diseases they incur. In *Pritchard*, the jury withheld express warranty liability by finding that the plaintiff had not relied on the defendant's advertisements and that the plaintiff had also assumed the risk. In *Cipollone*, the jury did find both a negligent failure to warn and the breach of an express warranty, but it added a finding that the plaintiff was herself 80 percent at fault, and therefore should be denied a recovery. A second-wave design defect case that will be discussed below is *Horton v. American Tobacco Co.*, decided by a Mississippi jury in 1990. In this case, the plaintiff's evidence somehow persuaded the jury that the design of cigarettes renders them unreasonably dangerous; the jury hence found that the tobacco company was "liable" for the victim's lung-cancer death. In a manner reminiscent of *Cipollone*, however, the jury then awarded zero damages. As the jury foreman later explained to the press, "We decided both parties were at fault" (Blum 1990). However, the trial judge had instructed the jury that if it found both parties negligent it should apply principles of comparative negligence and award the plaintiff a proportionate recovery.[32]

All these jury rulings were optional, in the sense that contrary rulings were clearly permitted by the evidence. Indeed, in some instances juries have seemingly violated the law in reaching their verdicts. Thus in *Pritchard* the jury went well beyond the evidence in finding that the plaintiff had assumed the risk; in *Cipollone* the jury illicitly applied the comparative negligence defense to an express warranty claim; and in *Horton* the jury neglected the judge's instructions on comparative negligence in finding zero damages. (All three cases raised issues relating to the smoker's own responsibility.) A common observation about the tort system is that juries are prone to resolve doubts in favor of badly injured plaintiffs who are suing corporate defendants. While I accept this generalization as commonly accurate, the counterexample of these tobacco verdicts shows that its validity does have significant limits. Tobacco companies have been able to secure favorable jury verdicts even though they have not taken advantage of a common litigation strategy. When a corporate defendant faces a significant number of tort claims, it often seeks to settle those claims in which the "facts" look good for plaintiffs, so as to avoid any jury verdicts that might send signals to other plaintiffs that the cases can be successful. In the tobacco litigation, however, the companies have perceived a larger reputational advantage in categorically refusing to offer settlements; they therefore have deprived themselves of the flexibility that other corporate defendants enjoy in selecting which cases will finally be heard by juries.

In trying to explain the pattern of jury verdicts, the quality of the parties' lawyering should certainly be given consideration. In some cases—for example, the first-wave *Pritchard* and the second-wave *Galbraith*—the lawyers for plaintiffs performed inadequately in ways that help explain the juries' defense verdicts. However, in other cases—for example, *Cipollone*—the quality of plaintiff's legal effort has plainly been first-rate. In the meantime, the lawyering on the defendant's side has been in almost all instances ambitious and effective. In each case, for example, defendants have filled the record with evidence that supports their side of the case. While this evidence has not been so strong as to lead courts to take factual issues away from juries, the evidence has obviously made it much easier for juries to finally render factual evaluations favoring the companies. Moreover, company lawyers have engaged in extensive efforts to better understand the psychology and thinking of jurors:

> Lawyers stage secret full-dress mock trials to test the reactions of lay people to the industry's legal arguments. Before actual trials, pollsters take the public pulse on issues such as cigarette advertising, information that might be helpful to the lawyers in picking a jury. After trials, interviewers grill jurors for hours in an effort to reconstruct deliberations minute by minute.[33]

Major efforts of this sort are, of course, quite expensive. The companies are in a position to outspend the plaintiffs partly because the companies have very ample financial resources. An additional explanation focuses on the disparity in the stakes that the parties face in any individual case. What a plaintiff's lawyer, operating under a contingent fee, can afford to spend on that case is primarily a function of the size of that case's possible damage award. For the tobacco companies, however, any such award would predictably encourage large numbers of other victims to proceed with suits against the companies. Given these considerations, what the company saves by winning a verdict in any individual case is vastly more than what the individual plaintiff loses. This circumstance helps explain the ability of companies to spend lavishly in defending against liability.

Still, many corporate defendants make elaborate efforts to defend against liability, and still suffer expensive defeats when cases finally get decided by juries. Something more than a differential in lawyering, then, seems necessary to explain the jury verdicts in the tobacco cases. That something seems to be the sense that juries have that the smoker bears personal responsibility for his or her current disease. To be sure, in tort litigation it is common for juries to ignore or downplay risky conduct that the plaintiff has engaged in (for example, his careless use of a power tool that is alleged to have some design flaw). What is unique about the tobacco cases is that the plaintiff's conduct in smoking cigarettes is *consciously* risky; not only that, but it is conduct that is *repeatedly* undertaken by the plaintiff over very long periods of time.

To be sure, the $400,000 verdict in *Cipollone*, although in key respects a disappointment for the plaintiffs' bar, does mark one dent in the industry's previous armor of invulnerability. If in some future case a plaintiff is able to secure an unambiguously favorable jury verdict, that verdict will be important in establishing that cigarette cases are not unwinnable. But it by no means follows that this verdict would be a turning point: that later juries would routinely rule in favor of plaintiffs. Rather, when subsequent cases do go to juries, one should probably expect a continuing pattern of jury skepticism. Indeed, the public's increasing perception of smokers as moral deviants (a perception described in other chapters in this volume) might make future juries even more unwilling to exercise their discretion by ruling in favor of smokers' tort claims.

The most recent evidence of jury attitudes toward the responsibility of both smokers and tobacco companies comes from *Kueper v. R. J. Reynolds*, a suit by a plaintiff dying of lung cancer (who alleged that his addiction prevented him from quitting smoking). Despite a good presentation of evidence by the plaintiff, in January 1993 an Illinois jury ruled against him and aquitted the company.

Strict Products Liability

In the second wave of tobacco cases, plaintiffs have been able to rely on the doctrine of strict products liability, a doctrine that was nurtured by courts during the 1960s and 1970s. As noted, however, even this doctrine requires that the plaintiff identify some defect in the defendant's product. That is, for strict liability purposes, it is not sufficient that the product is highly dangerous; it must be defective as well. In *Roysdon v. R. J. Reynolds Co.*, a 1988 case brought by a plaintiff whose smoking had allegedly caused his vascular disease,[34] the plaintiff argued that a product is automatically defective whenever it foreseeably causes a disease or injury. This argument, however, is unsupported by either legal doctrine or common usage, and it was properly rejected by the federal appellate court. By now, a well-established typology exists for the defect concept: there can be defects in manufacture, defects in design, and defective warnings. It is certainly possible for cigarettes to include manufacturing defects. In one case, for example, a foreign substance in a cigarette caused it to burst into a small fire as the plaintiff was smoking it, singeing his nostrils and mustache.[35] In this case the court affirmed the plaintiff's right to a recovery. But manufacturing defects of this sort are uncommon in cigarettes, and plainly, cigarettes that explode while being smoked are not what the Surgeon General has in mind in declaring that cigarettes are a major public-health hazard. When cigarettes do cause lung cancer or heart disease, it is not because of manufacturing defects. Nor, on first analysis, is there anything obviously defective about the design of cigarettes. Moreover, since 1966 cigarette packages have indeed warned smokers of the hazards of smoking. It is possible, then, that cigarettes provide an effective example of a product that is extraordinarily dangerous yet nevertheless nondefective. Before this assessment is confirmed, however, the concepts of design defect and inadequate warning should be give further consideration.

Design Defect

A doctrine of negligent design was already in the law by 1960; the more recent concept of defective design permits a more aggressive review of a company's design choices. What standards do modern courts rely on in determining defectiveness? Some opinions state that a design is defective if it poses dangers that exceed what ordinary consumers expect. By treating consumer knowledge as the relevant fact, this criterion reflects the implied warranty background of the modern products liability doctrine. The Restatement of Torts, in discussing products that are not defective because they comply with consumer expectations, refers to "ordinary sugar" that may be deadly to diabetics, "good whiskey" that can produce a variety of harms, and "good tobacco," which may likewise be harmful.[36] This language was added to the Restatement during its drafting in 1961, at about the same time that Judge Goodrich was preparing his separate opinion on implied warranty in the

Pritchard case; and as Professor Rabin reports, Goodrich was then the Director of the American Law Institute, which supervises the drafting of the restatements.

This Restatement language obviously provides a strong doctrinal explanation for why litigation dried up in the years after 1965, when the Restatement was published. Plaintiffs declined to sue because the Restatement seemingly declared that their suits would be losers. Indeed, so long as courts continue to rely on the consumer expectations standard as explained by the Restatement, the plaintiff's task of proving design defect in a cigarette case remains very difficult.[37] In *Roysdon*, for example, the court, in denying the plaintiff's design defect claim, pointed out that the plaintiff had not shown that "the defendant's cigarettes present risks greater than those known to be associated with smoking."[38] In this case the plaintiff was suffering from a severe peripheral vascular disease that had resulted in the amputation of his left leg below the knee. According to the court, "whether there was [consumer] knowledge regarding Mr. Roysdon's specific medical problem is irrelevant in the light of the serious nature of the other diseases known [by consumers] to be caused by cigarette smoking."

By the mid-1970s, however, many courts had begun relying on a risk/benefit standard of design defect as either a supplement to or substitute for the consumer expectations test. Under this standard, a design is deemed defective if there is a safer alternative design that seems on balance to be a good idea. The 1953 *Business Week* article had closed by quoting a cigarette company official as stating, "if we are guilty and they find out what causes cancer, we'll remove it from cigarettes" ("Cigarette Scare" 1953, p. 68). If that harmful agent had ever been clearly identified and if it could have been conveniently removed from cigarettes, the failure to remove it could have resulted in findings of design defectiveness.

In second-wave cases such as *Forster v. R. J. Reynolds Tobacco Co.*, plaintiffs have indeed alleged design defect, and courts have generally ruled that plaintiffs can proceed ahead with these allegations. As the Minnesota Supreme Court suggested in *Forster*, however, "it is unclear what plaintiffs have in mind" in making their allegation.[39] The Surgeon General has reported that there are more than four thousand "compounds" in tobacco smoke, and the anticigarette literature frequently alleges that cigarettes include many dangerous additives. In *Horton v. American Tobacco Co.*, the judge issued a pretrial ruling that the plaintiff could proceed with his allegation of inappropriate additives.[40] In this case the plaintiff had secured evidence indicating that the company had sprayed its tobacco with DDVP (dimethyl dichlorovinyl phosphate) before forming the tobacco into cigarettes. The plaintiff's expert, however, was willing to testify only that DDVP was a "possible carcinogen." With evidence this equivocal, the plaintiff chose not to present this argument to the jury.

Cipollone is one case in which the plaintiff did offer evidence of a major design alternative. That evidence showed that in the early 1970s Liggett & Myers had developed (and then decided not to market) a "palladium cigarette." Such a cigarette would add a palladium catalyst and a nitrogen salt to the tobacco. However, the trial judge, while acknowledging the relevance of this evidence to the issue of design defect, ruled that the plaintiff's presentation had failed to satisfy tort law's causation requirement (a requirement that, as noted, is frequently troublesome in toxic tort litigation). First, Mrs. Cipollone's doctor, while testifying that she would definitely have tried a palladium cigarette had it been marketed, acknowledged that he "could not predict" whether she would have liked it and continued to buy it. Secondly, the evidence suggested that smoking palladium cigarettes beginning in 1971 would have reduced Mrs. Cipollone's risk of contracting lung cancer by only about 12 percent; therefore, even if after 1971 she had smoked these cigarettes exclusively, the jury would not have been able to find that her cancer probably would have been avoided.[41]

It should be emphasized that the "design" of cigarettes has changed dramatically since the early 1950s. During the "tar derby" of the late 1950s, almost all cigarettes significantly reduced their nicotine and tar levels, and new brands of filter cigarettes proliferated, offering "low" nicotine and tar. The last fifteen years have seen the introduction of brands with "ultra low" nicotine and tar levels. Consider the smoker, now suffering from lung cancer, who during the last thirty years has smoked only an unfiltered regular brand of cigarette, such as Camels. In the abstract, this smoker might be able to argue that the filtered designs of the low and ultra-low brands suggest something about the defectiveness of the design of Camels. In practice, however, this argument would likely turn out to be self-defeating. For the plaintiff chose to buy Camels, even though the more safely designed brands were available for purchase. The plaintiff would therefore find it difficult to show causation: that he would have continued to smoke Camels had the company redesigned it to comply with ultra-low standards.[42] To make essentially the same point in a somewhat different way, the jury would almost certainly find that the smoker has assumed the risk.

The obvious point is that in designing cigarettes there is a trade-off between consumer safety and consumer pleasure or satisfaction. Consumers smoke in order to secure that satisfaction; interference with satisfaction is therefore a factor that any risk/benefit analysis would need to take seriously into account in considering a plaintiff's design defect claim. For that matter, consumers may be less willing to purchase cigarettes whose taste is inadequate. Kent was one of the first filter cigarettes, in the early 1950s. Its Micronite filter was quite effective in curtailing nicotine and tar. Consumers complained, however, that Kents were like "smoking through a mattress"; eventually, "popular demand forced Kent to loosen up its filter" (Wegman 1966, p. 681). R. J. Reynolds recently test-marketed a so-called "smokeless cigarette": a cigarette-like product that was wholly lacking in tar. (This product eliminates not only the tar risks to smokers, but also the secondhand smoke that can be annoying or harmful to bystanders.) Consumer response proved weak, however, and Reynolds has now dropped the product. I am unaware of any plaintiffs who are currently contending that the option of this smokeless cigarette suggests the design defectiveness of more ordinary cigarettes.

As noted above, Kent's Micronite filter in the mid-1950s contained asbestos; this filter may be the cause of recent instances of mesothelioma. Given the feasibility of alternative designs for filters (and also consumers' unawareness of what may have been the special danger in the Kent filter), claims against Kent by victims of asbestos-induced diseases may prove to be winners.[43] However, the very fea-

tures of feasible alternatives and consumer ignorance that make these claims somewhat promising highlight the lack of promise in the design defect claims brought by
smokers whose diseases are attributable to the tobacco that is in all cigarettes.

Indeed, frustrated in their efforts to identify a design alternative that would
enable them to show a design defect pursuant to the risk/benefit test, plaintiffs in
recent years have attempted to refocus that test in a rather ambitious way. They have
argued that cigarettes constitute a product that, at a generic level, fails the risk/bene-
fit standard. That is, they allege, all the health risks associated with cigarettes
exceed all the benefits for which cigarettes may take credit. For purposes of this
argument, the alternative that cigarette companies should have pursued was that of
not even offering their products for sale. In cases in the early and middle 1980s
involving products other than cigarettes, courts in New Jersey and Louisiana endorsed the idea that manufacturers can be liable for products that are in this sense
"unreasonably dangerous per se."[44] However, such an approach to liability is plainly problematic. For one thing, gathering and weighing evidence on all the benefits
and all the detriments of a particular genre of products would enormously strain the
capacity of any court (and the financial resources of any plaintiff). Second, when
products are generically hazardous, their hazards are likely to be appreciated, at
least in a rough way, by consumers who buy the product. To rule the product
tortious on risk/benefit grounds would be to suggest that the product should not be
marketed at all, and therefore to deprive consumers of the opportunity to make up
their own minds about whether the product is on balance worthwhile. Also, deciding whether to place explicit or implicit bans on products may well be a function
better suited for politically responsible legislatures than for decision making by ad
hoc lay juries.

Acknowledging these problems, most courts (quite properly, in my view) have
declined to endorse a generic risk/benefit liability standard for product cases. The
standard has therefore been unavailable in tobacco cases. In *Hite v. R. J. Reynolds
Tobacco Co.*, for example, a Pennsylvania court ruled that the test is not accepted in
Pennsylvania;[45] and in *Kotler*, a federal court came to the conclusion that the test
has not been authorized by Massachusetts law.[46] Even in New Jersey and Louisiana,
the judicial adoption of the generic risk-benefit test has produced a legislative
backlash. The legislatures in those two states have recently adopted statutes declaring
that products are free of liability if their hazards are appreciated by ordinary consumers.[47] Courts in New Jersey and Louisiana have ruled, however, that these statutes
do not apply retroactively. The courts have therefore allowed plaintiffs who filed
their cases before the statutes were enacted to proceed with their generic arguments.[48] None of these cases has yet come to trial.

Post-1965 Inadequate Warnings

The federal Cigarette and Advertising Act of 1965 went into effect in January 1966.
It required that all cigarette packages contain the mild warning "Caution: Cigarette
Smoking May Be Hazardous To Your Health." In 1970, an amendment to that act
changed this warning to read "Warning: The Surgeon General Has Determined That
Cigarette Smoking is Dangerous To Your Health." In 1972, a consent decree involv-

ing the FTC and the major cigarette companies required the latter to "clearly and conspicuously" display on cigarette advertisements the same warning that appears on cigarette packages. The exact size of such warnings on advertisements was clarified in 1981. The Labeling Act was further amended in 1984 to require that four new specific health warnings be rotated on cigarette packages and advertisements. One of these warnings specifies that "smoking causes lung cancer, heart disease, emphysema, and may complicate pregnancy." A second indicates that "quitting smoking now greatly reduces serious risk to your health." Smokeless tobacco did not operate under any federal warning requirement until 1987. In that year, however, a 1986 federal statute went into effect requiring the rotation of three warnings on smokeless tobacco packages and advertisements.

Obviously, the person who has smoked subsequent to 1966 cannot argue that the tobacco companies have given him *no* warning of the hazards of cigarette smoking. Modern products liability, however, requires the furnishing of a warning that can be deemed "adequate." Under the expanded common law standards, the federally mandated warnings could be regarded as "inadequate" in a variety of ways. As far as substance is concerned, the original 1966 warning employed very tentative language: "may be hazardous . . . ." Even the 1970 warning did not specify the diseases that might be caused by cigarette smoking, nor did it quantify the extent of cigarette risks. And even the current warning makes no mention of the extent to which cigarette smoking can be addictive.[49] Moreover, if the substance of the federal warnings can be criticized, their style—their effectiveness in communication—can be criticized as well. Arguably, the warnings should be larger than they now are, and their graphics should be more vivid. One scholar, for example, has suggested the inclusion of a skull-and-crossbones (Levin 1987).

Yet what about the federal statute? If the defendant complies with a statutory requirement, is a tort jury entitled to rule that the defendant should have done more? Interestingly, American common law tradition has tended to answer this question in the affirmative. That tradition regards safety regulations as typically intending to establish no more than minimum requirements, and it suggests that proposed regulations are often weakened by the political power of those being regulated. (In fact, cigarette company opposition helps explain why addiction is not included in the congressionally mandated warning.)

Yet American law does acknowledge that particular statutes *can* include language that validly "preempts" any further obligations that tort law might seek to impose. Is the Federal Labeling Act preemptive in this way? The Labeling Act, in its 1969 amended form, contains an explicit section on preemption, which specifies that no statement except for the federal warning "shall be required on any cigarette package," nor should state law impose on cigarette advertising any "requirement or prohibition" that goes beyond what is set forth in the federal statute itself.[50] If a state court jury rules that the company's warning is inadequate and that the company should therefore bear liability, does that ruling count as a "requirement"? This is the issue that was recently considered by the Supreme Court in *Cipollone*,[51] and that managed to fracture the Court badly. An opinion for two justices, written by Justice Scalia, would have found all the plaintiff's claims preempted; Justice Blackmun's opinion, speaking for three justices, would have found none of those claims preempted; the plurality opinion, written by Justice Stevens, attempted to achieve a compromise, finding preemption for some claims but not for others. When the Stevens opinion votes in favor of preemption, it joins with the Scalia opinion to create a decisive pro-preemption majority; when the Stevens opinion is opposed to preemption, it joins with the Blackmun opinion to create a dispositive majority. In this odd sense the Stevens plurality opinion speaks for the full Court.

That opinion clearly holds that smokers' claims are barred insofar as they allege that the warnings provided in cigarette ads are incomplete or inadequate. The opinion has commonly been read as further holding that claims of inadequate warnings on cigarette packs are likewise preempted. On this second point, however, the opinion, closely inspected, turns out to be ambiguous; much may depend on whether the package itself can be regarded as part of the "advertising or promotion" of the cigarettes. But the opinion is entirely unambiguous in reaching a third conclusion: that smokers cannot claim that the favorable messages contained in cigarette advertising have improperly diluted or neutralized the warnings on packs or in ads that otherwise would be deemed legally adequate.

Still, according to Justice Stevens, an additional range of claims is not preempted. Smokers are not barred from alleging that company ads have created express warranties; that those ads have contained fraudulent misrepresentations; that companies have intentionally concealed facts in situations in which state law mandates the disclosure of those facts through "channels of communication other than advertising or promotion"; or that companies have conspired to issue fraudulent misrepresentations or intentionally conceal facts in the ways described above.

As both the Scalia and Blackmun opinions point out, the technical legal reasoning relied on by the Stevens plurality is unconvincing and even self-contradictory. Yet there is a core of common sense in the plurality's results. The federal interest in a coherent warning program would be unduly impaired if a jury in Massachusetts could find that the warning should mention addiction while an Oregon jury rules that the warning should include a skull-and-crossbones and a Florida jury concludes that the warning should set forth actual data on the probability of disease. Thus, it was proper for the plurality to rule that providing the Surgeon General's warning essentially satisfies the companies' own obligation to warn. Even so, giving that warning should hardly confer on companies the license to lie or to make false promises.

At an abstract level, then, *Cipollone* comes up with defensible holdings. The problem comes in figuring out what those abstract holdings mean in the real world. In explaining a company's potential liability for intentional concealment, the plurality opinion gives the example of a state law that *both* obligates companies to disclose hazards to a state administrative agency *and* confers on the smoker the right to sue for harms somehow caused by the company's failure to disclose. But the opinion does not suggest that any state actually has a law that fits this pattern. Moreover, it is difficult to identify other ways in which modern tort law obliges manufacturers to provide information through "channels of communication other than advertising" and the warning that accompanies the product itself. Professor

Laurence Tribe, the Cipollone family's appellate advocate, speaks of companies furnishing information through a toll-free telephone number, but no modern tort opinion has ever suggested that manufacturers operate under such an obligation.

As for the concepts of express warranty and fraudulent misrepresentation, their legal meaning is familiar. The problem comes in trying to identify any cigarette advertisements or public representations that could properly be classified under these headings. The Stevens opinion, to illustrate express warranty, hypothesizes an advertisement in which a company "promise[d] to pay a smoker's medical bills if she contracted emphysema. . . ." Yet this hypothetical, while no doubt analytically useful, is unrelated to the reality of actual cigarette company advertisements and promotions. As noted, since 1955, FTC guidelines have tended to prohibit companies from making explicit health claims. What kinds of company ads, then, might be susceptible to criticism? First, advertisements promoting ultra-low brands highlight those brands' nicotine-and-tar numbers. But the publication of nicotine-and-tar data is itself required by the FTC, and the testing is done under FTC specifications. These ads frequently rely on some variation of the theme that "if you're worried about smoking, our brand is the right choice." As such, they can fairly be read as conveying the claim that the particular ultra-low brand is safer than the all-cigarette average. But this claim may well be correct; at the very least, it is not fraudulently false.

A second possibility: companies routinely run ads associating smoking with healthy, glamorous women and healthy, virile men. But the law of express warranty and false representation draws a line between statements of fact and expressions of opinion; and the images contained in such ads probably fall on the "opinion" side of this divide. (Consider, for example, a new car ad showing beautiful women draped around the car; such an ad—though doubtless effective in encouraging sales— hardly counts as an express warranty that the car buyer will have an abundant romantic life.) Furthermore, since 1972, all of these ads have included the Surgeon General's warning—which makes it just about impossible to characterize the ads as warranties or representations of good health.

Again, the tobacco industry, through its supposedly independent Council for Tobacco Research (CFR), has frequently issued public statements that the causal connection between smoking and disease remains unproven. In fact, by now almost all scientists believe that a strong causal link between cigarettes and cancer has been convincingly established. Those scientists nevertheless are led to concede that science has not yet demonstrated what the exact causal mechanism is. Especially in these circumstances, it would be inappropriate for courts to denounce as tortious the merely agnostic position on causation that the industry has publicly adopted.[52]

Moreover, even the smoker whose lawsuit *is* able to identify an express warranty or a willful misrepresentation will then encounter the tort doctrine of causation. Under misrepresentation law, a plaintiff must show that he reasonably relied on the defendant's statement; under the law of express warranty, as clarified by the Court of Appeals in *Cipollone*, the company can defeat liability by showing that the consumer did not actually believe the company's representation. In this regard, keep in mind that the Surgeon General's warning has been on every pack since 1966 and on every advertisement since 1972; moreover, the hazards of smoking have been a frequent topic in social conversations and media presentations. In any lawsuit, the tobacco company, during discovery, would be able to scrutinize the plaintiff's entire career as a smoker, learning of all the instances in which the plaintiff had been exposed to information about cigarette health hazards and counseled by friends or family to cut down on smoking. For that matter, most long-term smokers have been advised by their doctors to discontinue smoking; if the plaintiff has rejected this advice, it will be hard for a jury to find that he would have quit smoking had advertising images been less glamorous or had the tobacco industry formally acknowledged the various dangers of smoking. In *Cipollone*, the defense was able to present the jury with a binder containing more than three hundred newspaper articles on the hazards of smoking that Mrs. Cipollone might well have read. In any later case, the defense will certainly be able to prepare even more extensive binders and to present those binders to the juries. While Mrs. Cipollone died in 1984, these later cases will concern plaintiffs who continued to smoke through the 1980s and into the 1990s, and ordinary American life is increasingly pervaded with signs and signals about the hazards of smoking.[53]

In short, in those suits that *Cipollone* permits, plaintiffs will not have an easy time of proving company misstatements; moreover, plaintiffs will find it difficult to persuade juries that company misbehavior in communications has been the actual cause of their continued smoking. *Kueper*, mentioned above, is the one case that has gone to trial since *Cipollone*; and in January 1993 an Illinois jury rejected all the plaintiff's claims of company fraud. To be sure, suits that focus on companies' irresponsible conduct might turn out to be a public-relations embarrassment for the industry, and influencing public opinion is often a principal function of test-case litigation.

Absolute Liability: A Brief Analysis

A number of commentators have claimed that tobacco companies have somehow achieved an "immunity" from modern products liability, an immunity that the commentators find both curious and unjustified (e.g., Garner 1980). This claim of "immunity," however, misses a key point about modern products liability doctrine. While that doctrine imposes strict liability, it does so only when the underlying product contains a defect. And cigarettes provide an example of products that are highly dangerous yet not obviously defective. Manufacturing defects are not much of a problem; claims of design defect are weak; and claims of warning defects face an uphill fight, given not only the Labeling Act but also the broad media coverage of the hazards of smoking.

Other scholars, while acknowledging the defect requirement in products liability, portray this requirement as having been so broadly defined and administered by the judiciary as to turn products liability into a de facto practice of near absolute liability—that is, a practice rendering the manufacturer liable for almost all harms occasioned by the use of its product (e.g., Priest 1985). In my judgment, this portrayal is as a general matter false (Schwartz 1992). At the very least, the cigarette cases certainly provide one very important setting in which the portrayal is false: one in which plaintiffs have not been able to manipulate the defect concept in any way that would facilitate large numbers of recoveries, let alone anything resembling absolute liability.

It is easy to explain, then, why absolute liability has not prevailed so far in the cigarette cases. Moreover, so long as courts adhere to a meaningful defect requirement, absolute liability will not prevail in the future. However, from the perspective of underlying products liability policy, the option of absolute liability should here be given further consideration. Leading judicial opinions have set forth broad rationales for products liability.[54] These rationales include giving manufacturers incentives for developing safer designs for products; achieving better resource allocation by raising the price of dangerous products and hence reducing their sales; and spreading among all consumers of a product the product-related losses of only a few. Several scholars, relying on these rationales, have recommended that products liability withdraw its defect requirement and impose absolute liability on product manufacturers.[55] This proposal might be thought to have special appeal in the context of cigarettes, since cigarettes, as noted, are products that are capable of causing serious harms even when they are used by consumers in altogether ordinary and proper ways.

In assessing the possibility of a rule of absolute liability as applied to cigarette companies, the attributes of such an application should be pointed out. Consider, first of all, the levels of litigation that would be generated. Currently, about sixty thousand products liability personal injury claims are filed in federal and state courts each year. According to the Surgeon General's report, 434,000 people die each year on account of cigarettes. Even if the number of suits is no more than the number of deaths, the adoption of an absolute liability rule for cigarette manufacturers would clearly increase the products liability litigation rate in a dramatic fashion. To be sure, given a rule of unconditional liability, the issues in many of these suits could be easily resolved. A substantial number of suits, however, would raise issues of causation that could prove quite vexing. What to do, for example, with victims, like Galbraith, whose cause of death may (or may not) be lung cancer? What to do with the heart-disease or bladder-cancer victim whose specific disease may (or may not) be due to smoking? What to do with the victim, like Cipollone, who has smoked several companies' brands of cigarettes in the course of her lifetime? There are many harms—for example, cervical cancer and infant mortality—whose general causal connection with smoking remains somewhat uncertain; what to do with the suit brought by the victim of one of these harms? Recent programs involving black lung, swine-flu vaccine, and children's vaccines demonstrate the capacity of the American legal system to generate high levels of claiming when compensation is made broadly available.

The financial magnitude of absolute liability should also be taken into account. To develop a quite conservative estimate, assume that claims result only from smoker deaths, and assume further that the average award for wrongful death is only $250,000. Given the Surgeon General's estimate of 434,000 fatalities each year, the annual cost of liability for tobacco companies would be about $100 billion. The issue of the incidence of this cost will be considered below. Assume first that the incidence falls on cigarette smokers. Americans purchase about thirty billion packs of cigarettes each year; absolute liability would hence increase the price of a pack by more than $3. Assume now (as will be suggested below) that the incidence of liability, at least for the first years of the new rule's application, would fall on the cigarette companies themselves. If so, then even one full year of absolute liability would apparently wipe out these companies. (In 1990, American tobacco companies achieved net profits of almost $5 billion on sales of $76 billion. When RJR Nabisco went private a few years ago, the implicit value placed on the company by the transaction was in the range of $25–29 billion.) Ironically, the very magnitude of the dangers associated with cigarettes counsels against the adoption of a broad products liability remedy. Classic products liability theory tends to assume that the costs of product-related accidents are in some sense moderate, so that those costs can be distributed among consumers or borne by companies without major market dislocations. But in the context of cigarettes, this assumption proves quite false.

On the question of incidence, one *would* expect companies to pass on to consumers the cost of liability insofar as the cigarettes they now sell will foreseeably lead to future smoker harms (and hence company liability). Yet given how the American tort system typically works, the rule of absolute liability, if adopted, would almost certainly be applied by the judiciary in a largely retroactive way (Schwartz 1983). That is, the rule would govern the claims of smokers who currently are suffering disease yet who began their smoking twenty-five or forty years ago. Indeed, such claims would inevitably preoccupy the legal system for many years after the adoption of such a rule. And the liability cost entailed by these claims would remain with the companies. A company cannot retroactively adjust the price at which earlier cigarettes were sold, and no company would add a huge surcharge to the price of its *current* cigarettes to take into account the liabilities accruing on account of *past* cigarette sales. (Among other things, if cigarette companies tried to implement such surcharges, new producers, uninhibited by past liabilities, would come in, offer cigarettes at unsurcharged prices, and effectively take over the market.) In these retroactive applications, absolute liability would be futile in achieving its goals of spreading losses across all consumers, allocating resources, and improving product safety: the choices rendered in the past by manufacturers (and consumers) cannot be influenced by the incentives afforded by a liability rule adopted in the present.

Consider, then, absolute liability insofar as it might be prospectively applied. The products liability rationales that can be invoked to support absolute liability tend to rest on a key assumption: that consumers are unaware of the hazards in the products they buy. (If consumers do know of these hazards, then the market, unsupplemented by liability, can do a reasonably good job in furnishing safety incentives and providing proper resource allocation; moreover, consumers can begin to make their own arrangements for insuring themselves against the possibility of serious loss.) In the context of cigarettes, however, any assumption that current consumers are completely ignorant is obviously inaccurate. Whether or not consumers by now have *full* knowledge of cigarette hazards, they clearly have acquired *considerable* knowledge. Indeed, that knowledge, operating through the market, has over time been considerably effective in achieving the results associated with absolute liability. On a per-capita basis cigarette sales have declined sharply, and cigarette nicotine-and-tar levels are now much lower than they used to be.

To be sure, substantial knowledge is not equal to complete knowledge, and the phenomenon of addiction can make it difficult for consumers to act rationally on the basis of whatever knowledge they do possess. To highlight these points, consider finally the application of the absolute liability rule to teenagers who naively now begin to smoke, who may in the future be discouraged by addiction from quitting, and who may then in the more distant future become afflicted with disease.[55] Even in these applications, the absolute liability proposal does not prompt enthusiasm. For one thing, addiction is hardly an absolute. (For every American who currently smokes there is another American who has given up smoking.) Society has an interest in encouraging smokers to quit; and offering the smoker a guarantee of full compensation should his smoking result in disease would be an odd way to promote that interest. For another, whatever the safety advantages of absolute liability in other product contexts, it simply does not seem realistic to believe that absolute liability would lead to significant future improvements in the safe design of cigarettes; ultra low is probably the best the industry can do. Furthermore, the problem of brand-switching would make it difficult for tort law to aptly minimize the liability of the company that does develop a better design. (Take the long-term smoker who several years before the onset of his disease had switched from regular cigarettes to an ultra-low brand. How could a court calculate the percentage of the ultra-low company's liability?) To be sure, absolute liability, by confronting the smoker with a price increase reflecting the hazards of smoking, would significantly reduce the demand for cigarettes; however, this result could also be achieved by a proper recalculation of the excise tax on cigarettes. Finally, even in the best of circumstances tort law is an awkward instrument for the delivery of compensation to accident victims. In the context of cigarette liability, this awkwardness would be magnified not only by all the causation problems discussed above but also by all the other implications of an interval of thirty to fifty years between the time that the teenager begins purchasing cigarettes and the time that the diagnosis of disease leads him to file his claim. How, for example, can a tobacco company, seeking to set aside adequate reserves, predict now what diseases will be treatable and indeed curable fifty years hence? And what happens to the potential liability of the company that goes out of business fifteen years after the rule of absolute liability is adopted?

Conclusion

The harms occasioned by cigarette smoking and other tobacco products raise dramatic issues of public policy. American tort law since 1960 has included a considerable inventory of doctrines, many of which were potentially available to cigarette plaintiffs who sued in the 1960s. These lawsuits ended up in failure, but the explanation of this lies more with the choices rendered by juries rather than with the legal opinions issued by courts. The more recent lawsuits have been able to rely on more contemporary tort doctrines. Yet despite these doctrines' generally abundant scope, they turn out to have no obvious application to cigarettes—products whose hazards (however extreme) are both inherent and reasonably well known by consumers. Moreover, given the features of the smoking problem in the 1990s, it is difficult to see how liability doctrines could be expanded (or the uncertainties in current doctrines resolved) in ways that would contribute to the development of an intelligent public policy. It is unlikely, for example, that a courtroom presentation by a tort plaintiff can succeed in establishing a safer, improved design for cigarettes. The warning mandated by Congress in 1984 is good enough to render uninviting the prospect of lawsuits complaining about that warning's inadequacy. It would be unwise to allow individual juries to make up their minds about whether the entire cigarette industry is a mistake. A rule of absolute liability, to the extent that it is applied retroactively, would be quite futile in achieving its desired results; not only that, but it would quickly wipe out all existing cigarette companies. Absolute liability, applied prospectively, would have the advantage of encouraging potential smokers to more fully consider the dangers of smoking; still, its limitations and disadvantages plainly counsel against its adoption.

Notes

1. 304 F.2d 70, 72 (5th Cir. 1962).
2. 350 F.2d 479, 482 (3rd Cir. 1965).
3. 317 F.2d 19 (5th Cir. 1963).
4. 893 F.2d 541, 576–77 (3rd Cir. 1990), aff'd in part and rev'd in part, 112 S. Ct. 2608 (1992).
5. Here and elsewhere I rely on information provided in the Surgeon General's Report (U.S. DHHS, Surgeon General 1989).
6. 866 F.2d 319, 321 (10th Cir. 1989). See Robinson 1986.
7. While the hazards of secondhand smoke have recently been recognized, it is hard to see, given current doctrine, how these hazards could lead to tort claims against the manufacturers of particular brands of cigarettes. Those hazards do raise issues concerning the liability of employers, other building owners, and private individuals (such as parents) who smoke in the presence of potential victims (such as children). However, these issues are beyond the scope of this chapter.
8. 158 F. Supp. 22, 25 (D. Mass. 1957).
9. 674 F. Supp. 1149, 1155 (E.D. Pa. 1987).
10. 295 F.2d 292, 296–97 (3rd Cir. 1961).
11. 350 F.2d 479, 483 (3rd Cir. 1965).
12. 350 F.2d at 479, 486 (3rd Cir. 1965). Here the court took the defendant's advertisements into account as bearing on whether the plaintiff had assumed the risk. "[I]t is difficult to perceive how the plaintiff, a cabinet-maker with no scientific background, could have been charged with notice or knowledge of a danger, which the defendant, with its professed superior knowledge, extensively advertised did not exist." *Id.*
13. 893 F.2d at 549. Godfrey himself underwent surgery for lung cancer in 1959.
14. 893 F.2d at 551.
15. *Id.*
16. 328 F.2d 3, 12–13 & n.13 (8th Cir. 1964).
17. 926 F.2d 1217, 1232–35 (1st Cir. 1990).
18. 295 F.2d at 300.

19. 350 F.2d at 482.

20. 926 F.2d at 1220.

21. 893 F.2d at 553–54. See Singer 1988. The case also suggests problems tobacco companies face in presenting their arguments. For litigation and public relations reasons, these companies do not want to concede that cigarettes are in fact dangerous; and for public relations reasons, they certainly do not want to argue that consumers behave "unreasonably" in buying cigarettes. In a case like *Cipollone*, then, the company was willing to argue only that the victim had deliberately encountered whatever risks there are in smoking. The company therefore needed the cooperation of the jury in order to fill out all the elements of the affirmative defense.

22. An alternative explanation is that the jury did not believe that Mrs. Cipollone had in fact relied on the company's express warranty, and hence doubted that this warranty was really the "cause" of her cancer. Yet this explanation seems wrong: for if the jury had denied the causal relevance of the express warranty, it would not have awarded Mr. Cipollone $400,000 on account of the express warranty.

23. 683 F. Supp. 1487, 1490–93 (D.N.J. 1988).

24. In a more recent New Jersey case, a trial judge ruled in early February 1992 that the plaintiff had gathered enough evidence of industry fraud to secure discovery of industry documents, despite claims of attorney-client privilege. Haines v. Liggett Group, Inc., 140 F.R.D. 681 (D.N.J. 1992). But an appellate court has since vacated that ruling on account of procedural irregularities. Haines v. Liggett Group, Inc., 975 F.2d 81 (3d Cir. 1992). The district court judge in both *Cipollone* and *Haines* was Lee Sarokin. In both cases he employed strong rhetoric as to the moral irresponsibility of the industry. In *Haines*, the appellate court concluded that this rhetoric had created an "appearance" of bias, and that Sarokin should therefore be removed from the case. At this point, Sarokin chose to withdraw from *Cipollone* as well.

25. Ross v. Phillip Morris & Co., 328 F.2d 3, 8 (8th Cir. 1964); *Green*, 304 F.2d at 72.

26. Ross, 328 F.2d at 8.

27. Tort law in the United States is state law. When a tort plaintiff sues a defendant in federal court, the federal judge is obliged to apply the substantive tort law of the relevant state. If that law is uncertain, one option available to the federal judge is to certify the issue to the relevant state supreme court.

28. 154 So.2d 169, 179 (Fla. 1963). The current balance of scholarly opinion favors a knowability limitation in products cases generally.

29. 409 F.2d 1166 (5th Cir. 1969).

30. Id. at 1167 (Coleman, J., dissenting). The dissenters had originally been in the majority when the case was first heard by a "panel" of the Fifth Circuit. See 391 F.2d 97 (5th Cir. 1968). For over a year, then, the apparent view of the Fifth Circuit was that cigarette companies were fully liable for lung cancers under the implied warranty doctrine.

31. 295 F.2d at 296, 302 (Goodrich, J., concurring in result).

32. The plaintiff, in appealing the jury's verdict, is relying on the apparent discrepancy between the judge's instruction and the jury's reasoning.

33. Gray 1978. This article also describes how tobacco companies, through hardball lawyering tactics, seek to make life as painful as possible for the smoker who begins a lawsuit.

34. 849 F.2d 230, 236 (6th Cir. 1988).

35. Liggett & Myers Tobacco Co. v. De Lape, 109 F.2d 598 (9th Cir. 1940). This case was decided before the era of strict liability. The plaintiff secured a recovery by using the device of *res ipsa loquitur* to establish the company's negligence.

36. Restatement (Second) of Torts, 402A comment i (1965).

37. Each year, eighteen hundred Americans die in fires produced by smoldering ciga-

rettes. In *Lanke v. Futorian Corp.*, 709 P.2d 684 (Okla. 1985), the plaintiff argued that the fire could have been avoided had the design of the defendant's cigarette not included certain chemicals, or if the cigarette had been designed so as to be self-extinguishing. (Self-extinguishing cigarettes are currently being marketed.) In denying liability, the court reasoned that consumers appreciate that cigarettes can cause fires and therefore refused to consider the alternative designs proposed by the plaintiff.

38. 849 F.2d at 236.

39. 437 N.W.2d 655, 661 (Minn. 1989).

40. 5.1 Tobacco Products Liability Reporter 2.1 (1989–90).

41. 683 F. Supp. at 1493–94. Recall that Mrs. Cipollone had begun smoking in 1942. The expert testimony was unclear as to what the lung-cancer risk reduction would be for the person who smoked only palladium cigarettes throughout her lifetime.

42. Indeed, in recent years the company has marketed filtered and ultra-low varieties of Camels as well as the traditional unfiltered Camels.

43. Yet in *Ierardi v. Lorrilard*, the plaintiff was unable to show that Kent was the brand he had smoked. Moreover, several of the *Ierardi* jurors evidently doubted that the amount of asbestos in Kent's filter was significant enough to have been the cause of actual cancers (Geyelin and Lambert 1991).

44. See Halphen v. Johns-Manville Sales Corp., 484 So. 2d 110 (La. 1986); O'Brien v. Mushkin Corp., 94 N.J. 169, 182, 462 A.2d 198 (1983).

45. 478 A.2d 417 (Pa. Super. Ct. 1990).

46. 926 F.2d at 1225–26.

47. Such a statute has also been adopted in California; indeed, the California statute refers specifically to tobacco. The liability-denying effects of the statute have been given a broad interpretation in American Tobacco Co. v. Superior Court, 208 Cal.App.3d 480, 255 Cal. Rptr. 280 (1989).

48. See *Cipollone*, 893 F.2d at 555–78; Gilboy v. American Tobacco Co., 582 So.2d 1263 (La. 1991); Dewey v. R. J. Reynolds Tobacco Co., 121 N.J. 69, 577 A.2d 1239 (1990).

49. See Garner 1980; see also Rogers v. R. J. Reynolds Tobacco Co., 557 N.E.2d 1045, 1055 (Ind. Ct. App. 1990).

50. 15 U.S.C. 1334 (1988 ed.).

51. 112 S. Ct. 2608 (1992).

52. The record in *Cipollone* suggests other possible claims of fraudulent misrepresentations: (1) CTR supposedly set up by companies as an independent effort to ferret out the truth about smoking, may well be a public relations "hoax" designed merely to deflect concerns about cigarettes; (2) CTR may have issued statements referring to nonexistent studies denying a causal relationship between cigarettes and cancer; and (3) CTR may have ghost-written articles appearing in journals like the *National Enquirer* which themselves deny such a causal relationship. See Freedman and Cohen 1993. While none of these claims of fraud is frivolous, none is an obvious winner, and several were rejected, at least in part, by the *Cipollone* jury. Moreover, all would carry with them problems of tort causation of the sort described in the text.

53. The Surgeon General's 1989 report gathers evidence suggesting that significant numbers of consumers are unaware of or underestimate many of the specific risks of smoking (U.S. DHHS, Surgeon General 1989, p. 244). However, recent studies by Kip Viscusi find that the average person in fact overestimates the overall cancer and morbidity risks entailed by long-term smoking (Viscusi 1990; Viscusi 1992). While smokers volunteer lower estimates than nonsmokers, even their estimates are too high. To be sure, our research project has become aware that other social scientists question the adequacy of Viscusi's methodology.

54. See Escola v. Coca-Cola Bottling Co., 24 Cal. 2d 453, 461–63, 150 P.2d 436, 440–41 (1944) (Traynor, J., concurring).

55. For discussion, see Schwartz 1991. The idea of cigarette company absolute liability is

sympathetically considered in Ausness 1988. A compensation plan as an alternative to absolute liability is presented in Ausness 1990.

56. Many states have statutes prohibiting the sale of cigarettes to minors. In *Kyte v. Phillip Morris, Inc.*, 408 Mass. 162, 556 N.E.2d 1025 (1990), a divided Massachusetts court ruled that the plaintiff had not proved that Phillip Morris was engaged in a "civil conspiracy" with the Store 24 convenience-store chain to sell cigarettes to minors in violation of the Massachusetts statute. The plaintiffs were themselves minors who had purchased cigarettes from Store 24; addiction was the injury they claimed to have suffered on account of the illegal sales. A year later, the plaintiffs' direct suit against Store 24 led to a settlement in which the chain agreed to demand proof of age from young would-be cigarette purchasers. See Freedman 1991. This is not really tort law; rather, it is a creative use of private litigation to achieve prospective compliance with a statutory norm.

8

Disparate Treatment of Smokers in Employment and Insurance

Stephen D. Sugarman

This chapter focuses on disparate treatment of smokers and nonsmokers in the overlapping arenas of employment and insurance. The first section identifies public policy justifications for such treatment. The heart of the chapter, section II, considers several objections to disparate treatment. Smokers' rights laws, a new response to disparate treatment, are discussed in section III.

The Case for Disparate Treatment

In recent years, a small, but apparently growing, number of employers, both public and private, have begun openly treating smokers worse than nonsmokers. Some require employees who smoke to make larger contributions to employee benefit plans (such as group health and group life insurance).[1] Some offer financial rewards in their "wellness" programs to nonsmoking employees. Some go so far as to refuse to hire people who smoke off the job. It is much more difficult to identify employers who actually fire existing employees because they smoke, although tough controls on smoking at work may well have the effect of encouraging some smokers to quit their jobs (rather than quit smoking).

In the past two decades, more and more sellers of individual private insurance policies have begun to charge insured smokers higher rates for life insurance, health insurance, and disability insurance, and even occasionally for auto and homeowner's insurance. Although social insurance programs, like Medicare, don't currently disfavor smokers, they might (for example, by demanding larger monthly "premiums"), and some have suggested that they should.

These ideas and practices have gained considerable recent attention (Muchnik-Baku 1992; Stout 1991; Bureau of National Affairs 1990a and 1990b; New York Business Group on Health 1990). It is not yet clear whether disparate treatment of smokers in these ways represents an important trend or merely a modest, and perhaps only temporary, deviation from traditional practice. Especially because of this uncertain future, it is an apt time to explore whether these practices seem well advised or counterproductive.

From the public policy perspective, three basic stances are open to society: to encourage (or require) this differentiation, to discourage (or prohibit) it, or to leave its extent to be determined by private decisionmaking (by the market, so to speak). In fact, government cannot take a completely hands-off policy; in its roles as employer and provider of insurance, government must decide whether or not it will treat smokers and nonsmokers alike.[2] Of course, public policy need not take a common stance with respect to the full range of disparate treatments examined here. For instance, the law might ban the practice of refusing to hire smokers, require private term life insurance to contain nonsmoker discounts, and leave unregulated the pricing of group health insurance to smoking and nonsmoking employees.

Advocates of such disparate treatment are often unclear about what, if anything, government should actually be doing to influence employers and insurers. Moreover, they sometimes misdirect their calls to the insurance industry when their real target should be the employer (in the case of employee group insurance plans, for example).[3] Nor are they always altogether clear about the reasons why they favor disparate treatment (for some illustrative proposals, see ASH 1987b; Somers 1984: Stokes 1983; and Brailey 1980).

Nevertheless, I have identified three different public policy arguments that may be advanced on behalf of disparate treatment:

- One rationale is equity based. It rests first on the factual belief that smokers disproportionately use insurance and employee benefit programs, and second on the moral assertion that, absent disparate treatment of smokers and non-smokers, smoking costs are unfairly "externalized" to nonsmokers (or, in some interpretations, employers) who are forced to "subsidize" smokers. Supporters of this argument typically assume that smoking is, at least in important respects, a voluntary activity[4]—although it is by no means clear that this is a necessary predicate to this argument.
- A second rationale is incentive based. Here, too, smoking is seen as a matter of choice, and the underlying belief is that disparate treatment will cause some smokers to stop smoking (or smoke less) and will cause other people to remain nonsmokers. Paternalism generally lies behind this desire to use incentives to shape conduct: smokers would be better off if they quit or would not relapse after having previously quit. Disparate treatment might also be justified on self-paternalism grounds, however—as pressure that is privately welcomed by many smokers (and former smokers) as a tool to help them quit (or not relapse).[5]
- A third rationale for disparate treatment is that it helps tobacco-control advocates maintain public attention on the risks of smoking. In turn, the more vividly people see that smoking is dangerous, the easier it may be for tobacco-control advocates to secure the adoption of smoking-control policies generally. Disparate treatment may, for example, facilitate the following argument: "Each year about 400,000 Americans die too early from smoking. That's why term life insurance costs smokers up to twice what it costs nonsmokers. But smoking typically starts in childhood. So we need your support now to elimi-

nate cigarette sales from vending machines in all places accessible to minors."
In short, disparate treatment may serve a valuable rhetorical or symbolic
function.

It is critical to understand that private actors may have self-interested reasons for
disparate treatment that are rather different from the public health and antismoking
rationales just offered. For example, insurers may charge different premiums to
smokers and nonsmokers, not because of a belief that uniform premiums are unfair
to nonsmokers, but rather in order to avoid adverse selection and to have available a
competitively priced product. So, too, employers may utilize disparate treatment as
an incentive mechanism, not because they think it would be better for smokers, their
families, and society for them to quit, but because they believe that the more
smoker-employees they have, the more they are burdened with higher health care
costs, greater absenteeism, higher employee turnover, greater difficulties in maintaining smoke-free work places for nonsmokers, and lower employee productivity
in general. Disparate treatment may also be thought to improve the morale of
nonsmokers with consequent benefits to the enterprise. (The extent to which these
beliefs are true is another matter.)

Two implications follow from this insight: First, private adoption of disparate
treatment may in fact have little to do with the clamor for such practices from public
health and antismoking advocates. Second, absent self-interested reasons or legal
requirements, private actors may well be unresponsive to disparate treatment advocacy.[6] This is not to deny that disparate treatment advocacy could have an indirect
impact; for example, it might rile up employees and consumers, forcing employers
and insurers to become responsive.

Qualms About Disparate Treatment

There is, of course, another side to the disparate treatment debate, and it is that side
to which I will devote my main attention here. Perhaps disparate treatment is
inequitable, the symbolism of disparate treatment is all wrong, and the intended
incentive effect will backfire or will simply be inconsequential. These are possible
direct rejections of the tobacco-control campaign's justifications for disparate treatment. Other objections might acknowledge at least some of the force of those
justifications, but counter that disparate treatment has more-than-offsetting social
costs which make it, on balance, undesirable. Indeed, from this side of the argument, it may be socially unacceptable to permit private decisions to discriminate
against smokers for whatever reason (although actually preventing such discrimination may also be difficult).

To be sure, it is not necessarily an all-or-nothing matter; as already noted, some
disparate treatment might be urgent, some intolerable, and some simply innocuous.
It is also important to realize that, although some public-health and antismoking
advocates favor disparate treatment in the realms examined here, not all do; some
strongly oppose such practices, others are largely indifferent.

Privacy

One objection to the disparate treatment of smokers draws upon the value of privacy.[7] The privacy claim rejects interference in people's personal lives by government and others with power. Examined more closely, privacy has several meanings, many of which are potentially relevant here. The thrust of this discussion will not be that disparate treatment of smokers constitutes an *illegal* violation of privacy (although it might be in some circumstances).[8] Rather, I mean to emphasize that the privacy invasions that occur or are threatened by disparate treatment are morally troubling.

Most centrally, privacy concerns the right to be left alone—to be free to do in your home (or in other private places) what you want, including smoke, if that is your wish. This value is broadly protected by court decisions applying the Fourth Amendment's prohibition against unreasonable searches and seizures. As a deterrent to police interference with people's right to be left alone, these decisions exclude from criminal and related proceedings incriminating evidence that has been illegally obtained (e.g., without a search warrant) in violation of the right of privacy of the accused.

These days, few deny that employers ought to be allowed to make the workplace smoke free or to serve only healthy food in the employee cafeteria. It may even be generally acceptable for employers to conduct suitable group-exercise sessions for employees, mimicking media accounts of Japanese business practices. But these behavior regulations all concern the work day. Disadvantaging people with respect to work because they smoke off the job is a different matter, and frightening to many. While, of course, no one is currently imagining police bursting unannounced into smokers' homes, conditioning continued employment on not smoking clearly infringes upon the in-home freedom otherwise enjoyed by smokers. Furthermore, some fear this will lead to the opening of a dangerous Pandora's Box, with the powerful enterprises of this nation having far too much influence over the private lives of ordinary citizens.

Indeed, in the view of some, this is already happening: smoking is but one private behavior that employers and insurers are identifying as the basis for disparate treatment. Those employers who "risk-rate" employee contributions to the firm's group health insurance plan may well require extra payments, not only from those who smoke, but also from those who are overweight and who have high cholesterol counts (both often indicating poor diet and/or inadequate exercise).

The same goes for "wellness" programs. While these programs traditionally include free health screening, dietary advice, and lunchtime exercise classes, some employers have recently added financial payments to employees meeting certain "healthy" criteria. Typically, rewards (say, $10 a month) are paid not only to non-smokers (and those smokers participating in a smoking cessation program), but also, for example, to those who have normal blood pressure (or adopt a regime to lower theirs) and to those who agree regularly to wear auto safety belts.

So, too, those few employers who formally announce that they won't hire people based upon lifestyles that risk poor health may target not only smokers. Those with high cholesterol, excess body fat, and the like have also been explicitly denied jobs for those reasons. (The extent to which employers informally pass over job applicants who display indicators of poor health prospects is a matter about which there is little hard information.)

The picture is roughly the same in the private, individual-insurance realm. Several personal lifestyle factors, including whether the applicant smokes, are typically taken into account in the underwriting process. Life insurers often have special rate tables for smokers and nonsmokers that they do not have for other groups. In term life insurance, for example, published smoker rates are not infrequently at least 50 percent more than those of nonsmokers with substantial differences at all ages.[9] Moreover, some insurers in other lines have routine discount amounts that they offer to nonsmokers (other things being equal), such as 10 percent in health insurance and 25 percent in disability insurance. Although the treatment of those with high blood pressure or excess weight, for example, is usually not quite so standardized, nevertheless, on an individualized basis they may be denied life, health, or disability insurance coverage altogether, or placed in a much higher premium category.[10]

This outlook has been facilitated, I believe, because in our culture, one's health is increasingly viewed more as a matter of choice than chance. With bad health linked to smoking, drinking too much, eating the wrong things, failing to exercise, and engaging in dangerous activities (sexual and other), commentators increasingly tie early death, disability (both permanent and temporary), and the use of health care services to personal lifestyle decisions. Some fear that disparate treatment based on "lifestyle" may spread even further. Consider the privacy implications if employers and insurers next disfavor those who spend their time at home watching too much (or too little) TV or those who don't marry and have children (or who do) on the ground that one group is healthier and/or more productive than the other.

Yet a different notion of privacy involves the protection from intrusion. This sense of the right is invaded, for example, by unauthorized wiretaps, eavesdropping, and "peeping Toms." A key objection here is to unwarranted monitoring of one's conduct. So, too, a policy of disparate treatment of smokers raises an image of non-worktime monitoring: company investigators talking with neighbors about one's conduct and snooping on the weekend to see if one is smoking. Here the privacy interests of nonsmokers are equally at risk.

Thoughtful employers, of course, appreciate employee concerns about their privacy, and employers are also concerned about the cost of monitoring rules that distinguish smokers from nonsmokers. These factors together push some employers to rely exclusively on employee assurances: "I haven't smoked in twelve months." Insurers, too, typically start simply by asking for this sort of representation. If that is all that is required, then the intrusion concerns are minimized. But the danger is that some employees and insureds will make misrepresentations (and secretly smoke); that, of course, undermines the enterprise's objectives. Moreover, if other employees learn about the misrepresentations and nothing is done about them, then the negative morale costs incurred may outweigh any gains the program might have had in the first place. (Insurer representatives I interviewed suggested that perhaps up to 10 percent of insurance applicants misrepresent their nonsmoking status.)

Insurers might put off worrying about fraud until a claim has been made, and when they then find out that the insured lied and was a smoker after all, they may be able to void the contract and deny the insured and/or his heirs the insurance benefit. Indeed, in some jurisdictions the rules are quite harsh on insureds, who may have their insurance contract voided if they lied about their smoking status, even if they end up dying (or becoming sick or disabled) for reasons wholly unrelated to smoking.[11] On the other hand, a subsequent challenge of the insured's smoking status may be barred by the normal two-year incontestability clause in life insurance (or other insurance); and in any case, many insurers are not likely to be content with the hope that they might uncover something later that was concealed from them at the outset. (Employers, even if they could void benefits to secret smokers, may be more reluctant to take advantage of such rights in the employee's time of need.)

In keeping with these conflicting pressures, many employers and insurers who distinguish among smokers and nonsmokers have chosen to use what they consider to be inexpensive and easy-to-administer tests of compliance—such as blood, saliva, and breath tests that check for cigarette use. However, many also consider it privacy-invading to make people give urine or blood, or even saliva or breath, for external appraisal. Analogously, this accounts for one objection to randomized blood testing for the use of illegal drugs.

One fear here is that once a smoking-control regime requires employees and insurance applicants to submit their, say, blood for testing for the presence of nicotine, other things can be detected as well (e.g., whether the person is HIV-positive or has used illegal drugs), and word of that finding might be spread in ways that the employee believes are highly privacy invading. More generally, greater employer and insurer attention to individual health risks from smoking threatens to put everyone's medical records into the hands of more and more people.

In addition, widespread compulsory testing can be seen to violate people's right to bodily integrity. Beyond that, smoking itself, of course, also involves the private use of one's body. The connection between the right to privacy and the control over one's body has been made most importantly in the area of sexual and reproductive freedom. The U.S. Supreme Court's recognition of a woman's constitutional right to an abortion as part of the right to privacy is but the most discussed example of an array of rights that people currently enjoy concerning control over their bodies. Body searches by the police are also restricted by the Fourth Amendment because of this idea. Indeed, this meaning of privacy partly explains the vigorous objection by some motorcyclists to mandatory helmet-wearing laws.

Most employers who have treated their employees differentially in insurance and wellness programs make participation voluntary. They provide discounts or incentive payments for those who choose to join the program and then test "healthy." No one proposes making a smoker take a job reserved for a nonsmoker and forcing him to stop smoking; and no one is required to apply for a life or health insurance policy with a nonsmoking discount. Hence, as a formal matter, those smokers who are eager to protect their ability to smoke outside of work and those smokers and nonsmokers alike who are eager to shield themselves from scrutiny by others can do so. But, of course, they must pay for their privacy. If strong privacy rights really are at stake here, most people would probably have grave doubts about the fairness of making people pay in these ways to protect those rights. Imagine, for example, the furor that would be created if insurers and ordinary employers refused to hire, or imposed higher financial charges on, those who engage in sexual intercourse at home. Or consider the actual furor that has been created by allegations that insurers disfavor gays and those who work in occupations that stereotypically are dispropor- tionately associated with gays—for example, florists, antique dealers, and so on (Stone 1990).

On the other hand, sweeping claims to privacy may go too far. First of all, secrecy is considered, at least in some cases, to be trumped by the public's legiti- mate right to know; our persistent interest in the personal doings of political aspi- rants is a good example. Perhaps even more important, what one party asserts is a personal matter can be seen by other people as having undesirable external effects on them or third parties. The abortion battle is, of course, partly about this; so, too, is the strong push for drug testing of those who perform acutely sensitive jobs, such as airline pilots.

In the smoking context, some see the external effects as equally important: smokers are blamed for imposing burdens on employers, fellow employees and insureds, the health care system, and family members. And, as a possible analogy, no one doubts that it is a matter of public concern when people who get drunk in the privacy of their own homes then go out and run others down with their automobiles (or come into work drunk and cannot perform their jobs). Any response to this argument from the smoker's perspective requires, I think, the introduction of a more general point, to which I now turn.

Individualized Treatment

Another widely shared value in our society is that of individualized fair treatment. Along with this ideal often comes the insistence that judges or other neutral moni- tors should ensure fidelity to it. And from this value arises a second cluster of objections to disparate treatment of smokers.

The clamor for individualized fair treatment is well reflected, with respect to actions taken in the public sector, in the widespread demand since the late 1960s for due process of law: in welfare determinations, school disciplinary proceedings, juvenile courts, driving-license revocations, civil commitments to mental institu- tions, transfers of children from one foster family to another and of nursing home patients from one facility to another, and so on. At the heart of due process is the notion that each person is to be treated individually, on the merits, and with dignity. The goal is accurate application of rules and standards to every case, giving the person being measured an opportunity to be heard and fairly judged.

In a similar vein but outside the constitutional context, individuals have suc- cessfully pressed in recent years for an end to "arbitrary" and rule-of-thumb treat- ment by private actors, as illustrated, for example, by the growth of lawsuits for "wrongful discharge," by attacks on banking and insurance "redlining" (where, in its purest form, service is simply excluded from specific neighborhoods), and by efforts to prevent landlords from simply refusing to rent, say, to families with children.

Individual smokers may make similar objections when they are subject to a firm rule that treats all smokers alike. This is because normally an employer cannot demonstrate that off-work smoking affects how the *individual* employee currently performs on the job, her absentee rate, or her use of health care services—even if the employer may have some data on general tendencies of employees who smoke. The same goes for an insured's judgment about an individual smoker applicant. While many people who smoke will eventually get lung cancer, emphysema, or heart disease as a result, most won't.

This means that, although many smokers would concede that they are at risk of ill health from cigarettes, at the same time they would insist that they are not now ill in the conventional way that term is used. Hence, when they are subjected to disparate treatment, they see themselves as being penalized, not because they cost the company more today or because they have been shown to perform worse at present, but rather because of speculation that they might do so in the future. They may legitimately view themselves as being judged on the basis of statistics and not as individuals. (Feelings of injustice are likely to be greatest if the individual smoker considers herself to be a productive worker, in good health, and so on.)

Our national civil rights laws (starting most significantly with the federal Civil Rights Act of 1964) are, in an important respect, but a special example of the demand for due process in response to perceived impermissible group treatment. At their core (putting aside issues of affirmative action and "quotas"), civil rights laws stand for the proposition that members of legally protected groups must not be treated in terms of an unacceptable stereotype. For example, rather than assuming that women simply cannot be fire fighters, these laws insist that we find out whether any particular female applicant is actually fit for the job. This same drive for individualized treatment explains the age-discrimination laws and the end to mandatory retirement.

In this regard, smokers may be able to invoke disability discrimination laws, such as the Americans with Disabilities Act (ADA) (P.L. 101–336) that was adopted by Congress in 1990 and recently came into effect. This law, and similar state laws protecting the disabled, generally require that a person must have an impairment or handicap before she can invoke it. At first blush it might seem that merely being a smoker would not in itself qualify a person as disabled or handicapped; indeed, as just explained, the smoker's point is that she isn't currently impaired.

However, under the ADA and similar laws, if a prospective employee is rejected because he or she is "regarded as" having a qualifying impairment, he or she may be protected by the statute after all.[12] Suppose, for example, an apparently healthy young person is accepted for a job subject to a preemployment physical exam and that exam uncovers a congenital back problem previously unknown to and not currently bothering the job applicant. If the employer, now fearing this condition may lead to a back injury and high replacement, retraining, or benefit costs, rejects the applicant, this will be illegal (or at least some courts so have held[13]) because the employer is seen as "regarding" the person as having a qualifying impairment when there is nothing about the person which prevents him or her from now performing the job. (Case law, at least in some jurisdictions, has clearly rejected the defense that the employer fears increased costs from hiring this employee.[14])

It is certainly possible that the refusal to hire a smoker would be subject to the same analysis if the employer bases that decision on fears of higher costs in the future from health claims and absenteeism owing to disabling conditions brought about from smoking. The core idea of the ADA, after all, is that disabled people are capable of work (at least where "reasonable accommodations" are made for them) that employers have too quickly assumed they cannot do, and that the disabled are entitled to an individualized appraisal of their ability, not a blanket rejection based on stereotypes. As expanded by the "regarded as" concept, it is just as improper to deny a job to a person with a potentially disabling condition as it is to refuse to hire someone with an actually disability who can still do the job in question. Whether the ADA and similar laws will actually be interpreted to apply to smokers in this way is uncertain; at present there is insufficient case law to say much more as a legal matter.[15] But in many respects the analogy to the job applicant with the congenital back problem is striking.

Even if otherwise within the reach of the ADA, some employer practices are specifically authorized by the act. Key here is specific language that exempts certain insurance pricing practices that have actuarial validity. However, none of the examples about such pricing practices in either the legislative history or the regulations go precisely to the sorts of disparate treatment of smokers addressed in this chapter.[16] Furthermore, it is by no means clear that group health and group life plans that disfavor smokers, to say nothing of wellness plans, would have sufficient data support to qualify as exempt from ADA coverage on actuarial grounds.

Although the individualized treatment ideal remains potent, there are arguments against insisting upon its application to all circumstances. First, many argue that rules of thumb are often fair and efficient and that the demand for individualized treatment properly applies only to the use of arbitrary categories. For example, many would strongly defend some uses of rules of thumb such as insisting that a job applicant have a college degree or have previously been employed in this field of work. Our experience in administrative law teaches that uniform treatment achieved through rule-making proceedings is sometimes superior to individualized adjudication. In public assistance, for example, there may be advantages all the way around in providing all poor people with a standardized grant, rather than empowering a welfare worker to decide whether some individual claimants need more, and others less, for blankets, cooking equipment, bus fare, and the like.

As for determining whether a rule of thumb is arbitrary or not, some argue that, at least in the private sector, market forces themselves generally will serve to police decision making by employers and insurers so as to prevent the use of inefficient rules of thumb. On this view, external monitoring of enterprise decision making (by courts or public agencies, for example) is wasteful and unduly burdensome on business.

Furthermore, a sweeping attack on rules of thumb strikes at the heart of the whole basis for insurance classifications. Insurance, after all, is about risk pooling in the face of uncertainty about the future. If people could be charged only on the basis of their known individual future, it would no longer be insurance. But if insurers were required to go to the other extreme and treat all insureds alike, as though they all had the same predicted future, this would create other problems. If insurers had to charge everyone the same price, the first concern from the insurer's point of view would be that the individual company would be subject to adverse selection (getting too many high-risk and not enough low-risk customers). This is because, although the precise future of individuals may be uncertain, a group of people with certain characteristics is often known to have a greater or lesser chance of incurring the loss that is being insured, and those who are in the higher-risk class may well realize this about themselves. On a "one-price" basis, insurance may become especially attractive to the higher-risk people. Out of fear of attracting too many of the latter customers, companies would be under great pressure to engage in secret ways of doing business that would exclude high-risk applicants anyway (such as not having agents open offices in certain places).

If this strategy were unsuccessful, the concern then becomes that low-risk people would then decide that the insurance is too expensive (because they would be subsidizing the claims made by the high-risk class). If low-risk people began withdrawing from the market, this could create a spiral effect that either drastically reduced, or possibly completely destroyed, the market for the insurance in question; that is, the more the low-risk people drop out, the more money the insurers have to charge those remaining; the more money charged, the more other low-risk insureds will be forced out. These considerations argue strongly against the individualized-treatment norm and in favor of allowing insurers to classify on the basis of actuarially valid rules of thumb.

Nevertheless, in some situations states already legislatively bar certain insurance classifications that might otherwise be actuarially justified, such as establishing life insurance premiums on the basis of race, and, in a few places, pricing auto insurance on the basis of gender. Moreover, even where the relevant insurance classification practices are currently legal, complaints are continually raised about some of them. For example, many motorists detest being charged more for auto insurance not because of their own driving record, but because of a high accident rate in the neighborhood in which they live. (This objection was partly responsible for the passage in California in 1988 of the initiative petition called Proposition 103, which sought to eliminate the use of "territorial rating" in auto insurance.) And many obstetricians are outraged because they are charged more for medical malpractice insurance, not because they have committed medical malpractice in the past, but because others in their specialty have.

These latter objections to statistics-based group treatment may appear to draw their moral force from the idea that a person is being unfairly put in a higher-cost risk pool for reasons that are beyond her control. To deal more generally with the question of who may be fairly thought of as inside or outside of any risk pool, I want to introduce yet a third broad social value—collective responsibility.

Collective Responsibility

Collective responsibility for misfortune has been much emphasized in the past two or three decades. At base here are public judgments that in certain circumstances social intervention is needed so that people will be taken care of and treated alike—which would not be the result were the matter left to be determined privately (and through the market).

The adoption in 1965 of Medicare (perhaps best seen as publicly provided health insurance for the elderly) is an important example of this idea. Simply put, everyone who qualifies for Social Security at age sixty-five is entitled to medical and hospital services funded by the government. Moreover, to the extent that modest individual payments are required in the form of premiums, deductibles, and coinsurance payments, all Medicare participants are treated alike. The current chorus of demands that America adopt some sort of universal national health insurance plan also draws broadly on the idea of a collective duty to provide reasonably equal access to health care for all.

Other recently adopted programs reflecting this ideal include California's fund to compensate victims of the 1989 earthquake, Virginia's and Florida's funds to compensate seriously neurologically disabled newborns, and the congressionally created fund to provide compensation for children injured or killed by the side effects of childhood vaccines.

How critical is the innocence of the claimant to the invocation of collective responsibility ideal? Many health and mortality risks remain largely beyond an individual's control. Some people contract certain diseases or suffer certain accidental injuries despite their best efforts at avoidance. Others are genetically predisposed to suffer (and perhaps die) from particular ailments. Yet insurers and employers have a selfish financial reason to take into account the health and life expectancy of workers and insureds whether or not those with poor prospects can do anything about it.

The collective responsibility value leads many to conclude that it would be unfair to permit differential treatment in employee group health insurance plans, for example, on the basis of factors that are beyond the employee's control. They would find it outrageous, for instance, for an employer to demand higher premiums from employees who have contracted multiple sclerosis (or have been diagnosed as at risk for that disease), and would favor laws that precluded such differential treatment.

Turning to the smoking context, the first issue is whether smoking is really a matter of choice. Is it best understood as a voluntary "lifestyle" (as the earlier discussion in this chapter has implicitly assumed), or is it better seen as an addiction that began in childhood when the young person was too immature to make an informed choice? This is obviously a controversial issue that has not been laid to rest by the Surgeon General's recent report on smoking as an addiction. We know that as many people have quit as continue to smoke; yet we also know that most who smoke have tried to quit and have failed. Once more the parallel with other "indicators" of unhealthy lifestyles is revealing. High blood pressure or obesity may also sometimes be beyond the individual's control.

One possible way for employers to finesse the "choice" issue is to grant favorable treatment both to those who are not smokers and to those who agree to participate in a program designed to help them to quit. In fact, employers who treat smokers disparately seem rather more willing to adopt this stance in wellness programs than in insurance pricing and hiring practices. But even then, for some "hooked" smokers, forcing them to try one more "stop smoking" program may be worse than fruitless.

For supporters of the idea of collective responsibility, differential treatment may even be inappropriate where we are convinced that those seeking equal treatment have chosen to engage in riskier behavior. Consider, for example, our current practices toward those people who through negligence allow themselves to become injured, ill, or killed. Although tort law has traditionally paid considerable attention to the fault of the victim in awarding compensation for losses, carelessness (even knowing carelessness) is generally ignored when it comes to awarding benefits in social security, workers' compensation, and public and private health insurance schemes. Such conduct by the victim could be the occasion for the reduction or denial of benefits in those programs, but it is not. Rather, collective protection in these programs is generally extended even to those who have put themselves in a position to draw disproportionately on the common fund. To be sure, there are extreme situations, generally involving deliberate self-injury, which are treated differently, and such conduct in effect excludes the actor from the community.

Where do smokers fit? Those supporting the idea of collective responsibility are likely to want to set narrow limits on the category of those who may be excluded. Smoking probably would not be put in the same category as acts such as self-maiming and suicide, because the latter typically involve more certain and immediate consequences. Rather, smoking is more apt to be categorized along with dangerous driving. (Of course, people may feel differently about disparate treatment before and after times of need; we may be reluctant to deny care to those who hurt themselves while driving dangerously, but not reluctant to charge dangerous drivers more for auto no-fault insurance.)

Objections to disparate treatment are intensified when a rule of thumb has the effect of singling out for worse treatment a group that has traditionally been subject to what society now considers impermissible discrimination. In this respect, it should be understood how the 1964 Civil Rights Act might possibly be invoked to prevent employers from discriminating against smokers if the consequence would be to disadvantage, say, African-Americans.

Title VII of the 1964 Civil Rights Act protects various groups (including racial and religious minorities and women) from employment discrimination. As the law has developed, two classic sorts of lawsuits may be brought. One is the "disparate treatment" case, where an employer explicitly treats women differently from men, for example. But protected groups may also bring cases under Title VII on what is known as the "disparate impact" theory.[17] Given that smoking may be associated with lower socioeconomic status, and the concentration of blacks in lower-status jobs, a finding of disparate impact is by no means a speculative possibility in firms whose black workers are largely restricted to and largely comprise the blue-collar ranks. Title VII plainly covers differences in employee benefits—not just job access, promotions, and salary levels—although some legal experts detect a reluctance of courts to use the disparate impact theory aggressively in the employee benefit context.

Once the claimants have proved disparate impact, the question becomes whether the employer's practice is justified by business necessity. The phrase "business necessity" is somewhat misleading, because such a "necessity" need not be truly proved in any strict sense. Its precise meaning has not been clarified by the new definition set out in the 1991 amendments to the Civil Rights Act (Congressional

Quarterly 1991; Gewirtz 1991). So how those amendments will be interpreted remains highly uncertain.

Nevertheless, a demonstration that the employer could readily accomplish its goals in a different way would probably serve to discredit a claim that the disparate treatment is a business necessity. For example, if a firm refused to hire smokers in order to provide a smoke-free workplace, and this practice had a disparate impact on blacks, the practice might be struck down on the ground that the employer could simply insist on a smoke-free workplace—a far less restrictive approach.

But suppose the employer practice challenged is that existing employees who smoke are charged more for insurance; no obvious alternative practice is available. Would this practice pass the "business necessity" test after a finding of disparate impact? It is difficult to predict with confidence. In any event, once the disparate impact has been identified it can become a basis for agitation and strife quite apart from its legality.

On the other hand, the call for collective responsibility and uniform treatment clashes with resurgent political emphases on self-reliance. This viewpoint is often heard from conservative quarters in debates on the American welfare system. It seeks to resonate with older American ideals of rugged individualism and personal accountability. Put in the smoking context: if employers and insurers choose to disfavor you because you smoke, that is your problem; nonsmoking workers and insureds should not have to share their more favorable premium rate, wage level, or employee benefit package with you.

In the end, I believe that the pressure for collective responsibility is most powerful when what is at stake is seen as part of the basic social safety net. Compare our attitudes toward health and life insurance. Concerning life insurance, there is relatively little public resistance to underwriting decisions based on an insured's mortality risk, regardless of whether that risk is under the control of the insured. Except for certain socially objectionable classifications (such as race), only actuarial soundness determines the legitimacy of the insurer's risk categories. If a life insurer wants to charge more or even refuse coverage to someone who has a long history of cancer in the family, or who has multiple sclerosis, or who has high blood pressure (even if it can't be controlled through medication, exercise, and diet), or who shows some genetic "defect" in a blood test, that is generally thought to be a legitimate practice—at least so long as there is a statistical basis for the differentiation. Moreover, the market is counted upon to play a useful policing role here: if an insurer arbitrarily sought to either charge some people more or refuse to sell to them without any actuarial basis for the distinction, it would simply lose good business to other carriers. In light of this, it seems difficult to object to nonsmoker discounts.

The central role of life insurance is to provide for the income needs of survivors or the retirement needs of the insured. These are matters of important public concern. Nevertheless, the families of nearly all breadwinners in America are already partially protected through the Social Security system, which provides a basic level of life insurance. On the death of a worker or former worker covered by Social Security, the system pays monthly benefit payments to dependent elderly spouses and to dependent minor children and their surviving caretaker parent. And, of course, Social Security also provides a basic pension for nearly all retirees. Hence, because life insurance today is best viewed as a voluntary add-on to our Social Security insurance base, the pressure to apply the collective responsibility value there is lessened.

By contrast, for most people, health insurance provided through the private sector is not supplementary, but rather is basic. To be sure, the elderly and the poor rely upon publicly funded Medicare and Medicaid for their health care protection. But most of the rest of us depend for our primary protection upon work-based protection. This makes the force of the collective responsibility principle greater, and makes us less willing to defer to market forces even where health insurance is privately provided.

Suppose that all of us were randomly signed up for health insurance with different insurers while we were still in the womb and continued with the same insurer throughout our lives. In that case, there would be no issue about excluding "preexisting conditions" when people buy insurance, and insurers would face no adverse selection problems either. Under this scenario, to charge people more only when it is shown they need or will need the insurance more seems unacceptable. But in the real world some people do acquire health insurance when they already have health problems or known health risks. This is where the moral conflict arises in permitting differential treatment in individual health insurance plans. On the one hand, it is hard to resist the insurers' concerns about adverse selection and preexisting conditions; yet to allow those factors to be taken into account undermines the equal provision of a basic service (and because of that, some states are now considering legislation that would require health insurers to take all comers at uniform rates).

In contrast with individual insurance, group health insurance has traditionally been thought of as the general collective responsibility of those participating. Moreover, reenforcing the community solidarity notion, group health insurance has traditionally not excluded "preexisting conditions" in the way individual health insurance has.

Of late, because of market pressures, the tradition of rating group health insurance according to a geographic community has broken down. As a result, when employers with a fair number of employees fund their health-care plan through insurance today, that insurance is very likely experience rated—that is, it is based upon the claims experience of the employees in that firm (whether better or worse than average).

But the destruction (through experience rating) of the idea of sharing health care burdens across the greater geographic community need not also mean the destruction of the community within the enterprise when a social function of the enterprise is to provide a key element of the basic safety net. And it is within-the-workplace community sharing, after all, that is at stake in proposals to differentiate among employees and would-be employees based upon whether they smoke.

Of course, employer concerns about excess health care costs of smoking employees is only part of a more general concern employers have about rapidly escalating health-care costs. Employers can contain health-care costs in a variety of ways. They can reduce the quality of their health-care plan. They can shift to provider networks that are committed to more carefully managed care. They can try directly to save money and over time reduce utilization though higher deductibles or coin-surance requirements. (Some firms can encourage older employees who are more likely to draw more heavily upon the health plan to retire; but many large firms today are committed to providing continued health care benefits for retirees.)

Finally, they can simply shift more premium costs onto employees. And here some firms might find it advantageous to do so through risk-rating dangerous lifestyles. That way perhaps only some of the employees need face higher costs, and the plan might be presented to the workforce as an incentive scheme designed to reduce the overall health-care bill for everyone. The policy question nonetheless remains whether an employer's wish to adopt this approach should be trumped by the collective-responsibility norm when the employer is the source of the basic health-care service. In this respect it is perhaps noteworthy that I have been able to find no serious discussion of imposing smoker/nonsmoker health insurance differ-entials in countries with national health-care systems. In those countries, if smokers are to be asked to pay more, it is through the tax system.

Of course, smokers in America also pay special state and federal excise taxes which are imposed on the sale of tobacco products. This raises a "macro-fairness" question. Even if smokers do disproportionately use medical services, by dying younger they are also less of a burden on both the Social Security system (Shoven et al. 1989) and presumably the private pension systems of employers who have defined benefit plans (since those plans are structured to favor longer-service em-ployees). And when both these factors and the excise taxes are taken into account, it can be argued that smokers already pay, or perhaps more than pay, their way—that is, assuming the lost productivity of smokers who work fewer years because of their smoking is considered a private loss to them and not a separate cost to the society (Manning et al. 1989; see also Schelling 1986b). From this wider perspective, to make smokers pay more for basic health care may also seem unfair.

Desirable Incentive Effects?

So far, I have considered whether the trio of values—privacy, individual fair treat-ment, and collective responsibility—may lead some to the conclusion that disparate treatment of smokers by insurers and employers is an unfair practice, at least in some contexts. Nevertheless, were disparate treatment actually to change smoking behavior, this benefit might, in the view of some, trump those other concerns.

At $10 a month in lowered insurance premiums or wellness program benefits, it is fair to conclude that few smokers will actually be enticed to quit smoking. Thirty-three cents a day is a modest, although not trivial, addition to the typical smoker's current cost of cigarettes. But coming in the form they do, these wellness and insurance charge differentials are likely to have even less impact than would an equivalent new tax on each pack purchased. This is because the smoker would be aware of the tax (in the form of the higher price) each time he buys the product. By contrast, given administrative realities, the financial disadvantages imposed by insurance and wellness plans are effectively one-time or once-a-year charges. And once the smoking employee decides that it isn't worth, say, $120 in the next year to stop smoking, the marginal burden of continuing to smoke disappears. Moreover, the smoker is not likely to be reminded of his decision regardless of what is printed on his monthly pay stub. It is fair to point out, however, that to the extent that these schemes have little behavioral bite, they primarily amount to a tax on private lifestyle rather than a coercive alteration of private conduct; as such, they may be somewhat less offending of privacy values.

Differential premiums for smokers and nonsmokers in individual life, health, and disability insurance policies are also not likely to have an important impact on smoking behavior. Although the amounts involved may be substantial, especially in term life insurance, the smoking applicant typically won't become eligible for the lower rates for at least one year into the future, and only provided that he immediately quits and continues not to smoke for the full period. It is possible that learning about the premium difference from a life-insurance salesman is the final straw that secures the resolve of a relatively few smokers to quit (although some of those surely would relapse before the year is out). But for most smokers, the decision to quit or not is dominated by other factors; the prospects of lower future insurance premiums is simply too tenuous a reward. Perhaps they just purchase less insurance, or none at all (thereby leaving their dependents at greater risk).

Denying a person a job if she smokes, by contrast, might well have an impact— either forcing her to quit, or forcing her to take an otherwise less-desired job (if available). And if most employers were to adopt this policy, it could well become quite effective in forcing many people to stop smoking. Indeed, it is the very fact that such a policy is potentially so coercive that makes it especially objectionable to those groups such as the American Civil Liberties Union (ACLU) which are eager to protect people's off-work privacy rights.

Smoking-control advocates who favor disparate treatment of smokers in insurance and wellness plans have not seemed willing to take a visible public stance urging employers to refuse to hire smokers. Of course, they realize that some smokers would be unable to quit even if their job depended on it and that others would intensely dislike quitting even if they could. At the same time, smoking-control advocates must appreciate that gaining access to a job is itself considered to be a kind of basic right in our society. The upshot is that, in the smoking context, moderate incentive devices that promise, at best, to affect only those on the verge of stopping (or otherwise starting) smoking may be more acceptable than potentially far more effective behavioral channeling devices that threaten much greater penalties. In the end, I suppose, this is because denying smokers jobs feels too much like outright prohibition, which itself is something that most smoking-control advocates probably would not favor (for adults) even if it could be enforced.

Appropriate or Necessary Symbolism?

With respect to the symbolic or rhetorical function of disparate treatment of smokers, it is by no means clear that this is important in the way it might have been fifteen to twenty-five years ago. Then, when the connection between smoking and higher mortality rates was less widely accepted and more vigorously contested, it was useful for tobacco-control advocates to be able to point to the fact that life insurers were increasingly offering nonsmoker discounts. Having this old industry with its staid and cautious image putting its money behind the proposition that smoking kills was good ammunition for the cause.

Today, however, it is much less clear that this sort of support is needed. Studies now show that nearly everyone believes that smoking is dangerous. Yet, it is disingenuous to point to certain insurance classifications and other disparate treatments of smokers in support of the proposition that smoking is the cause of anything: actuarial soundness and causation are not the same thing.

To take one illustration from a different context, when auto insurers charge young men more than young women, they are not necessarily capturing real gender differences. Rather, gender under age twenty-five may simply be a good proxy for how much overall driving you do or how much driving at night you do. But insurers might find it administratively simpler to use the proxy of gender than to try to tie rates to the underlying explanation. The point here is not that using such proxies is an unacceptable insurance practice in some situations (although young men who drive little may be justly angered by it). It is rather that many people find it inappropriate to rely on correlation for rhetorical purposes that imply (or assert) causation.

Turning to the smoking context, it may also be factually correct that people who smoke are involved in proportionately more auto accidents than those who don't. But probably only a very small portion of that excess accident rate is caused by the smoker attending to her cigarette instead of the road. Rather, being a smoker might, in effect, be a proxy for other factors that are more properly understood to be the underlying causes of higher auto accident rates. That is, there might be a fairly strong correlation between smoking and drinking before driving, or between smoking and having an aggressive and risk-taking personality, and so on (DiFranza et al. 1986; Grout et al. 1983).

As a different example, suppose a correlation study shows that smokers are decidedly more often absent from work than are nonsmokers. This might suffice to support certain employer and insurer practices that differentiate smokers from nonsmokers. But what if, on more careful study, it turns out that what is really being captured by the smoking variable is an employee's socioeconomic status? (For doubts about whether smoking causes greater absenteeism, see Bonilla 1989, and Tollison and Wagner 1988:25). Then to point to the increased absenteeism as a symbol of the dangers of smoking would seem inappropriate.

This same point may apply even to the question of differential health care use by smokers and nonsmokers. A consulting firm studied the utilization of health care benefits by employees of the Control Data Corporation, and its well-publicized report revealed that smokers had higher average claims levels than nonsmokers (Milliman and Robertson 1987). But this study does not appear to have adjusted for several other factors that might differentiate smokers from nonsmokers. For actuarial purposes this may not matter, but for rhetorical purposes it should.

Backlash: Smokers' Rights Legislation

As of mid-1992, about half of the states have passed some form of legislation protecting the rights of smokers in employment (McGrath 1992). A few states have considered and so far rejected such legislation, and others are currently considering enacting smokers' rights laws. The laws being considered and enacted by the states vary widely in the scope of the protection that they offer to smokers. This is a very new phenomenon that could potentially have a sharp impact on the ability of employers to differentiate between smokers and nonsmokers.

The majority of states with legislation protecting the employment rights of smokers have used language similar to that of traditional civil rights laws. They make it illegal for an employer to require as a condition of employment that a person abstain from smoking during nonworking hours, and they prohibit an employer from discriminating with respect to hiring, firing, compensation, terms, conditions, or privileges of employment because an employee smokes during nonworking hours.

Many states with these types of statutes make at least two exceptions for employers. For example, under the laws in South Dakota, New Mexico, and Colorado, employers can place restrictions on smoking during nonworking hours if these restrictions relate to a bona fide occupational requirement and are reasonably and rationally related to the employment activities or if restricting smoking outside the workplace is necessary to avoid a conflict of interest. These exceptions might, for example, permit fire departments and the American Cancer Society to refuse to hire smokers.

On the other hand, some states create much more limited rights for smokers. The Colorado and South Dakota statutes, for example, cover only discrimination in decisions to terminate employees. Virginia prohibits discrimination only against smokers who are state employees. Oregon allows discrimination against smokers when a collective bargaining agreement limits off-duty smoking.

Most of these statutes clearly preclude most employers from refusing to employ smokers, and that is their primary purpose. However, many of these statutes also seek to prevent disparate treatment in insurance and wellness plans. In Title VII litigation, the U.S. Supreme Court has rejected the argument that employers who charge smokers more than nonsmokers for their insurance are requiring only that each employee pay for the risk he or she creates and hence are not "discriminating." The Court's reasoning is that the core point of the antidiscrimination laws is that employers should treat people as individuals and not stereotypically as part of a group.

On the other hand, some smokers' rights laws (for example, South Dakota and New Jersey) do specifically allow employers to make distinctions between employees in the type or cost of health or life insurance provided based on whether the employee is a smoker.

The smokers' rights movement is a recent one. The majority of the legislation in this area has been passed in the last three years. The tobacco industry—not smokers themselves—has in fact been the major proponent of smokers' rights legislation.

Obviously, the industry would also like to diminish the stigma attached to smoking and provide smokers as a group with a rallying point. The other main proponent of smokers' rights legislation is the ACLU, which, as noted above, does not want employers to be able to regulate the legal activities of their employees outside of the workplace.

The primary opponents of the legislation have been public-health and antismoking groups. These groups make the policy argument that smokers should be given incentives to quit, not expansive rights to continue a destructive habit; however, these groups don't seem willing to argue that employers should be enticed or required to refuse to hire smokers. Traditional civil-rights proponents have also sometimes joined the battle against smokers' rights laws. They argue that smokers should not be a protected group, because the right to smoke is not as important as other rights such as freedom of religion, and that elevating smoking to a civil right would diminish the traditional importance of the other protected categories.

Smokers' rights laws have not yet been aimed at insurers. Moreover, although the issue has not yet been resolved, it is possible that attempts by these state smokers' rights laws to control what employers wish to do through their employee benefit plans (i.e., group insurance pricing practices and wellness plan features) will be deemed preempted by federal employee benefit regulation under the law known as ERISA (Employee Retirement Income Security Act of 1974).[18] Were that to come about, the smokers' rights laws would be left with hiring, promotion, and firing decisions as their basic target. This core protection would make it unnecessary in those states for smokers to attack disadvantageous practices in the more indirect ways discussed earlier—relying on disability rights laws and traditional employment discrimination laws.

Conclusion

Important values are at stake in the decision to permit, encourage, or prevent employers and insurers from treating smokers worse than nonsmokers. For their part, opponents of disparate treatment appeal to recognized privacy rights and to the strong norm that people should be judged as individuals rather than as stereotypes. Furthermore, they resist having smokers treated as outcasts, as beyond the circle of those for whom we feel a sense of collective responsibility. I have also expressed doubts about both the public health need for this disparate treatment on symbolic grounds, and the ability of this sort of disparate treatment to significantly change smoking behavior (short of a widespread refusal to hire smokers). Nevertheless, supporters of disparate treatment unquestionably can draw on a certain sense of fairness on behalf of their position: why should nonsmokers subsidize smokers in any respect?

The right policy choice is made more complicated here for several reasons. First, because government itself is the largest employer in America, as well as the provider of all sorts of insurance or insurance-like programs, it is difficult for it to escape taking a stance. Second, private enterprises—both employers and insurers have their own legitimate financial interests at stake, interests we normally permit them to pursue without public interference. Yet these same private enterprises control access to certain basic needs in our society—health insurance and jobs.

In other contexts our society has sharply restricted the ability of those with economic power to use rules of thumb in making decisions about individuals. But those people who are protected ordinarily have an unchangeable status for which they are not responsible (e.g., race, gender, and disability). Are smokers really to be thought of in similar ways? Although smokers are now (perhaps unfairly) despised in many circles (a traditional basis for civil-rights protection), many in the public would more readily classify smokers along with drunk drivers and drug addicts than with the blind, the elderly, and religious minorities in terms of their claims to legal protection. As other chapters in this book explore in more detail, the increasing concentration of poorer and less-educated people in the smoking population has generated more stigma than sympathy. This is perhaps symptomatic of the general decline of liberalism and the growing impatience with self-destructive conduct that have marked the past dozen years.

Given my values, I'd like to see employers tread lightly, giving smokers who can do the work an equal opportunity to be hired. The health insurance pricing problem faced by employers could be happily eliminated if the United States were to join most other modern industrial societies and provide sensible access to health care through a single national program that treated all Americans alike. (I admit that it may be wildly optimistic to expect the United States to adopt such a national health insurance plan in the short run.) With basic health care taken care of by the government scheme, private insurers would sell only supplementary health, life, and disability insurance, which are themselves supplemental to basic public programs like Social Security. In that environment, since insurance serves the function of spreading risk created by individual private conduct, actuarially justified premium differences between smokers and nonsmokers should be allowed. But it would not be seemly for antismoking advocates to make too much of the fact. Furthermore, with a national health insurance scheme, employers would have considerably less interest in offering significant financial rewards to nonsmokers through their wellness plans, and would probably choose to discourage smoking primarily though a combination of the sponsorship of smoking cessation programs and controls on smoking at the workplace.

Public efforts to discourage smoking and make smokers "pay their way," as the public sees it, .would be pursued primarily at the point of smoking itself—by manipulation of the excise tax imposed on the purchase of cigarettes and, perhaps, by advertising and other educational campaigns against smoking. This approach has the virtue of avoiding many of the privacy problems created by disparate treatment by employers and insurers. Moreover, by taxing, in effect, the act of smoking, rather than treating people differently because of predicted individual consequences of smoking, smokers (whether rationally or not) are less likely to feel that they are treated as stereotypes. (Analogously, drivers who object strongly to paying higher auto insurance premiums because they live in areas with higher accident rates are not likely to have the same objection to differential premiums based upon miles driven.)

Those who believe more in the virtue of leaving economic decisions wherever possible to the market and those (often the same people) who have a stronger commitment to personal responsibility and its application to smokers are likely to draw the line somewhat differently. Moreover, I will be quick to admit that telling employers not to refuse jobs to smokers, for example, is not the same as fully achieving that goal, as our experience with civil-rights laws generally makes clear. Nonetheless, in the spirit of tolerance, I think it far better, where the distinction is possible, to aim our public health pressures at smoking, rather than at smokers.

Notes

1. This is a rather new development in the group health field (Schauffler, this volume), and still exceedingly rare in employment-based group life and group disability plans. Arguably, section 79 of the Internal Revenue Code stands in the way of some employers charging differential premiums for smokers and nonsmokers in their life insurance plans. In the regulations implementing that section, the Internal Revenue Service (IRS) has published a premium table in which premiums vary by age. Section 1.79–0 of the regulations then provides that if some employees are charged more and others less than the table amounts (given their ages), those charged less are deemed to receive taxable income equal to the difference between their premiums and the rates in the table. Historically, the main idea behind this provision was to discourage employers from favoring older and typically higher-paid employees by charging all employees the same premiums for life insurance; which practice, of course, would benefit the older employees as a group. Many firms would find, however, that if they adopted nonsmoker differentials, nonsmokers at all ages would be charged less than the table amounts, and smokers more. Thus, on the face of it, the non-smokers would have to give up some of their discount in federal income tax, and the enterprise would be burdened with complicated tax-reporting obligations. Given its history, whether the tax law would actually be interpreted to yield this result is rather uncertain, as was revealed to me in telephone interviews with officials of various insurers and employers. Coors Brewing Company, for example, offers a supplemental group life insurance plan with rates for smokers and nonsmokers on either side of the rates in the IRS's table, but does not treat its nonsmokers as receiving taxable income. Some employers, it turns out, have sufficiently good mortality experience with their workforce that, even with nonsmoker discounts in place, both smokers and nonsmokers would pay less than the tax table amounts; in that case, interestingly enough, the nonsmokers wouldn't owe any additional federal income tax after all. In a recent private ruling, the IRS adopted a creative solution allowing differential premiums without subjecting nonsmokers to tax: it decided that the employer could elect to treat the insurance as two separate policies, thereby avoiding the section 79 problem. Private Ruling 9149033, 1991 PRL Lexis 1964.

2. Some state and local government units formally distinguish between smokers and nonsmokers; the states of Colorado and Kansas, for example, differentially charge for health insurance. Within the federal government, however, despite the leadership role in the tobacco control campaign of individual national leaders and certain federal departments, smokers are not charged more for insurance, given financial incentives to quit, or formally refused employment.

3. Group insurance policies (health, disability, and life) are overwhelmingly provided through employment (American Council on Life Insurance 1990; Bucci 1991), and, generally speaking, what is offered (or provided) to employees is driven by the desires of employers,

not insurers. This is certainly true for employers with a significant number of employees. The matter of whether insurers charge employers more because they employ a disproportionate number of smokers is a different question. First of all, most medium and large employers are effectively experience-rated so that the cost of their plans simply reflects the experience of their own employee base. Hence, if smokers cost the plans disproportionately more, the cost to the employer is more without any special pricing practices by insurers that single out smokers. Second, and even more to the point, even if insurers were to charge employers more based upon the smoking practices of their employees (a practice engaged in by some insurers of firms with few employees), the employers are still free to treat all employees alike, or not, as they wish.

4. A position paper prepared by the antismoking group Action on Smoking and Health (ASH) argues that state insurance laws requiring premiums not to be "discriminatory" actually require smoker/nonsmoker differentials (ASH 1987a). Putting aside whether or not this legal argument is correct (and many would be unconvinced), ASH rests its case on the assumption that smoking is voluntary.

5. For more general discussions of the role of public policy in changing lifestyles, see, e.g., Goodin 1989; Schelling 1986a; Walsh and Gordon 1986; and Wikler 1978.

6. For example, sometimes the important extra health-care costs associated with an employee's health-threatening lifestyle are not likely to occur until well into the future, so that a firm may actually be little concerned about their impact on its health insurance program. Chain-smoking employees in their twenties may illustrate the point; if they continue to smoke, they face greatly elevated risks of lung cancer, emphysema, and so on—but, in the main, not for many years to come.

7. For more general concerns about the connections between loss of privacy and unfavorable treatment in employment, see Nelkin and Tancredi, 1989; Stone 1986.

8. The American Civil Liberties Union (ACLU) has started a national project aimed at employers who, in the ACLU's view, illegally invade people's privacy rights by refusing employment to those with indicators of unhealthy lifestyles outside of work. And the ACLU is involved in several states in litigation against government employers in cases of this broad sort. At least one of these cases involved smoking. Arlene Kurtz v. City of North Miami, Dade County, Florida, Circuit Case No. 91–3165 CA-15 (smoker). Others, for example, involve obesity (Cook v. State of Rhode Island, Dept. of Mental Health, Retardation and Hospitals, 783 F. Supp. 1569 (D.R.I. 1992), and high cholesterol (Maltby and Rosenthal 1991).

9. In permanent life insurance, the premium differentials are smaller because so much of the premium actually goes for the savings/investment feature of the policy rather than for insurance against the pure risk of mortality.

10. Indeed, the National Association of Insurance Commissioners (NAIC) has taken some measures to try to encourage insurers to make these distinctions. And in Delaware, home of the most active commissioner in the NAIC on this topic, special efforts have been made to get health insurers to adopt routine premium increases and decreases based on a variety of health indicators. Under the Delaware scheme, an insurance policy following this pattern can become "certified." See Delaware Insurance Regulation 60, Certificate and Standards for Health Plans or Policies (1989). But so far as I have been able to determine, no insurer has yet applied for "certified" status.

11. Mutual Benefit Life Insurance Company v. JMR Electronics Corp., 848 F.2d 30 (2d Cir. 1988); New York Life Insurance Company v. Johnson, (923 F.2dd 279 (3d Cir. 1991); Old Line Life Insurance Company of American v. Superior Court, 228 Cal. Appl. 3d 855, 279 Cal. Reptr. 80 (1991).

12. See 42 U.S.C.A. 12102(2)(C) and 29 CFR 1630.2(g) and (k).

13. Sterling Transit Co. v. Fair Emp. Practice Comm'n, 121 Cal. App. 3d 791, 195 Cal. Rptr. 548 (1981).

14. See id.

15. Most of the attorneys we interviewed who represent the disabled expressed doubt about whether the ADA or similar state laws would, in the end, cover smokers. The Equal Employment Opportunity Commission (EEOC) regulations implementing the ADA have been issued, but how they will be enforced is unclear, and they do not make completely clear how the "regarded as" idea is supposed to be interpreted.

16. See 42 U.S.C.A. § 12201(c) and 29 CFR § 1630.16(f).

17. See Griggs v. Duke Power Co., 401 U.S. 424 (1971).

18. ERISA's preemption clause is found at 20 U.S.C.A. section 1144. Assuming that smokers aren't already protected against such discrimination by federal law (such as by the Americans with Disabilities Act), state attempts to regulate employee benefit plans on behalf of smokers through state civil rights laws are probably invalid. Shaw v. Delta Air Lines, Inc., 463 U.S. 85 (1983]).

9

Health Insurance Policy and the Politics of Tobacco

Helen Halpin Schauffler

What role should health insurers play in reducing tobacco use in our society? Are the goals of health insurance compatible with public-health objectives for health promotion and disease prevention? This chapter examines three policy options for health insurers to influence tobacco use. The first two policies target the behavior of individual policy holders and reflect the two basic functions of health insurance: the collection of premiums and the payment of claims for covered benefits. To influence tobacco use among their policy holders, health insurers can risk-rate health-insurance premiums based on smoking status, in the form of discounts for nonsmokers or surcharges for smokers, or they can pay or reimburse for smoking-cessation services as covered benefits, such as physician counseling for smoking-cessation, participation in smoking-cessation programs, or use of smoking-cessation aids such as nicotine gum. A third policy option goes beyond these individualistic approaches, relying instead on the power of the health-insurance industry to influence the development of public policy on tobacco.

In reviewing the involvement of health insurers with respect to these policies, I have uncovered several surprising results. First, despite the widespread attention that risk-rating and payment for smoking-cessation have received in the published literature, popular press, and public policy documents, the health-insurance industry has moved very slowly to adopt either of these measures. Risk-rating premiums based on smoking status is limited to a very small segment of the health-insurance market, and only one indemnity health-insurance carrier in the country routinely includes smoking-cessation as a covered benefit. Understanding the health-insurance industry's reluctance to use smoking status in their policies makes the second major finding, that health insurers are actively engaged in lobbying to influence public policy on tobacco, all the more unexpected. Yet I found that behind the scenes the health-insurance industry has been involved in a radical restructuring of political alliances to change the social and structural factors affecting tobacco use.

This analysis of the relationship between health-insurance policy and tobacco use is organized into two parts. First, I explore the political ideologies, underlying causal models, power relationships, and class biases associated with each of the three policy alternatives.[1] Second, for each of the three policy alternatives, I review the history and current status of policy development, including major barriers to implementation, and I draw conclusions regarding the extent to which each policy can be expected to contribute toward achieving the public-health objectives of reduced tobacco use and a smoke-free society.

A Political Framework for Health Insurance Policy and Tobacco

Risk Rating Insurance Premiums: A Libertarian Approach

A policy of risk-rating health-insurance premiums based on smoking status reflects a libertarian political ideology and a set of values that stresses personal responsibility and views health-insurance and medical care as part of the reward system. Under this system, the rewards are distributed based on each individual's effort to earn them (Donabedian 1973). Persons who do not smoke are rewarded with lower health-insurance premiums. While individuals are not prohibited from engaging in lifestyle practices that are harmful to their health, the reward system uses incentives to influence their choices.

A policy of risk-rating insurance premiums based on smoking status also reflects a story of secondary economic harm. Under a libertarian framework, the justification for interfering with individuals' lifestyle choices is not to benefit those individuals, but to prevent harm to others (Mill 1987). This story says that smoking causes indirect or secondary financial harm to others, as the increased costs associated with tobacco-related diseases translate into higher taxes and higher health-insurance costs for nonsmokers. This policy requires that smokers, with full knowledge of the resulting secondary economic harms, must assume responsibility for the costs generated by their willful behavior through higher health-insurance premiums.

In short, proponents of risk-rating health-insurance argue primarily on the basis of equity, suggesting that it is not fair for nonsmokers to have to subsidize the higher health-care costs of smokers. The enemy in this story and the target of the policy is the smoker, with the goal not so much to change future behavior, but rather to punish or reward the status quo.

A policy of risk rating health-insurance premiums based on smoking status not only places the insurer and the smoker in adversarial positions, widening the cleavage between them, but it also divides policy holders into two camps, smokers and nonsmokers, fostering and building on the resentment of one group against the other. The policy creates a climate of conflict and singles smokers out for retribution. For critics, this approach amounts to blaming the victim (Crawford 1977; Stone 1986; Wikler 1987). Smokers are at increased risk of premature morbidity and mortality. In addition to paying for the consequences of their actions in terms of their own health status, they are also held accountable for the economic consequences of their choice to smoke: smokers pay a pound of flesh and a pound of gold.

The effect of a risk-rating policy is to shift the burden of out-of-pocket costs for health-insurance from nonsmokers to smokers. Implementing such a policy requires that the insurance company or employer exercise its authority over the relatively powerless position of the smoking employee or policy holder. Ironically, the way in which the policy is implemented and its objectives may actually decrease the individual liberty of policy holders. In many cases, participation in a risk-rating policy is not voluntary and policy holders are left with no options, other than declining health-insurance coverage, except to pay what is asked.

A policy of risk-rating premiums using smoking status also produces differential class effects. The majority of the beneficiaries of private health-insurance are not smokers, and premium differentials are likely to have little impact on total income of the small percentage of middle- and upper-class beneficiaries who do smoke. The burden of this policy alternative falls most heavily on lower-income or fixed-income smokers, among whom smoking is more common. These smokers not only feel higher premiums more sharply but also are more likely to have the fewest social supports for quitting and the least access to smoking-cessation programs. One further adverse consequence of the practice of risk-rating may be that many of the families and individuals who are identified as high risk will be priced out of the private health-insurance market altogether, contributing to the growing number of people in the United States with no health insurance.

Paying for Smoking Cessation Services: An Egalitarian Approach

A policy of health-insurance coverage for smoking-cessation reflects a more egalitarian political ideology that places health insurance and medical care outside of the reward system (Donabedian 1973). Under this framework, the cost of health insurance is equal for all members of the community, regardless of lifestyle behaviors, and the smoking-cessation benefit is available to all policy holders. Health insurance under an egalitarian value system functions as an entitlement, rather than a reward or penalty. The objectives of policies developed within this political framework are to work toward equality by providing equal opportunities to achieve shared goals.

Under this policy option, the smoker is viewed not as the enemy, but as a victim of tobacco addiction or of immature or uninformed decision making. This is a much softer version of blaming the victim (Crawford 1977; Stone 1986; Wikler 1987). While the individual is seen as responsible for her behavior, it is understood that the consequences were not necessarily fully appreciated or were unforeseen, and certainly were not purposeful. Proponents of this policy argue that teenagers did not understand the consequences of smoking when they made the choice to smoke, that many older smokers did not have information on the harms of smoking when they initiated the habit, and that smokers have no idea how difficult it will be to quit when they start smoking. The target of the policy is not the individual as much as it is the smoking behavior. The individual is viewed as basically good, since she wants to quit—and more than 90 percent of smokers want to quit (U.S. DHEW 1979)—and addiction-causing tobacco and nicotine are identified as the villains.

The goal of health-insurance coverage for smoking-cessation programs is to assist smokers to quit smoking. Insurance coverage for smoking-cessation treatments removes financial barriers to access for the individual smoker. The policy is also targeted at changing the behavior of the public-health community and medical-care providers by giving them an incentive in the form of payment or reimbursement to increase the supply of smoking-cessation programs, making them more available to smokers.

Politically, a policy of payment for smoking-cessation places the insurer and the smoker in an alliance, positioned on the same side of the battlefield in the fight for smoking-cessation. The policy is based on a shared goal of smoking-cessation and a shared understanding of the difficulty of quitting (a majority of smokers have tried to quit one or more times, U.S. DHEW 1979). In fact, in contrast to the libertarian approach, the policy shifts funds to the smoker from the nonsmoker through the reallocation of insurance resources. On the other hand, the policy also allows smokers to retain autonomy over their own behavior, because the benefit is triggered only by the smoker's choice.

Health-insurance coverage for smoking-cessation is most likely to benefit low-income populations where the prevalence of smoking remains highest and financial barriers to smoking-cessation programs are greatest.

Influencing Public Policy on Tobacco: A Structuralist Approach

The third policy alternative of influencing public policy on tobacco rejects the individualistic approaches offered by the first two, and instead uses the power and resources of the health-insurance industry and large self-insured employers to challenge the political and economic institutions that support the production and distribution of tobacco.[2] This policy option reflects what may be called a structuralist's perspective, targeting policy to the interaction between government and industry (Tesh 1988).

The enemies in this story are the tobacco industry and government policy that supports it. From this perspective, the tobacco industry, as well as Congress and the administration, know full well the consequences of protective tobacco policies for pubic health, use of medical-care services, and expenditure of public and private resources. Yet the tobacco industry intends to maintain, if not increase, the use of tobacco products in the United States and abroad by identifying new populations and marketing strategies, and the federal government continues not only to subsidize the production and marketing of tobacco products, but also to shelter them from vigorous consumer health and safety regulation. The federal government has not regulated tobacco commensurate with its knowledge and concern about the public-health implications of tobacco use. The story concludes that the actions of the government and the tobacco industry succeed in meeting their objectives: supporting the financial viability and profitability of a major economic institution—tobacco.

Smokers here are viewed as merely a product of the political, economic, and social structures in which they live, which currently support and encourage the production and use of tobacco products. Smokers are viewed as victims in this story, and they are held relatively blameless. More-widespread smoking cessation is not thought achievable merely by helping or coercing individuals to change their behavior. Rather, significant and real change will require changing the structures that support the continuation of smoking in our society (Iglehart 1986; Lundberg and Knoll 1986; Kottke et al. 1988).

The tobacco industry's financial resources to fight government regulation have been far greater than the public resources available to the antismoking forces to make smoking socially unacceptable. Moreover, politically, the tobacco industry has had the advantage of having highly concentrated interests (Wilson 1980). Cigarettes are manufactured in only three states (North Carolina, Virginia, and Kentucky) by six firms (Friedman 1975). The resources of the antismoking movement have been comparatively diffuse. Thus, the battle has been uneven.

The structuralist approach seeks to redress this imbalance by putting equally concentrated and powerful interests, the health-insurance industry and large employers, on the side of the antismoking forces. Smoking represents an enormous financial risk to the health-insurance industry and an increasing liability for large employers who share heavily in the economic consequences associated with tobacco-related diseases. However, this approach rests on the assumption that it is in their interest to challenge existing government regulations protecting the tobacco industry, and to participate in the social movement against tobacco use.

While the burden of stopping smoking under this approach continues to fall disproportionately on the lower classes, given their higher prevalence of smoking, a policy targeted at influencing the relationship between government and the tobacco industry is more sensitive to class issues, as it does not place the burden of behavior change or financial accountability directly on smokers. Instead, it targets the behavior of institutions to affect the availability and accessibility of, as well as attitudes toward, tobacco products.

Policy Impact and Political Feasibility

More than 75 percent of all people under age sixty-five in the United States have private health insurance provided primarily through employment-based group plans rather than individual policies. Private insurance is offered in many forms, including Blue Cross and Blue Shield plans, commercial insurance, health maintenance organizations (HMOs), preferred provider organizations (PPOs), and, increasingly, health insurance provided directly through an employer who self-insures for employee medical-care costs. Publicly financed health insurance for the poor under Medicaid covers approximately 6 percent of all Americans, and among the elderly, 95 percent are Medicare beneficiaries, with an additional 4.6 percent of older persons having other forms of health insurance (military or private policies). Approximately 85 percent of all Americans have some form of health insurance coverage. Thus, not only can health insurance policy influence the smoking behavior or tobacco use of most Americans, but health insurers and large employers also represent the health-care interests of the majority of the voting public. And yet until very recently both private and public health insurers have largely ignored smoking in the design of their policies and in their political activities.

The first few preliminary scientific studies linking tobacco use to cancer emerged in the 1920s and 1930s (Broders 1920; Lombard and Doering 1928; Pearl 1938), about the same time that private health-insurance plans began to develop in the United States (Starr 1982). However, it was not until the 1980s that public-health officials began to suggest that health insurers should join in the effort to reduce tobacco-related disease. Life-insurance companies began to use smoking status to risk-rate premiums almost immediately following the release of the first Surgeon General's Report on Smoking and Health in 1964 (U.S. DHEW 1964a). The first health-insurance company did not follow suit until 1980. In 1988, the Surgeon General suggested that all health insurers should cover smoking-cessation treatments as part of routine benefits (U.S. DHHS, Surgeon General 1988), and yet three years later only one health insurer in the nation had done so. What explains the growing interest in using health insurance policy to influence tobacco use on the one hand, and the reluctance of the insurance industry to adopt these policies on the other? What explains the apparent rejection of individualistic approaches to tying health insurance to tobacco use, while at the same time the insurance industry is becoming increasingly active in lobbying for antismoking legislation?

Risk Rating Health Insurance Premiums Using Smoking Status

Risk-rating of health-insurance premiums using smoking status has developed as the result of two major trends. First, increasing competition within the private health-insurance market in the United States has pushed insurers to find ways to make their products more attractive to healthy and lower-risk populations, and to decrease the access of unhealthy or high-risk populations. Second, the increasing availability of epidemiological and actuarial data on smoking, which could be used for underwriting purposes, has made it possible for insurers to use smoking status as the basis for differentiating premiums. Each of these trends is reviewed briefly.

Increasing Competition in Health Insurance. Unlike most other industrialized nations, the United States has never adopted a universal health-insurance program for its citizens, and health insurance is not viewed as a social responsibility. Instead, a system of private health-insurance developed, which was eventually supplemented with public insurance for those who were priced out of the market: Medicaid for the very poor, and Medicare for the disabled and elderly. Initially, private health insurers adopted some of the values associated with social insurance programs by spreading risks evenly across members of a community. However, increased competition in the industry ultimately forced most health insurers to differentiate their rates, abandoning risk sharing and opening the door to risk-rated health insurance.

Blue Cross and Blue Shield plans developed initially using a community rating structure, where all group subscribers paid the same rate, reflecting the average cost of health care in the community. Community-rating was intended to make health insurance affordable for all members of the community, for high-risk as well as low-risk groups. To compete with "the Blues," the commercial insurers priced their group health insurance using an experience-rating structure, charging groups differential rates based on their prior medical-care costs. Experience-rating enabled the commercial insurers to offer lower and more competitive rates to healthier groups. For a while, the Blues remained at a competitive advantage because of their non-profit tax-exempt status and their close relationships with hospitals, giving them discounted hospital rates (Starr 1982). However, the increased competition between the Blues and the commercial insurers for the healthier, lower-risk groups ultimately led to the erosion of the practice of community rating in health insurance. By 1960, a majority of Blue Cross and Blue Shield plans were using experience rating for groups (Starr 1982) and by 1990, fewer than one-third still offered community rates. The trend away from community rating to experience rating represents a radical shift in the underlying philosophy of private health insurance in the United States.

As part of this trend, health insurers more recently have begun to move from group experience rating to individual risk rating, using risk factors such as smoking status, as a way to further differentiate expected health-insurance costs, protecting themselves financially from adverse risks, and making their products more attractive to nonsmokers.

Increasing Availability of Epidemiological and Actuarial Data. Risk-rating health insurance based on smoking status depends on the availability of actuarial data differentiating the claims experiences of smokers and nonsmokers. The first Surgeon General's Report on Smoking and Health (U.S. DHEW 1964a) provided the earliest comprehensive epidemiologic data on the effects of smoking on mortality, which was used almost immediately by life-insurance companies in offering premium discounts to nonsmokers (Cowell 1985). This practice has grown to such an extent that by 1987, nearly 80 percent of life-insurance companies were offering smoking discounts on individual life-insurance policies (CCPI 1987).

Before 1980, no health-insurance company in the United States linked tobacco use with health-insurance premiums or benefits (Brailey 1980). In fact, the idea of tying health-insurance policy to tobacco use was not proposed in the professional medical-care literature until the early 1980s (Brailey 1980, Greenwald 1981; Stokes 1983; Somers 1984; Veatch and Steinfels 1984). It was not until 1987 that the first comprehensive data on the impact of smoking on medical-care costs became available. Milliman and Robertson, Inc., an actuarial consulting firm, published data from 1981 through 1984 on health-care utilization and costs by smoking status for Control Data Corporation employees (Milliman and Robertson 1987). This study found that people smoking one or more packs of cigarettes per day have annual medical claims 18 percent higher than those who do not smoke, have 25 percent more hospital days, and are 29 percent more likely to have medical-care expenditures over $5,000 compared with people who do not smoke. The Milliman and Robertson, Inc., report estimated that on average smokers have $10 per month per employee higher claims compared with nonsmokers. A study that estimated the costs of smoking to the Medicare program in an elderly population found that smoking is associated with 16 percent higher Medicare claim costs compared to nonsmokers controlling for other risk factors, demographics, and prior utilization of health care services. The authors estimate that in 1984 and 1985 the increased costs directly associated with smoking in the elderly is $312 per year per Medicare enrollee (95 percent CI, $156, $468) or $26 per month (Schauffler et al. 1993). The availability of these preliminary data may help remove a major barrier to more widespread adoption of premium differentials based on smoking status.

Nonetheless, a great deal of uncertainty remains over how to price health-insurance premiums based on smoking status. At the same time that Milliman and

Robertson released their report, the National Association of Insurance Commissioners (NAIC) compiled health insurance claims data by smoking status from eight commercial insurers and five Blue Cross plans (NAIC 1987). These data showed wide variation in the claims experiences of smokers and nonsmokers. While the claims experience for all Blue Cross and Blue Shield plans justified at least a 19 percent nonsmoker discount, similar to that found for the Control Data employees, the claims experience for half of the commercial insurers did *not* support nonsmoker discounts (NAIC 1987; Pashos 1989). The reasons for the variation are unknown but may be the result of misrepresentation of smoking status by policy holders, the classification of former smokers as nonsmokers, or failure to control for the presence of other known risk factors such as elevated blood pressure, cholesterol, relative weight, and other lifestyle risks, which might overwhelm the effects of smoking. The data suggest that while considerable progress has been made in documenting the claims experiences of smokers and nonsmokers, a great deal more work is needed to develop actuarially sound differentials for health insurance.

Policy Adoption Among Private Insurance Carriers. The practice of using smoking status as the basis for risk-rating premiums for *individual* health insurance policies has grown rapidly among private health insurance companies over the past ten years. A 1987 NAIC survey of 603 insurance companies offering health insurance in the state of Illinois and all Blue Cross/Blue Shield plans in the United States found that 14 percent of commercial health insurers and 16 percent of the Blue Cross/Blue Shield plans offered individual policies with either discounts for nonsmokers or surcharges for smokers (NAIC 1987). A 1991 survey of 280 insurance companies licensed to sell health insurance in the state of California indicates much more widespread adoption of these policies by commercial insurers over the past four years. Of the 54 percent of companies responding to the survey, 35 percent of the companies who write health insurance indicated that they have sold individual policies with a rating structure that utilizes smoking status—that is, either nonsmoker discounts or smoker surcharges (Schauffler and Gentry 1993).

However, one critically important feature of private health insurance as it has developed has prevented widespread adoption of individual risk rating. Most health insurance is sold and priced differently than other forms of insurance, such as auto or life insurance, which are sold primarily to individual policy holders with premiums actuarially based on an individual's past experiences or characteristics. In sharp contrast, only 20 percent of private health insurance is sold as individual (or family) policies. Most Americans get their health insurance through an employer or other large group, and individual characteristics traditionally have not been used to set health-insurance premiums within groups.

Nevertheless, private health insurance companies have also begun to experiment with nonsmoker discounts for *group* policies. For example, King County Medical Blue Shield of Washington State offers discounts to employer groups that have prohibited smoking in indoor work areas and where 90 percent of the employees have been nonsmokers for at least a year (Wright 1991). Groups must file a certificate stating that they qualify for the discount, and for small groups with fewer than twenty-five employees, each nonsmoking employee must submit a certificate. The stated objectives of this discount program are to attract new, healthy business groups and to encourage employers to make their workplaces smoke-free.

Policy Adoption Among HMOs. Very little is formally known about HMO practices and policies regarding risk-rating based on smoking status. The Group Health Association of America has never surveyed its members with respect to risk-rating practices. In 1981, the federal HMO Act was amended to allow HMOs to move away from straight community rating to become more competitive. The amendments permit HMOs to set their community rates by class (industry, age, sex, and family size). Smoking status was not included in the list of accepted class variables. However, federally qualified HMOs can apply for a waiver from the Health Care Financing Administration to use smoking status as a classification factor in setting rates.

The only HMO to apply for such a waiver has been the Contra Costa Health Plan in California (Washington 1990). The rationale given in requesting the waiver was "to reflect utilization differences and enhance competitiveness with other plans" (Contra Costa Health Plan 1986). The request was prepared by Milliman and Robertson, Inc. (1987), the consulting actuaries who published the employer data on the health care costs attributable to smoking. The waiver requested a 5 percent discount for nonsmoking and a 9 percent surcharge for smoking. The nonsmoker/smoker differential is applied only to policies written to small employer groups and is based on the proportion of smokers and nonsmokers in each group. But just because an HMO charges an employer less because it has a disproportionately high nonsmoking workforce does not mean that individual employee contributions, if any, are based on smoking status.

Risk-rating has also been applied to HMO enrollees who have individual or family policies. Group Health Cooperative of Puget Sound has instituted a premium discount program for individual and family enrollees called Healthpays (New York Business Group on Health, Inc. 1990). Discounts under this plan are available only to individuals who meet seven low-risk criteria, one of which is nonsmoking status.[3]

Policy Adoption at the State and Federal Levels. There has been very little movement to regulate the use of risk-rated premiums at the state level using smoking status (Levinson 1990). In 1984, NAIC (NAIC 1985) adopted a model regulation, referred to as the "wellness" regulation, that if adopted by a state would require that all health-insurance policies written in the state provide economic incentives to insureds to practice healthy lifestyles, including smoking cessation.

While no state has adopted the NAIC wellness regulation, two states, Colorado beginning in 1987 and Kansas beginning in 1988, are risk-rating health insurance for employees of state government using smoking status. These two states use very different approaches in implementing their policies. In Colorado, state employees get a discount of $6 per month if neither the employee nor her dependents have used tobacco products in the last year (Pashos 1989; Penner 1989). Participation in the Colorado program is voluntary and only a small proportion of those thought to be eligible for the discounts have applied.

Using the threat of penalty instead of the promise of reward, Kansas state employees who smoke must pay a $10 per month surcharge. Participation in the

Kansas program is mandatory, and the only way to avoid the surcharge is for employees to certify in writing that they do not use any tobacco products (New York Business Group on Health 1990). The proportion of state employees required to pay the surcharge is equivalent to the proportion of smokers in the state of Kansas. However, when surveyed, 42 percent of Kansas state employees responded that they thought such a policy was unfair, and following the implementation of the policy, the state saw an increase in the number of employees who chose not to be covered by health insurance (Penner 1990).

At present, none of the federally financed health insurance programs (Medicaid or Medicare) risk-rate beneficiary contributions based on smoking status. Two bills sponsored by Senator Durenburger in 1985 (S357 and S358) proposed to offer a small nonsmokers discount on premiums for Part B of Medicare, which pays for physician services for elderly and disabled beneficiaries. Neither of the proposed bills ever got reported out of committee.

Policy Adoption Among Employers. One trend in health insurance that has the potential to extend the use of risk-rated health insurance to a majority of the population is self-funded employer health-insurance plans. In response to rising health-care costs, many large employers, who have been the major purchasers of private health insurance, have begun to self-insure, assuming the risk for their employees' medical-care expenses. Recent estimates suggest that more than half of these firms now self-insure (Rublee 1986). Corporations that self-insure are at direct financial risk for employee health-care costs, and thus may have an incentive to adopt risk-rating of health-insurance premiums based on smoking. As employers take on the role of insurer, they may look to risk-rating as a way to shift the increasing costs of health insurance onto high-risk employees, rewarding low-risk employees with lower health-insurance premiums.

However, a recent survey of 280 large employers (more than five hundred employees) in the state of California suggests that the practice of risk-rating employee contributions to health insurance has not been widely adopted (Schauffler 1993a). Of the 66 percent of companies responding to the employer survey, only 2 percent indicated that they offer employees health-insurance policies with a rating structure that utilizes smoking status for nonsmoker discounts or smoker surcharges. (In all cases, risk-rating using smoking was done only by self-insured employers for their indemnity health-insurance plans.) In fact, only 9 percent of corporations had ever considered the idea of using smoking status to risk-rate health insurance, and more than three times as many corporations who had considered risk-rating using smoking status had rejected it as had adopted it (Schauffler 1993a).

Conflict in Values. Experience to date suggests that a conflict remains in the underlying values associated with group health insurance and the practice of risk-rating premiums. Warner and Murt (1984) make this point succinctly when they state that "risk rating is the antithesis of risk sharing." The conflict is fundamentally over an ethic of community, security, and social responsibility on the one hand, and goals of efficiency, economic equity, and individual responsibility on the other. The practice of risk-rating insurance based on smoking status has not been adopted by most large employers, who view health insurance as a valued employee benefit. It has not been adopted by state and federal health insurance programs for the poor, elderly, and disabled, for whom health insurance is an entitlement, designed to protect them financially, fulfilling their basic need as members of our society for access to health care.

Potential Policy Impact. Can we expect premium differentials based on smoking to alter tobacco use? There are no data available to suggest that health-insurance premium differentials of $10 per month (the current industry average) are large enough to motivate a change in smoking behavior (Greenwald 1981; Warner and Murt 1984). In fact, if $10 per month were enough of a financial incentive to induce smoking cessation, then the cost of purchasing cigarettes alone for a one-pack-a-day smoker would serve as an even greater financial incentive to quit. Evaluating the impact of a premium differential in terms of its marginal impact on income also suggests that it is not significant enough to effect behavioral change. Even for a smoker earning minimum wage, $10 per month is only slightly more than 1 percent of monthly income.

Some policy analysts have tried to equate the effect of premium differentials with an equivalent cigarette tax (Penner 1989). The $10 per month premium would be the equivalent of a 16¢ tax per pack for a two-pack-a-day smoker. (Penner 1989). Warner estimates that a 16¢ per pack increase in the tax on cigarettes would induce 4 percent of smokers to quit (Warner and Murt 1984) However, it is difficult, if not misleading, to extrapolate from the effect of one policy to the other. The tax is tied directly to the purchase of tobacco products and is experienced every time tobacco is purchased. The premium differential is linked to tobacco use, not the purchase of tobacco products. It occurs only monthly, and it is implemented automatically without much reminder or notice, as the premium is deducted from the paycheck before the employee ever sees it. In addition, the smoker can reduce the effect of the tax by cutting back on the number cigarettes. In contrast, the premium differential is an all-or-nothing proposition. The only way to reduce a surcharge or qualify for a discount is to quit smoking altogether, and most policies require that a policy holder not have smoked for at least twelve months in order to qualify as a nonsmoker. The "reward" is not immediate, and the change in behavior has to be sustained over a long period of time. It is unlikely that an incentive that is so indirectly tied to a behavior and that is received so long after the behavior change can have much effect on the target behavior (Stone 1989).

If a premium differential of $10 per month is not sufficient to change tobacco use significantly, does it make sense to increase the differential substantially beyond what is actuarially justified to where smoking cessation is stimulated for a significant number of smokers? The answer depends on the goal of implementing a risk-rating policy. If the goal is simply one of making smokers pay their fair share of the cost, then a differential premium set above the actuarial value would not be justified. But if the goal is to induce substantial smoking cessation through premium differentials, then it might be necessary to create much larger differentials than indicated actuarially.

However, increasing the premium differential beyond its actuarial value raises new questions of equity, this time for smokers. The tables would be turned completely. Instead of nonsmokers subsidizing smokers, a risk-rating policy whose objective is smoking cessation will most likely create inequities such that smokers subsidize health insurance for nonsmokers.

Recent analyses of the equity issue concerning whether or not smokers pay their way relative to the costs they inflict on society suggest that smokers may already be paying more than their fair share (Manning et al. 1989; Schelling 1986b). While nonsmokers subsidize smokers' group health and life insurance, smokers subsidize retirement benefits and long-term nursing-home care for nonsmokers. Manning et al. (1989) conclude from their economic analysis that, taking into account these cross-subsidizations and the present level of excise tax on cigarettes, smokers currently subsidize nonsmokers, rather than the other way around. Schelling (1986b) in his economic analysis concludes that smokers who die fifteen years early are a net financial benefit to society, as they pay taxes through their productive years and never cash in on their retirement benefits. Leu and Schaub (1983) conclude from their projections of health-care costs for smokers and nonsmokers that the health-care costs of smokers and nonsmokers are comparable over a lifetime, with the difference being that the costs for smokers occur earlier and the costs for non-smokers occur later in life. Based on these analyses, a policy of risk-rating based on a goal of smoking cessation will most likely further exacerbate any present inequities in favor of nonsmokers.

Potential for Achieving Public Health Objectives. Current trends would suggest that to stay competitive and reduce financial risk, the health-insurance industry will continue to use smoking status as the basis for setting premiums for individual policy holders and their families. However, adoption of these policies for group health insurance has been much slower, and has met with much more resistance and concern. Many health-insurance companies indicate that they are unwilling to offer a new group health insurance product that they can not price actuarially, for which there is little market demand, for which there will be added administrative costs, and for which there is no evidence on cost-effectiveness (Schauffer 1993a).

In summary, the majority of people who have group health insurance, either public or private, have not been subject to risk-rating policies. At present, the practice of risk-rating in health insurance has been limited primarily to a very small segment of the population: people who are self-employed, who work in small businesses or in low-wage occupations without health-insurance benefits, or who are out of work *and* who can afford the increasing costs of individual private health insurance. Current trends among large employers suggest that to the limited extent that differential premiums based on smoking status have been adopted, they represent only one piece of a more comprehensive policy targeted at smoking-cessation, which also includes worksite smoking restrictions and support of smoking-cessation programs for employees and their dependents as part of worksite wellness or health promotion programs (Schauffler 1993a). Only to the extent that smoking differentials have symbolic value and represent one more patch on the quilt of activities directed toward a smoke-free society are health-insurance premiums likely to influence tobacco use. The public-health community probably cannot look to widespread adoption and implementation of risk-rating health insurance based on smoking status to contribute significantly to achieving goals of smoking-cessation and the reduction of tobacco-related disease.

Health Insurance Coverage for Smoking Cessation

There is no ambiguity over the goal of health-insurance coverage for smoking cessation. To the extent that the costs of smoking-cessation services act as a barrier both to receiving services and to offering them, financing and reimbursement for smoking cessation will increase accessibility and availability of smoking-cessation programs. However, there remains a great deal of uncertainty over whether or not payment for smoking cessation will increase quit rates among smokers, whether or not payment for smoking cessation is cost-effective, and what kinds of smoking-cessation treatments should be reimbursed. These uncertainties, which are guided largely by economic considerations, combined with a historical lack of commitment to disease prevention in health insurance, hinder adoption of this policy option (Schauffler and Parkinson 1993).

Bias of Insurance Against Prevention. Health insurance as it developed in the United States has been biased against disease prevention, and health insurers have never been convinced that paying for prevention will save them money or help them to control costs. As a result, the industry has been very slow to adopt policies intended to promote health and prevent disease.

From the start, the primary objective of private health insurance was to protect individuals from the high costs associated with the treatment of acute illness and, most important, the costs of hospitalization. Disease-prevention services, which are routine and relatively low-cost items, have not been considered appropriate services to insure, consumers have not demanded them, and as a result they have been excluded systematically and explicitly from most health-insurance products as they developed in the United States. For example, the Medicare program, which in 1965 was modeled after Blue Cross and Blue Shield plans, in Section 1862 prohibits reimbursement of preventive services. The small number of preventive services that recently have been added specifically to Medicare and other private and public health-insurance plans (immunizations and screening tests, such as mammography and pap smears) have been limited to those which have been demonstrated through research to be cost-effective, and reflect the bias in medical care for technology over evaluation and management services (Schauffler 1993b). Rarely have any health education and counseling services for lifestyle behaviors been covered under health insurance. Smoking is no exception.

Policy Adoption by Private Insurance Carriers. The Health Insurance Association of America reports that King County Medical Blue Shield in Washington State is the only health insurer in the country that provides coverage for smoking-cessation as a routine part of its group benefits package. The benefit covers 75 percent of the costs of smoking-cessation programs, up to a total of a $500 lifetime benefit per policy holder, without an increase in rates (Wright 1991). The insurer contracts with selected smoking-cessation vendors in the community to accept payment based on prevailing charges as payment in full for policy holders.

In a 1991 survey of insurance companies licensed to sell health insurance in California, of forty-eight companies responding that sold health insurance, only one indicated that it offered a smoking-cessation benefit and it reported that it had not sold any policies with this benefit. In fact, only twelve percent of the health insurance companies surveyed indicated that they had ever considered offering smoking-cessation benefits, and none of these companies had plans to add a smoking cessation benefit in the future (Schauffler and Gentry 1993).

Policy Adoption Among Employers. Health-insurance plans with smoking-cessation benefits are more widespread among employers, and are limited primarily to the HMO plans they offer their employees. A recent survey of large corporations (more than five hundred employees) in California found that 15 percent of large employers offer a health-insurance plan with smoking-cessation benefits (Schauffler 1993a). All of the corporations that offered smoking-cessation benefits as part of an indemnity insurance plan were self-insured. Consistent with the findings from the health-insurer survey, no corporations offered smoking-cessation benefits under a commercially available indemnity health-insurance plan. Of those who offered smoking-cessation benefits under commercially available health insurance, approximately 90 percent were provided by HMOs, with the remainder provided by PPOs. In all cases, smoking-cessation benefits were offered as part of a more comprehensive package of preventive services. Of those employers who had ever considered offering health insurance with smoking-cessation benefits, approximately 75 percent had chosen to do so (Schauffler 1993a).

Cost-Effectiveness of Smoking Cessation. Shortly after the first Surgeon General's Report on Health Promotion and Disease Prevention was published in 1979 (U.S. DHEW 1979), identifying smoking as the single most preventable cause of disease, a number of papers were published suggesting disease prevention as the most promising route to controlling health-care costs (Stokes 1983; Somers 1984). While at the time little evidence was available on the effect of behavior change on health-care utilization and costs (Russell 1986), the cost-control argument for prevention became an important marketing strategy in promoting the development of corporate wellness and health promotion programs and in encouraging health-care providers and health insurers to invest in disease prevention.

One of the major barriers to adoption of smoking-cessation benefits by health insurers is that little information is available on the impact of payment of such benefits on health-care costs, and on the cost-effectiveness of covering smoking cessation services (Schauffler and Parkinson 1993). Surprisingly few research studies on the cost-effectiveness of smoking-cessation interventions have been conducted. While many estimates have been made of the costs of smoking and the benefits of quitting (Oster et al. 1984; Rice et al. 1986; Cady 1983), there have been only a few studies of the cost-effectiveness of smoking-cessation programs. Only two studies evaluating the cost-effectiveness of physician counseling against smoking were identified (Cummings et al. 1989; Oster et al. 1986), and only four studies were identified that estimate the relative cost-effectiveness of smoking-cessation classes, contests, or self-help programs (Pashos 1989; Marks et al. 1990; Windsor et al. 1988; Altman et al. 1987). Several of the studies that have been done are analyses of cost-effectiveness based on the experience of a hypothetical population or have other methodological limitations, particularly with respect to cost-estimation. In addition, it is difficult to compare the findings across studies because they use different outcome measures of effectiveness (per year of life saved, per life saved, per low birth weight prevented, and per quit), and are done from different perspectives (cost-effective for whom?) (Schauffler and Parkinson 1993).

Nonetheless, the authors of all of these studies reach the same conclusion: smoking cessation, regardless of the methods used, is at least as cost-effective as other widely accepted medical practices. Physician counseling for smoking cessation was found to cost $748 to $2,020 per life year saved (Cummings et al. 1989). The authors conclude that additional physician visits for smoking cessation may be cost-effective and may warrant reimbursements by insurers. The cost-effectiveness of adding nicotine gum to physician counseling for smoking cessation was also found to be relatively cost-effective, at $4,113 to $9,473 per year of life saved (Oster et al. 1986).

A comparison of the cost-effectiveness (measured in terms of cost per quit) of a smoking-cessation class, a smoking-cessation contest, and self-help materials found that the self-help materials were the most cost-effective ($22 to $144 per quit), followed by the contest ($129 to $239 per quit), with the class being the least cost-effective ($235 to $399 per quit) (Altman et al. 1987). The authors conclude that all of the programs are relatively cost-effective, and caution against rejecting any of these smoking-cessation programs on the basis of the rankings of their cost-effectiveness ratios. Different types of programs may meet the needs of different smokers, and it may be important to offer a variety of methods to help people quit smoking.

Three of the studies that have estimated the cost-effectiveness of smoking cessation have been done for pregnant women, estimating the cost per infant life saved and the cost per low birth weight prevented. Pashos (1989) estimated that smoking-cessation programs cost $100 to $325 per low birth weight prevented and $20,000 to $41,528 per infant life saved. Marks et al. (1990) estimated that the cost-effectiveness of a smoking-cessation program for pregnant women is $4,000 per low birth weight prevented and $69,542 per perinatal death prevented. Taking into account the costs of neonatal intensive care for low-birth-weight infants, Marks et al. (1990) estimate that over $3 can be saved for every $1 spent on smoking-cessation programs for pregnant women. The authors of this study conclude that insurers should offer smoking cessation to all pregnant women who smoke, and that doing so would not only save money for treatment of low-birth-weight infants, but would also save lives at relatively little cost.

Public Policy Development.   Recently, public policy makers have begun to urge health insurers to pay for smoking-cessation benefits. Implementation, however, is lagging far behind policy development (Schauffler and Parkinson 1993). In conjunction with the release of the 1990 Surgeon General's Report on the Benefits of Quitting Smoking (U.S. DHHS 1990), several leading policy makers, including the Surgeon General, the Director of the Centers for Disease Control, and the Secretary of the Department of Health and Human Services, all agreed that the benefits gained from quitting smoking are great enough that both public and private health insurers should pay for programs to help people quit, and that insurance coverage of smoking-cessation programs is potentially a highly cost-effective element in the nation's health policy agenda (Hilts 1990). Louis Sullivan, Secretary of the Department of Health and Human Services, concluded in his letter transmitting the Surgeon General's report (U.S. DHHS 1990) to Congress that

> the evidence is overwhelming that smoking cessation has major and immediate health benefits for men and women of all ages. Smoking cessation increases overall life expectancy and reduces the risk of lung cancer, other cancers, heart attack, stroke and chronic lung diseases such as emphysema. Given the enormous benefits of smoking cessation, and the fact that good smoking-cessation programs can achieve abstinence rates of 20 to 40 percent at one year follow-up, these programs are likely to be extremely cost-effective compared with other preventive or curative services. Therefore, I would encourage health insurers to provide payment for smoking cessation treatments that are shown to be effective.

Evidence of Policy Impact. Nevertheless, insurance companies counter that neither the research base nor the experiential base exists to guide policy development for smoking-cessation benefits. The only study that evaluates the effect of health-insurance payment for smoking cessation on quitting is the INSURE study (INSURE Project 1988). The INSURE study, supported by the life- and health-insurance industry, was an eight-year multisite study of preventive-services benefits provided by primary-care physicians. This study compared adult patients at study sites with those at control sites and found that a statistically significant greater proportion of patients in the test sites quit smoking. While these findings are important in establishing the effect of insurance payments on quit rates, this study tested only one method of smoking cessation, physician counseling, and did not evaluate the cost-effectiveness of payment for smoking cessation.

Other evidence on the effect of participant out-of-pocket payments on quit rates are mixed. Some studies suggest that participant payments increase quit rates, supporting the theory that the smoker is more motivated to quit, having made a financial commitment. Other studies suggest that free programs are associated with higher quit rates, supporting the theory that lowering the price increases access to and utilization of services and associated quit attempts (Schwartz 1987). A great deal more research is needed to assess the effects of payment for smoking cessation and participant copayments on quit rates (Parkinson et al. 1992).

Selecting Treatments for Coverage. Another barrier to including smoking-cessation benefits in health insurance is uncertainty over what types of smoking cessation programs to cover. In a review of smoking-cessation methods from 1978 through 1985, Schwartz (1987) concludes that, "any number of methods (or combination of them) can help smokers achieve abstinence." While most smokers quit on their own, many use self-help materials and additional guidance to quit on their own, and others who have been unable to quit on their own look for assistance from health professionals or groups to help them quit.

Recent surveys suggest that only 7 percent of smokers have quit using special smoking-cessation services, such as hypnosis and acupuncture, or smoking-cessation classes. Thus, the number of persons who may be helped by payment for smoking cessation may be quite small. This assumes, however, that those who are still smoking have the same ability to quit without assistance as those who have quit in the past. This assumption has been challenged by suggesting that those who have been able to quit on their own probably have, and those who are still smoking are the hardcore smokers who are addicted and may need cessation techniques other than quitting cold turkey or gradually cutting back. Recent research on the characteristics of persons who use assisted methods of smoking cessation confirms that they are heavy smokers who have previously made several unsuccessful attempts to quit smoking (Fiore et al. 1991).

Most smoking-cessation interventions achieve median quit rates at one year of between 18 and 40 percent. Based on an analysis of 416 smoking-cessation trials, Schwartz (1987) found that the median quit rates at one year follow-up for each of the following methods were as shown in Table 9-1.

One way in which health insurers can avoid the issue of which smoking-cessation methods to cover is to select a payment mechanism that recognizes the value of having a range of available alternatives. Similar to the payment mechanism established by King County Medical Blue Shield of Washington, a maximum dollar amount payable per beneficiary for smoking-cessation treatments can be established by the insurer prospectively, letting the smoker choose how the benefits are spent up to the maximum.

Quality Concerns. To address concerns over the quality of smoking-cessation services, the insurer can selectively contract with a set of preferred providers of smoking-cessation programs representative of the range of treatment alternatives available in the community (Schauffler and Parkinson 1993; Schauffler and Rodriguez 1993). The insurer can establish criteria for selecting eligible smoking-cessation programs, such as having a medical director or demonstrated quit rates of at least 20 percent at one-year follow-up. A recent meta-analysis of thirty-nine controlled trials of smoking interventions in medical practice identifies several other characteristics associated with successful programs (Kottke et al. 1988). These

Table 9-1. Smoking Cessation Method Quit Rates at One-Year Follow-up

Method	Percentage
Self-help methods	18.0
Educational techniques	25.0
Withdrawal groups	28.0
Nicotine gum alone	11.0
With behavioral therapy	29.0
Individual hypnosis	19.5
Acupuncture	27.0
Physician advice alone	6.0
With more than counseling	22.5
With pulmonary patients	31.5
With cardiac patients	43.0
Multiple programs (several methods)	40.0

characteristics include face-to face advice by both physician and nonphysician counselors, using both group and individual interventions, and using two or more intervention modalities with three or more reinforcing sessions. To the extent that insurers are willing to dictate the structure and methods of smoking cessation they will reimburse, they can influence the availability of more-effective programs.

Class Bias. Class bias may make the provision of smoking-cessation benefits less desirable from the perspective of the insurance companies. The majority of the beneficiaries of private health insurance are not smokers, and payment for smoking cessation may not be a significant barrier to quitting smoking for middle- and upper-class smokers. Lack of demand for this benefit from the consumer market and the allocation of additional benefits to a segment of the market (low-income smokers) that is perceived as already consuming more than its fair share of health-insurance dollars may also help to explain why health insurance coverage for smoking cessation is rare (Schauffler and Parkinson 1993).

Adverse Selection. A final barrier to adding smoking-cessation benefits to health insurance is the potential for adverse selection—the risk of attracting large numbers of smokers who select an insurance plan because it has smoking-cessation benefits. If all insurance companies offered smoking-cessation benefits (either voluntarily or under state mandates) as part of their standard benefit packages, the likelihood of biased selection by smokers would be reduced. But if only one or a few health insurance companies in an area offer smoking-cessation benefits, they risk attracting a group of beneficiaries with higher-than-average costs, putting the insurance company at a competitive disadvantage.

Policy Adoption by Public Insurance. It is also unlikely that publicly financed health insurance will be adding smoking-cessation benefits in the near future. A former administrator of the Health Care Financing Administration, which administers the Medicare and Medicaid programs, in a memorandum responding to the 1990 Surgeon General's report that recommended insurance coverage for smoking cessation, stated "we do not believe that the Medicare and Medicaid programs should be expanded at the federal level to include smoking-cessation programs." The memorandum goes on to say that "we believe that the Medicare program is an inappropriate source for smoking-cessation services," and, "we do not believe that the information contained in this report justifies a mandate that states cover smoking cessation services as a part of Medicaid" (HCFA 1990).

The reasons given for these conclusions are similar to those expressed by private health insurers. They include the fact that most people stop smoking without assistance, Medicare and Medicaid are intended to pay for "needed medical services" and smoking-cessation services are not medical services, there is little demand by beneficiaries for smoking-cessation programs, and smoking-cessation programs are not unavailable due to lack of funding. In addition, reasons given specific to Medicare include little evidence on either the effectiveness of smoking-cessation treatment for the elderly or the relative cost-effectiveness of smoking cessation for the elderly compared to other preventive services. The HCFA clearly rejects a policy of coverage for smoking-cessation benefits in publicly financed insurance, and proposes instead that the "laudable goal" of smoking cessation for Americans is more appropriately achieved through "education and inducement" to "convince individuals to stop doing health harming behaviors" (HCFA 1990).

Potential for Achieving Public Health Objectives. Neither public nor private health insurers currently view payment for smoking cessation as being in their interest. The health insurers who have offered smoking-cessation benefits are limited primarily to HMOs, which have traditionally offered greater preventive-services benefits compared with indemnity insurance plans. Only recently have a very few self-insured employers begun to add smoking-cessation benefits to their plans. For most smokers, health insurance will continue to exclude payment for smoking-cessation services. As a result, the public-health community can expect that only a small proportion of smokers will be covered for smoking-cessation benefits in the near future, contributing only marginally to reducing tobacco-related disease.

Influencing Public Policy on Tobacco

The health-insurance industry's involvement in influencing public policy on tobacco has evolved very rapidly over the past ten years from encouraging individual insurance companies and their clients to adopt worksite smoking policies to an involvement in active lobbying on Capitol Hill in support of a broad range of tobacco-control policies. This transformation, from no health-insurance industry involvement in public policy on tobacco for fifteen years following the publication of the first Surgeon General's Report on Smoking and Health (U.S. DHEW 1964a) to a position of committed involvement in supporting federal, state, and local legislation on tobacco, is the result of several factors. Health-insurance industry executives have become increasingly aware of the importance of the relationship of tobacco to disease, and the health consequences of smoking for both smokers and nonsmokers. The consumer groups and major voluntary associations in the public-health field, which had been the early leaders seeking aggressive public action on smoking, invited the support of other groups such as the health-insurance industry. In addition, the experience of working with consumer groups to influence governmental health and safety regulation of other risks provided the insurance industry with a model for successfully collaborating to influence public policy concerning tobacco.

Ownership of the Smoking Problem. Following the release of the first Surgeon General's Report on Smoking and Health in 1964, public-health groups were mobilized to launch an aggressive educational campaign to try to reduce and prevent smoking. It was thought that if smokers were made aware of the health consequences of smoking, they would choose to quit. The smoking problem was initially defined as one of persuading smokers to quit for their own good.

It was not until the 1980s, when reports of the adverse health effects of secondary or passive smoking were publicized widely (U.S. DHHS, Surgeon General 1986), that nonsmokers, who had become a clear majority since 1964, began to develop a strong sense that they too were being wronged by smoking. This evidence shifted the battle lines by giving nonsmokers a self-interest in the fight against smoking.

The new objectives of the antismoking movement became to prohibit smoking in public places (making smoking a completely unacceptable social behavior) and to discredit the tobacco industry. Some adopted a goal of a smoke-free society by the year 2000 (Koop 1984). As compelling scientific evidence that cigarettes are addicting became available (U.S. DHHS, Surgeon General 1988), the smoker has come to be viewed even more as a victim of the tobacco industry. The shift in the locus of responsibility for the smoking problem away from the individual to the tobacco industry has helped to stimulate the creation of new political coalitions in the antismoking movement and has led to demands for an expanded role for public policy on tobacco (American Cancer Society 1987c).

Development of Political Coalitions. Over the last ten years, three major coalitions have evolved with a priority of influencing public policy on tobacco. Separate coalitions first developed among the voluntary health associations and the health-insurance industry. Eventually, the voluntarily agencies and insurance industry groups joined forces with consumer groups and private business to create a political coalition with the potential to have a major impact on the development of public policy on tobacco.

Consumer groups, particularly a group called Action on Smoking and Health (ASH), which was formed in 1968, first took the lead in lobbying for tobacco legislation and regulation (U.S. DHHS, Surgeon General 1989). ASH also relied on a legal action strategy to try to force legislators and regulatory bodies to address cigarette smoking. The three major voluntary health associations who are directly concerned with the health risks associated with smoking—the American Heart Association (AHA), the American Lung Association (ALA) and the American Cancer Society (ACS)—initially played a comparatively passive role in public policy development (U.S. DHEW 1964a). From 1964 through 1969, the voluntaries were involved in testifying in public hearings related to tobacco and in providing scientific data to House and Senate committees, but they did not actively support the enactment of specific tobacco legislation (U.S. DHHS, Surgeon General 1989).

In 1982, the three major voluntary health associations formed the Coalition on Smoking OR Health to coordinate federal legislative activities related to tobacco (U.S. DHHS, Surgeon General 1989). The coalition, which has been a major force in the new antismoking movement, works with other groups to support federal smoking-control policies, including warning labels on tobacco products, regulation of advertising, restriction of smoking in public, increasing the excise tax, and reducing price supports on tobacco.

The roots of the health-insurance industry's involvement in influencing public policy on tobacco are found in the creation of the Center for Corporate Public Involvement (CCPI) (Karson 1991). The Health Insurance Association of America (HIAA), the trade association representing the health-insurance industry, and the American Council of Life Insurers (ACLI), the trade association representing the life-insurance industry, joined forces in 1977 to create CCPI to address community and social issues affecting both industries.[4] Within one year of its creation, CCPI identified health education and health promotion as a high priority area and created an Advisory Council on Health Promotion, a group of national experts on health promotion and disease prevention that advises the life- and health-insurance industries in setting policy. In 1980 the Advisory Council on Health Promotion recommended, and the CCPI concurred, that insurance companies, as employers, should adopt worksite nonsmoking policies for their employees, and should encourage their client companies to do likewise. CCPI published a nonsmoking guidebook for insurance companies and employers in 1982 which was widely distributed.

The idea of combining the forces of consumer groups with the insurance industry around tobacco policy arose as a result of their cooperation in another arena of public policy. The consumer groups and insurance industry had earlier been successful when they joined forces to support automobile safety legislation (Roper 1991). In 1987, representatives of the Consumer Federation of America and the insurance industry trade associations, ACLI, HIAA, and the American Insurance Association (AIA), began talking about the possibility of identifying additional areas where they could agree and work together cooperatively to achieve shared goals. Largely as a result of their influence on public policy in auto safety, the consumer groups, public-health voluntary associations, insurance industries, and business interests created the Coalition for Consumer Health and Safety. One of the seven priority issues the coalition identified for consumer health and safety is cigarettes.

Lobbying in Support of Public Policy on Tobacco. The coalitions rely primarily on lobbying to exert their influence. Before 1984, most of the lobbying efforts by HIAA, ACLI, and CCPI had been limited to issues directly affecting the regulation of the life- and health-insurance industries, as the insurance industry had been reluctant to spend its political capital on noninsurance issues. By 1984, however, the health-insurance industry began to get involved independently in lobbying for federal legislation addressing tobacco. CCPI not only endorsed the 1984 Comprehensive Smoking Education Act, which required that four health warnings be rotated on cigarette packages and advertisements, but also endorsed active lobbying of its member organizations in support of the bill.

The Coalition for Consumer Health and Safety, which now represents thirty-seven insurance industry, business, consumer, and public-health groups, focuses its activities primarily at the federal level, meeting with lobbyists and legislators, endorsing legislation, writing letters, testifying at public hearings, and informing member organizations of upcoming legislation. The coalition supports federal, state, and local legislation addressing restriction of smoking in public places and on all modes of transportation, nonsmoking policies and smoking cessation programs at the worksite, regulation of the sale and distribution of tobacco products, enforcement of laws restricting tobacco sales to minors, and financing for public education on the hazards of tobacco (Coalition for Consumer Health and Safety 1989).

Most recently the HIAA, independently as well as though its memberships with CCPI and the Coalition for Consumer Health and Safety, supported the Tobacco Product Education and Health Protection Act of 1991 (S1088), introduced by Senator Edward Kennedy of Massachusetts. The Washington Business Group on Health, which represents the interests of large employers and which is also a member of the Coalition for Consumer Health and Safety, also independently endorsed the Kennedy bill. This bill is comprehensive in its scope as it seeks to expand education and research efforts, establishes new regulatory provisions, repeals federal preemption of state and local restrictions on advertising, and establishes an Office of Regulatory Affairs to enforce regulatory provisions using fines, imprisonment, or product seizure.

The health-insurance industry has sponsored the proposed smoking legislation, and individual health insurance company executives wrote letters in support of the bill; moreover, Senator Kennedy's staff approached CCPI to get insurance company executives even more involved in lobbying through direct, personal contact with key senators who were undecided or opposed to the bill. At the CCPI meeting held in Phoenix, Arizona, in February 1991, not only did the health- and life-insurance companies recommend continued support for the comprehensive antismoking bill, but they recommended that CEOs contact key legislators to support the bill as needed and appropriate. Both the ACLI and HIAA boards ratified these recommendations (Karson 1991).

Evidence of Impact. Each of the coalitions points to evidence of its impact on public policy and tobacco. ASH and its leaders are largely credited with adoption of the Federal Communications Commission (FCC) rules that the Fairness Doctrine be applied to cigarette advertising and the adoption of no-smoking sections on airlines (U.S. DHHS, Surgeon General 1989).

The Coalition on Smoking OR Health is credited with numerous successes for antismoking legislation, including the enactment of the 1984 Comprehensive Smoking and Education Act, the 1985 extension of the 16¢ federal excise tax on cigarettes and the ban of smoking on commercial airline flights of two hours or less, and the enactment of the 1986 Comprehensive Smokeless Tobacco Health Education Act, which banned advertising of smokeless tobacco on electronic media and required warning labels on smokeless tobacco products (U.S. DHHS, Surgeon General 1989).

CCPI credits itself with having had a major impact on industry adoption of nonsmoking policies (Karson 1991). By 1990, more than 90 percent of life- and health-insurance companies had nonsmoking policies, and 40 percent had adopted total bans on smoking in the worksite.

The Coalition for Consumer Health and Safety identifies significant accomplishments in influencing policies on tobacco in Congress and the federal agencies, such as the 1990 ban on smoking on all domestic commercial airline flights of six hours or less. Other activities of the coalition include the development of proposed model state legislation addressing tobacco consumption by children, and the distribution of documents prepared by the Environmental Protection Agency (EPA) addressing the health effects of passive smoking and environmental tobacco smoke. The coalition has adopted as future priorities passing stronger federal tobacco-control and health-protection legislation, increasing federal funding for research and information dissemination by the Centers for Disease Control Office on Smoking and Health, working with state and local governments to pass model legislation addressing tobacco use in children, and supporting EPA's development of stronger regulatory and legislative proposals to reduce environmental tobacco smoke.

Potential Conflicts of Interest. A potential barrier to insurance-industry involvement in influencing public policy on tobacco is conflict of interest: some individual companies have ties to the tobacco industry; others are concerned that it is not in the insurance industry's interest to support regulatory policies against another industry. These conflicts, however, have had only a very limited impact on the insurance industry's support and pursuit of antitobacco legislation. When CCPI first began to discuss supporting federal legislation on tobacco, some questions were raised by its members over supporting legislation targeted at another industry, but their concerns were not sufficient to override the consensus to support antismoking legislation. The only insurance company on the CCPI Committee that voted against supporting the 1984 Smoking and Education Act was owned by a tobacco company (Karson 1991).

Four life-insurance companies are owned by tobacco companies, creating a conflict of interest for them in supporting regulation of tobacco products and smoking ("Tobacco Companies Charge Smokers Double" 1990). Loews Corporation owns Lorillard Tobacco Company and CNA Life Insurance Company. American Brands owns American Tobacco Company and Franklin Life and Southland Life Insurance companies. BAT owns Brown and Williamson Tobacco and Farmers Life Insurance Company. However, these four insurance subsidiaries of tobacco corporations represent only 0.5 percent of the seven hundred health and life insurance companies in the United States, resulting in little effect on policy development by the insurance industry as a whole.

In discussing the issue of excise taxes on tobacco products, several life-insurance executives argued that the insurance industry should not take a position in support of taxing another private industry, particularly since they were engaged in fighting proposed legislation to increase taxes on insurance (Karson 1991). As a result, CCPI did not support maintaining the increase of the federal excise tax on tobacco in 1987. However, the health-insurance industry did not concur with CCPI's rejection of increased excise taxes, and HIAA independently approved a policy statement supporting an increase in the federal excise tax on cigarettes, provided the tax revenue was used for health-care purposes (Marsh 1991).

Potential for Achieving Public Health Objectives. The health-insurance industry, in cooperation with other private business and consumer interests, in the last ten years has increasingly become involved in supporting public policy on tobacco. It has supported policies that increase public education on the health hazards of tobacco, stronger warning labels on tobacco packaging, development of worksite smoking policies, enactment of clean indoor air legislation, and increased excise taxes on cigarettes as long as the revenue is used for health care. In its endorsement of the Tobacco Product Education and Health Protection Act of 1991, the insurance industry has indicated its support for enforcement of sales-to-minor laws, restrictions on advertising, disclosure of product additives and tar and nicotine levels, and enforcement of regulatory provisions on tobacco.

Not surprisingly, the Tobacco Institute, representing the interest of the tobacco industry, was very critical of the Kennedy bill, charging it with creating inefficiency in government by creating a "duplicate bureaucracy to do what is already being done in federal agencies". The Bush administration also voiced clear opposition to the Kennedy bill. In testifying before the Senate Labor and Human Resources Committee in February 1990, the Secretary of Health and Human Services called the bill "unnecessary" even as the Bush administration was releasing new data on the health effects of passive smoking on children and the increased risk of cancer for workers exposed to environmental tobacco smoke. The administration's position was that the authorizations and requirements of the bill will not "measurably add to our current or planned efforts" ("Anti-Tobacco Legislation Passes" 1991).

The efforts of the health-insurance industry to influence public policy on tobacco, in conjunction with consumer groups, the life-insurance industry, employers, and public-health and voluntary agencies, has produced a powerful political alliance. It remains to be seen just how effective that alliance will be over time against the tobacco industry and its supporters in Washington. While the Tobacco Product Education and Health Protection Act of 1991 was passed by the Senate Committee on Labor and Human Relations, it was not scheduled for a floor vote in the 102d Congress. It is not clear whether this bill will be re-introduced in the 103d Congress in its present form. The only portions of the bill that may be implemented in the 102d Congress are provisions related to the enforcement of the sales-to-minors laws, which have been added to the drug abuse block grants in the reauthorization bill for the Alcohol, Drug Abuse and Mental Health Administration. However, it seems clear that the public-health community's best hope for achieving goals of a smoke-free society and reduced tobacco-related disease, disability, and death through the actions of health insurers lies in the continued efforts of the health-insurance industry in trying to influence public policy on smoking.

Notes

1. The political analysis of these policy options is based on a framework developed by Deborah Stone in her book, *Policy Paradox and Political Reason* (1989).

2. The development of this policy option was stimulated by Sylvia Noble Tesh's book, *Hidden Arguments: Political Ideology and Disease Prevention Policy* (1988).

3. The other criteria are height/weight ratio, seatbelt use, aerobic exercise, drug use, alcohol use, and driving habits.

4. CCPI is run by a joint committee of CEOs from life- and health-insurance companies, and policies endorsed by the CCPI are ratified independently by ACLI and HIAA.

10

Symbols and Smokers: Advertising, Health Messages, and Public Policy

Michael Schudson

It is widely believed that Madison Avenue is enormously successful in persuading the public to buy what it wants to sell. This belief in the power of advertising is vigorously championed by the advertising industry as it awards itself prizes for creative advertising, as it promotes its services to prospective clients, and as ancillary firms in market research urge their expertise upon the advertising agencies themselves. Cultural critics who mistake the surface glitter of advertising for the heart of what makes a consumer society tick also encourage popular confidence in advertising's efficacy. In the popular view, advertising has almost magical potency (Schudson 1991).

But there is reason to question whether commercial advertising has found a direct route to the hearts and minds of consumers. The clearest testimony to the difficulties of successful advertising is that most advertisers organize their advertising expenses to minimize the amount of *persuading* they expect the advertisements to do. That is, most advertisements are directed to target audiences who already use the product in question; the advertisement tries simply to interest the consumer in an alternative brand of a product they already use. Moreover, most advertising aims to reach especially heavy users of a particular product category. It also seeks to reach consumers at moments when they are most likely to want to use a particular product: soups are advertised in winter, iced tea in summer, toys before Christmas.

Within these limits—that advertisers direct advertising primarily to people who already use a product, particularly people who use a product heavily, especially at times culturally sanctioned as periods of appropriate use—what do advertisers expect to achieve with advertising campaigns? Not very much. They may seek by advertising not to lose their share of a market, or they may hope to modestly increase their share of the market. For example, most new cigarette brands come and go within months. It is not easy to develop a successful new brand for a mature market. In the world of cigarettes, a company needs to gain roughly 0.5 percent of the cigarette market to establish a new brand (Loeb 1983, p. 27). If 50 percent of a population of four hundred people smokes cigarettes, then for a firm to create a successful new cigarette brand it can ignore the two hundred people who do not smoke at all and try simply to convince one of the two hundred smokers to switch to the new brand. But most commercial advertising and marketing campaigns designed by the best Madison Avenue agencies fail to achieve just that (Schudson 1984). Advertising typically attempts little and achieves still less.

The skeptical view of advertising I am suggesting here runs counter to popular mythology about Madison Avenue, but it is consistent with the conventional understanding that sticks and stones break bones but words will never hurt us. The saying that "the pen is mightier than the sword" is arresting precisely because it is incongruous. Certainly in public policy battles for health and safety, the pen of public education seems less forceful than the sticks and stones of legal prohibitions and prosecutions or the carrots and sticks of tax exemptions and taxes (Adler and Pittle 1984). Automobile safety belt usage increased sharply when states imposed penalties for not wearing seat belts but barely inched up over the many years when public service announcements urged people to "buckle up" (U.S. Congress 1985). AIDS awareness programs have been less effective in changing the behavior of targeted groups than expected (Hornik 1988). Health messages in the mass media appear to be less effective than taxation in discouraging alcohol and tobacco consumption (Raftery 1989, p. 1246; Daynard 1988, p. 10; U.S. DHHS, Surgeon General 1989, pp. 474–543). Educational efforts alone did little to reduce illegal tobacco sales to minors, in one two-year trial, until coupled with stepped-up legal enforcement (Feighery et al. 1991).

Even so, public health advocates and government officials often have high hopes that mass-media public-health campaigns will promote public understanding and that bans on alcohol and tobacco advertising will promote public health. Certainly there is strong reason to believe that, even when the effects of isolated health-information campaigns are modest, the growth of medical knowledge about the harmful effects of smoking and the growing diffusion of this knowledge in the general population have over the past several decades been the key reason for the decline in smoking. Moreover, optimism about informational campaigns is partly pragmatic. It is normally easier to sell educational efforts to legislatures or to the public than to enact coercive regulatory measures: closing gay bathhouses or requiring automatically operated seat belts in cars or restricting smoking in public places. Optimism is also based on faith in human rationality and the power of information to influence behavior. If this optimism is justified, it reasonably leads to two different public policies: restricting or banning advertising for dangerous products or designing public-health promotional messages for the mass media on the model of commercial advertising.

Without denying that there may be important reasons to use the mass media for public-health messages, I want to question the underlying premise that commercial advertising is a highly effective activity and an appropriate model for public-health initiatives. I want to suggest that commercial advertising for cigarettes as well as for other products normally has only slight effect in persuading people to change their attitudes or behaviors. I want to suggest, further, that public-health messages about smoking normally face a different set of problems and prospects than commercial advertising. Efforts both to restrict cigarette advertising and to counter it with health education make sense if the expectations of policy makers about these efforts are realistically modest.

The Effectiveness of Commercial Advertising

If the role of advertising is generally as circumscribed as I have suggested, why do big corporations with good accountants and eyes on the bottom line spend so much money on advertising? There are several answers to this. The first and most important answer is: they don't. In most product areas, advertising expenses represent a very small percentage of total expenses in producing and marketing a product. In many product lines, including cigarettes, advertising expenses represent well less than half of the total marketing and sales-promotion expenses. In 1990, tobacco companies spent about four cents (4.2) in advertising for every dollar in cigarette sales. This was more than some familiar advertisers—the advertising-to-sales ratio was 2.8 percent for department stores, but about the same as electric housewares (4.5 percent) and greeting cards (4.1 percent) and household furniture (4.0 percent) and just a little less than hospitals (5 percent) ("Advertising-to-Sales Ratios" 1990, p. 24). To consumers, advertisements are generally the most visible and memorable part of the sales efforts of major corporations, but they are rarely the most important.

The second answer is that corporations believe that the small difference advertising and promotion can make in defending market share and in shifting people among brands of a given product is important. In a large market, a percentage point or two of market share is a large enough difference to have major consequences for bottom-line profits. It may be of little consequence in the greater scheme of things if Coca-Cola's market share grows from 24 percent to 25 percent, but that is a difference of great significance to Coca-Cola. Major advertising for a well-known cigarette brand like Virginia Slims yields it "only" 3 percent of the cigarette market, but that is more than enough for a profitable brand.

A third answer is that corporations do not know why they spend money on advertising. They may be fearful of what might happen if they failed to. They also may derive a set of important indirect and unmeasurable benefits from advertising. Advertising, even if it does not affect the mind of a consumer, may affect the mind of an investor. Investors at annual meetings like to see the latest reel of slick, national television advertisements for products their company produces. Company employees—particularly the company sales force—also are impressed by highly visible national advertising campaigns, and the sales force feels itself supported in the field when national advertising makes their company a household name. And if retailers believe, rightly or wrongly, in the power of advertising, they then stock widely advertised products and brands, consumers then buy what they find in stock, and the retailers' superstitious belief in the power of advertising is in their minds confirmed. These indirect powers of advertising may be a very important consequence of advertising, although they operate regardless of whether consumers are moved by an advertisement to change their way of life. Other indirect influences of advertising could also have significant influence on consumer behavior. For instance, the evidence is now very strong that tobacco advertising in magazines, particularly in popular women's magazines, has swayed editors to avoid publishing articles on the topic of the health dangers of smoking (Warner 1986). These may also be factors that lead tobacco companies to vigorously defend their freedom to advertise because they are factors that help give a lock on the market to companies with major marketing capacities.

With respect to cigarettes specifically, there are several sources of evidence about the effectiveness of advertising. I will review what is known from econometric studies, from our own and other nations' experience of advertising bans, and from what can be inferred from general knowledge about both the advertising industry and the character of cigarette consumption.

Econometric Studies

A large number of econometric studies try to model the effects of aggregate advertising on aggregate tobacco sales or consumption (Schmalensee 1972; Hamilton 1972; Schneider et al. 1981; U.S. DHHS, Surgeon General 1989, p. 503). To make a long story short, these studies find either no overall relationship between advertising and sales or a small, statistically significant positive relationship. There are long debates in the literature between those who would like to find no relationship, notably the tobacco industry, which wants to prevent government limitations on advertising, and those who want to find a positive relationship, notably public-health advocates who seek to build a case for government restrictions on tobacco advertising. Whether the results turn out to be no relationship or a small positive relationship does not seem to me a matter of great moment. In terms of a general relationship between cigarette advertising and cigarette smoking, the available econometric evidence is equivocal and the kind of materials available to produce the evidence leave much to be desired.[1]

Evidence from Advertising Bans and Limitations

A second approach to gathering data on the role of advertising in cigarette consumption is to turn to evidence from the American ban on television tobacco advertising as well as evidence from more comprehensive advertising bans in other countries.

In the period 1968 through 1970, cigarette advertising appeared on television along with anticigarette advertising. Beginning in 1971, all tobacco advertising was removed from television. In studies of the effect of the ban on tobacco consumption, the result was at first astonishing: per capita cigarette consumption, which had been declining since 1966, soon after the publication of the 1964 Surgeon General's Report, leveled off and then increased in the first few years after the television advertising ban. The most widely cited study of the effects of the ban explains that the antismoking commercials were much more powerful than the prosmoking commercials. According to this study by James Hamilton, procigarette advertising increased per capita consumption of cigarettes 76 cigarettes per year over the period 1950 to 1970 while the anticigarette advertising from 1968 through 1970 decreased per capita consumption 507 cigarettes per year (Hamilton 1972, p. 401). Others concur that the ban, by eliminating the powerful antismoking commercials, boosted tobacco consumption in the short run, whatever its long-run and more indeterminate effects may be (Schneider et al. 1981; Warner 1979).

Defenders of tobacco advertising point out that in countries with little or no advertising, people smoke. In communist countries, the growth in cigarette consumption has sometimes been much greater than in the West. This is a telling point against advertising bans only if proponents of advertising bans argue that advertising is the *sole* cause or *primary* cause of smoking. No responsible antitobacco activist holds this view. On the other hand, antitobacco activists who point to downward trends in smoking where advertising bans have been enacted (Norway) are equally unpersuasive. No country with enough political clout to pass an advertising ban has used an advertising ban exclusive of other measures against tobacco consumption (Warner 1986, p. 372). The advertising bans, then, though on the surface offering a natural experiment, provide evidence as difficult to evaluate as econometric data.

Inferences from General Knowledge

In the absence of definitive evidence from econometric studies or evaluation of advertising bans, we can still make reasonable inferences from what is generally known about advertising effects and what is specifically known about how people take up the cigarette habit.

A major issue between the tobacco industry and its opponents is whether advertising is designed to affect a company's market share by stealing consumers of other brands to the company's own brand or whether it is designed to attract new smokers. The tobacco industry regularly claims that advertising affects market share, not the size of the total market, and that advertisements are designed to influence current smokers, not to attract new ones. Opponents of tobacco advertising say this is patently absurd on both empirical and logical grounds (Chapman 1989, p. 1266). Empirically, it is plain that tobacco advertising is placed in media where teenagers and preteens see it. Since almost all smokers begin smoking before they are out of their teens, this seems an obvious attempt to "get them while they're young." Logically, the tobacco market, like any market, has to be renewed as consumers who use the product die off. Since tobacco smoking kills people, the rate of turnover caused by death is higher in this market than in most markets, and so the need to attract new, young consumers is accelerated.

Moreover, opponents of tobacco say, relatively few smokers switch brands in a given year. Luk Joossens, a Belgian researcher and consumer activist writes, "Brand-switching among adult smokers is very limited: the market share of the different brands differs annually, in general, less than 1 percent. Smokers show strong brand loyalty. Adults' smoking habits are well established and their addictive behaviour makes them less receptive to advertising messages" (Joossens 1989, p. 1279). American researchers Joe Tye, Kenneth Warner, and Stanton Glantz write, "In the cigarette business, actual brand-switching is very limited. Cigarettes enjoy one of the most tenacious brand loyalties of any consumer product; in a given year only about 10 percent of smokers switch brands" (Tye et al. 1987, p. 493). Even at that, since just two major cigarette manufacturers in the United States control the lion's share of the market, and each of them produces multiple brands, there is a strong likelihood that brand switching will be between brands produced by the same manufacturer (Tye et al. 1987, p. 494).

The question raised here is whether advertising has only the power to effect the modest behavioral change of brand-switching or else an influence great enough to produce in a consumer the more significant behavioral change of initiating smoking or perhaps stalling a resolve to quit. How is this question to be settled? It may not be possible to ultimately resolve the matter, but I do think the weight of evidence strongly suggests that, as a general rule, advertising is more likely a factor of importance in reinforcing existing social habits than in stimulating new ones. When it appears that advertising has produced a large behavioral change, chances are that it has in fact only reinforced and symbolized social trends already underway. Some examples may help put this in perspective. The advertising campaign in the late 1920s to attract women to smoking cigarettes and the Virginia Slims cigarette campaign begun in 1968 have been heralded as cases where advertising was largely responsible for producing a dramatic shift in consumer behavior. Yet in both cases—and these are some of the most dramatic examples used to tout the power of advertising—the advertising campaign followed rather than preceded the behavior it supposedly engendered.

Cigarette Sales in the 1920s

In the 1920s, large numbers of women began smoking cigarettes. While their usage represented only 10 to 15 percent of all cigarette consumption by the early 1930s, women before World War I had smoked rarely and had scarcely ever smoked in public, so the change was a dramatic one (Bonner 1926, p. 21). While women had been pictured in cigarette advertising before the late 1920s, they had been pictured as onlookers who might enjoy the aroma of the man's cigarette but there were only intimations, at most, that women themselves might smoke. As late as 1924 the editor of a tobacco trade journal wrote that the industry found the habit of women smoking so novel that "it would not be in good taste for tobacco men as parties in interest to stir a particle toward or against a condition with whose beginnings they had nothing to do and whose end, if any, no one can foresee" (Schudson 1984, p. 192). In 1926, an advertising trade journal held that the tobacco industry was aware of the increasing importance of women in the smoking market but feared a prohibition-like response if it advertised directly to them. Tobacco manufacturers feared stirring up reformers and precipitating a backlash (Bonner 1926).

This changed dramatically within a few years, once the cigarette habit among women of respectable social status was reasonably well established. By 1927, Lucky Strike used famous women opera singers and actresses in advertisements recommending cigarettes and testifying that they were soothing to the throat. By 1928, Lucky Strikes were advertised as a diet-conscious alternative to eating candy: "Reach for a Lucky instead of a sweet." In New York's 1929 Easter Parade, public relations agent Edward L. Bernays arranged for ten women to light up cigarettes as "torches of freedom," and he gloatingly recalls in his autobiographical account of his public relations triumphs that this created a storm of interest and front-page news stories and photographs.

But Bernays was no genius in realizing he could get women smoking in public onto the news pages. Women smoking in public had been on the news pages, without any public relations impresario at work, for nearly a decade. Several developments made this possible. First, World War I brought women into new roles and new situations. Women war-workers took up the cigarette habit overseas and women working in factories at home took up the habit, too. Second, the war cut off supplies of Turkish tobacco, and milder blends, easier for inexperienced smokers to get used to, began to dominate the market. Third, there was a visible women's movement in the 1920s and women's right to smoke in public became an important symbol of women's equality. Fourth, news coverage of the women's movement, including its battles on the cigarette front, was prominent. Conspicuously placed *New York Times* stories on skirmishes over smoking rules at women's colleges (a topic also very well covered in college newspapers) or front-page stories on conflicts over women smoking on railroad trains, streetcars, or ocean liners were common several years before tobacco companies began picturing women smokers in their ads.

The increasing attention tobacco companies paid to women after 1927 no doubt helped legitimate women's smoking, but did it "cause" women to smoke? The tobacco marketers took advantage of a social change well underway.

Virginia Slims 1968–Early 1970s

Joe Tye, Kenneth Warner, and Stanton Glantz among many others in the public health field, have suggested the Virginia Slims advertising campaign may be related to increased smoking among young women, pointing out that Virginia Slims was introduced to the market in 1968 and began its vigorous and widely noted advertising campaign ("You've come a long way, baby") at the very time (1968–1974) when smoking among teenage girls was increasing. This was especially suspicious because smoking among teenage boys in those same years was decreasing. While Tye, Warner, and Glantz do not assert unequivocally that the Virginia Slims advertised caused the increase in teenage girls' smoking, they certainly leave the implication that they believe it a strong contributing factor (Tye et al. 1987, p. 500). Is this right?

Probably not. Between 1955 and 1966, cigarette smoking increased among American women of all ages from 24.5 percent of all women to 32.3 percent, at a time when smoking decreased among men from 54.2 percent to 50 percent. Using figures for 1968 instead of 1966, the comparison would be a drop for men from 54.2 percent to 47 percent and an increase for women from 24.5 percent to 31.2 percent (U.S. DHHS, Surgeon General 1988, p. 566). Any tobacco marketers reading the evidence of the Public Health Service or their own market reports would have wanted by the mid-1960s to find a way to target women, because women, not men, were the leading edge of growth in the domestic cigarette market. The Virginia Slims campaign followed a growth in cigarette smoking among women, including teenage women. It took advantage of a trend already begun.

The Virginia Slims campaign and the campaigns for several other brands aimed at women attracted some controversy and some protests, especially from feminist groups. More recently, the Virginia Slims sponsorship of athletic events has occasioned public controversy, too. But did Virginia Slims advertising and promotion increase smoking among young women? Did it stimulate the trend with which its introduction coincided? Perhaps. I have no evidence that it did not. I would be shocked, indeed, if such a widely noted campaign had no effect at all. But I would be equally surprised to find the Phillip Morris promotional efforts to have anything like the effect of the larger social forces leading women to smoke in this period. These include:

- An increase in women's labor force participation from 35.5 percent in 1960 to 40.8 percent in 1970 to 47.7 percent in 1980. Since women employed in the paid labor force smoke in larger numbers than housewives, this would seem to be a significant factor at least for women eighteen and older (U.S. DHHS 1980b, p. 74).
- Generally increasing affluence and family income through 1973.
- Gradual liberalization of morals and manners, less control of teenagers by parents, and more egalitarian attitudes toward young people, especially women.
- Rapid rise and attention to the "women's movement" in exactly the same period, 1968 to 1974, a movement that seems to have influenced younger women first. As late as 1967, feminist concerns were ridiculed in left-wing social movement circles, but within a very short time thereafter this would not be possible (Chafe 1991, p. 205). In 1962, two-thirds of American women in a Gallup poll said they did not think they were victims of discrimination. In 1974, two-thirds said they were (Chafe 1991, p. 211).

More women entered science and engineering fields and many more women entered traditionally male professions of law, business, and medicine. In the early 1970s, opinion about women's roles was transformed on college campuses. In the 1950s and 1960s, less than 10 percent of entering classes in these professional schools was female; by the mid 1980s, more than 40 percent was. Women represented 10 percent of doctorates awarded in 1971 and 30 percent by the 1980s (Chafe 1991, p. 222).

All these features of women as a market for cigarettes did not go unnoticed by the tobacco industry. Marketers became well aware that women offered them significant marketing opportunities, and they adjusted their product lines and marketing efforts accordingly (Ernster 1985, p. 337). Virginia Slims has been a marketing success, but it seems to be again a case where success comes to marketers who ride the wave of powerful social trends.

Charles Ramond, one-time editor of the *Journal of Advertising Research*, reviewed the literature on the relation of advertising to sales, and concluded that the effect of advertising on sales "is always less than that of population, income and other environmental variables." He adds, "Advertising's effect on sales is almost always less than that of other marketing forces" (Schudson 1984, p. 88). I agree. The opinions I express here, however distant from popular views, are not unusual. They are adapted from the mainstream opinion of economists and others engaged in advertising research, and I think they are almost irresistible given the evidence we have. Commercial advertising is not a sure-fire way to sell an idea or change a behavior, even a small behavior. Advertising is unpredictable; notably successful advertising campaigns are rare and even these typically result from supporting or reinforcing existing social trends.

Then what is all that advertising for? As Kenneth Warner has observed, it may achieve ends other than the extremely difficult one of initiating new smokers. It may affect people more open to prosmoking messages and more attentive to them than nonsmokers typically are. It may encourage former smokers to start again. It may encourage current smokers to smoke more. It may weaken current smokers' resolve to quit (Warner 1986, pp. 59–60). For smoker and nonsmoker alike, it may help create a sense of the social acceptability of smoking. It *is* evidence, after all, of the social acceptability of smoking. It indicates that smoking can be done legally and publicly. Compare this, for example, to the furtive advertising of condoms or sexual aids. The public advertising of cigarettes greases the cultural skids for smoking.

There is one important feature of cigarette smoking that these general considerations do not confront: almost all smokers become smokers as teenagers. About 85 percent of smokers begin smoking while children or teenagers (Pierce 1991, p. 390). The adult nonsmoker is relatively invulnerable to cigarette advertising. Past the usual point of initiation and past many of the usual reasons for taking up smoking, the adult nonsmoker is likely to be very inattentive to the ads around him or her. (This argument is weaker for nonsmokers who are *former* smokers.) For adults, there is little doubt that cigarette advertisers are indeed seeking to find brand-switchers or to keep their own customers brand-loyal or in other ways to strengthen smokers' allegiance to smoking. They are not proselytizing for new smokers.

But the case with teenagers and younger children may be different. Teenagers are typically less secure in their identities than most groups in the population, and their age-appropriate task is in part to experiment with different adult identities. They are more subject to social pressure and more attuned to advertising than most groups in the population. A Belgian study found that teenagers noticed advertisements more often than adults and were more familiar with cigarette brands than adults (Rombouts and Fauconnier 1988). Teenagers buy the most heavily promoted cigarette brands disproportionately (McNeill et al. 1985, pp. 271–72). It seems likely that advertising helps contribute to the fact that adolescents think a large majority of people their age smoke when, in fact, it is 15 to 30 percent (U.S. DHHS 1980b, p. 285). They "exaggerate the prevalence of smoking, believing smoking is the norm" (Silvis and Perry 1987, p. 369). Almost all adolescents believe smoking is a health hazard but "few believe it is a threat to *their health*. Since most adolescents believe that they can stop smoking whenever they wish, chronic diseases are not seen as a threat" (Silvis and Perry 1987, p. 363).

Tobacco companies insist that their advertising is exclusively directed to maintaining or increasing market share. Critics find this claim preposterous. It is and it isn't. Market share could logically justify cigarettes' substantial promotional budget. At the same time, the industry dies unless children and teenagers start to smoke. The best face one can put on the industry's behavior is that they are seeking to encourage in teens an emotional attachment to a cigarette brand but are hoping they will not start smoking until their eighteenth birthday (and that they will not wait a day longer). If tobacco firms do not win the loyalty of people in their teens, they will have to attempt the harder task of weaning them away from one brand to another later on.

No one knows for sure how big a factor cigarette advertising is in leading teens to smoke. That tobacco companies locate advertising in media they know reach large concentrations of teenagers and children is clear, despite industry denials. Recent studies showing that even six-year-olds are familiar with advertising for Camel cigarettes and that Camel has become one of the leading brands for first-time smokers certainly suggests some connection (DiFranza et al. 1991; Fischer et al. 1991; Pierce et al. 1991). The best that could be said for the industry is that it believes advertising to youths has no effect in attracting to smoking people who would not become smokers without advertising. The advertising then simply reproduces for new smokers the "market share" strategy. If the industry assumes that some given percentage of teens will become smokers regardless of advertising, then advertising to teens can be defended as simply an effort to get the teens to adopt a given brand.

This is a dubious but not an absurd argument. It is reasonable to assume that most teens who choose to smoke would do so with or without advertising.

However, can it be asserted with equal assurance that *all* teens who choose to smoke would do so with or without advertising? That would seem rash indeed. It is reasonable to believe that some teens become smokers or become smokers earlier or become smokers with less guilt or become heavier smokers because of advertising. For some teens, surely advertising is a contributing factor to their decision to smoke.

How many is "some"? Twenty percent of teen smokers? Two percent? Two-tenths of a percent? No one knows. But let us assume that cigarette advertising is an important contributing factor to a decision to smoke in just two of every one hundred teens who become smokers. That would mean that advertising is seriously detrimental to the health prospects of twenty thousand minors a year, since about a million minors take up smoking in the United States each year (Pierce 1991, p. 390). Suppose that advertising is a contributing factor to a decision to smoke in just two of every *one thousand* teens who become smokers. That still means advertising represents a significant health danger to two thousand minors a year. Should society not do what it can to protect these two thousand or twenty thousand children this year, or these twenty thousand or two hundred thousand children in the next decade, from the dangers of tobacco?

Toward a Rationale for Public Health Mass-Media Efforts

If advertising can lead smokers to smoke more or if it can turn former smokers into backsliders or if it legitimates smoking or if its power is to be present at the right place at the right time to coax vulnerable teenagers over the edge, then can counteradvertising lure smokers to smoke less? or keep former smokers securely abstinent? or delegitimate smoking? or be at the right place at the right time for the vulnerable teenagers?

While both commercial and public-health advertising may be efforts to persuade the general public to change an attitude or behavior, they are not truly parallel efforts. The cards are stacked against the public-health message in ways that commercial advertising does not have to deal with. This is so in three respects.

First, commercial messages are ordinarily addressed to consumers already favorably inclined toward the product advertised, while health and safety messages are generally addressed to the people "least disposed to listen to their message" (Adler and Pittle 1984, p. 164). A commercial advertisement for a cigarette, for instance, addresses people who are for the most part already addicted to cigarettes. A "smoking is dangerous to your health" message is also addressed to people addicted to cigarettes but, obviously, while the nature of this audience works in favor of the commercial advertisement, it works against the success of the health message. (Ninety percent of current smokers express a desire to quit; this desire is at least some degree of counterforce to the addiction of smokers and may make smokers a more receptive audience for health messages than one would otherwise imagine [Flay 1987, p. 4].)

Second, we conventionally measure the effectiveness of commercial and public-service campaigns differently. The measure for the commercial advertising is straightforward, in principle (in practice, it is rarely possible to isolate the effect of advertising from other causes of sales): if the increased costs of advertising are more than offset by increased income from sales, the ad campaign is a winner. If this means market share increases 1 percent or 0.1 percent, the ad campaign has succeeded. A public-information campaign, on the other hand, that led 1 percent of the target population to buckle their seat belts, or recycle their garbage, or dispose properly of their toxic wastes, or install smoke alarms, or inspect their homes for radon, or consider rationally the cancer risks of chemically sprayed apples, or weigh the costs and benefits of nuclear power plants, would no doubt be judged a failure. Public information campaigns normally seek to affect a substantial segment of the population. (*Should* such campaigns be rated failures? Not if the costs of the campaign were less than the benefits in lives saved and health improved and the money could not have been more effectively spent in some other way.)

Third, commercial advertising has a kind of psychological advantage over public-health communication. Commercial advertising takes the side of the consumer, in a sense, promoting a product and its consumer benefits when they are oriented to desires known to be present in the consumer. Everyone would like a peanut butter that tastes good, although they may differ as to how important this is. Any advertisement that promotes a peanut butter that tastes good or any advertisement that promotes a product that would save the consumer money flatters a sentiment or desire that the consumer has. The consumer is asked simply to consider trying an alternative product to suit present dispositions. The ad does not ask the consumer to change his or her dispositions.

A public-health communication may be different in this respect. The health message pushes the consumer toward a behavior that the communicator claims is in the interest of the consumer. This may well be true—seat belts save lives, smoking cessation saves lives, and presumably people seek long lives. But the communicator, not the consumer, is here defining the consumer's interests, and this is necessarily paternalistic or preachy, no matter how cautiously it is presented. The commercial advertisement is more often saying "try this, you'll like it" than "do this, it's good for you." It therefore does not have to overcome the resistance that a paternalistic approach will automatically arouse.

Not all differences between commercial advertising and public-health communication make public-health communication the harder task. Messages have greater influence when communicators themselves are highly credible with their audience. Commercial advertising is widely distrusted. Health messages coming from civic organizations or government agencies with strong track records for reliability are more likely to be believed than messages from commercial firms. Nevertheless, the ambitions in public-health messages for changing behavior are so much greater than in commercial advertising that the analogy between the persuasive task of commercial advertising and that of public-health messages is not a good one.

William DeJong and Jay Winsten have argued that pessimism about public-health mass-media campaigns is based on evidence of media campaigns that were too short, that a small proportional success rate may still mean a large numerical success because of the large size of the audience reached, and that recent research suggests media campaigns are successful when properly designed. This means they should carefully identify their target audience, design campaign materials carefully in accord with research on the target audience, key the messages to the audience's current levels of knowledge and existing needs and motives, and make commitments to long-term programs (DeJong and Winsten 1989). Brian Flay's review of antismoking media campaigns supports this view. Flay reviewed a wide range of mass-media antismoking campaigns and concluded that mass-media campaigns, especially using broadcast media, "have produced changes in the smoking behavior of statistically and socially significant, though small, portions of the smoking population" (Flay 1987, p. 1). This is consistent with the apparent success of counteradvertising on television from 1968 to 1970. Flay concludes that mass-media campaigns can create knowledge, attitude, and behavior change; that the more intensive the publicity, the better. A recent public-health campaign in Australia provides support for the view that a well-planned antismoking media campaign can make a difference (Pierce et al. 1990).

Public-health media campaigns may work, but they may also be worth undertaking even without evidence of direct effectiveness. Warning labels may be merited even if there is no easy way to measure effectiveness, even if the effectiveness of the symbols in and of themselves cannot ever be measured, even in principle. This, it seems to me, is the presumption behind most educational efforts. We know, in the end, when education works when, by education, we mean some evident behavioral change: a person learns or fails to learn to swim, a person stops smoking or does not stop smoking. But it is rarely possible to know, even in something so simple as a swimming class, what particular effort or what cumulation of efforts does the trick, overcomes the child's fear of the water or teaches the brain or muscles that a certain pattern of fluttering and floating and floundering can sustain a body aloft in the water. One thing works for one child, another thing works for another child. This is not to say there is no point to general instruction, only that general instruction by itself will not necessarily "take." What does take and when? If swim instructors knew that, this would be a much easier matter than it is. But does the inefficiency of swim instruction mean that it should be abandoned? More people would drown this way. Fewer people would learn to swim.

Public-health advertising may be worth undertaking not because it is especially effective but because it is inexpensive. It is a bargain-basement strategy in several respects. Relative to other possible interventions, it costs little. It is inexpensive in terms of the time and energy required to arrange it. There are highly qualified professionals at advertising agencies to design an advertising campaign and place the ads in the medium most likely to be cost-effective. An advertising campaign requires no long-term investments. It has very little in the way of sunk costs. It is an intervention that, once begun, can be easily terminated. It can be terminated with little visible human cost, unlike, say, hiring and then having to fire a corps of health-outreach workers.

Health advertising may also be a likely strategy because it may have similar indirect advantages for people in the health professions that commercial advertising has for people in the business world. It gives them a sense of feeling noticed and important. It bucks them up with a sense of their public prominence. It motivates them.

Third, public-health media campaigns do (or can) provide information. They are potentially educational, whether they persuade people to change behavior or not. At a time when the vast majority of the population, including the vast majority of smokers, recognizes that smoking endangers health, the educational value of health advertising would seem limited. But, in fact, people who believe cigarettes are, in general, dangerous may still have very little specific information about what precisely the dangers of cigarettes are. There is evidence that large proportions of the population underestimate the role of smoking in heart disease, do not know that lung cancer is more common now in women than is breast cancer, do not know the dangers of smoking during pregnancy, and underestimate the risks of cigarette consumption relative to other environmental health risks. There remains a large educational job, one that I think the recent glitzy advertising campaign in California did not take into consideration. Even if people do not act on the information they gain from a media campaign, the information gain is not thereby trivial. Many more people believe they should stop smoking than in fact quit successfully, but it is not trivial that their friends and children and other people around them learn from them that they believe their habit to be harmful and would like to give it up. It does not seem to me wise, ever, in a society committed to democratic values, to be overly skeptical of the worth of education.

Policy Options: The Question of an Advertising Ban

An alternative public-health strategy is not to create health messages but to restrict or ban commercial messages that promote dangerous products. Advertising bans have been on the public agenda in one form or another at least since the television advertising ban in 1971. The American Medical Association endorsed a ban on all tobacco promotion in 1985 and the American Cancer Society and American Heart

Association followed suit in 1986 (Warner et al. 1986, p. 379). There are other proposals besides those for a ban. One is for "tombstone advertising," that is, a prohibition on models, slogans, music, or lifestyle depictions in tobacco advertising, allowing only a simple statement of what the product and brand is and perhaps a display of the package. This would do little good if it led tobacco firms to simply shift more of their marketing dollars to promotion rather than advertising. Another proposal calls for counteradvertising. There are no serious constitutional objections to either of these proposals. Indeed, I see no objections at all. But neither has excited a wave of grass-roots interest.

I am persuaded that normally more speech is better than less, and that First Amendment values should ordinarily prevail. Some in the public-health community are inclined to see the First Amendment issue as a "smoke screen" (Warner 1985; Amos et al. 1991; Minkler et al. 1987). Certainly the tobacco industry's sudden discovery of the value of the First Amendment after decades of using their advertising muscle to discourage free discussion of the dangers of tobacco in popular magazines is an astonishingly shameless hypocrisy. And the Supreme Court's *Posadas* decision seems to leave the road clear to advertising bans on cigarettes.[2] Still, questions of free speech deserve serious consideration.

The Supreme Court in the past two decades has extended First Amendment protection in part, not in full, to commercial speech and has done so, I believe, for generally good reasons. In the *Central Hudson* case, the Court established a sensible test to determine when government can legitimately infringe on commercial speech. The *Central Hudson* test is that if the commercial speech concerns a lawful activity and is not misleading or fraudulent, then it can only be restricted if (a) the government's interest in doing so is substantial, (b) the restrictions help the government attain its interest, and (c) no less-restrictive remedy would serve that interest as well.[3]

The *Posadas* case turned this around. In finding that Puerto Rico was within its rights to prohibit advertising of gambling casinos even while permitting the casinos to operate, the Court specifically mentioned that governmental jurisdictions have been found to have the power to regulate products or activities deemed harmful "such as cigarettes, alcoholic beverages, and prostitution" in a wide range of ways, including not only outright bans on the product or activity but restrictions on "stimulation of its demand."[4] Justice Brennan offered an eloquent dissent, holding that there is no reason to provide commercial speech less protection than other types of speech "where . . . the government seeks to suppress commercial speech in order to deprive consumers of accurate information concerning lawful activity."[5] This dissent would offer some hope to those who would prefer a "tombstone advertising" set of restrictions rather than an outright ban on advertising.

In the case of tobacco, the evidence of the health consequences of smoking provides overwhelming justification of a legitimate governmental interest. Whatever doubts one may have about how effective tobacco advertising is in encouraging and legitimating smoking, it is pointless to argue that restricting or banning tobacco advertising would make *no* difference at all. Banning tobacco advertising would save some lives. Whether there are better measures than an advertising ban to improve public health with respect to smoking is a harder question. Would legislation requiring tobacco advertisers to contribute a percentage of their advertising budgets to a fund for the production of antitobacco advertisements be a better direction? The evidence on the effectiveness of counteradvertising in 1968 to 1970 is not settled, but it tends to suggest that the counteradvertising was more effective than the commercial advertising. Or it may be that the interaction is exactly what mattered: that the mix of advertising and counteradvertising showed up the hypocrisy of the commercial advertising or simply kept alive a running debate. Since that running debate has plenty of social and cultural support now that it did not have in 1968, it is unlikely that ads and counterads would have the same kind of effect today. The lessons of 1968–1970 (even if they were clear) may not be transferable. Still, it is at least arguable that this is a case where the rule that "more speech is better than less" applies. Counteradvertising may be not only a less restrictive means than an advertising ban to achieve a legitimate governmental objective but it may be more effective.

If we compare the policies of an advertising ban, the provision of counteradvertising, and tombstone advertising regulations, their desirability varies according to what criterion we are applying. In terms of providing the least challenge to First Amendment doctrines, counteradvertising (more speech is better than less) would be the best policy, tombstone advertising next best, and an advertising ban the least desirable. In terms of achieving a governmental objective of public health, we do not have evidence adequate to say whether counteradvertising would prove more effective than an advertising ban or less effective; we could reasonably, but not certainly, presume that tombstone advertising regulations would be somewhat less effective than the alternatives. In terms of the convenience, economy, and effectiveness of enforcement, a total advertising ban would be easier to administer than tombstone advertising regulations or counteradvertising efforts. In terms of political feasibility, I suspect that tombstone advertising regulations would be the easiest to pass, since tombstone advertising offers no significant First Amendment problems, unlike a ban, and, unlike counteradvertising, requires no public expenditure of funds or complicated financial scheme to ensure that the tobacco industry underwrites counterads.

Any of these strategies, I think, would make good public policy, given that the public health is of overriding importance and the restrictions these remedies impose on free speech apply only to commercial speech for a product that kills people when used as directed. There may be a slope here to other products or services (alcohol is the next case to look at), but I do not think it is a very slippery one.

It may be that the advertising ban is the best strategy because its simplicity and boldness may attract and motivate public support. Alternatively, the public may be more effectively mobilized if the symbolic aspects of smoking policy are disaggregated. Instead of one general effort for advertising bans, waged at the federal level and with the First Amendment as a major issue, efforts at state and local advertising restrictions might make more strategic sense. Tobacco advertising on billboards, for instance, represents 13 percent of outdoor advertising revenue in 1989, down from 40 percent in 1979 (Outdoor Advertising Association of America, May 28, 1991 press release). But why should it exist at all? Surely it is a form of advertising easily available to minors that should be entirely eliminated. Since this would be a restriction on speech of the "time, place, and manner" sort, it has smoother sailing on constitutional grounds. Or consider the placement of cigarette vending machines in locations accessible to minors. That is another issue that can be separately lobbied and legislated. What about banning the distribution of free samples of cigarettes? Each of these separate efforts takes work, but each is a vivid reminder to public-health workers and their supporters of the hypocrisy of the tobacco industry and the seriousness of the battle at stake.

Conclusions

Because cigarette advertising is a less powerful marketing tool than many people think, banning it is not likely to have a dramatic impact on the prevalence of smoking. Even so, advertising is one of the factors in the environment that encourages children and adolescents to start smoking, and there is ample justification for efforts to find public policy remedies that attack cigarette advertising.

Conceptually, the advertising issue has been separated from other public policy issues. Talking about a cigarette or picturing a cigarette is not the same as thrusting one into the hands of a consumer. But the line between advertising and promotion is wavy and there is a gradation from the billboard to the free sample that all comes out of the same part of a company's budget. On the public-health side, public education is not exclusively a symbolic activity, nor are more coercive or regulatory efforts without significant symbolic dimensions. Even at law, where speech is protected in ways action is not, commercial speech is far from absolutely protected. It is closer to an act of selling than it is to a speech act of advocacy, judging from the tricky distinction the Federal Trade Commission has made in considering its jurisdiction over the tobacco companies' "free speech" ads.

If advertising is less powerful than its critics usually claim, this is no cause to ignore it, and if health education meets with only limited success, this is no grounds for despair. There is good evidence that the American Cancer Society report on smoking in 1953 and the Surgeon General's Report on smoking in 1964 both had very large effects on smoking behavior (Schneider et al. 1981). In 1953, publicity about the dangers of smoking (particularly in *Reader's Digest*, a magazine that does not accept tobacco advertising) led to a decline in smoking and, among the many who still smoked, a sharp swing toward the use of filtered cigarettes. In 1964, publicity led to a sharp decline in smoking. Educational efforts to chip away at the rock of addiction are not always slow. In these instances, dramatic, legitimate, convincing, newsworthy evidence greatly affected both smokers and, in elaborate defensive maneuvers, the tobacco industry. Educational efforts in the mass-media are no panacea, either by themselves or in conjunction with other tobacco control measures, but there are good grounds for a measured, continued faith in the uses of education.

Notes

1. There are overwhelming difficulties in specifying the econometric models.

Time-lag problems. Might the effect of advertising be delayed? This seems plausible but, unfortunately, is recalcitrant to measurement. Should the model estimate the relation of advertising spending at time t to sales at t + one day? Or t + three months? Or a certain percentage of t + 1 and a different percentage of t + 2 and yet another percentage of t + 3? We know very little about how quickly the effect of advertising "wears out" or whether there might be a "sleeper effect" of advertising or whether "wear out" depends on the quality of the advertisement, the novelty of the product, the season of the year, or what.

Marginal rate problem. Kenneth Warner and colleagues have pointed out that econometric modeling is designed to estimate the value of the next marginal increase or decrease in the independent variable (advertising) on the dependent variable (sales). This may not provide useful information for public policy, especially as the question of banning all tobacco advertising outright is considered (Warner et al. 1986, p. 371). The existing studies that estimate the relationship between advertising and consumption based on data from a time period of relatively high levels of both advertising and consumption are not designed for extrapolation to a time period in which there is no advertising at all. Moreover, if advertising is designed both to affect market share and to increase market size, then "the rational level of advertising expenditure will exceed that which increases aggregate consumption" (Warner 1986, p. 68). If the marginal advertising dollar affects market share, not market size, then any statistical relationship between aggregate advertising and aggregate consumption will be reduced.

Direction of causation problem. Just what is the dependent variable and what is the independent variable? Econometric modeling does not ordinarily sort this out but operates on the common-sense assumption that advertising, designed to have an effect on sales, is the independent variable. Is it? Studies of how businesses actually establish advertising budgets indicate that the actual, real-world relationship is that last year's sales volume may be used as a standard for determining this year's advertising budget (Schudson 1984, p. 17). When business is good, advertising budgets grow; when business is slow, advertising contracts (Horovitz 1991). Thus increases in sales over the years will lead to increases in advertising budgets over the years and a positive relationship will turn up without any evidence that advertising stimulates sales (Boddewyn 1989, p. 1256).

Measurement problems. Do advertising expenditures, invariably accepted in econometric models as an appropriate measure of consumer advertising exposure, fairly represent public exposure to advertising? All models of cigarette advertising and smoking take advertising expenditure to be a plausible index of advertising effectiveness. It may be. But it may not be. It leaves out quality differences, of course. Not all advertising is equally effective; some advertising may even be counterproductive (Warner 1986, p. 67). It also takes no account of the medium of advertising. In the United States since the television advertising ban in 1971, tobacco companies have increased their advertising budgets, moving to larger outlays in magazines, newspapers, and billboards. Still, for this increased expense they reach fewer people than they did with television ads and they reach them in less dramatic and focused ways. "Advertising expenditure" is no more adequate a proxy for advertising reach than it is for advertising quality.

Of course, notice of cigarettes has returned to television in the increased popularity of "movie channels" in cable television that show films where people smoke and in the television broadcast of sporting events at stadiums that have prominent cigarette billboards or in the television broadcast of sporting events sponsored by cigarette companies or cigarette brands. According to one estimate, on NBC's ninety-three-minute 1989 Marlboro Grand Prix, there were 4,997 images of Marlboro signs, 519 of Marlboro billboards, 249 of the Marlboro car, making the brand name visible forty-six of the ninety-three minutes of the telecast (Will 1990). But does this kind of background exposure have less, as much, or more effect than the horde of sixty-second commercials that used to appear on prime-time television before the ban? We have no measure of this.

"Advertising" as opposed to "advertising and promotion," is not, in any event, the variable that should be measured. Tobacco companies have not only redistributed advertising expenses among media but have shifted advertising dollars to promotion, that is, to forms of sales promotion that do not use normal media channels and generally provide the audience not only an image of a product but some tangible reward. Promotion thus prominently includes the distribution of free samples, promotional discounts provided to retailers to display a cigarette brand advantageously, the provision and redemption of coupons, the sponsoring of contests and give-aways, or the sponsorship of public entertainment. Tobacco firms, like other companies, may also pay movie producers for prominently displaying their brand in a film. While advertising represented 75 percent of all advertising and promotional expenditures for cigarettes in 1975, it represented only 32 percent by 1988 ("Cigarette Advertising—United States, 1988" 1990, p. 263).

There is also a problem in measuring tobacco consumption. Most studies use as their measure the total number of cigarettes people consume, but an argument has been made that the better measure, with very different implications for public policy, is the total amount of tobacco people consume. Public-education efforts, notably the Surgeon General's report of 1964, can be shown to have had much greater impact on consumption if one uses total tobacco, rather than total number of cigarettes, consumed (Schneider et al. 1981, p. 609).

2. Posadas de Puerto Rico Assoc. v. Tourism Co. of Puerto Rico, 478 U.S. 328 (1986).

3. Central Hudson Gas & Elec. Corp. v. Public Serv. Comm'n, 447 U.S. 557, 564 (1980).

4. Posadas de Puerto Rico, 478 U.S. at 346.

5. *Id*. at 350 (Brennan, J., dissenting).

References

Action on Smoking and Health (ASH). 1987a. Why Charging Smokers More for Health Insurance Is Both Fair and Legal. *Smoking and Health Review* May:7.

————. 1987b. ASH Helps Persuade Government to Let Smokers Pay More for Health Insurance. *Smoking and Health Review* July:1.

Adler, Robert, and Pittle, R. David. 1984. Cajolery or Command: Are Education Campaigns an Adequate Substitute for Regulation? *Yale Journal on Regulation* 1:159–93.

Advertising-to-Sales Ratios, 1990. 1990. *Advertising Age*. 13 August:24.

Agnew, Joe. 1987. Alcohol, Tobacco Marketers Battle New Ad Restraints. *Marketing News* 21(30 January):1.

Akiba, S.; Keto, H.; and Blot, W. J. 1986. Passive Smoking and Lung Cancer among Japanese Women. *Cancer Research* 46:4804–07.

Allen, Henry. 1988. Ah, Those Smoky Yesterdays. *Washington Post* 15 June:C1.

Altman, David G.; Flora, June A.; Fortmann, Stephen P.; and Farquhar, John W. 1987. The Cost-Effectiveness of Three Smoking Cessation Programs. *American Journal of Public Health* 77(February):162–65.

Altman, Lawrence K. 1990. The Evidence Mounts on Passive Smoking. *New York Times* 29 May:C1.

American Cancer Society. 1982. *The Most Often Asked Questions About Smoking Tobacco and Health and the Answers*, sections 4, 24, 26.

————. 1987a. *Facts on Lung Cancer*.

————. 1987b. *The Truth About Alcohol Use—Statistics, Facts and Figures*.

————. 1987c. *Smoke Signals: The Smoking Control Media Handbook*.

American Council on Life Insurance. 1990. *Life Insurance Fact Book*.

American Law Institute (ALI). 1961. *Proceedings of the Thirty-Eighth Annual Meeting*. Philadelphia, Penn.: American Law Institute.

————. 1965. *Restatement (Second) of Torts*. St. Paul, Minn.: American Law Institute Publishers.

Amos, Amanda; Jacobson, Bobbie; and White, Patti. 1991. Cigarette Advertising and Coverage of Smoking and Health in British Women's Magazines. *Lancet* 337(8733):93–96.

Anti-Tobacco Legislation Passes Senate Committee. 1991. *Nation's Health* August.

Ausness, Richard C. 1988. Cigarette Company Liability: Preemption, Public Policy and Alternative Compensation Systems. *Syracuse Law Review* 39:897–971.

————. 1990. Compensation for Smoking-Related Injuries: An Alternative to Strict Liability in Tort. *Wayne Law Review* 36:1085–1148.

Banner, Ann. 1991. Roseville City Council Takes First Step to Ban Open Displays of Cigarettes in Stores. *St. Paul Pioneer Press* 13 June:1A.

Barlas, Stephen. 1990. Bill Poses Threat to Cigarette Ads. *Marketing News* 24 (19 February):1–2.

Barol, Bill. 1986. Cocaine Babies: Hooked at Birth. *Newsweek* 28 July:56.

Barrett, Paul M. 1992. Tobacco Industry Faces Fresh Legal Danger After Justices' Ruling. *Wall Street Journal* 25 June:A1.

Beauchamp, Dan. 1988. *The Health of the Republic*. Philadelphia, Penn.: Temple University Press.

Becker, Howard. 1963. *The Outsiders*. New York: Free Press.

Belasco, Warren. 1989. *Appetite for Change: How the Counterculture Took on the Food Industry, 1966–1988*. New York: Pantheon Books.

Bell, Jonathan W. 1985. France: The Tobacco Crop in 1985: Situation and Prospects. *Tobacco International* 15 November:24.

Bellah, Robert; Madsen, Richard; Sullivan, William; Swidler, Ann; and Tipton, Steven. 1985. *Habits of the Heart: Individualism and Commitment in American Life*. Berkeley and Los Angeles, Calif.: University of California Press.

Beltramini, Richard F. 1988. Perceived Believability of Warning Label Information Presented in Cigarette Advertising. *Journal of Advertising* 17:26–32.

Berger, Peter, and Luckman, Thomas. 1967. *The Social Construction of Reality: A Treatise on the Sociology of Knowledge*. Garden City, N.Y.: Anchor Books/Doubleday.

Best, Joel. 1979. Economic Interests and the Vindication of Deviance: Tobacco in Seventeenth Century Europe. *The Sociological Quarterly* 20(Spring):171–82.

Bloor, F. 1992. What Can the Sociologist of Knowledge Say about 2 x 2 = 4? Unpublished lecture, 13 January, University of California, San Diego.

Blum, Andrew. 1990. Blurred Decision. *National Law Journal* 8 October:7.

Boddewyn, Jean J. 1989. There Is No Convincing Evidence for a Relationship Between Cigarette Advertising and Consumption. *British Journal of Addiction* 84:1255–61.

Bohannon, Paul. 1967. Introduction. In *Law and Warfare*, edited by Paul Bohannon. Garden City, N.Y.: Natural History Press.

Bonilla, Carlos E. 1989. *Determinants of Employee Absenteeism*. Washington, D.C.: National Chamber Foundation.

Bonner, Lin. 1926. Why Cigarette Makers Don't Advertise to Women. *Advertising and Selling* 7 (20 October).

Bourdieu, Pierre. 1984. *Distinction: A Social Critique of the Judgment of Taste*. Cambridge, Mass.: Harvard University Press.

Bourdieu, Pierre, and Passeron, Jean-Claude. 1977. *Reproduction in Education, Society and Culture*. London and Beverly Hills: Sage Publications.

Boyers, Charles. 1916. A City Fights the Cigarette Habit. *The American City* 14 (April):369–70.

Brailey, Allen G., Jr. 1980. The Promotion of Health Through Health Insurance. *New England Journal of Medicine*302:51–52.

Brandt, Allen. 1990. The Cigarette, Risk, and American Culture. *Daedalus* 119:155–76.

Brennan, Thomas. 1990. Review of *Drink and Social Reform*, by Patricia Prestwich. *Journal of Social History* 23(Summer):859–61.

Briggs, B. Bruce. 1988. The Health Police Are Blowing Smoke. *Fortune*, 25 April:349–50.

Broders, A. C. 1920. Squamous-Cell Epithelioma of the Lip. A Study of Five Hundred and Thirty Seven Cases. *Journal of the American Medical Association* 74:656–64.

Brodeur, Paul. 1985. *Outrageous Misconduct: The Asbestos Industry on Trial*. New York: Pantheon Books.

Bruce, James; Miller, James; and Hooker, Donald. 1909. The Effect of Smoking upon the Blood Pressures and upon the Volume of the Hand. *American Journal of Psychology* 24:104–16.

Bucci, Michael. 1991. Growth of Employer-Sponsored Group Life Insurance. *Monthly Labor Review* October:25–32.

Burch, P.R.J. 1983. The Surgeon-General's "Epidemiologic Criteria for Causality": A Critique. *Journal of Chronic Diseases* 36:821–36.

———. 1984. The Surgeon-General's "Epidemiologic Criteria for Causality": Reply to Lillienfeld. *Journal of Chronic Diseases* 37:148–57.

Bureau of National Affairs (BNA). 1990a. Reduced Plan Rates Offered to Employers of Non-Smokers. *Benefits Today* 9 March:73.

———. 1990b. Employers Use Cash Incentives to Encourage Healthy Lifestyles. *Benefits Today* 6 April:103.

———. 1991. SHRM-BNA Survey No. 55: Smoking in the Workplace, 1991. *Bulletin to Management* 29 August.

Cady, Blake. 1983. Cost of Smoking. *New England Journal of Medicine* 308:1105.

Calabresi, Guido. 1970. *The Costs of Accidents: A Legal and Economic Analysis*. New Haven, Conn.: Yale University Press.

Calfee, John E. 1986. The Ghost of Cigarette Advertising Past. *Regulation* November/December:35–45.

Calgary Health Services. 1986. *Smoking By-Laws in Canada*.

Canadians Fired up over Cigarette Tax. 1991. *San Francisco Chronicle* 23 May:C5.

Carter, R. Brudenell. 1906. Alcohol and Tobacco. *The Living Age* 32 (25 August):479–93.

Center for Corporate Public Involvement (CCPI). 1987. *1987 Report of the Life and Health Insurance Business*. Washington, D.C.

Chafe, William. 1991. *The Paradox of Change*. New York: Oxford University Press.

Chapman, Simon. 1989. The Limitations of Econometric Analysis in Cigarette Advertising Studies. *British Journal of Addiction* 84:1265–74.

Cigarette Advertising—United States, 1988. 1990. *Morbidity and Mortality Weekly Report* 27 April:263.

Cigarette Scare: What'll the Trade Do? 1953. *Business Week*. 5 December:59.

Cigarette Smoking is a Health Hazard. 1964. *Newsweek* 20 January:48–50.

Cigarettes. 1958. *Consumer Reports* December: 628–36.

Cigarettes Called Peril to Health. 1964. *San Diego Union* 12 January:1.

Cigarettes in France. 1985. *Market Research Europe* July:17–20.

Classified Ads—Personal. 1991. *New York Review of Books* 18 July:47.

Clearing the Air for Nonsmokers (editorial). 1984. *New York Times* 19 December:A38.

Coalition for Consumer Health and Safety. 1989. Cigarette Consumption. *Consumer Health and Safety Agenda* March:45–47.

Cohen-Solal, Jean Martin. 1982. Antismoking Actions in France: Five Year Results. *World Smoking and Health* Summer:20–23.

Collishaw, Neil. 1991. Interview. *Health and Welfare Canada* 15 March.

Congressional Record. 5 March 1991. S2675.

Congressional Quarterly. 7 December 1991. Civil Rights Act of 1991. 3620–22.

Contra Costa Health Plan. 1986. *Request for Community Rating by Class (CRC) to the Office of Financial Management, Health Care Financing Administration*. 5 November:1.

Corelli, Rae. 1987. Crackdown on Smoking. *Maclean's* 22 June:24–27.

Cort, David. 1959. Cigarettes, Cancer and the Campus. *The Nation* 15 August:69–71.

Cosco, Joe. 1988. Tobacco Wars. *Public Relations Journal* 39:14–19.

A Counterblast Against Tobacco. 1909. *New York Times* 2 October:17.

Cowell, M. J. 1985. An Insurance Company Perspective on Smoking. *New York State Journal of Medicine* July:307–09.

Crawford, Robert. 1977. You Are Dangerous to Your Health: The Ideology and Politics of Victim Blaming. *International Journal of Health Services* 7:663–80.

————. 1979. Individual Responsibility and Health Politics in the 1970s. In *Health Care in America*, edited by Susan Reverby and David Rosner. Philadelphia, Penn.: Temple University Press.

Criticized Panel Backs the Condemnation of Second-Hand Smoke. 1990. *New York Times* 6 December:A6.

Cummings, Steven R.; Rubin, Susan M.; and Oster, Gerry. 1989. The Cost-Effectiveness of Counseling Smokers to Quit. *Journal of the American Medical Association* 261:75–79.

Dahl, Jonathan. 1990. Smokers Go Out of Their Way to Beat Restrictions on Lighting up in Flight. *Wall Street Journal* 23 April:B1.

Dalla-Vorgia, P. 1990. An Evaluation of the Effectiveness of Tobacco-Control Legislative Policies in European Community Countries. *Scandinavian Journal of Social Medicine* 18:81–89.

Davis, Noel Pharr. 1968. *Lawrence and Oppenheimer*. New York: Simon and Schuster.

Dawley, Harold H., and Baldwin, Joe. 1983. The Control of Smoking: Smoking Rate in Designated Smoking and No-Smoking Areas. *International Journal of the Addictions* 18:1033–38.

Dawley, Harold H., and Burton, McKay C. 1985. Smoking Control in a Hospital Setting. *Addictive Behaviors* 10:351–55.

Dawley, Harold H.; Morrison, M.; and Carol, S. 1980. A Comparison of Hospitalized Veterans' Attitudes Toward Smoking and Smoking Cessation over a Four Year Period. *Addictive Behaviors* 5:241–45.

Daynard, Richard A. 1988. Tobacco Liability Litigation as a Cancer Control Strategy. *Journal of National Cancer Institute* 2 March:9–13.

DeJong, William, and Winsten, Jay A. 1989. *Recommendations for Future Mass Media Campaigns to Prevent Preteen and Adolescent Substance Abuse*. Cambridge, Mass.: Center for Health Communication, Harvard School of Public Health.

DelVecchio, Rich. 1991. Smokers Feeling Lonely and Angry. *San Francisco Chronicle*, 6 August:1.

Dickey, Glenn. 1991. Coliseum Smoking Ban Has A's Fans Fired Up. *San Francisco Chronicle* 14 June:D3.

DiFranza, Joseph R.; Richard, John W.; Paulman, Paul M.; Wolf-Gillespie, Nancy; Fletcher, Christopher; Jaffe, Robert D.; and Murray, David. 1991. RJR Nabisco's Cartoon Camel Promotes Camel Cigarettes to Children. *Journal of the American Medical Association* 266:3149–53.

DiFranza, Joseph R.; Winters, Thomas H.; Goldberg, Robert J.; Cirillo, Leonard; and Biliouris, Timothy. 1986. The Relationship of Smoking to Motor Vehicle Accidents and Traffic Violations. *New York State Journal of Medicine* 86:464–67.

Doll, Richard, and Hill, A. Bradford. 1952. A Study of the Aetiology of Carcinoma of the Lung. *British Medical Journal* 2:1271–86.

Donabedian, Avedis. 1973. Basic Values Relevant to Medical Care Administration. *Aspects of Medical Care Administration*. Cambridge, Mass.: Harvard University Press.

Do They—or Don't They? 1959. *Newsweek* 21 December: 80–81.

Douglas, Mary, and Wildavsky, Aaron. 1982. *Risk and Culture: An Essay on the Selection of Technical and Environmental Dangers*. Berkeley, Calif.: University of California Press.

Dr. Burney's Alarm. 1959. *Newsweek* 7 December:66.

Dunn, Percy. 1906. Tobacco Amblyopia. *The Lancet* 1 December:1491–93.

Elias, Norbert. 1978. *The Civilizing Process*. Volume I. New York: Pantheon.

Elson, John. 1991. Busybodies: New Puritans. *Time* 12 August:20.

Environmental Tobacco Smoke and Cardiovascular Disease. 1992. AHA Council on Cardio-pulmonary and Critical Care Position Paper. *Circulation* 86(2):1–4.

Ernster, Virginia L. 1985. Mixed Messages for Women: A Social History of Cigarette Smoking and Advertising. *New York State Journal of Medicine* July:335–40.

Eysneck, Hans J. 1986. Smoking and Health. In *Smoking and Society*, edited by Robert Tollison, 17–87. Lexington, Mass.: Lexington Books.

Feighery, Ellen; Altman, David G.; and Shaffer, Gregory. 1991. The Effects of Combining Education and Enforcement to Reduce Tobacco Sales to Minors. *Journal of the American Medical Association* 266:3168–71.

Fiore, Michael; Novotny, Thomas; Pierce, John; Hatzandrieu, Evridiki; Patel, Kantilal; and Davis, Ronald. 1989. Trends in Cigarette Smoking: The Changing Influence of Gender and Race. *Journal of the American Medical Association* 261:49–55.

Fiore, Michael C.; Novotny, Thomas E.; Peirce, John P.; et al. 1991. Methods Used to Quit Smoking in the United States: Do Cessation Programs Help? *Journal of the American Medical Association* 263:2760–65.

Fischer, Paul M.; Schwartz, Meyer P.; Richards, John W.; Goldstein, Adam O.; and Rojas, Tina H. 1991. Brand Logo Recognition by Children Aged 3 to 6 Years. *Journal of the American Medical Association* 266:3145–48.

Flay, Brian. 1987. *Selling the Smokeless Society: 56 Evaluated Mass Media Programs and Campaigns Worldwide*. Washington, D.C.: American Public Health Association.

Flinn, John. 1991. No-Smoking Laws Have Tobacco Industry Fuming. *San Francisco Examiner* 13 May:A1.

France to Ban Tobacco and Alcohol Advertising by 1993. 1990. *UPI Wire* 13 December.

Freedman, Alix M. 1988a. Tobacco Firms, Pariahs To Many People, Still Are Angels to the Arts. *Wall Street Journal* 8 June:1.

———. 1988b. Smokers' Rights Campaign Suffers from Lack of Dedicated Recruits. *The Wall Street Journal* 11 December:28.

———. 1991. Chain to Enforce Ban on Minors Buying Tobacco. *Wall Street Journal* 18 June:B1.

Freedman, Alix M. and Cohen, Laurie P. 1993. How Cigarette Makers Keep Health Questions 'Open' Year After Year, *Wall Street Journal* 11 February:A1.

French Ad Ban. 1990a. *Wall Street Journal* 7 June:B6.

———. 1990b. *Wall Street Journal* 29 March:A8.

Freour, P. 1986. French Doctors to the Aid of Smokers. *World Health Forum* 7:388–9.

Friedman, Kenneth M. 1975. *Public Policy and Smoking-Health Controversy*. Lexington, Mass.: D.C. Health and Company.

Fuchs, Victor. 1979. Economics, Health and Post-Industrial Society. *Milbank Memorial Fund Quarterly/Health and Society* 57:153–82.

Garfinkel, L. 1981. Time Trends in Lung Cancer Mortality Among Non-Smokers and a Note on Passive Smoking. *Journal of the National Cancer Institute* 66:1061–66.

Garner, Donald. 1980. Cigarette Dependency and Civil Liability: A Modest Proposal. *Southern California Law Review* 53:1423–26.

Garrison, Michael J. 1987. Should All Cigarette Advertising Be Banned? A First Amendment and Public Policy Issue. *American Business Law Journal* 25:169–205.

Gewirtz, Paul. 1991. Fine Print. *The New Republic* 18 November:10.

Geyelin, Milo, and Lambert, Wade. 1991. Jury Rejects Cigarette-Asbestos Lawsuit. *Wall Street Journal* 19 November:B10.

Gidmark, David. 1986. Jury Reaction in *Galbraith* Case. *Tobacco Products Liability Reporter* 1.5:4.45.

————. 1987a. Interview with Melvin Belli and Paul Monzione [Belli's cocounsel]. *Tobacco on Trial* April:1.

————. 1987b. Jury Reaction in *Roysdon v. R. J. Reynolds. Tobacco Products Liability Reporter* 3.1:4.1.

————. 1988. The *Horton* Case. *Tobacco on Trial* 12 February:1.

Giles, Geoffrey. 1990. Review *Drink and Social Reform*, by Patricia Prestwich. *American Historical Review* 95:840–41.

Gilles, C. R.; Hale, D. J.; Hawthorne, V. M.; and Boyle, P. 1984. The Effect of Environmental Tobacco Smoke in Two Urban Communities in the West of Scotland. *European Journal of Respiratory Diseases* 65(Supp. 133):121–26.

Gladwell, Malcolm. 1990. Virginia Slims Tournament Is Backed by "Blood Money," Sullivan Charges. *Washington Post* 24 February:A3.

Glantz, Stanton. 1987. Achieving a Smokefree Society. *Circulation* 76(October):746–50.

Glantz, Stanton A., and Daynard, Richard A. 1991. Safeguarding the Workplace: Health Hazards of Secondhand Smoke. *Trial* June:37.

Glassner, Barry. 1989. Fitness and the Post-Modern Self. *Journal of Health and Social Behavior* 30(June):180–91.

Goad, G. Pierre. 1991. Canada's Tobacco-Ad Ban is Overturned by Judge. *The Wall Street Journal* 29 July:B1.

Goldstein, Michael. 1991. *The Health Movement: Promoting Fitness in America*. Boston: Twayne Publishers.

A Good Beginning (editorial). 1908. *New York Times* 5 May:6.

Goodin, Robert E. 1989. *No Smoking: The Ethical Issues*. Chicago: University of Chicago Press.

Gooding, Judson. 1992. France: An Ambivalent War Against Smoking. *The Atlantic Monthly* June:50–56.

Gottlieb, Neil H., et al. 1990. Impact of a Restrictive Work Site Smoking Policy on Smoking Behavior, Attitudes, and Norms. *Journal of Occupational Medicine* 32:16–23.

Gottsegen, Jack J. 1940. *Tobacco: A Study of Its Consumption in the United States*. New York: Pitman.

The Government Report. 1964. *Time Magazine* (n.d.):42.

Gray, Patricia Bellew. 1978. Tobacco Firms Defend Smoker Liability Suits with Heavy Artillery. *Wall Street Journal* 29 April:1.

Greenwald, Mathew. 1981. Health Promotion and Health Insurance. In *Strategies for Public Health* Number 16, edited by K. Y. Ng Lorenz and Doria Lee Davis, 259–66. New York: Van Nostrand Reinhold Company.

Grimond, John. 1991. For Want of Glue: A Survey of Canada. *The Economist* 29 June:4.

Grout, P.; Cliff, K. S.; Harman, M. L.; and Machin, D. 1983. Cigarette Smoking, Road Traffic Accidents and Seat Belt Usage. *Public Health*, 95–101.

Gusfield, Joseph. 1991. Benevolent Repression: Popular Culture, Social Structure and the Control of Drinking. In *Drinking: Behavior and Belief in Modern History*, edited by Susanna Barrows and Robin Room. Berkeley and Los Angeles, Calif.: University of California Press.

————. 1992. Science and the Textual Culture of Health. Unpublished lecture, 24 March, Princeton University, Princeton, N.J.

————. Forthcoming. Nature's Body and the Metaphors. In *Cultivating Differences*, edited by Michelle Lamont and Michel Fournier. Chicago, Ill.: University of Chicago Press.

Hamilton, James L. 1972. The Demand for Cigarettes: Advertising, the Health Scare, and the Cigarette Advertising Ban. *Review of Economics and Statistics* 54:401–11.

Havender, William. 1982a. About Knowledge and Decisions (review essay on Thomas Sowell's *Knowledge and Decisions*). *Regulation* March/April:47–50.

————. 1982b. Assessing and Controlling Risks. In *Social Regulation: Strategies for Reform*, edited by Eugene Bardach and Robert A. Kagan. San Francisco, Calif.: Institute for Contemporary Studies.

Health Care Financing Administration (HFCA). 1990. Memorandum from Gail Wilensky, Administrator, Health Care Financing Administration, to Karen Deasy, Associate Director for Policy, Office on Smoking and Health, Public Health Service. 6 September.

Hensler, Deborah R.; Felstiner, William L. F.; Selvin, Molly; and Eberner, Patricia A. 1985. *Asbestos in the Courts: The Challenge of Mass Toxic Torts*. Santa Monica, Calif.: Rand Institute for Civil Justice.

Hewitt, Patricia J. 1991. When the No-Smoking Rule Is a Bad Habit. *Wall Street Journal* 8 May:A14.

Hilts, Philip, J. 1990. Health Gains Seen in Smokers Who Quit. *New York Times* 25 September.

Hirsch, Albert. "The Public Health Lobby in France." Unpublished manuscript.

Hocking, Bruce; Borland, Ron; Owen, Neville; and Kemp, Geoffrey. 1991. A Total Ban on Workplace Smoking Is Acceptable and Effective. *Journal of Occupational Medicine* 33:163–67.

Hornik, Robert. 1988. Evaluation Strategies: Comparable Findings from Australia, Sweden and the United Kingdom. *AIDS Health Promotion Exchange* 1:9–11. Geneva, Switzerland: World Health Organization.

Horovitz, Bruce. 1991. No Room This Season for Splashy Print Ads. *Los Angeles Times* 17 December:D6.

House, James; Kessler, Ronald; and Herzog, A. Regula. 1990. Age, Socioeconomic Status and Health. *Milbank Quarterly* 68(3):383–411.

Hubbell, Charles. 1904. The Cigaret Habit—A New Peril. *The Independent* 56:375–78.

Hudzinski, Leonard G., and Frohlich, Edward. 1990. One Year Longitudinal Study of a No-Smoking Policy in a Medical Institution. *Chest* 97:1198–1202.

Huntington, Samuel. 1983. *American Politics: The Promise of Disharmony*. Cambridge, Mass.: Belknap Press.

Ibrahim, Michael. 1976. The Cigarette Smoking/Lung Cancer Hypothesis. *American Journal of Public Health* February:132–33.

Ibrahim, Youssef M. 1990. French Plan to Restrict Ads: Less Wine and No Smoking. *New York Times* 29 March:D1.

Iglehart, John K. 1986. The Campaign Against Smoking Gains Momentum. *New England Journal of Medicine* 314(April 17):1059–64.

Inciardi, James. 1986. *The War on Drugs: Heroin, Cocaine, Crime and Public Policy*. Mountain View, Calif.: Mayfield Publishing Co.

INSURE Project. 1988. Final Report of the INSURE Project. New York.

Irvine, Reed. 1991. The Dioxin Un-Scare—Where's the Press? *Wall Street Journal* 6 August:A14.

Jason, Leonard A., and Clay, Roy. 1978. Modifying Smoking Behaviors in a Barber Shop. *Man-Environment Systems* 8:38–40.

Jason, Leonard A.; Clay, Roy; and Martin, Michael. 1979–80. Reducing Cigarette Smoking in Supermarkets and Elevators. *Journal of Environmental Systems* 9:57–66.

Jason, Leonard A., and Liotta, Richard F. 1982. Reduction of Cigarette Smoking in a University Cafeteria. *Journal of Applied Behavior Analysis* 15:573–77.

Jaynes, Gerald D., and Williams, Robin, eds. 1989. *A Common Destiny: Blacks and American Society*. A National Research Council Report. Washington, D.C.: National Academy Press.

Jenkins, John A. 1989. *The Litigators*. New York: Doubleday.

Joossens, Luk. 1989. The Influence of Advertising on Tobacco Consumption: Comments on Boddewyn and Chapman. *British Journal of Addiction* 84:1279–81.

Kagan, Robert A. 1989. On the Visibility of Income Tax Law Violations. In *Taxpayer Compliance: Social Science Perspectives*, edited by Jeffrey Roth and John Scholz. A National Research Council Study. Philadelphia, Penn.: University of Pennsylvania Press.

———. 1991. Adversarial Legalism and American Government. *Journal of Policy Analysis and Management* 10:369–406.

Karson, Stanley J., Executive Director, Center for Corporate Public Involvement. Interview with the author, July 1991, Washington, D.C.

Keeton, W. Page, Owen, David G., Montgomery, John E., and Green, Michael D. 1989. *Products Liability and Safety* (2d ed.). Westbury, N.Y.: Foundation Press.

Kerr, Peter. 1990. Smokers' Rights Bill Is Test for Florida. *New York Times* 20 February:A9.

Kerr, Robert. 1990. EPA Smoke Report Should Fuel the Fire. *San Francisco Examiner* 2 September:A3.

Kett, Joseph. 1977. *Rites of Passage: Adolescence in America*. New York: Basic Books.

Kleiman, Mark. 1992. *Against Excess: Drug Policy in Moderation*. New York: Basic Books.

Koop, C. Everett. 1984. A Smoke-Free Society by the Year 2000. Presented as the Julia M. Jones Lecture at the Annual Meeting of the American Lung Association, Miami Beach, Florida, May 20.

Kottke, Thomas E.; Battistia, Ronald N.; DeFriese, Gordon H.; and Brekke, Milo C. 1988. Attributes of Successful Smoking Cessation Interventions in Medical Practice. A Meta-Analysis of 39 Controlled Trials. *Journal of the American Medical Association* 259:2883–89.

Kyle, Ken. 1990. Canada's Tobacco Legislation: A Victory for the Health Lobby. *Health Promotion* Spring:9–12.

Lachance, Victor, and Collishaw, Neil. 1989. Tobacco Control in Canada. *Proceedings of the European Conference on Tobacco Priorities and Strategies*, 1–3 November: The Hague.

LaFollette, Marcel. 1990. *Making Science Our Own: Public Images of Science 1910–1955*. Chicago: University of Chicago Press.

Lamont, Michelle. Forthcoming. *Money, Morals and Manners*. Chicago: University of Chicago Press.

Langley, Monica. 1986. The Tobacco Institute Loses Political Power as Attitudes Change. *Wall Street Journal* 14 November:17.

Latest on Smoking and Cancer. 1955. *U.S. News and World Report* 17 June:45–47.

La Vecchia, C., et al. 1991. Smoking and Cancer with Emphasis on Europe. *European Journal of Cancer* 27:1–103.

Laugeson, M., and Meads, C. 1991. Tobacco Advertising Restriction: Price, Income and Tobacco Consumption in OECD Countries, 1960–1986. Unpublished manuscript.

Leichter, Howard. 1991. *Free to be Foolish: Politics and Health Promotion in the United States and Great Britain*. Princeton, N.J.: Princeton University Press.

Lender, M. E., and Martin, James Kirby. 1987. *Drinking in America: A History* (revised and expanded edition). New York: Free Press.

Leu, Robert E., and Schaub, Thomas. 1983. Does Smoking Increase Medical Care Expenditures? *Social Science and Medicine* 17:1907–14.

Levin, Bruce A. 1987. The Liability of Tobacco Companies—Should Their Ashes Be Kicked? *Arizona Law Review* 29:195–245.

Levin, Myron. 1988. The Tobacco Industry's Strange Bedfellows. *Business and Society Review* 65:11–17.

Levin, Myron. 1989. Tobacco Industry Unharmed by Landmark Defeat in Smoker Death Case. *Los Angeles Times* 31 December:A41.

Levine, Joshua. 1991. Don't Fry Your Brain. *Forbes* 4 February:116–17.

Levinson, David N. 1990. Financing Cessation Services. In *Smoking Cessation: The Organization, Delivery and Financing of Services*. Smoking Behavior and Policy Conference Series, 13–14 July 1989. Cambridge, Mass.:Harvard University.

Lewis, W. H. 1957. *The Splendid Century: Life in the France of Louis XIV*. Garden City, N.Y.: Doubleday Anchor.

Lillienfeld, Abraham. 1983. The Surgeon General's Epidemiologic Criteria for Causality: A Criticism of Burch's Critique. *Journal of Chronic Diseases* 36:837–45.

Lipman, Joanne. 1990. Opponents Aim Another Slam at Virginia Slims Tennis Name. *Wall Street Journal* 1 March:B6.

Lipset, Seymour Martin. 1991. *Continental Divide: The Values and Institutions of the United States and Canada*. New York: Routledge.

Loeb, Margaret. 1983. Marketing: Giving Smokers Added Value Is Tobacco Firms' Latest Idea. *Wall Street Journal* 30 June:27.

Lombard, Herbert L., and Doering, Carl R. 1928. Cancer Studies in Massachusetts: Habits, Characteristics and Environment of Individuals with and without Cancer. *New England Journal of Medicine* 198(April 26):481–87.

Lukes, Steven. 1973. *Individualism*. Oxford: Basil Blackwell.

Lundberg, George D., and Knoll, Elizabeth. 1986. Tobacco: For Consenting Adults in Private Only. *Journal of the American Medical Association* 255:1051–53.

McAufliffe, Robert. 1990. The FTC and the Effectiveness of Cigarette Advertising Regulation. *Journal of Public Policy and Marketing* 7:49–64.

McGrath, Dennis J. 1992. New Laws Give More Rights to Smokers; Employers' Acts Are Restricted. *Minneapolis Star Tribune* 17 May:1A.

McNeill, Ann D.; Jarvis, Martin J.; and West, Robert J. 1985. Brand Preferences Among Schoolchildren Who Smoke. *Lancet* 2(8449):271–72.

Maltby, Lewis L., and Rosenthal, John. 1991. Lifestyle Discrimination Threatens Employees' Private Lives. *ACLU Civil Liberties* No. 373:5.

Manning, Willard G.; Keller, Emmett B.; Newhouse, Joseph P.; Sloss, Elizabeth M.; and Wasserman, Jeffrey. 1991. *The Costs of Poor Health Habits*, 24–25, 62–85. Cambridge, Mass.: Harvard University Press.

———. 1989. The Taxes of Sin: Do Smokers and Drinkers Pay Their Way? *Journal of the American Medical Association* 261:1604–09.

Marks, James S.; Koplan, Jeffrey P.; Hogue, Carol J.; and Dalmat, Michael E. 1990. A Cost-Benefit/Cost-Effectiveness Analysis of Smoking Cessation for Pregnant Women. *American Journal of Preventive Medicine* 6(5):282–89.

Marsh, Alan. 1987. *The Dying of the Light*. Smoke-Free Europe Publication No. 7. Copenhagen and Geneva: World Health Organization.

Marsh, Melanie, Public Relations and Communications, Health Insurance Association of America (HIAA). Interview with the author, July 1991. Washington, D.C.

Matlack, Carol. 1990. Smoke-Free Advertising. *National Journal* 14 February:452–55.

Michalowska, Anika, and Rosenbaum, Andrew. 1990. Fight Looms Over French Ad Ban Vote. *Advertising Age* 2 July:4.

Mill, John Stuart. 1987. *On Liberty*. Harmondsworth, England: Penguin Books Ltd.

Millar, Wayne J. 1988. Evaluation of the Impact of Smoking Restrictions in a Government Work Setting. *Canadian Journal of Public Health* 79:379–82.

Miller, Lois Mattox, and Monahan, James. 1954. The Facts behind the Cigarette Controversy. *Reader's Digest* July:1–6.

Milliman and Robertson, Inc., and Control Data. 1987. *Health Risks and Behavior: The Impact on Medical Costs*. Brookfield, Wisc.: Milliman and Robertson, Inc.

Minkler, Meredith; Wallack, Lawrence; and Madden, Patricia. 1987. Alcohol and Cigarette Advertising in Ms. Magazine. *Journal of Public Health Policy* 8(Summer):164–79.

Mintz, Morton. 1990. No Ifs, Ands, or Butts. *Washington Monthly* July/August:30–37.

———. 1991. Marketing Tobacco to Children. *The Nation* 252:577–96.

Mitchell, Mark L., and Mulherin, J. Harold. 1988. Finessing the Political System: The Cigarette Advertising Ban. *Southern Economic Journal* 54:855–62.

Monkkonen, Eric. 1975. *The Dangerous Class*. Cambridge, Mass.: Harvard University Press.

Morris, Norval, and Hawkins, Gordon. 1977. *Letter to the President on Crime Control*. Chicago, Ill.: University of Chicago Press.

Muchnik-Baku, Sonia, ed. 1992. *The Challenge of Financial Incentives and Risk Rating: A Collection of Essays and Case Studies*. Washington, D.C.: Washington Business Group on Health.

Nadelmann, Ethan A. 1989. Drug Prohibition in the United States: Costs, Consequences and Alternatives. *Science* 1 September:939–47.

National Association of Insurance Commissioners (NAIC). 1985. Resolution on Financial Incentives, December 1984. *NAIC Proceedings 1985* 1:638.

———. 1987. Smoker-Nonsmoker Experience Survey Report. *NAIC Proceedings 1987* 2:648–722.

National Library of Medicine. 1975–1981. *Index Medicus*. Washington, D.C.: Government Printing Office.

———. 1982–1989. MEDLINE database.

National Research Council. 1986. *Environmental Tobacco Smoke: Measuring Exposures and Assessing Health Effects*. Washington, D.C.: National Research Council.

Navarro, Vincente. 1976. The Underdevelopment of Health of Working Americans: Causes, Consequences and Possible Solutions. *American Journal of Public Health* 66:538–47.

Nelkin, Dorothy. 1987. *Selling Science: How the Press Covers Science and Technology*. New York: W. H. Freeman.

Nelkin, Dorothy, and Tancredi, Laurence. 1989. *Dangerous Diagnostics: The Social Power of Biological Information*. New York: Basic Books.

New York Business Group on Health. 1990. *Risk-Rated Health Insurance: Incentives for Healthy Lifestyle*. Discussion Paper, Vol. 10, supplement no. 1, May. New York: New York Business Group on Health.

Norr, Roy. 1952. Cancer by the Carton. *Reader's Digest* December:7.

Norton, John E., ed. 1981. *The Anatomy of a Personal Injury Lawsuit* (2d ed.). Washington, D.C.: The Assocation of Trial Lawyers of America Education Fund.

Novak, Viceca. 1989. Conservatives and Corporations Plug Into Black Power. *Business and Society Review* Fall:32–39.

Office of the City Manager. 1989. *Annual Report on the Smoking Pollution Control Ordinance*. Oakland, California.

Office of the City Manager. 1990. *Annual Report on the Smoking Pollution Control Ordinance*. Oakland, California.

O'Hagan, John W. and Carey, Kevin M. 1988. The Proposal for Upward Alignment of Tobacco Taxes in the European Community: A Critique. *British Tax Review* 8:329–48.

Oster, Gerry; Colditz, Graham A.; and Kelly, Nancy L. 1984. The Economic Costs of

Smoking and Benefits of Quitting for Individual Smokers. *Preventive Medicine* 13:377–89.

Oster, Gerry; Huse, Daniel M.; Delea, Thomas E.; Colditz, Graham E. 1986. Cost-effectiveness of Nicotine Gum as an Adjunct to Physician's Advice Against Cigarette Smoking. *Journal of the American Medical Association* 256:1315–18.

Ostry, Sylvia. 1985. Government Intervention: Canada and the United States Compared. In *Canadian Politics: A Comparative Reader*, edited by Ronald G. Landes. Scarborough, Ontario: Prentice-Hall Canada.

Outdoor Advertising Association of America. 1991. Billboard Industry Announces New Code of Advertising Practices. Press release, May 28.

Packer, Herbert. 1968. *The Limits of the Criminal Sanction*. Stanford, Calif.: Stanford University Press.

Parliament Gives Boost to Antismoking Campaign in France. 1990. *Japan Times* 29 December:19.

Pashos, Chris L. 1989. *The Role of Health Insurers in Promoting Smoking Cessation*. Ph.D. diss., Harvard University.

Parkinson, Michael J.; Schauffler, Helen H.; Kottke, Thomas; et al. 1992. Report of the Tobacco Policy Research Group on Reimbursement and Insurance in the United States. *Tobacco Control* 1:S52-S56.

Pearl, Raymond. 1938. Tobacco Smoking and Longevity. *Science* 87(4 March):216–17.

Penner, Maurice. 1989. Economic Incentives to Reduce Employee Smoking: A Health Insurance Surcharge for Tobacco Using State of Kansas Employees. *American Journal of Health Promotion* 4(1):5–11.

———. 1990. *The Ethics of a Health Insurance Surcharge on Employee Smokers in a Group Health Places*. Paper presented at the Annual Meeting of the American Public Health Association, New York, N.Y., October 2.

Pertschuk, Mark. Interview with the Executive Director, Americans for Nonsmokers' Rights, 23 October 1990.

Pertschuk, Michael. 1986. *Giant Killers*. New York: W. W. Norton.

Petersen, Donald J. and Massengill, Douglas. 1986. Smoking Regulations in the Workplace. *Personnel* May:27–31.

Pfohl, Stephen. 1984. The Discovery of Child Abuse. *Social Problems* 24:310–23.

The Pharmacology of Tobacco Smoke (editorial). 1909. *Journal of the American Medical Association* 30 January.

Pierce, John P. 1991. Progress and Problems in International Public Health Efforts to Reduce Tobacco Usage. *Annual Review of Public Health* 12:383–400.

Pierce, John; Fiore, Michael; Novotny, Thomas; Hatzandreu, Evridiki; and Davis, Ronald. 1989. Trends in Cigarette Smoking in the United States: Educational Differences Are Increasing. *Journal of the American Medical Association* 261:56–60.

Pierce, John P.; Gilpin, Elizabeth; Burns, David M.; Whalen, Elizabeth; Rosbrook, Bradley; Shopland, Donald; and Johnson, Michael. 1991. Does Tobacco Advertising Target Young People to Start Smoking? *Journal of the American Medical Association* 266:3154–58.

Pierce, John P.; Macaskill, Petra; and Hill, David. 1990. Long Term Effectiveness of Mass Media Anti-Smoking Campaigns in Australia. *American Journal of Public Health* 80:565–69.

Polich, J. Michael; Ellickson, Phillip; Reuter, Peter; and Kahan, James. 1984. *Strategies for Controlling Adolescent Drug Use*. Paper No. R-3076-CHF. Santa Monica, Calif.: Rand Corporation.

Popper, Edward T., and Murray, Keith B. 1989. Communication Effectiveness and Format

Effects on In-Ad Disclosure of Health Warnings. *Journal of Public Policy and Marketing* 8:109–23.

Priest, George L. 1985. The Invention of Enterprise Liability: A Critical History of the Intellectual Foundations of Modern Tort Law. *Journal of Legal Studies* 14:461–527.

Rabin, Robert L. 1976. Lawyers for Social Change: Perspectives on Public Interest Law. *Stanford Law Review* 28:207–61.

———. 1988. Tort Law in Transition: Tracing the Patterns of Sociolegal Change. *Valparaiso University Law Review* 23:1–32.

———. 1991. Some Thoughts on Smoking Regulation. *Stanford Law Review* 43:475–96.

Raffel, Marshall, and Raffel, Norma. 1989. *The U.S. Public Health System*. Toronto: John Wiley and Sons.

Raftery, James. 1989. Advertising and Smoking—A Smoldering Debate? *British Journal of Addiction* 84:1241–46.

Ramirez, Anthony. 1990. Smoking Is Ruled Cause of a Death But Jury Declines to Award Damages in Suit Against a Tobacco Company. *New York Times* 26 September:B4.

Raz, Joseph. 1979. *The Authority of Law*. New York: Oxford University Press.

Repace, James. 1985. Risks of Passive Smoking. In *To Breathe Freely: Risk, Consent, and Air*, edited by Mary Gibson. Totowa, N.J.: Rowman and Allanheld.

Reynolds, W. Richard. 1991. Canadian Dollars Cross the Border. *San Francisco Chronicle* 2 September:1.

Rice, Dorothy P.; Hodgson, Thomas A.; Sinsheimer, P.; et al. 1986. The Economic Costs of the Health Effects of Smoking, 1984. *Milbank Quarterly* 64:489–547.

Riding, Alan. 1990. What Price Tobacco Ads? A Countdown in France, and France Is New Front in Battle Over Tobacco Ads. *New York Times* 9 April:D8.

Riesman, David; Denny, Ruel; and Glazer, Nathan. 1950. *The Lonely Crowd*. New Haven, Conn.: Yale University Press.

Rigotti, Nancy. 1989. Trends in the Adoption of Smoking Restrictions in Public Places and Worksites. *New York State Journal of Medicine* 89:19–26.

Rigotti, Nancy A.; Bourne, David; Rosen, Amy; Locke, John A.; and Schelling, Thomas C. 1992. Workplace Compliance with a No-Smoking Law: A Randomized Community Intervention Trial. *American Journal of Public Health* 82:229–34.

Rigotti, Nancy A.; Stoto, Michael; Kleiman, Mark; and Schelling, Thomas. 1987. *Implementation and Impact of a City's Regulation of Smoking in Public Places and the Workplace: The Experience of Cambridge, Massachusetts*. Paper presented at the Sixth World Congress on Smoking and Health, November 11, Tokyo, Japan.

Robb, Christina. 1991. Child Deficits Tied to Smoke Breathed by Mothers at Work. *Boston Globe* 17 July:1, 17.

Roberts, Katherine, and Scardino, Albert. 1985. A Trial Opens in a New Wave of Cigarette Suits. *New York Times* 17 November:8E.

Robinson, Ray. 1986. Snuff Maker Not Liable in Teen's Death. *National Law Journal* 7 July:23.

Roehrich, H., and Gold, M. 1988. Cocaine: Origin, Significance, and Findings. *Yale Journal of Biology and Medicine* 61:149.

Rombouts, K., and Fauconnier, G. 1988. What Is Learnt Early Is Learnt Well? A Study of the Influence of Tobacco Advertising on Adolescents. *European Journal of Communication* 3:303–22.

Roper, Barbara, Consumer Federation of America. Interview with the author, July 1991, Washington, D.C.

Rosenberg, Charles. 1962. *The Cholera Years*. Chicago, Ill.: University of Chicago Press.

Rosenstock, Irwin M.; Stergachis, Andy; and Meany, Catherine. 1986. Evaluation of Smoking Prohibition Policy in a Health Maintenance Organization. *American Journal of Public Health* 76:1014–15.

Rosewicz, Barbara, and Karr, Albert R. 1990. Smoking Curbs Get a New Lift from EPA Plan. *Wall Street Journal* 21 June:B1.

Rothstein, Mervyn. 1990. Uneasy Partners. *New York Times* 18 December:B1, B8.

Rublee, Dale A. 1986. Self-Funded Health Benefit Plans. *Journal of the American Medical Association* 255:787–89.

Rushford, Greg. 1990. Pressing Tobacco's Cause: Where There's Cigarette Smoke, There's Fire, Covington Finds. *Legal Times* 16 April:1.

Russell, Louise B. 1986. *Is Prevention Better than Cure?* Washington, D.C.: The Brookings Institution.

Says Schoolgirls Smoke. 1905. *New York Times* 20 February:12.

Schauffler, Helen H. 1993a. Integrating Smoking Control Policies into Employee Benefits: A Survey of Large Corporations in California. *American Journal of Public Health.*

———. 1993b. Disease Prevention Policy Under Medicare: An Historical and Political Analysis. *American Journal of Preventive Medicine* 9.

Schauffler, Helen H.; D'Agostino, Ralph B.; Kannel, William B. 1993. Risk for Cardiovascular Disease in the Elderly and Associated Medicare Costs: The Framingham Study. *American Journal of Preventive Medicine* 9.

Schauffler, Helen H., and Gentry, Daniel. 1993. *Smoking Control Policies in Private Health Insurance: Results of a Statewide Survey.* Berkeley, Calif.: University of California.

Schauffler, Helen H., and Parkinson, Michael J. 1993. Health Insurance Coverage for Smoking Cessation Services. *Health Education Quarterly* 20.

Schauffler, Helen H., and Rodriguez, Tracy. 1993. Managed Care for Preventive Services: A Review of Policy Options. *Medical Care Review* 50.

Schelling, Thomas C. 1986a. Whose Business Is Good Behavior? In *American Society: Public and Private Responsibilities*, edited by Winthrop Knowlton and Richard Zeckhauser.

———. 1986b. Economics and Cigarettes. *Preventive Medicine* 15:549–60.

———. 1991. *Addictive Drugs: The Cigarette Experience.* Unpublished manuscript. RAND Drug Policy Research Center.

Schmalensee, Richard. 1972. *The Economics of Advertising.* Amsterdam: Elsevier North-Holland Publishing.

Schmidt, William E. 1991. Smoking Permitted. *New York Times* 8 September:31.

Schneider, Lynn; Klein, Benjamin; and Murphy, Kevin M. 1981. Government Regulation of Cigarette Health Information. *Journal of Law and Economics* 24:575–611.

Schoenborn, Charlotte, and Boyd, Gayle. 1989. Smoking and Other Tobacco Use, 1987. *National Center for Health Statistics: Vital Health Statistics* 10:69.

Schudson, Michael. 1984. *Advertising: The Uneasy Persuasion.* New York: Basic Books.

———. 1991. Delectable Materialism: Were the Critics of Consumer Culture Wrong All Along? *The American Prospect* Spring:26–35.

Schwartz, Gary T. 1983. New Products, Old Products, Evolving Law, Retroactive Law. *New York University Law Review* 58:796–852.

———. 1991. The Myth of the Ford Pinto Case. *Rutgers Law Review* 43:1013–68.

———. 1992. The Beginning and the Possible End of the Rise of Modern American Tort Law. *Georgia Law Review* 26:601–702.

Schwartz, Hillel. 1986. *Never Satisfied: The Cultural History of Diets, Fantasies and Fat.* New York: The Free Press.

Schwartz, Jerome L. 1987. *Review and Evaluation of Smoking Cessation Methods: The United States and Canada, 1978–1985*. NIH Publication No. 87–2940. Washington, D.C.: National Cancer Institute, Division of Cancer Prevention and Control.

Select Committee on Narcotics Abuse and Control. 1987. *The Crack Cocaine Crisis*. 15 July 1986. Washington, D.C.: Government Printing Office.

———. 1990a. *Drug Crisis in Hawaii*. 13 January 1990. Washington, D.C.: Government Printing Office.

———. 1990b. *The Reemergence of Methamphetamine*. 24 October 1989. Washington, D.C.: Government Printing Office.

Shabecoff, Philip. 1989. 3 U.S. Agencies, to Allay Public's Fears, Declare Apples Safe. *New York Times* 17 March:A10.

Shopland, Donald R.; Eyre, Harmon J.; and Pechacek, Terry F. 1991. Smoking-Attributable Cancer Mortality in 1991: Is Lung Cancer Now the Leading Cause of Death Among Smokers in the United States? *Journal of the National Cancer Institute* 83(21 August):1142–48.

Shoven, John; Sundberg, Jeffrey; and Bunker, John. 1989. The Social Security Cost of Smoking. In *The Economics of Aging*, edited by David Wise. National Bureau of Economic Research. Chicago: University of Chicago Press.

Silvis, Gregory L., and Perry, Cheryl L. 1987. Understanding and Deterring Tobacco Use Among Adolescents. *Pediatric Clinics of North America* 34(April):363–79.

Singer, Amy. 1988. They Didn't *Really* Blame the Cigarette Makers. *The American Lawyer* September:30–37.

Skolnick, Jerome H. 1975. *Justice Without Trial*. New York: Wiley.

———. 1978. *House of Cards: Legalization and Control of Casino Gambling*. Boston, Mass.: Little, Brown.

Tobacco Companies Charge Smokers Double for Life Insurance. 1990. *Smokefree Air* September:3.

Smoking and Cancer. 1955. *Time Magazine* 13 June:67–69.

Smoking and Cancer (cont'd). 1958. *Time Magazine* 5 May:61.

———. 1959. *Time Magazine* 27 April:73.

Smoking and Health. 1962a. *Newsweek* 18 June:74–75.

Smoking and Health. 1962b. *Newsweek* 19 November:74.

Smoking Declines at a Faster Pace. 1992. *New York Times* 22 May:A12.

Smoking Is Not a Civil Right. 1990a. *The Times* (Trenton, N.J.) 29 October:A12.

The Smoking Report (editorial). 1964. *New York Times* 12 January:IV–12.

Sobel, Robert. 1978. *They Satisfy: The Cigarette in American Life*. Garden City, N.Y.: Anchor Press.

Some Cigaret Figures (editorial). 1914. *Literary Digest* 8 August.

Somers, Anne R. 1984. Why Not Try Preventing Illness as a Way of Controlling Medicare Costs? *New England Journal of Medicine* 311:853–56.

Sonnenberg, Stephen M.; Blank, Arthur S., Jr.; and Talbott, John A., eds. 1985. *The Trauma of War: Stress and Recovery in Viet Nam Veterans*. Washington, D.C.: American Psychiatric Press.

Spector, Malcolm, and Kitsuse, John. 1977. *Constructing Social Problems*. Menlo Park, Calif.: Cummings Publishing Co.

Stanwick, Richard S.; Thomson, Margaret P.; Swerhone, Patricia M.; Stevenson, Lindsay A.; and Fish, David G. 1988. The Response of Winnipeg Retail Shops and Restaurants to a Bylaw Regulating Smoking in Public Places. *Canadian Journal of Public Health* 79(July/August):226–30.

Starr, Paul. 1982. *The Social Transformation of American Medicine*. New York: Basic Books.

Sterling, Theodore. 1975. A Critical Reassessment of the Evidence Bearing on Smoking as the Cause of Lung Cancer. *American Journal of Public Health* 65:939–53.

Stevens, William K. 1990. Asbestos Debate Re-emerges in Dispute Over Building Hazard. *New York Times* 26 June:C4.

Stokes, Joseph, III. 1983. Why Not Rate Health and Life Insurance Premiums by Risks? *New England Journal of Medicine* 308:393–95.

Stone, Deborah A. 1986. The Resistible Rise of Preventive Medicine. *Journal of Health Politics, Policy and Law* 11:671–96.

———. 1989. *Policy Paradox and Political Reason*. Glenview, Ill.: Scott, Foresman and Co.

———. 1990. The Rhetoric of Insurance Law: The Debate over AIDS Testing. *Law and Social Inquiry* 385–407.

Stout, Hilary. 1991. Paying Workers for Good Health Habits Catches on as a Way to Cut Medical Costs. *Wall Street Journal* 11 November:B1.

Stubbed Out. 1992. *The Economist*, 7 November 58.

Sullivan, Walter. 1964. Cigarettes Peril Health, U.S. Report Concludes. *New York Times* 12 January:I1.

Sumner, William Graham. 1959. *Folkways*. New York: Dover.

Tax and Price Support Issues Causing Tobacco Interests' Solidarity to Crack. 1986. *National Journal* 26 October:2423–27.

Tempest, Rone. 1990. France's Anti-Anti-Smoking Campaign. *San Francisco Examiner* 6 June.

Tesh, Sylvia Noble. 1988. *Hidden Arguments: Political Ideology and Disease Prevention Policy*. New Brunswick, N.J.: Rutgers University Press.

Tobacco Products in France. 1988. *Marketing in Europe* No. 308:37.

Tobacco Products Liability Project (TPLP). 1988. Discovery Documents Accompanying Press Release, March 26 (on file with editors).

Tollison, Robert D., and Wagner, Richard E. 1988. *Smoking and the State*. Lexington, Mass.: Lexington Books.

Townsley, William E., and Hanks, Dale K. 1989. The Trial Court's Responsibility to Make Cigarette Disease Litigation Affordable and Fair. *California Western Law Review* 25:275–322.

Troyer, Ronald J., and Markle, Gerald. 1983. *Cigarettes: The Battle over Smoking*. New Brunswick, N.J.: Rutgers University Press.

Tye, Joe B.; Warner, Kenneth E.; and Glantz, Stanton A. 1987. Tobacco Advertising and Consumption: Evidence of a Causal Relationship. *Journal of Public Health Policy* 8:492–509.

Underwood, Nora, et al. 1987. The Growers' Despair. *Macleans* 22 June:30–32.

U.S. Congress. House. Committee on Appropriations. 1985. *Hearings on Department of Transportation and Related Agencies Appropriations for 1986*. Testimony of Diane Steed, National Highway Traffic Safety Administration (77–80) and Joan Claybrook, President, Public Citizen (179–80). 99th Cong., 1st sess. Washington, D.C.: Government Printing Office.

U.S. Department of Agriculture. 1990. *Agricultural Statistics*. Washington, D.C.: Government Printing Office.

U.S. Department of Health, Education and Welfare (U.S. DHEW). 1954. *Vital Statistics of the United States*. Public Health Service, National Office of Vital Statistics, Vol. II. Washington, D.C.: Government Printing Office.

———. 1964a. *Smoking and Health*. Report of the Advisory Committee to the Surgeon

General of the Public Health Service. Washington, D.C.: Government Printing Office.

————. 1964b. *Public Health Service Publication No. 1103-D*. Summary of the Report of the Surgeon General's Advisory Committee on Smoking and Health. Washington, D.C.: Government Printing Office.

————. 1979. *Healthy People: The Surgeon General's Report on Health Promotion and Disease Prevention*. Washington, D.C.: Government Printing Office.

U.S. Department of Health and Human Services (U.S. DHHS). 1980a. *The Health Consequences of Smoking for Women*. Washington, D.C: Government Printing Office.

————. 1980b. *Promoting Health Preventing Disease: Objectives for the Nation*. Washington, D.C.: Government Printing Office.

————. 1990. *The Health Benefits of Smoking Cessation*. Washington, D.C.: Government Printing Office.

————, Office on Smoking and Health. 1986. *Smoking and Health: A National Status Report*. Rockville, Md.

————, Surgeon General. 1986. *The Health Consequences of Involuntary Smoking*. Washington, D.C.: Government Printing Office.

————, Surgeon General. 1988. *The Health Consequences of Smoking: Nicotine Addiction*. Washington, D.C.: Government Printing Office.

————, Surgeon General. 1989. *Reducing the Health Consequences of Smoking: 25 Years of Progress*. Washington, D.C.: Government Printing Office.

————. 1992. *Smoking and Health in the Americas*. Washington, D.C.: Government Printing Office.

U.S. Environmental Protection Agency (EPA). 1992. *Respiratory Health Effects of Passive Smoking: Lung Cancer and Other Disorders*. Washington, D.C.: Government Printing Office.

————. What Is Known and Unknown About Smoking and Cancer. 1957. *U.S. News and World Report* 26 July:56–75.

U.S. Smoking Declines to 28%. 1991. *New York Times* 9 November:A9.

Veatch, Robert, and Steinfels, Peter. 1984. Who Should Pay for Smoker's Medical Care? *Hastings Center Report* 4(November):8–10.

Veblen, Thorstein. 1934. *The Theory of the Leisure Class*. New York: The Modern Library, Inc.

Verhovek, Sam Howe. 1990. At Love Canal, Land Rush on a Burial Ground. *New York Times* 26 July:A1, B2.

Vestal, David D. 1989. The Tobacco Advertising Debate: A First Amendment Perspective. *Communications and the Law* March:53–67.

Victor, Kirk. 1987. Strange Alliances. *National Journal* 15 August:2076–81.

Viscusi, W. Kip. 1990. Do Smokers Underestimate Risks?. *Journal of Political Economy* 98:1253–69.

————. 1992. *Smoking: Making the Risky Decision*. New York: Oxford University Press.

Vogel, David. 1986. *National Styles of Regulation*. Ithaca, N.Y.: Cornell University Press.

————. 1989. *Fluctuating Fortunes*. New York: Basic Books.

————. 1991. When Consumers Oppose Consumer Protection: The Politics of Regulatory Backlash. *Journal of Public Policy* 10:449–70.

Wagner, Susan. 1971. *Cigarette Country*. New York: Praeger Publishers.

Walsh, Diana Chapman, and Gordon, Nancy P. 1986. Legal Approaches to Smoking Deterrence. *Annual Review of Public Health* 7:127–49.

Warner, Kenneth E. 1979. Clearing the Airwaves: The Cigarette Ad Ban Revisited. *Policy Analysis* 5(Fall):435–50.

————. 1985. Cigarette Advertising and Media Coverage of Smoking and Health. *New England Journal of Medicine* 312:384–88.

————. 1986. *Selling Smoke: Cigarette Advertising and Public Health*. Washington, D.C.: American Public Health Association.

Warner, Kenneth E.; Ernster, Virginia L.; Holbrook, John H.; Lewit, Eugene M.; Pertschuk, Michael; Steinfeld, Jesse L.; Tye, Joe B.; and Whelan, Elizabeth M. 1986. Promotion of Tobacco Products: Issues and Policy Options. *Journal of Health Politics, Policy and Law* 11:367–92.

Warner, Kenneth E.; Linda Goldenhar; and Catherine G. McLaughlin. 1991. Cigarette Advertising and Magazine Coverage of the Hazards of Smoking: A Statistical Analysis. Unpublished manuscript.

Warner, Kenneth E., and Murt, Hillary A. 1984. Economic Incentives for Health. *Annual Reviews of Public Health* 5:107–33.

Washington, W. Delano T., compliance officer, Office of Compliance, Office of Prepaid Health Care, Health Care Financing Administration, Department of Health and Human Services. Correspondence with the author, 20 December 1990.

Wegman, Richard. 1966. Cigarettes and Health: A Legal Analysis. *Cornell Law Quarterly* 51:678–759.

Weiss, William. 1975. Smoking and Cancer: A Rebuttal. *American Journal of Public Health* 65:954–55.

Westerman, Jean. 1990. Standing Up Sitting Down. *Philip Morris Magazine* November-December:43.

What Britons Are Told About Lung Cancer and Tobacco. 1957. *U.S. News and World Report* 2 August:84–86.

What Is Known and Unknown About Smoking and Cancer. 1957. *U.S. News and World Report* 26 July:56–75.

Whelan, Elizabeth. 1984. *A Smoking Gun: How the Tobacco Industry Gets Away with Murder*. Philadelphia, Penn.: George F. Stickley Co.

Whiteside, Thomas. 1971. *Selling Death: Cigarette Advertising and Public Health*. New York: Liveright.

Wikler, Daniel I. 1978. Persuasion and Coercion for Health: Ethical Issues in Government Efforts to Change Life-Styles. *Health and Society* 56:303–38.

Wikler, David. 1987. Who Should Be Blamed for Being Sick? *Health Education Quarterly* 14:1.

Will, George. 1990. Tobacco's Targets. *Washington Post* 25 February:B7.

Williams, David. 1990. Socioeconomic Differentials in Health: A Review and Redirection. *Social Psychology Quarterly* 53:81–99.

Wilson, James Q. 1968. *Varieties of Police Behavior*. Cambridge, Mass.: Harvard University Press.

————. 1980. *The Politics of Regulation*. New York: Basic Books.

————. 1990. Drugs and Crime. In *Drugs and Crime*, edited by James Q. Wilson and Michael Tonry. Chicago, Ill.: University of Chicago Press.

Windsor, Richard A.; Warner, Kenneth E.; and Cutter, Gary R. 1988. A Cost-Effectiveness Analysis of Self-Help Smoking Cessation Methods for Pregnant Women. *Public Health Reports* 103:83–88.

Wright, Pamela, Advertising Coordinator, King County Medical Blue Shield. Correspondence with the author, 8 November 1991.

Wynder, Ernest L., and Graham, Evarts A. 1950. Tobacco Smoking as a Possible Etiologic Factor in Bronchiogenic Carcinoma: A Study of Six Hundred and Eighty-Four Proved Cases. *Journal of the American Medical Association* 143:329–36.

Zimring, Franklin E. 1975. Firearms and Federal Law: The Gun Control Act of 1968. *Journal of Legal Studies* 4:133.

Zimring, Franklin E., and Hawkins, Gordon. 1971. The Legal Threat as an Instrument of Social Change. *Journal of Social Issues* 27:33.

———. 1973. *Deterrence: The Legal Threat in Crime Control*. Chicago, Ill.: University of Chicago Press.

———. 1992. *The Search for Rational Drug Control*. New York: Cambridge University Press.

Zola, Irving. 1972. Medicine as an Institution of Social Control. *Sociological Review* 20:487–504.